Praise for *The Religion of Democracy*

"Historian Kittelstrom brilliantly presents the historic relationship between Christianity and social progress in American history."
—*The San Francisco Chronicle*

"Kittelstrom's history stands out for its deeply textured treatment of each of these profoundly important thinkers, permitting appreciation of the influences that brought them to an enlightened view of faith and its socio-political implications. This timely, important work by an excellent scholar is part of the *Penguin History of American Life* series."
—*Publishers Weekly* (starred review)

"Historian Kittelstrom examines the lives and the writings of seven prominent American liberals and suggests that today's pluralistic political liberalism is a direct descendant of the religious liberalism that emerged in, and transformed, the eighteenth and nineteenth centuries. . . . The result is a lively and erudite reminder of pluralism's deep roots in American soil, and religion's role in putting them there."
—*Booklist*

"Kittelstrom explores the private and intellectual lives of each individual and provides new insights into the cultural history of liberalism. . . . Readers will appreciate the skillful weaving of primary sources into a compelling chronicle of an idea told through individual experiences."
—*Library Journal* (starred review)

"This book challenges contemporary conversations that conflate secularism and liberalism and expands the scholarly understanding of liberalism in the US. Highly recommended."
—*CHOICE Magazine*

"*The Religion of Democracy* is an extremely well-researched and interesting description of the sustaining arguments and tenets of the American Reformation, as well as an informative portrayal of the complex lives of some of its central figures."
—*Christian Century*

"*The Religion of Democracy* is a stunning history of the opening of the American mind. Through a shrewd study of seven subtle thinkers, Kittelstrom explores the place of belief, faith, and virtue in the intellectual traditions that lie behind American liberalism. A fascinating, important, and resonant book."
—Jill Lepore, author of *Book of Ages* and *The Secret History of Wonder Woman*

"Amy Kittelstrom here pours new life into intellectual history for scholars and concerned citizens, whether they are religious or not. She traces the commitments of present-day civic liberalism—free inquiry, cultural pluralism, public education, and compassion for the disadvantaged—not to the rise of secularism but to the Christian theological liberalism of New England at the time of the American Revolution. She finds these origins in what she terms, appropriately, an American Reformation."
—Daniel Walker Howe, Pulitzer Prize-winning author of *What Hath God Wrought: The Transformation of America, 1815–1848*

"Turning the pages of this remarkable book, I found myself moved not only by its intellectual range and the lucidity of Kittelstrom's prose but also by its central theme, the emergence in nineteenth-century America of an ethical commitment to democracy's highest moral and practical possibilities—in effect, a 'religion of democracy.' An illuminating story, for our times as well as for what it tells us about the past."
—David D. Hall, Harvard University; author of *A Reforming People*

PENGUIN BOOKS

THE RELIGION OF DEMOCRACY

Amy Kittelstrom is a scholar of modern thought and culture who lives and works in the North Bay Area of California. She currently serves on the editorial board of the *Journal of American History* and is an associate professor at Sonoma State University. Her research has been supported by fellowships from the Center for Religion and American Life at Yale, the Charles Warren Center for the Study of American History at Harvard, and the Center for the Study of Religion at Princeton. Her next book will place the twentieth-century writer James Baldwin in deep historical context.

THE
Penguin History
of
AMERICAN LIFE

FOUNDING EDITOR
Arthur M. Schlesinger, Jr.

BOARD MEMBERS
Alan Brinkley, John Demos, Glenda Gilmore, Jill Lepore
David Levering Lewis, Patricia Nelson Limerick, James McPherson
Louis Menand, James H. Merrell, Garry Wills, Gordon Wood

James T. Campbell
*Middle Passages: African American
Journeys to Africa, 1787–2005*

François Furstenberg
*In the Name of the Father:
Washington's Legacy, Slavery,
and the Making of a Nation*

Karl Jacoby
*Shadows at Dawn: A Borderlands
Massacre and the Violence
of History*

Julie Greene
*The Canal Builders: Making
America's Empire at the
Panama Canal*

G. Calvin Mackenzie and
Robert Weisbrot
*The Liberal Hour: Washington and
the Politics of Change in the 1960s*

Michael Willrich
Pox: An American History

James R. Barrett
*The Irish Way: Becoming American
in the Multiethnic City*

Stephen Kantrowitz
*More Than Freedom: Fighting
for Black Citizenship in a White
Republic, 1829–1889*

Frederick E. Hoxie
*This Indian Country: American
Indian Activists and the Place
They Made*

Ernest Freeberg
*The Age of Edison: Electric Light and
the Invention of Modern America*

Patrick Allitt
*A Climate of Crisis: America in the
Age of Environmentalism*

Amy Kittelstrom
*The Religion of Democracy:
Seven Liberals and the American
Moral Tradition*

The

RELIGION

of

DEMOCRACY

SEVEN LIBERALS AND THE
AMERICAN MORAL TRADITION

AMY KITTELSTROM

PENGUIN BOOKS

PENGUIN BOOKS
An imprint of Penguin Random House LLC
375 Hudson Street
New York, New York 10014
penguin.com

First published in the United States of America by Penguin Press, an imprint of
Penguin Publishing Group, a division of Penguin Random House LLC, 2015
Published in Penguin Books 2016

THE LIBRARY OF CONGRESS HAS CATALOGED THE HARDCOVER EDITION AS FOLLOWS:

Kittelstrom, Amy.
The religion of democracy : seven liberals and the American moral tradition / Amy Kittelstrom.
pages cm
Includes bibliographical references and index.
ISBN 978-1-59420-485-2 (hc.)
ISBN 978-0-14-310813-9 (pbk.)
1. Politicians—United States—Biography.   2. Intellectuals—United States—Biography.
3. Christians—United States—Biography.   4. Liberalism—United States—History.
5. Democracy—United States—History.   6. Christianity and politics—United States—History.
7. United States—Politics and government.   8. United States—Intellectual life.
9. United States—Religion.   10. United States—Moral conditions.   I. Title.
E176.K58 2015
261.7—dc23
2014036666

Printed in the United States of America
1   3   5   7   9   10   8   6   4   2

Designed by Meighan Cavanaugh

For my grandfather
LEE M. KITTELSON (1915–2011)
and my children
TRAEGER LEE and SEELAH BEDE

because the meaning of the past hinges on the future

No single soul is capable of the whole image of God; it always reflects but a part of the truth, and must seek the complement of what is revealed to its own individuality in what is revealed to other individuals, who have other stand-points. He can comprehend the whole horizon only by a progressively widening, sympathetic, mutual intercourse with his fellow creatures.

—REV. WILLIAM ELLERY CHANNING, C. 1825,
AS RECOLLECTED BY ELIZABETH PALMER PEABODY

The divine can mean no single quality, it must mean a group of qualities, by being champions of which in alternation, different men may all find worthy missions. Each attitude being a syllable in human nature's total message, it takes the whole of us to spell the meaning out completely.

—WILLIAM JAMES, *The Varieties of Religious Experience* (1902)

CONTENTS

====

PREFACE
TO THE PAPERBACK EDITION

I have been so pleased with the reception of this book, and yet so mindful of its defects, that it is a relief to fix some of them and to add this preface to the paperback edition. The most galling of my errors was having left out one of my key pieces of evidence, which I had hoarded gleefully for years and then overlooked in the rush to press. Introducing it now also gives me the chance to engage with the initial critical response to the book and to offer appreciation to my audiences.

This is a book about how an originally Christian, eighteenth-century idea changed into a universal modern idea. Some New England Christians believed that every human being is a moral agent endowed with the sacred faculties of reason and conscience, a faith that their Christian and post-Christian intellectual descendants transformed into a "religion of democracy" in which the human right to dignity—to freedom and equality—became a practical faith for driving moral action. This transformation helped produce the modern concept of universal human rights.

I had already been working on the book for over a decade before I reread the United Nations Universal Declaration of Human Rights of 1948. This time, Article I jumped out at me like never before:

> All human beings are born free and equal in dignity and rights. They are endowed with reason and conscience and should act toward one another in a spirit of brotherhood.

The preamble calls human rights a "faith."[1] I have not done the necessary research to reconstruct how this language got into the Declaration, but even in the nineteenth century, the principles and vocabulary of what I call the American Reformation, which helped produce the religion of democracy, circulated around the Anglophone world and beyond. In the twentieth century the pacifist work of American liberals like Jane Addams—the subject of my chapter seven—helped create an international vocabulary for talking about human rights. Since Addams was a mentor to Eleanor Roosevelt, so central in the making of the Declaration, the language is not surprising. But it is revealing.

The United Nations (UN) draws criticism on many fronts, and this is not the place to field that criticism, but one frequent charge carries particular relevance here. The overbearing role of the United States in the UN may have made the organization ethnocentric, unduly friendly to unregulated capitalism, and biased in its approach to international affairs, but the actual conduct of the US and UN in the Cold War and its aftermath is a distinct issue from the ideal of human rights articulated in the Declaration. Similarly, the actual human rights record of the United States differs from the democratic ideals examined in this book, ideals that helped produce the modern liberalism of the New Deal but failed to prevent white supremacists from implementing it.[2] The language of Franklin Delano Roosevelt's famous Four Freedoms speech of

1941 is obvious in the 1948 Declaration, which claims that "a world in which human beings shall enjoy freedom of speech and belief and freedom from fear and want has been proclaimed as the highest aspiration of the common people." Just who the common people might be and how many human beings actually believe in universal human rights, however, are open questions.

And they are important questions, which I raise by giving them a history in this book. Academic reviews, from which I will have much to learn, have not yet appeared, but the early popular response has taught me a lot about the American reading public, which I am glad to find is still capable of taking in ideas more nuanced than 140 characters can describe. I did my best to avoid isms as much as possible in this book, but nevertheless secularism, pragmatism, pluralism, Romanticism, socialism, and many other complex intellectual constellations simply had to be covered in these pages in order to reconstruct the history my research unearthed. Readers with the fortitude to abide theological and philosophical complexity get rewarded, I hope, with dashes of poetry and drama, but stamina is required to grasp the whole of it.

I find that different angles of my research get reflected by different audiences, which is quite educational. I initially was pleased to see that the politically progressive journal *The American Prospect* chose Susan Jacoby, an independent scholar whose work on the history of free thought is vital to understanding American religious history, to review my book along with the important new book by the Princeton historian Kevin M. Kruse. His *One Nation, Under God* explains how, from the 1930s onward, the newly powerful corporate giants of twentieth-century America added "under God" to the Pledge of Allegiance and helped create a more jingoistic America with a new Christian identity. His work provides a vivid indicator of how the religion of democracy got submerged in the twentieth century under the modern forces of consumer culture, industrial capitalism, and Cold War politics. Jacoby seems mostly friendly to Kruse's work, but her resistance to mine shows even in the subtitle of her review: "the tension between religiosity and secular government goes back to the nation's founding." Since my argument holds, instead, that a particular religious orientation actually produced a variant of secularism—such that the liberal Jew Horace Kallen wrote a book by its light called *Secularism is the Will of God* (1954)—I could see that she had not taken my argument in. Upon examination, her response indicates the anti-religious bias in so-called leftist culture, which both inhibits modern progressivism's political effectiveness by alienating potential allies and belies the pluralistic convictions of early twentieth-century progressives like Jane Addams. At the same time, a full-throated defense of American civil liberty and atheist rights is politically necessary and often beleaguered in a political culture rife with religious symbols.[3]

Some readers seem to think that I make my argument based solely on the seven liberals whose perspectives govern each chapter. The book's subtitle is somewhat misleading in this respect, as those seven figures are vehicles for connecting to many other historical actors in the creation of this religion of democracy. "There are no Catholics or Jews in her book," charged Jacoby. Was the pope not Catholic, I wondered? Rabbis not Jewish? There are numerous Catholics and Jews in my book, which includes them in a historical narrative that begins exclusively Anglo-Protestant and becomes leavened with ethnic variety over time. My story, far from being blind to the contrast between the diversity of American peoples and the various exclusivities of American privilege, instead reconstructs intellectual, ethnoracial, and economic privilege by tracking the dissemination of ideas through embodied thinkers and their actual, lived connections to one another and to ideas through social experience recorded in texts, letters, and educational records.

Since my research began with the pivotal thinker William James and networked outward from his Harvard setting, I found that a segregated American history was reflected in a segregated world of ideas—and that the elite New England liberals who form the early backbone of my narrative produced ideas that victims of discrimination and their allies used to fight segregation, elitism, and unearned privilege.

These ideas disseminated far and wide in modern American culture. When the great twentieth-century writer James Baldwin described democracy, he sounded a lot like the Boston minister William Ellery Channing, the subject of my chapter three who named "self-culture" as the right and duty of every American. "Democracy," Baldwin said in a conversation with the anthropologist Margaret Mead in 1970, "should not mean the leveling of everyone to the lowest common denominator. It should mean the possibility of everyone being able to raise himself to a certain level of excellence." The purpose of the moral agent is progress, but racism taught the African American youth of Baldwin's day that "he won't ever have any control over his own destiny, which is the most demoralizing thing that there is." The events of police brutality and racial injustice that have become public since my book's debut show that the gap between democratic ideals and daily American reality remains large.[4]

Between the dogmatic rationalism of a Jacoby and the dogmatic Protestantism of some of my other critics, there appears to be a broad and varied readership whose insights and questions have stimulated my thinking and cast fresh light on material I have lived with for most of my adult life. The patrons of libraries and bookstores, viewers of C-SPAN Book TV and listeners of public radio, churchgoers and theologians, pagans and modern mystics have all responded to my work with wisdom, knowledge, and the reflection of long experience. I am grateful to many individuals and institutions that have fostered conversation around my book and it is a pleasure to acknowledge some of them here: Salon.com; Dolores Ornelas and her radio program *Encuentro de Mundos*; A Great Good Place for Books and the Montclair Presbyterian Church of Oakland, California; Book Passage in the San Francisco Ferry Building and C-SPAN; Hobo Wine Company and Copperfield's Books; Kelsey Crowe and Help Each Other Out; Lilian Calles Barger and New Books in American Studies; Village Books of Bellingham, Washington; Marc Wheeler and Jessica Paris of Coppa in Juneau, Alaska, Hearthside Books, and the Juneau Public Library Association; Rev. Dr. C. Welton Gaddy and his *State of Belief* radio program; The Elliott Bay Book Company and KUOW of Seattle, Washington; Anne Hill and Dream Talk Radio; Robert Moluf and St. Thomas' Episcopal Parish of Washington, DC; Dr. R. Albert Mohler, Jr., and his *Thinking in Public* radio program; Carrie Kaufman, host of *State of Nevada*, KNPR Las Vegas; Robert Schmidt and Stuart Goodnick and their *Mystical Positivist* program on KOWS, Sonoma County. You and your communities teach me that there is, indeed, a public intellectual life in America—and that it is worth fighting for.

A.K.
Sonoma County
December 2015

The

RELIGION

of

DEMOCRACY

INTRODUCTION:
AN AMERICAN REFORMATION

Somehow the word "godless" got hitched to the word "liberal." The story of this coupling has something to do with the Cold War against Soviet communism, but behind this unholy union lies a much more interesting history of how some American elites led a very different fight against—well, elitism. Seven liberals, whose lives interconnected across two centuries through shared readings, relationships, and concerns, were so far from godlessness that the pursuit of truth and virtue dominated their lives. The history they lived shows that after the Protestant Reformation in Europe came an American Reformation that built a moral tradition into democracy.

John Adams, the irascible, prideful second president of the United States, did not consider all people fit to vote, yet he thought every man had the right to make up his own mind over what to believe about politics, religion, or anything else—not only the right, but the duty to think for himself, because the only being who really knows everything is God.

The maiden aunt of Ralph Waldo Emerson made no fame for herself in a lifetime that began just before the American Revolution and ended in the middle of the Civil War. Mary Moody Emerson spoke her mind, though, fearlessly and freely. In this fierce liberty she was not only being a good American, she was being a good Christian.

Rev. William Ellery Channing never suffered for want of anything. He lived in an era when the wealthy regarded laborers almost as a separate species, but he called himself a working man to show his solidarity with the new laboring classes of his early industrial age. He believed that all individuals, including slaves and women, deserved the freedom to think and act by their own best lights, and he believed this because of his Christian faith in what lay inside each soul and what potential all of God's creatures could reach.

William James, the most important philosopher in American history, also wanted for nothing, but he never became a Christian. He did not appear to be much of a democrat, either, with his distaste for uneducated speech and his regard for European standards of excellence. Yet he professed to believe in a "religion of democracy" that took the sacred equality of all individuals as a postulate from which real human progress might flow.

The Scottish immigrant Thomas Davidson fell from Christian grace early in life while learning all he could about modern science, ancient and modern philosophy, human languages, religion, and culture. Yet he was more evangelistic than secular. The good news he wanted to spread was how free individuals interacting in all their diversity could make progress together—even Jews, even women, even workers in an age rife with prejudice of all kinds.

William Mackintire Salter, son of a minister, also fell from Christian grace as a young man despite his most earnest religious commitment. Actually, his earnestness gave him the integrity to face his growing belief that Jesus Christ was not the one and only uniquely divine being ever to be born. Salter became a post-Christian religious leader who called on the state to treat workers as equals with bosses during the industrial crisis of the late nineteenth century. Against the laissez-faire establishment, Salter asked for social justice as sacred justice.

The social thinker and activist Jane Addams did more than ask for social justice—she lived for it. Rather than giving the poor what she thought they needed, she lived among them as she believed Jesus would have done. Through community, she built relationships that taught her what all humans share, a longing for pleasure and beauty as well as security and shelter and a sense of purpose in life. She connected workers and bosses, social scientists and politicians, educators and ministers, philanthropists and activists from around the world. She wanted governments to tend human needs. And she wanted common human needs to drive global change.

The long cultural and intellectual lineage indicated by these seven thinkers stretches back to classical liberalism, the political commitment of a society to replace coercion with consent. Their genealogy extends forward all the way to modern liberalism, the moral commitment of a society to the collective needs of all its members, regardless of their differences. Between the ideal of modern liberalism that has never been realized and the theory of classical liberalism that has never been dismantled—and amid contrary historical currents, like discrimination and exploitation, that undermine both—these liberals and the rest of their intellectual family tree helped Americans and others think about why human beings ought to treat one another as equals who deserve to be free. This book is a history of that idea.

This history mostly took place in arguments, over dinner tables, beside campfires, aboard steamers, in the pages of journals, and inside people's heads. Of all the inner lives depicted in this book, that of

William James may be the most illustrative because he more than anyone tried to gather up the threads of ideas and values spun by his ancestors and to weave them into the new cloth of the modern era. The effort drove him to complete collapse at age twenty-four. He lost his strength, his energy, even his power of concentration as he squirmed beneath the oppressive weight of a life he now found loathsome. Dark clouds were all James could see as he struggled to reconcile what he thought was true with what he thought was right. Meanwhile, he could not make himself act at all and often wanted to die. This went on for seven years.

"Spinal paralysis," James called his mental affliction. The phrase holds a lot of historical meaning. If the spine is physical, then the problem is material and the solution may be discovered rationally—through the use of reason, evidence, experimentation, and all the other empirical instruments of the Enlightenment, the intellectual transformation that originated in Europe and migrated, unevenly, around the globe. Beyond a doubt, James was a product of the Enlightenment who practiced the scientific method and heeded natural facts. This was true of everyone on his intellectual family tree. Yet most people think of the Enlightenment as a secularizing movement, spreading a loss of faith in religion along with its new faith in human progress. And there is nothing James and his kin cared for more than religion.[1]

The spine is not only physical. Call someone spineless, say they have no backbone, and you are saying something about their character, something grave. Cowards are not manly. The weak-willed are not trustworthy. James worried so much about his spinal paralysis because he cared so much about his free will, and this value came not from the Enlightenment, but from the Reformation. Actually, the concept of free will is much older than the sixteenth-century Protestant Reformation. An ancient Christian answer to the problem of evil—the problem of why bad things happen to good people when an all-good God is supposed to be all-powerful, a problem that bothered James although he never believed in that kind of God—free will is particularly important in the history of American democracy because of the role it played in the Reformation and the role the Reformation played in New England. Indeed, free will has everything to do with the democratic principles of liberty and equality.

Although the first William James in America arrived after the Revolution, the roots of Jamesian thought lie not with this paternal grandfather but with New England Christians who did not even anticipate that such a war would ever come, yet whose deepest convictions helped make it possible. Heirs to the Puritan tradition, these Christians believed that their ancestors had crossed the Atlantic in devotion to liberty of conscience, or the divine right of private judgment, the idea that God creates every human being a moral agent endowed with free will, which it is each individual's right and duty to exercise conscientiously in order to cultivate virtue and its ally, truth. New England Christians argued with one another over precisely what the truth may be—and they always had—but as the eighteenth century wore on, most of them came to agree that the British were violating the colonists' essential liberty, which they understood in both religious and political terms.[2]

Their devotion to Reformation Christian liberty made New England patriots extremists in the colonies when it came to the cause of independence, but by the time the war arrived they had started to disagree with one another over a fundamental matter of their faith, the very nature of truth. One side, the side the founding father John Adams practiced, believed that the truth could be known in full to no human being, and that humility and open-mindedness as well as sincerity and candor were therefore fundamental characteristics of piety. These Christians became the first people in the world to call themselves liberals, by which they indicated their commitment to open-minded moral agency. The other side of the New England Christian debate believed that ultimate truth was contained in Calvinist articles of faith and ought to be spread evangelically. This side, although its commitment to Calvinism loosened over time, has been contending ever since that the United States is a Christian nation, meaning a nation founded upon an evangelical Protestant faith dubbed orthodox. The argument between these splintering halves of New England Christianity produced a novel turn in thought and culture, an American Reformation.[3]

Up to now the American Reformation has been hard to see for two main reasons. The first is the very myth of orthodox American Christianity produced by the evangelical side of the debate, a useful fiction in a country with a sizable Protestant majority but a guarantee of religious freedom instead of an established religion. This myth, adopted by scholars and popular commentators alike, equates religion with Christianity, Christianity with supernatural belief, and Christian belief with a particular faith in the special saving grace of Jesus through his blameless death and glorious resurrection. This evangelical kernel of Christianity had certainly been part of the Puritan tradition—and of other American Christianities—but the revival movement of the eighteenth century separated this kernel from other beliefs and practices that had grown up with those traditions, delineating the evangelical doctrine starkly so that it alone became the essence of faith. The myth of orthodox American Christianity gave rise to a distinction between head and heart, or the intellect and the soul, making any departure from so-called orthodoxy appear as a falling away from religion, a decline from faith, a crisis, a move of revolt or rejection or outright warfare on religion that inexorably brings on secularization, which measures value by the merely natural or material rather than the ultimate or divine and is widely associated with modernity. Christians who deplore secularization and humanists who applaud it have both found this myth useful, but lifting the veil of orthodoxy from the actual complexity of American religious thought reveals that the liberals who departed from this alleged orthodoxy did so in fidelity to their Christian faith rather than in spite of it.[4]

The second reason the American Reformation has been hard to see is because of a myth some later liberals created. Actually, it's Ralph Waldo Emerson's fault. This son of a son of a son of a New England minister acted like he was making a complete break with his ancestral faith when he left the pulpit, but actually he left it on grounds of conscience, to develop his moral agency, to pursue virtue and truth as only he could see it. In other words, Emerson was an exemplary fruit of the American Reformation and did not fall far from the tree planted by his forefathers. But admirers of Emerson early in the academic study of American literature were snookered by his story about corpse-cold Boston Unitarianism and erected him king of what they called the "American Renaissance," a cultural and literary movement purportedly free of superstition, dogma, and other stale accretions of America's religious past. These scholars knew that Emerson's father had belonged to a small intellectual fellowship in Boston that produced a monthly journal out of weekly conversation over "a modest supper of widgeons and teal," as one such scholar put it in 1936, "with a little good claret." Yet they had no idea that Rev. William Emerson and his friends practiced moderation for the sake of reason not only because they had absorbed Enlightenment ideas from Great Britain, but also because free inquiry paired so well with free will.[5]

Looking at the historical contribution of New England as an American Reformation instead of an American Renaissance shows that a democratic approach to religion forged the real liberal tradition in America. The American Reformation began as an extended conversation among professing Christians whose basic premises were spare: the perfection of God and the moral agency of human beings. About everything else they argued. In the face of disagreements, liberals tried to maintain open minds and to believe in the possibility and desirability of progress—moral progress, human progress, and social progress dependent on each individual's growth in conversation with other individuals, rather than in opposition to them, in a society that rises together if it is to rise at all. Liberals strove to keep their minds open to other people's perspectives because they knew they were fallible, like all humans, which meant that their own opinions might be wrong, and also because they believed that all humans also bore within some unique quality of the infinite divine from which others might learn. Human beings are essentially equal, profoundly equal, as fellow fallen creatures of the same perfect God. They need freedom in order to exercise their divine right of private judgment—to heed their sacred inner voices of reason and conscience and to evaluate others' opinions—and they have a duty to use this freedom to express their perspective on truth as faithfully as they can. The American Reformation produced not only Christians who called themselves liberals but also liberal intellectual culture, in which both listening with humility and speaking with integrity are acts of piety.

Liberals were initially concentrated in New England, the most scholarly and pious—scholarly because pious—community of discourse in America, but many of their main talking partners were British. Their conversation always reached across the Atlantic. Liberals also stood squarely between the two other most powerful intellectual cultures in what became the United States, the revived Christians of the wider American populace and the rational elites of urban centers. Instead of elbowing out these two groups, their fellow Reformation Christians on the one side and their fellow acolytes of reason on the other, liberals connected them, holding hands with each and translating key terms and critical concerns for the goal of important compromises like declaring independence from Britain and adopting a Constitution for nationhood. The conversation liberals carried on over the eighteenth century and across the nineteenth created such a powerful turn in modern thought because they were moderates, because they were central interlocutors, because they balanced confidence in their own point of view with a commitment to considering other points of view. Most important, their very particular Christian perspective gave them the tools to create, over a long span of intellectual and cultural development, a universal platform for mediating human difference that must be called secular although it is rooted in religion.[6]

"Secular" and "liberal" are among the most loaded terms in the English language, carrying so much intellectual freight that no one can conscientiously use them without explaining how they are meant. Conscientiousness, of course, is just what the religious liberals of the Revolutionary era and beyond most valued. Freely chosen action "upon mature deliberation," as they would have put it, is right conduct for a moral agent. But liberals were not secular if secular is to mean something somehow opposing religion, or devoid of religion. Far from it. Moreover, they really did not know anyone who truly opposed religion (churches were another matter). The lightest touches on religion came from people like Thomas Jefferson, who conscientiously trimmed the Christian Bible to dimensions of his liking; he certainly was a moral agent who used his reason and his conscience. Yet Jefferson spent much less time contemplating infinity than John Adams, his comrade, foe, and friend. This put Adams comfortably—or rather uncomfortably—between Jefferson and Samuel Adams, a cousin of John's who adhered to a much more evangelical, uncritically biblical Christianity and who therefore cannot be called much of a liberal because once one becomes a liberal of any type, one becomes a critic, actively scrutinizing every possible article of belief or value "objectively," with an impartial eye and a mind buoyed by the reference point of perfect divine truth—which is, unfortunately, invisible, beyond the reach of human senses. Jefferson thought less about the invisible than either Adams did, while being a rational critic; the Adams cousins shared more than a last name; all three could be mapped onto a continuum devised from what scholars refer to by the terms republicanism, political liberalism, and Christianity, as well as several other key words of the modern period, such as civic humanism, tolerance, individualism, rights, and perhaps even modernity itself. John Adams may be the most representative figure of the early American Reformation because he fell most stoutly in the middle of all these markers and because he engaged in active conversation with the biggest variety of representatives from groups who leaned more strongly in one direction or another. He was "secular," then, insofar as he believed the public sphere ought to field all viewpoints. Insofar as Adams was "liberal," he both stood up for his own point of view and, acknowledging its partiality, remained open to revision. Each of these positions reflected his Christian conviction and piety.[7]

Liberals were ubiquitous in American public culture across the nineteenth century, yet always a numerical minority. Wary of party spirit, they were Federalists and then they were mostly Whigs and then Republicans, and then, at the end of the century, they became Mugwumps who declared themselves independent thinkers while still voting Republican for the most part. It is tempting to claim they became Democrats in the twentieth century, but by then the American Reformation was over and the conversation changed. Although liberals favored a consistent range of social and political positions over this long period, their most fundamental commitment was to their approach to truth. Against those who believed they already knew what was right and pursued policies to reflect this fixed truth, liberals advocated for truths they recognized as provisional and incomplete, and they were committed to listening to contrary opinions for any possible truths the opposition might hold and working dialogically toward consensus. At least in theory. This open-ended conception of truth was born of Christian humility in the eighteenth century, when the American Reformation tied equality and liberty to the human soul at the same moment these root concepts were being tied to American democracy. The democratic idea gradually became not only a political system but also, among liberals, a universal ideal for the social practice of treating others as equals, a "religion of democracy." The commitment to universal moral agency was what it meant to be liberal from the early republic into the twentieth century, the period covered in this book. Only with the New Deal did the word "liberal" come to indicate a political commitment to a federal government responsible for social welfare, a commitment that was indeed produced by the long conversation among liberals with one another and their ever-changing opponents but that, once held as a fixed truth, was no longer liberal in this historically grounded sense of the term.[8]

Two subtle ironies surround the history of this religion of democracy. The first is that the liberal Christians who set its wheels in motion acquired a reputation for softening their religion into mere morality, as though to focus on ethics were to focus on something other than real religion. From the liberal point of view, virtue is the fruit by which true faith is known. This charge is a by-product of the myth of orthodox Protestant Christianity, made especially potent by what happened during the middle period of the American Reformation. When Romantic ideas about universal inner divinity arose amid an exploding literary canon that was globally inclusive for the first time, Christianity's claims to exclusive truth started to look like hubris to some liberals. How could an open-minded moral agent be so sure a Hindu did not know God? Transcendentalists and others then left the Christian fold without really rejecting Christ. To the surprise of many faithful devotees of the

American Reformation, liberal Christians started battling their own intellectual and cultural progeny, post-Christian religious liberals who discovered the divine not only in the Christian Bible but far beyond it. This post-Christian turn marked the end of the American Reformation and the beginning of the religion of democracy in which no tradition could boast unique revelation but all individuals bore unique inner divinity.

The second irony around this history is that the chief sin of which these post-Christian religious liberals were accused was of discarding ethics altogether by indulging in a moral relativism that verged on nihilism. The charge is delivered with moral indignation if not outrage, as though giving credence to other points of view were not itself a moral commitment with venerable Christian roots. Tolerance looked like apathy to critics and piety to liberals.[9]

Just as there is more than a grain of truth in the myth of orthodox Protestant Christianity in America, there is more than a grain of truth in these criticisms of liberal morality, despite their logical incompatibility, but nuance matters. At least it did to liberals. When Calvinists said that humans were utterly and innately sinful, liberals rejoined that humans were instead subject to sinfulness, prone to sin, the very thing religion is supposed to mitigate. This then highlights another film across this history: the one trend in the history of American religion to resist the myth of orthodox Protestant Christianity is the history of liberal religion, which includes post-Christian, metaphysical, spiritual-but-not-religious, and other nonevangelical forms of religion in the genuine and robust history of religion in the United States—and then goes on to treat liberal religion as though it did away with sin, and as though liberal religion had nothing to do with politics. This interpretation is understandable. Liberals had pushed back hard against the grim Calvinist insistence on the utter determinism of human sinfulness. Then the liberals of the nineteenth century were succeeded by some extremely optimistic and often politically irrelevant religious liberals in the therapeutic atmosphere of the twentieth century. "You are a child of the Universe," said one famous credo, reassuring an affluent public that "no doubt the universe is unfolding as it should." No problem of evil there. In the nineteenth century, however, religious liberals both Christian and post-Christian emphasized the positive in order to pull behavior out of its heavy habitual path toward the negative for reasons never unconnected to the public sphere. And they did this by focusing Christian practice—and then post-Christian religious practice—on mental development, the training of the human mind.[10]

The ideal of mental development is not as elitist as it may sound. Indeed, it is not elitist at all, although its liberal version originated among elite Bostonians. Their development of a culture of lived virtue based on the principle of moral agency provided a major feeder for the modern notion of a universal human equality compatible with human diversity, the pluralism essential to modern liberalism. That knot of refined diners among whom the father of Ralph Waldo Emerson practiced temperance did not know they were paving the way for an egalitarian doctrine of universal human value, but as soon as they declared that the most important thing about a man was the way he used his mind, they opened the theoretical door for men and women of all classes and colors to pursue their most complete mental development as the most important aspect of their religious path, and therefore the most important contribution they could make to the good of society. By any demographic measure, whether race, class, gender, ethnicity, religious affiliation, or public sexual orientation, the early intellectual fellowships of the Boston liberals were strikingly homogeneous. But from the perspective of the liberals themselves—blind as they were, at the time, to the impact of socioeconomics on status and access—their fellowships were beautifully diverse because liberals varied so much in opinion, taste, and experience, and they bounced these differences off one another so productively.

The goal of mental independence, in which the moral agent resists the way of the herd and speaks freely with candor and humility, encouraged every individual to find and develop her or his own inner voice of the divine to join the human chorus for the sake of the common good. Liberals valued individuality, not individualism, and the reason they came out against slavery and for women's rights was because slavery and patriarchy prohibited self-culture. Later liberals found that unregulated capitalism did too. Meanwhile, their reading lists quickly grew to include continental Europeans and more—taking in Muslim, Persian, Hindu, Buddhist, and Confucian texts—while their correspondents and travel ranged beyond Western Europe around the globe. As their canon expanded over the nineteenth century, the small elite of Boston liberals steadily extended their circles outward from the Northeast across the American West to include women, Jews, immigrants, workers, Native Americans, and former slaves and their descendants in a vast network of liberal intellectual culture lived through educational institutions, sermons and addresses, books and periodicals, friendships, fellowships, associations, and reform movements.

It took about a hundred years, but by practicing an ethic of inclusivity and integrity, liberals developed some of the most diverse communities of discourse by any measure ever found in human history up to that point. They also helped make possible both the more diverse fellowships that followed them—the United Nations, for example—and the more specialized, such as the National Association for the Advancement of Colored People. The diversity of the liberal fellowships did not correspond in representative percentages to the demographic diversity of American society by the turn of the twentieth century, nor indeed to the diversity of human society. Long after they had theoretically breached the barriers of prejudice and discrimination, most liberal fellowships remained disproportionately Anglo-Protestant and middle class. Such fellowships reflected the long leadership of the liberal movement and the accumulation of liberal privilege, while also including delegates from America's many internal constituencies. The liberal fellowships produced a religion of democracy that fed into both American civil religion and international human rights.[11]

This book re-creates the ever-evolving liberal conversation from the eighteenth century to the twentieth by tracing the lived connections between thinkers through what they read and wrote, who they knew, where they went, and how they expressed their opinions. Each chapter overlaps chronologically with its neighbor as generations reach into one another, texts cross oceans and centuries, and languages blend and change. The chapters all center on a single historical figure as a vantage point for seeing into the problems and preoccupations of the time and listening in on arguments, learning vocabularies, and meeting other participants in the liberal conversation. These chapters are not so much biographies aimed at understanding the character or legacy of these specific historical actors as they are reconstructions of key controversies in which the actors participated. The historical guides whose voices govern each chapter were "Representative Men"—and women—in the sense in which Ralph Waldo Emerson used the term in 1850: "such as are good of their kind."[12]

Emerson was talking about heroic genius, inspired by Romantic poets, but he too was a liberal who learned almost as much from his aunt—who read those poets first—as he taught his readers, who read the Romantics too. He and they all believed that everyone is sacred and there are no sacred cows, making heroism the daily act of speaking boldly and listening meekly like a moral agent who fears no truth.

1.

John Adams, Reformation Christian

THE PROTESTANT MORAL ETHIC AND THE SPIRIT OF INDEPENDENCE

John Adams was a good son. A good son to his father, Deacon John Adams, who made shoes and tanned hides and farmed crops all to the glory of God, whom he served by lay leadership at their village church, a lifestyle of simplicity, modesty, and charity, and the regular enforcement of Christian order at home, where prayer, Bible study, and obedience were on the agenda of each day. Adams family values cornered on personal morality, so even if the son departed from doctrines held by his father, they agreed on the necessity of reining in the passions, cultivating virtue, and submitting to divine providence.

Adams always admired his father's moral character. "Nothing that I can say or do," avowed the son late in life, "can sufficiently express my Gratitude for his parental Kindness to me, or the exalted Opinion I have of his Wisdom and Virtue." If the letter of their beliefs differed—which there is no way of fully knowing because Deacon John Adams, like most yeomen in colonial America, left little written record behind—they shared not only the common practices of piety but also a common faith in what their minister called "the divine Right of private Judgment." As Reformation Christians, they felt free to disagree with other Christians plenty, yet even disagreement rested on the essential Protestant conviction they shared with other spiritual descendants of Martin Luther, who claimed a fundamental Christian liberty with his historic pledge: "Here I stand, I can do no other, so help me God."[1]

John Adams was a good son of New England too. He knew the ways of his forebears and kept them, hearing sermons twice every Sunday and recording their substance diligently in the homemade diary he started keeping at age seventeen, while a student at Harvard, where for more than a century gentlemen and yeomen alike had been sending their most favored sons as preparation for leadership in church and state. Adams wanted to become a minister, but the church was growing more internally contentious at the time Adams had to make his choice, and he feared it would not tolerate his convictions in a pulpit. He decided he could do more good in law, and in Boston. There, as the movement for independence gained momentum, Adams joined the fray by writing something he called "An Essay upon Forefathers Rock"—the Adams farm lay some thirty miles from Plymouth—because in order to argue against the injustice of the Stamp Act and for the independent character of the American people, Adams drew on his heritage, telling a story about the Puritans that subsumed the Pilgrims and had nothing to do with Calvinism or theocracy and everything to do with self-government.[2]

Adams was not only being a politician when he cast his ancestors as the originators of American political culture, lovers of liberty who bravely resisted "spiritual tyranny." He was being a historian. At the same moment that a group of New England Congregationalists calling themselves orthodox were narrowing down the memory of the Puritan tradition to its Calvinist creed, Adams narrowed it down to its particular moral ethic, one that valued the common good over self-interest, extolled the pursuit of knowledge as a way to worship God and his creation, and insisted on both the divine right of private judgment and the related, God-given "dignity of human nature," as Adams put it in the essay. New England Puritans allowed no earthly authority to stand between their consciences and their God, in Adams's telling, which made them nonconformists fitted for self-government as no other people ever had been. Independent thought and action was central to Puritan culture.[3]

John Adams was, most famously and self-consciously, a good Son of Liberty. In the revolutionary brotherhood he joined in 1766 and arguably even more so in his legal defense of their enemies four years later in the Boston Massacre trial, Adams tried to do what he thought was right regardless of received opinion, to treat others fairly even when he disagreed with their positions, and to represent his own views candidly while keeping his mind receptive to other perspectives and new information. How successful he was in these efforts is up to another kind of history to judge. On the question of how Adams understood liberty and what difference that understanding made to the course of American thought, however, these ethical commitments say a lot. Tolerance, impartiality, and candor were the social virtues of a moral agent, the ideal Christian type produced by the American Reformation that sprang up when new Enlightenment texts fertilized the old Puritan fields of greater Boston. In the theology of the American Reformation, divine moral perfection stood at the center, God being the sole possessor of absolute truth and justice, the very definition of good. Against the wisdom and universal benevolence of God, human limitations are woefully apparent—and this is why liberty matters. It is the necessary precondition for the fight against sin. Humans have a duty to exercise liberty because they have mental powers implanted within them, by divine agency, for the purpose of growing virtue by discerning right from wrong. This essential human moral agency mandates both acting with personal integrity and recognizing the common dignity of other equally limited, equally divinely created beings equally endowed with the rights of liberty: of private judgment, conscience, and free inquiry. Because of the American Reformation, whose theology Adams and others brought into the founding of the republic, the American idea was never only the freedom from interference by authority with individual thoughts and beliefs. It was always also the freedom to pursue what is both true and right.[4]

Being a good son did not mean that John Adams was a good person, necessarily. All reports about his vanity, sensitivity, and pride are true. His temper was easy to provoke. He never forgot a grudge. He lorded his superior knowledge over others and needled those he could prove to have been in the wrong. He judged the morals and manners of individuals and whole nations with the condescending eye of the smugly righteous, while worrying too much—much too much—about what others thought of him. His anti-Catholic bigotry and lack of leadership on the slavery question mark him as a New Englander of his time, and compared to other founders, especially Franklin and Jefferson, he never lost the air of the provincial. Yet this is precisely what makes him such an important figure for understanding the spirit of independence in the American founding and the religious dimension of liberalism. His early social experience with Christians of diverse doctrinal complexions, especially as a schoolmaster after college in a town west of Boston, factored as much in the making of his revolutionary convictions as his readings during those years of natural and moral philosophy, classical republican and Whig political theory, and heterodox Protestant theology from Europe. His intimacy with the culture that produced him fundamentally shaped how he used the intellectual resources of his age.[5]

In 1904 the German sociologist Max Weber chose Benjamin Franklin to represent the Protestant ethic in his famous study of capitalism, and reasonably so, for no American styled himself with savvier self-fashioning than the thrifty, practical, worldly, entrepreneurial, optimistic, and industrious Franklin of his *Autobiography* (1791). Franklin exemplified the American individualism that transferred to this world the efforts once reserved for the next. If Weber had chosen Franklin's contemporary Rev. Jonathan Edwards, who redesigned Calvinism for Lockean Americans, he would have discovered a rather different Protestant ethic. Edwards sternly subordinated the things of this world before the judgment of a wrathful God, who offered sinners the only moral progress they could get through the single doorway of repentance and conversion. Edwards provided the eighteenth century a modern salvation-oriented ethic increasingly favored by a revived Christian American majority. This Protestant ethic fostered a different kind of American individualism from that of Franklin, and a different kind of American "we."[6]

In John Adams, Weber would have found yet another Protestant ethic, a particular moral ethic, an ethic that provided the politically necessary middle ground between the otherworldliness of an Edwards and the worldliness of a Franklin. Adams could occupy this middle ground because he had a foot in each sphere, equally balanced between the traditional Reformation Christian world of most Americans and the modern rational humanist world of others. Both sides fed what hope Adams had in the human capacity for progress because the perfection of God provided both the tools and the rules for moral growth. At the same time, the more Adams learned about the record of human experience, the more his respect for the power of sin grew. He would never have made a daily chart of the virtues on the presumption that he could master them, as Franklin famously did, nor would he have been satisfied with the mere appearance of virtue, nor with virtue for the sake of prudence or self-interest. Virtue was a revolutionary principle for Adams. The obligation of its pursuit was incumbent on all of humankind because the human relation to a perfect God was the thing in which all were equal. This more than any other concept allowed Adams to pry apart the colonial relationship to the crown as well as the bands of hierarchy within the colonies. By the age of twenty-one, he earnestly believed that the business of life was "constantly to improve our selves in Habits of Piety and Virtue. . . . [T]he meanest Mechanick, who endeavours in proportion to his Ability, to promote the happiness of his fellow men, deserves better of Society, and should be held in higher Esteem than the Greatest Magistrate, who uses his power for his own Pleasures or Avarice or Ambition." Adams did his part to overthrow such corrupt magistrates because of his devotion to a religious faith that, by the time he was in his eighties, described the moral ground of "Universal Tolleration" in four words: "Be Just and Good."[7]

MORAL AGENCY IN THE AMERICAN REFORMATION

The American Reformation began in 1749 when the Adams family pastor delivered a sermon at the West Church of Boston. It was a rare treat for Parson Lemuel Briant to make the trip from Braintree to the colonial capital at all, much less to appear before a well-heeled congregation already primed by the cutting-edge preaching of its regular minister, Rev. Jonathan Mayhew, to appreciate Briant's message. It was not so rare for colonial New England ministers to favor one another with sabbaticals by trading pulpits, which was the only way they could develop their sermons for publication—that is to say, the only way they could become scholars—but Briant and Mayhew were limited to trading with one another because they had yet to break into the old boys' network that distributed such favors, the Boston Association of Ministers. In fact, neither ever did. Both were young and idealistic and both revered moral agency over prudence on the scale of human virtues, which means that both of them were outspoken too, and tactless. Both were to die rather young as well, but before they did they and their like-minded brethren influenced the Christian and civic faith of not only John Adams, but a large enough and powerful enough portion of the Congregational body that by the eighteenth century their new flavor of Christianity had won over Harvard, most of Boston's better sort, and much of the merchant class in New England.[8]

Jonathan Mayhew was another good son, whose parents carried the Puritan line in their very names. His mother, Remember, was a living symbol of the Reformation Christian injunction to bend all thoughts toward the divine. His father, Rev. Experience Mayhew, reflected in his name the centrality in Reformation Christian theology of each individual's experience of the divine in the life of their faith. And the "Missionary Mayhews," as the family became known around New England, really meant to include each individual in that doctrine; Experience was the fourth Mayhew minister to preach to the Native Americans on Martha's Vineyard. Fluent in the Massachusett language, Experience made a new translation of the Psalms and the Gospel according to John early in the eighteenth century. He later wrote two different books testifying to the religious conversions and faithful lives of the Pokanoket among whom he lived, believing—as many Puritans did not—that Indians were fully capable of Christian sainthood. Not far away and not much later, John Adams frequently visited the nearby homes of Ponkapoag and Neponset, who shared their bounty of fruit with him. By the early nineteenth century, though, New England Natives had lost so much economic power that "the Girls went out to service and the Boys to sea,"

Adams wrote in an 1812 letter to Jefferson, "till not a Soul is left. We scarcely see an Indian in a year."[9]

Jonathan Mayhew left the Vineyard ministry to his father and younger brother, but he kept up the family tradition in other ways. As a minister, he called on his parishioners to keep God's perfection in mind and to imitate it, and to do so not blindly but by the light of their own senses, including the internal evidence provided by reason and conscience. His choice of language, his extrabiblical references, and his willingness to stand up to the authority of tradition all mark him as a child of the Enlightenment—and reasonably so, since the Harvard Mayhew attended had been including Locke and his epigoni in its curriculum for three decades by the time Mayhew's generation came along. Yet Mayhew was among the first to integrate Enlightenment material into his Reformation Christianity. His theology was new and daring to a degree that delighted his congregation while offending some other ministers. The novelty of his sermons also earned him an honorary degree from the University of Aberdeen in Scotland, which fostered a variety of dissenting Protestantism that American Christians, first Mayhew and friends and later including many evangelicals, found enormously appealing into the last third of the nineteenth century. But in the mid-eighteenth century, Scottish and other dissenters were controversial in the colonies.[10]

Mayhew developed a reputation for Arminianism, the religion of free will and morality long a dirty word in Calvinist circles. This reputation convinced historians from the antebellum era to the present to depict him as a radical who destroyed core principles of the theology he inherited. Yet evidently he upheld enough other core principles of that tradition to retain the approval of his "Honor'd Father," as Jonathan addressed his letters to Experience, letters he carefully smoked before mailing whenever there was sickness raging in Boston. The elder Mayhew initially drew up a will dividing his property on the Vineyard equally between Jonathan and Jonathan's older brother, but by 1755—at the same time John Adams was worrying about his prospects in the ministry given how much he liked Mayhew's theology—Experience had changed his mind: "My Will now is that he shall have the Whole of it."[11]

One reason Jonathan and Experience Mayhew only became more harmonious over the years was their agreement on the proper character of Christian ministry. Both generations of Mayhews practiced the "plain style" of preaching favored among New England Congregationalists since the first generation, which meant that they severely disliked the new revival fevers burning in the colonies. When the famed Anglican evangelist George Whitefield came to Boston in 1747, Jonathan reported to his father that although the event was well attended, it was chiefly by "the meaner sort, excepting those that heard him from a Principle of Curiosity," as Mayhew himself did. Mayhew judged the last sermon Whitefield delivered to be as "low, confused, puerile, conceited, ill-natur'd, enthusiastick, & c. Performance as ever I heard in my life." The key word here is enthusiastic, for Old Lights like the Mayhews and New Lights like Whitefield and Edwards had a disagreement over intellectual style rather than doctrine. After all, Edwards was as Calvinist as they came, and his brand of Calvinism was soon to be scholasticized in New England by Congregationalists who then wielded Edwardsian theology against fellow Congregationalists in the Mayhew strain. The New Lights, in their thirst for conversion and its fruits, were united not so much by their doctrines as by their willingness to interpret passionate human emotions—what one historian calls "fits, trances, and visions"—as signs of divine grace, and to gear the style of sermons toward arousing those emotional states. The Old Lights disagreed, insisting that sobriety in both preacher and parishioner remained the optimal mode of religious instruction. As Briant attested from Mayhew's pulpit, Christianity is "a Doctrine of Sobriety, Righteousness and Piety."[12]

Possibly the most vocal opponent of the new revivalism, Rev. Charles Chauncy of Boston's First Church (or "Old Brick"), developed his contribution to the American Reformation out of his critique of the revival style. Chauncy, born a year after Edwards, was already settled at Old Brick when the first revivals began. Initially his response modeled the temperance he advocated. Distinguishing the Reformation Christian ideal from other approaches to belief in a 1739 sermon, for example, he explained that in the scripture "Compel them to come in," Christ "speaks, not of *physical*, but *moral* Compulsion; not of Compulsion by *outward Violence*, but *internal Persuasion*; that which is effected, not by *Fines, Imprisonments, Racks* and *Tortures*, but by Application to the *Understandings* of Men." Chauncy identified the Christian faith with a mild evangelism of reasoning and argumentation, sensitive to the mental states of individuals and protective of moral agency. By illustrating the specter of forceful compulsion with Inquisition-style Christianity, he defended and amplified the standard of sober, reasoned Christian faith against which revival methods contrasted so strongly. Enthusiastic evangelism stoked the very passions God had provided reason to contain. In the view of Reformation Christians like Chauncy, revivalist methods led to "Error in Principle," "wildness in Imagination," "Indecency in Language," and "Irregularity in Practice" among unreliable witnesses to a corrupted Christian faith. He challenged the Protestant credentials of revivalists, urging his hearers to imitate "the first Reformers," when Luther himself inveighed against the "pretended Prophets, who boasted of angelic Revelations, and immediate Converse with GOD." Chauncy placed his own theology squarely in the Reformation Christian tradition.[13]

Chauncy was among the few senior ministers in Boston to welcome Mayhew onto the scene in 1747. Before receiving the call from West Church, Mayhew had candidated for a congregation in Worcester, but he was handily beaten by a fire-and-brimstone preacher, Thaddeus Maccarty (who later found the town a new schoolmaster in a bright fresh Harvard graduate with excellent Christian character, John Adams). Mayhew was not popular in the provinces. Even in Boston many wondered whether his brilliance might not be suspicious in itself, but his career was safe so long as the people of West Church were happy with him. Chauncy—whose published sermons had earned him an honorary degree from the University of Edinburgh in 1742—quite liked Mayhew, and so did Ebenezer Gay (1696–1787), beloved pastor on Boston's South Shore at Hingham, another architect of the American Reformation and a former teacher of Mayhew's. Gay ordained Mayhew and later joined Chauncy in burying him. As the senior theologian of the American Reformation, Gay—who initially supported evangelical revivalism before gradually disassociating himself from it—articulated the definition of religion that distinguished the kind of Christianity to emerge from the American Reformation, a definition that remained remarkably constant across the nineteenth century even as Reformation Christians turned into liberal Christians who turned into post-Christian religious liberals. Religion, according to Gay, is *"An Obligation lying upon Men to do those Things which the Perfections of God, relative unto them, do require of them."* In other words, religion is not a set of beliefs but an action-generating principle.[14]

The action that religion obliges humankind to undertake is, of course, moral virtue. This was the subject that got Briant in trouble after his appearance at West Church. Mayhew had already preached—and published—on the issue, claiming in 1748 that the moral perfection of God places upon all "intelligent beings" the "obligation to practice what is usually called *moral virtue*; for by this we imitate God: and fall in with his benevolent design in creating and governing the world." Briant agreed. His 1749 sermon, however, was not simply an affirmation of Mayhew's point of view; it was a salvo fired at their fellow Congregationalists who seemed to preach otherwise. Briant's West Church sermon was called "The Absurdity and Blasphemy of Depretiating Moral Virtue," and it challenged the evangelical denial of the spiritual value of moral effort as an idea opposing the religion of Christ, a challenge Briant tethered to biblical proof. Briant used as his text Isaiah 64:6 ("All our Righteousnesses are as filthy Rag[s]"). He argued that this verse was specific to the cultural context in which it was uttered and could not mean that God's creatures are totally depraved, not when the Bible shows that moral virtue is "what Christ himself laid the chiefest Stress upon." Briant's evidence was the "divine Sermon on the Mount; which contains the Sum and Substance of his whole Doctrine." These radically moral teachings in the Gospel according to Matthew also provided the central text for three of Mayhew's published sermons, "The Love of God," "The Love of our Neighbor," and "The first and great Commandment." The Christ of the American Reformation saved humankind not by atonement but by mediating between earthly sin and heavenly perfection through the example of his life as supreme moral agent as well as the golden rule of his teaching.[15]

Undoubtedly this was shocking doctrine from a Calvinist perspective, but Briant was prepared for the reaction. He anticipated the criticism of his doctrinal antagonists, rebutting in advance by stating a principle he knew was shared across the Congregationalist spectrum—that of private judgment—and resting his case on it. To the expected objection that his sermon would feed a sense of sanctimoniousness and righteousness in its hearers, he responded simply, "I have no other Answer to make, but to leave every one to judge for himself, how groundless it is." The centrality of the divine right of private judgment was also the subject of one of Mayhew's 1748 sermons; it was the liberals' best tool for legitimizing doctrinal novelties. This principle was so deeply rooted in New England culture that the Massachusetts charter of 1691 had guaranteed all Reformation Christians "a liberty of Conscience." The architects of the American Reformation invoked this right again and again as they argued for their own interpretations as scripturally grounded, against the legitimacy of authority standing outside the individual, and for appeal to the standard of evidence. Objections must have grounds. Claims must stand on the strength of their argumentation. The conjoining of the Reformation Christian commitment to liberty of conscience with the Enlightenment standard of empirical discovery brought about something new, a practical approach for ascertaining truth and justice and for acting with moral virtue. Briant called this approach "right Reasoning."[16]

Right reasoning laid out the tools for building the understanding of what is true and the practice of what is right. Briant, Mayhew, Gay, Chauncy, and other ministers who read the new theology coming out of Britain used its Enlightenment tinges to specify how Christians should enlist their mental powers in developing their moral virtue in the direction of divine perfection. The first rule was for Christians to acknowledge that they are not yet in possession of truth. Call it humility, call it partiality, call it fallibility, it is objectively true from a Reformation Christian perspective that no one can claim to possess the whole truth any more than they can claim to be free of sin. Therefore all must continue to seek more truth. Briant urged his audience to listen to his sermon "in meekness of Wisdom," the remembrance that the only ultimate viewpoint belongs exclusively to God. Christians proceed open-mindedly, therefore, "in real Love to the Truth wherever we find it." The alternative to acknowledging human ignorance relative to God is swallowing doctrine that is not only false but downright dangerous in pretending to truth. "For with what Air of Infallibility soever Men may vent the Fictions of their own weak or disordered Brains for the Doctrines and Precepts of the Gospel," Briant complained, "the greatest Absurdities, the most palpable Nonsense" will get foisted upon those uncritical enough to believe it.[17]

The second rule taught the critical thinking necessary to discern between doctrines. Truth-seekers must be open-minded, honest, and sincere. They resist appeals to authority, tradition, or superstition, thinking for themselves and being both candid about what they think and willing to consider all claims. Mayhew stated such a rule in a 1748 sermon when he criticized the scribes and Pharisees in the time of Christ as "imposing upon the people" on the basis of their authoritative air, thereby acting without "such an unprejudiced and candid disposition as became inquirers after the truth." Briant skipped the Pharisees and went straight after "those who sustain the Character of *Teachers* in the Christian Church." At all of twenty-seven years old, he chided his fellow ministers that they are "under special Obligations to search the Scriptures daily, to give themselves to Study, Meditation and Prayer" so that they do not mistakenly expound doctrines "from particular Scraps of Scripture, and from the bare jingle of Words." Only with Christian teachers like these can parishioners "consider with themselves" what meaning to take away from scripture. The rule of critical thinking applies two ways, then, upon both the manner of preaching and the manner of listening. The good Christian is "the Sober, and the Sensible" evaluator of doctrine, who would "never receive any Thing for Truth only because 'tis spoken with an Air of Assurance and *Godly Tone*." The right of private judgment connotes a duty of critical thinking.[18]

The third rule of right reasoning directed the Christian to consider the effects of a doctrine as indicative of its degree of validity. If the fundamental reasonable Christian premise is the moral perfection of God, all other doctrines must be evaluated according to their ability to foster human virtue. Of the "false Gloss" that holds the Isaiah verse to mean that humankind can produce no goodness whatsoever, Briant warned against "the dangerous Consequences of admitting this Sense of the Text." Such a reading "tends to prejudice the most Sensible against the Christian Profession, and confirm Men in their Infidelity." Indeed, such a misreading amounts to "the most effectual Discouragement that could be given to the Practice of Christian Morality, and consequently one of the most fatal Snares that could be laid for the Souls of Men." The practical effect of some Calvinist doctrines was immorality and infidelity, not righteousness. Worst of all, some Christian teachers think so mistakenly about the role of grace in salvation, according to Briant, that "they conceive of it so as to destroy all moral Agency, and set themselves down with this vain Thought, that nothing on their Part is necessary to Salvation, but if they are designed for it, they shall *irresistably* be driven into Heaven, whether they will or not." A doctrine that saps Christians of moral agency cannot be true.[19]

This direct connection between articles of faith and moral behavior became one of the hallmarks of the American Reformation. As Mayhew put it in a sermon on "The Difference Betwixt Truth and Falshood, Right and Wrong," whether Christ's use of "right" refers to "what is *true in theory*, or what is *right in practice*, it will come to much the same thing at last." Seeing this is a matter of clear thinking. "If certain things are *true* in speculation, there must be some correspondent *fitness* of actions resulting therefrom," Mayhew explained. More pointedly, Briant averred that "no Scheme can be right, no Doctrine from God that abates the Motives of Vertue, or discourages the Practice of any one Duty." What is true begets what is right. What is right must be true.[20]

All of these rules blended Reformation Christian and Enlightenment principles. Fallibility works as well in experimental science as in Calvinism, and reason was held to be the voice of God within, alongside conscience. Right reasoning meant acknowledging fallibility, thinking for oneself, expressing one's views forthrightly, evaluating others' views with a mind both critical and receptive, and attending particularly to the moral effects of beliefs. This Christian mental training sharpened the precision with which the implications of truth-claims are brought to light. From this process, truth and morality as lived and understood by earthbound humans could no longer appear in black-and-white terms, either absolutely right or absolutely wrong. They appeared in shades of gray, all polluted by sin against the heavenly purity of Christ and his Father, but polluted to different degrees, differences with real moral meaning. Briant argued in his sermon that the doctrine of total depravity, in failing to distinguish between degrees of moral misconduct, equated "the Character of a very loose and abandoned People" with that of "the best Righteousness of the most improved Christians," ultimately insulting God's judgment. In one of his rebuttals to the fallout that ensued upon the sermon's publication, he was more specific. "I always tho't that so far as any Man is pure, (let it be in a greater or lesser Degree) he is not filthy." Moreover, for a New England tradition committed to "carrying on a *glorious Work* of Reformation in the Land," Briant thought it a terrible hindrance "to make personal Goodness of no Account, and to load it with the most Opprobrious Language, because we an't so perfect in the Practice of it, as some other superior Beings in the Universe."[21]

Finally, Briant presented the pursuit of moral virtue as the pursuit of happiness, which God wants for humankind. The God of the American Reformation was all-wise, all-knowing, and all-benevolent too. Mayhew called him "Parent of the world," characterizing his attitude toward humanity as one of "*loving-kindness*." Briant agreed that "it must be the grand Design, the ultimate View of God, in all his Dispensations, to promote the moral Rectitude and Happiness of his Creatures." This was much more significant than simply believing in an ordered universe and a rational conception of the deity. God lost none of his power by being defined by his benevolence. Instead, the starting premise of God's benevolence created a logical progression of inferences that all of his laws, moral and natural, tended toward the good, so that examining, understanding, and following those laws worked both to fulfill God's will and to effect human good. Salvation itself became reconfigured in the progressive terms of the American Reformation. Not a black-and-white deal done in a predestined moment or a rapturous one, salvation was a gradual drawing near the goodness of God through successive acts of moral agency. Virtue was not some arbitrary thing God wants for his own glory, but is consistent with his benevolence. "Either our Righteousness is of some Use and Significancy in the Affair of our Salvation," Briant pointed out, "or it is not. Either it has some Connection with, and actual Influence on our Happiness, or it is of no real Necessity as to us." This view of happiness is neither the simple contentment of prudence and self-interest nor the ultimate glory of heaven. It is the sign of God's love. Denigrating the importance of virtue denigrates the character and wisdom of God. To love God is instead to believe with Paul, with whose words from Titus 3:8 Briant closed his sermon, that moral actions "*are* GOOD, *and* PROFITABLE *unto Men*." In essence, the theology of the American Reformation challenged part of the doctrinal interpretation of the Protestant Reformation traditional in New England with arguments rooted in an equally traditional commitment to private judgment.[22]

Reaction to Briant's sermon came in two waves. The first, a pamphlet war, came from other provincial ministers taking to pulpits in direct challenge to Briant's theology, and Briant answering them. The second wave erupted in Briant's home congregation, when a brother of Deacon John Adams—Ebenezer Adams—agitated to have Briant removed from the pulpit, adding charges of personal and ministerial misconduct to those of false doctrine. Various councils of ministers and church members ensued. The controversy set the template for the rest of the American Reformation, during which Congregationalist ministers and laity argued among themselves and against one another over doctrinal matters, generating a flood of literature that refined the edges between doctrines, creating a polarization where before there had been a spectrum of difference. The later controversies have been well studied by scholars, who dub them "the Unitarian controversies," since they resulted in the schism within the Congregational Church that produced the Unitarian denomination in the nineteenth century. Here at the start of the American Reformation, though, the doctrine of the trinity was not at issue. Instead, as arguments against Briant sharpened the distinction between the orthodoxy his opponents claimed for themselves and the heresy they pinned to him, the once common ground of the divine right of private judgment became a battleground.[23]

The first to respond to Briant's sermon, published soon after its delivery, was Rev. John Porter of Bridgewater, who legitimated his own New Light heterodoxy via his attack on Briant. Porter delivered his response in one of Briant's competitor churches in Braintree six months after Briant's appearance at West Church, pointedly titling his sermon "The Absurdity and Blasphemy of substituting the personal Righteousness of Men in the Room of the Surety-Righteousness of CHRIST, in the important Article of Justification before GOD." Naturally, the sermon aimed to present the evangelical view of Christ's atonement of sins as the scripturally based one, expressing astonished outrage at how "some entertaining an high Opinion of their Gifts and Abilities" overlook the "text and context" of the "infallible" word of God in preaching otherwise. A textbook exposition of the justification of sinners by grace ensued. Yet Porter had to allow that Christianity did indeed prescribe "Duties of Piety, Righteousness, and Sobriety," and further that doctrines were to be judged in part by whether "*dreadful Consequences*" ensued. Porter simply insisted that the ill consequences followed what he named "the *modern Arminian Way*," which he contrasted with "the *good old calvinistical Way*." But his sermon, which was signed by five other ministers supporting his position against that of Briant, was not necessarily the good old way of New England's heritage. Neither John Cotton nor Increase Mather would have recognized the evangelical message in Porter's sermon, which he closed on an Edwardsian note, warning any wayward members of the flock to whom he preached, "You are this *Moment* upon the Brink of eternal Burnings: and should God cut the slender Thread of your Lives, you would be immediately beyond *all Hope* and Help for ever." The only solution to this plight is to repent and be saved at once.[24]

Briant's initial answer to Porter was relatively temperate—he entitled it "Friendly Remarks," anyway—and cheerfully denied both his Arminianism and Porter's Calvinism. The most significant feature of his reply was where he aimed for harmony, and how. Briant praised the degree of protection in their time of the "Freedom and Plainness of Speech (which is an essential Branch of that Holiness that becomes God's House forever)," clearly including Porter in this Reformation Christian value. "We are all agreed in the divine Right of *private judgment*," Briant concluded, a point Porter conceded in his next reply. Insisting again on his own fidelity to Calvin and Briant's to Arminius, Porter laid out his case and then handed off the verdict: "Let the World judge." When Rev. Samuel Niles chimed in—after Briant's "Some more friendly remarks" quite intemperately accused Porter of plagiarizing one of the English theologians he claimed to find so heretical—Niles upheld at least one plank of Briant's right reasoning when he claimed that his convictions "are not built on *Tradition*, or the Authority of our Fathers." The claim rang a little hollow, coming after the ministers who appended their signatures to Porter's initial criticism signed under the claim that Porter preached the truth "as it hath been taught in *these Churches* from the Beginning of *New England*." The fight was on.[25]

The venue shifted from the theoretical realm of the pulpit to the practical question of what to do about Briant. In addition to his error-ridden preaching, Briant had not performed public fasts adequately, nor taught the catechism. He had alienated his wife's affections to such a degree that she left him, accusing him of tippling and of "not using her well," as Jonathan Mayhew described the situation in a letter to his father. Briant was also in trouble for recommending that a parishioner read a dangerous book by an English dissenter, Rev. John Taylor. All of these instigations brought together "a Number of aggrieved Persons" in requesting an investigation, which materialized in the form of an ecclesiastical council made up of seven churches. They met at the end of 1752 "at the House of Deacon *John Adams*."[26]

Deacon Adams himself did not sign the document of grievance generated by that meeting, appearing to support Briant. Young John was off at Harvard by this point, so he could not witness the discussions, but he followed the drama through print and gossip. The council laid out the charges against Briant, including his refusal either to meet with the council or to call a church meeting. The members of the council notably insisted that they arrived at their grievance after engaging, in good Congregationalist fashion, in "a serious, deliberate and impartial Consideration."[27]

Briant was not dismissed. Despite the assembly of opponents to his ministry from other churches, his own church supported him. The congregation formed a committee to field the concerns of the ecclesiastical council, demonstrating in their report what good students of the American Reformation they were. The principles of right reasoning appeared throughout the short document. The committee praised Briant's sermons "as having a direct Tendency to inspire every unprejudiced Mind with the Love of Virtue and Goodness." They affirmed Briant's personal "Right of private Judgment" and, to the charge regarding the book recommendation, underscored the importance of conscience by explaining that "we can't but commend our Pastor for the Pains he takes to promote a free and impartial Examination into all Articles of our holy Religion, so that *all may judge of themselves, what is right*." The members of the committee did not necessarily agree with Briant's doctrines, noting in the report that "he may differ from some of us," but they insisted upon his "Right to judge for himself." Any "Difference in Opinion" between them was acceptable in light of the greater obligations of private judgment.[28]

Briant did not last long after this controversy, however. His wife stayed away. His health worsened, whether owing to the fondness for drink of which she had accused him or to some other cause history will never know. He asked for a leave of absence from his duties, and then died. He was thirty-two years old.

Yet he had set the American Reformation on its course, with effects far wider than a single sermon. By creating a big enough interest in the question of moral virtue, Briant had helped shape the careers of his opponents almost as much as of his allies. Although he did not oppose the Puritan tradition itself but only the legitimacy of appeals to tradition as reasons not to think for oneself, he lost the claim to orthodoxy in the fight against the neo-Calvinists, who thereby gained in their quest to legitimate the new evangelical focus on conversion. But the neo-Calvinists lost too. The new Boston Christianity of Briant and Mayhew seized the high ground of the divine right of private judgment, and from it generated rules of right reasoning that would prove potent in arguments of all kinds. By reformulating religion around the idea that God's perfection obligated humankind to act with moral agency, the American Reformation invested the individual with a new kind of sovereignty, and with it a new responsibility to behave with personal integrity. Now good Christians "will (if they are honest Men) with all Openness declare their Sentiments," said Briant, "and by the Force of right Reasoning endeavor to propagate them."[29]

A COSMOPOLITAN PROVINCIAL

John Adams at college read all the sermons and reports related to the Briant affair—and much else besides—with great interest. He was trying to decide between ministry and law, a pleasant state of suspension while he excelled in his classes, dabbled in the new scientific "Experimental Phylosophy," and argued with his friends. As he recalled to Jefferson more than half a century later, at the time he thought himself "a metaphysician," and his friends "thought me so too; for we were forever disputing though in great good humor."[30]

The disputes of this phase of the future statesman's life were formative. In his old age Adams often referred back to this era, especially the years he spent considering the ministry while teaching school in Worcester, as the time when he settled on his personal brand of religion, which he practiced with temperate zeal for the rest of his life. It was a religion in which the contrast between the good-natured disputes he had with his peers and the ecclesiastical disputes that almost brought down Briant was morally meaningful. It was a religion that had room for differences of opinion while uniting around moral conduct. It was a religion, as he declared to Jefferson near the end of their lives, consisting of a simple twofold active practice. "Allegiance to the Creator and Governor of the Milky-Way . . . and benevolence to all his creatures, is my Religion," Adams declared. Then he added, in Latin, that if Jefferson had any better ideas he should "candidly share them."[31]

Before Adams even entered college, he had heard Mayhew preach from Briant's pulpit a number of times and read his published sermons, one in particular with great avidity. It was the sermon that "made a Noise in Great Britain where it was reprinted and procured the Author a Diploma of Doctor in Divinity," Adams explained to Jefferson sixty-nine years later, enclosing a copy of what "was a tolerable Chatechism for The Education of a Boy of 14 Years of Age, who was destined in the future Course of his Life to dabble in so many Revolutions in America, in Holland and in France." Adams told Jefferson that he had "read it, till the Substance of it was incorporated into my Nature and indelibly engraved on my Memory." The sermon was called "A Discourse, Concerning the Unlimited Submission and Non-Resistance to the Higher Powers" (1750). It made the linkage between civil and ecclesiastical tyranny that Adams later harnessed for revolutionary purposes in his published response to the Stamp Act, on grounds that he also helped see into the Declaration of Independence. He gave credit where it was due, ever after describing Mayhew and Chauncy as responsible for the change in the people's hearts and minds that brought about the Revolution.[32]

Mayhew had gotten much of his argument from *The Independent Whig* (1721), a polemical work by an anonymous pair of English dissenters, John Trenchard and Thomas Gordon, who also produced the widely influential *Cato's Letters* (1724), which mixed liberal and republican political languages to create the radical Whig ideology later to prove so potent in American revolutionary thought. *The Independent Whig* burnished the anti-Catholic prejudice that Mayhew and Adams and everyone else in the American Reformation displayed. As Adams wrote in his diary after reading *The Independent Whig* in Worcester, "The Church of Rome has made it an Article of Faith that no man can be saved out of their Church, and all other religious Sects approach to this dreadfull opinion in proportion to their Ignorance, and the Influence of ignorant or wicked Priests." Fears of papacy ran deep in Anglo-American religious culture, of course, as did fears of papist principles infiltrating Reformation Christian circles. The new aspect of the radical Whig critique of "PRIEST-CRAFT and Nonsense," as Mayhew put it, was the idea that there is something wrong with claiming exclusive truth, and something downright tyrannical about imposing such a claim on others. The only aspect of religion everyone with their different sensory experiences and personal understandings can agree upon is the behavior that religion should produce, which is morality, "a social Virtue, or rather the Mother of all social Virtues," according to Trenchard and Gordon. "It wishes and promotes unlimited and universal Happiness to the whole World," they argued in one of the more serious moments of a rather playful text. Morality, the common ground of civil and religious society, "regards not a *Christian* more than a *Jew* or an *Indian*, any further than as he is a better Citizen; and not so much, if he is not." On the basis of morality and not authority, differences of doctrinal allegiance and what may be called culture are compatible with the fundamental equality with which all are born.[33]

Mayhew plastered *The Independent Whig*'s arguments about tyranny onto the Bible and the divine right of private judgment—in other words, onto the New England tradition. From a robust and reasoned defense of human dignity with extensive scriptural citations, he paired moral virtue, which God gave his creatures liberty in order to pursue, with the style of intellectual candor in which one's own opinions are spoken plainly and those of others respected. Tyranny of either church or state "degrades men from their just rank, into the class of brutes." Mayhew argued that the "spirit of civil and religious liberty" is promoted by overcoming divisions on the common ground of moral pursuit. "There are virtuous and candid men in all sects," after all, and "all such are to be esteemed." But "there are also vicious men and bigots in all sects; and all such *ought to be despised*."[34]

Tolerance? Not exactly. The idea of transcending sectarian divisions in the name of virtue did reflect the pioneering opinions of Locke and the radical Whigs, who advocated a "latitudinarian" style of Christianity that defined the church broadly enough to include different beliefs on grounds of prudence. Whether those beliefs were true or not, the latitudinarians thought, it was better for the church to tolerate them than to repress them. Yet in the American Reformation, the right of private judgment pointed to a duty of public expression too, evaluating the results of holding this or that belief by measure of the virtue or non-virtue such a belief produced. There was no shortage of judgment in Mayhew's sermon on unlimited submission in relation to civil power. He qualified the degree to which subjects ought to submit on Lockean grounds of consent and government's "subserviency to the general welfare." King Charles I was certainly judged by Mayhew as a vicious bigot with a taste for Rome, who "died an enemy to liberty and the rights of conscience," and Mayhew notably enumerated a long list of grievances against the king, prefiguring the Declaration of Independence. He offered evidence for his moral judgments, as well as for his claim that he had a right as a minister to comment on political concerns, which grounded his judgment in terms that could be considered by others. In an exercise of candor, he offered his point of view up to his reader's judgment. Exercising "the same *freedom*" with political questions as with "other doctrines and precepts of christianity," he assured his reader that he spoke so freely "not doubting but you will *judge* upon every thing offered to your consideration, with the same spirit of *freedom* and *liberty* with which it is *spoken*."[35]

John Adams carried this imprint on his mind into his Worcester years. He was twenty when he arrived, the protégé of Rev. Maccarty, whose sermons he heard most often and with whom he frequently dined. Maccarty's favorite expressions Adams recorded in his diary: "Carnal, ungodly Persons. Sensuality and voluptuousness. Walking with God. Unregeneracy. Rebellion against God." The litany rolled on and on, calling up the proud precise faith of a doctrine-driven Reformation Christian. Adams recorded these observations without judgment in his diary, which provides a patchy record of the breadth and diversity of Christian opinion in the hinterlands of Boston. Reading Protestant dissenters from Great Britain and taking tea with neo-Calvinists, Adams appeared to be on equally good terms with Maccarty as with the household of Major Gardiner Chandler, where Enlightenment ideas were on open spigot. One evening the company there "thought that the design of Christianity was not to make men good Riddle Solvers or good mystery mongers, but good men, good majestrates and good Subjects, good Husbands and good Wives, good Parents and good Children, good masters and good servants." In the objective tone of his diary, Adams appeared to set all these opinions down to consider at his own liberty.[36]

One such opinion is particularly illustrative of the early American Reformation in two respects, the first related to how the divine right of private judgment still served as common ground among Congregationalists and the second to the relationship between Adams and Mayhew. Adams took a spring journey from Worcester toward home. Setting off early after a drink of fresh milk, he stopped first at an uncle's house, then after his next stretch of riding he rested and fed his horse with one family of Clarks and later dined with another. Finally, he visited with a most interesting pair of ministers:

> Stopd to see Mr. Haven of Dedham, who told me very civilly that he supposed I took my faith on Trust from Dr. Mayhew, and added that he believed the doctrine of the satisfaction of J[esus] C[hrist] to be essential to Cristianity, and that he would not believe this satisfaction, unless he believed the Divinity of C[hrist]. Mr. Balch was there too, and observed that he would not be a Christian if he did not believe the Mysterys of the Gospel. That he could bear with an Arminian, but when, with Dr. Mayhew, they denied the Divinity and Satisfaction of J[esus] C[hrist] he had no more to do with them. That he knew not what to make of Dr. Mayhews two discourses upon the Expected Dissolution of all Things. They gave him an Idea of a Cart whose wheels want'd greazing. It rumbled on in a hoarse rough manner. There was a good deal of ingenious Talk in them, but it was thrown together in a jumbled confused order. He believed the Dr. wrote it in a great Pannick. He added farther that Arminians, however stiffly they maintain their opinions in health, always, he takes notice, retract when they come to Die, and chose to die Calvinists.[37]

This extraordinary passage with two obscure Reformation Christians in a classic New England town provides a snapshot of a friendly, critical conversation, an exemplary model of virtue and candor. It begins with a civil rebuke, the suggestion by Haven of Dedham that young John took his "faith on Trust," which is to say that he arrived at his convictions not by a process of sober deliberation but instead felt awed by Mayhew's doctorate or air of authority, never thinking for himself. Haven and Balch agreed on what was wrong with Mayhew's Christology, but Balch's criticism—at least the parts that Adams recalled—also provides a colorful and informal but serious and penetrating analysis of Mayhew's intellect, style, and argumentation. The remarks reflect the mind of a Christian who troubled to read the work of someone with whom he disagreed, and to develop an opinion for himself.[38]

One gets the sense that Adams paid such close attention to these observations because he was preoccupied with the prospect of becoming a minister, admitting to his diary on this period that "my Inclination I think was to preach." Being linked with such a controversial figure was one matter, concern enough that when he decided against the ministry, he gave his diary the reason of his "Opinion concerning some disputed Points." But equally vivid in this entry is how attentive Adams was to the matter of style, the form of the conversation. As when he recorded Maccarty's favorite phrases, and elsewhere when he commented on sermons—some of which he found "Frigid performances," others worth paraphrasing at great length—he constantly tested languages and concepts for possible adoption in his own faith and, potentially, his career. He copied sermons and theological tracts also, in order to impress them on his mind as he had Mayhew's work. "Writing Tillotson" was a frequent notation, which meant he had spent part of his day copying out in longhand the same English latitudinarian whom Briant had accused his opponent of plagiarizing. "We are told that Demosthenes transcribed the history of Thucididies 8 times, in order to imbibe and familiarize the elegance and strength of his stile," Adams observed one fine February day. "Will it not then be worth while for a candidate for the ministry to transcribe Dr. Tillotson's Works."[39]

Haven of Dedham was wrong about Adams. He did not take his faith from Mayhew, strictly, and certainly not on trust. Adams had one of the most restless, hungry minds in the colonies. He read, he listened, he disputed, and he contemplated a wide range of Reformation Christian opinions, testing them against his experience of his own inner awareness as well as his observations of others—their characters, their strengths, their weaknesses. Some of his reflections read like paraphrases verging on interpretations, others more like the application of principles to fresh experience, as when he cast his eye about his surroundings and reflected on the glory of God in arranging the universe. The dominant note of the diary, though, is his conviction of his own sin through meditative self-awareness and honest self-examination. "I find my self very much inclin'd to an unreasonable absence of mind, and to a morose, unsociable disposition," he confessed one Friday in February 1756. "Let it therefore be my constant endeavor to reform these great faults."[40]

Inattentiveness and misuse of his time were the chief faults for which Adams castigated himself, but his defects of character bothered him too, particularly his arrogance. "Good sense will make us remember that others have as good a right to think for themselves and to speak their own Opinions as I have," he reminded himself, before acknowledging that he was "to a very heinous Degree, guilty in this Respect." He detailed at length his specific tendencies to fail to exhibit tolerance and respect for others and then urged himself to take a better course. "I now resolve as far as lies in me, to take Notice chiefly of the amiable Qualities of other People, to put the most favourable Construction upon the Weaknesses, Bigotry, and Errors of others . . . and to labour more for an inoffensive and amiable than for a shining and invidious Character."[41]

But he was John Adams. The heat of discussion drew out his passions. A few days later he came home from an evening of spirited talk and faced it: "The Event Shews that my Resolutions are of a very thin and vapory Consistence." He never could live up to his own expectations for how his character should be, ardently though he prayed to "conquer my natural Pride and Self Conceit . . . acquire that meekness, and humility, which are the sure marks and Characters of a great and generous Soul, and subdue every unworthy Passion and treat all men as I wish to be treated by all." Instead of attaining this model Christian character, Adams struggled against his "sloth and negligence," his ambition and dissatisfaction, his ardor in argument and his inability to control the direction of his thoughts. He knew these were not the worst sins of humankind, and duly registered his disgusted disapproval of a licentious fop in Worcester, for example, "a fine Gentleman with laced hat and wast coat, and a sword" who accosted an impoverished local girl on his way home from the tavern, forced her into a stable, had his way with her, and finally pressed what he claimed to be three guineas upon her as compensation for the assault. "The 3 Guineas proved 3 farthings—and the Girl proves with Child, without a Friend upon Earth that will own her, or knowing the father of her 3 farthing Bastard." (Out of all the founding fathers, Adams may have been the least tolerant of irresponsible paternity.) Struggling to come to grips with sin was a crucial feature of his Worcester years.[42]

The repeated failure of his most concerted resolves ultimately drove Adams to a spiritual crisis of sorts, out of which emerged his personal religion. By the late summer of 1756, he again found himself acknowledging how little improvement he had made in the virtuous habits he aspired to. Now he considered his mental inconstancy against what he knew of the universe. "Why am I so unreasonable," he wondered, "as to expect Happiness, and a solid undisturbed Contentment amidst all the Disorders, and the continual Rotations of worldly Affairs?" He rattled off all the evidence found in nature for the impermanence of earthly satisfaction and the inevitability of disappointments, bringing his individual experience into the wider context of humanity, which is continually chastened by the swings between joy and misery. "Thus God has told us," through his authorship of nature, "that This World was not designed for a lasting and a happy State, but rather for a State of moral

Discipline, that we might have a fair Opportunity . . . to labour after a cheerful Resignation to all the Events of Providence, after Habits of Virtue, Self Government, and Piety." The accomplishment of perfection Adams now saw to be impossible, but the attitude of resignation—which he sometimes called submission—is an essential practice of virtue, and "this Temper of mind is in our Power to acquire." Such resignation to the higher wisdom of God he now sought to induce in himself. "The Scituation that I am in, and the Advantages that I enjoy, are thought to be the best for me by him who alone is a competent Judge of Fitness and Propriety," he reminded himself. "Shall I then complain? Oh Madness, Pride, Impiety."[43]

The next day, Adams settled a question that had been vexing him for a long time. Employing a logical proof based on the perfection of God and the relationship between rights, liberties, actions, and responsibilities, he considered the problem of original sin. He deduced what it said about God's character that he transmitted responsibility for the first sin to the rest of humanity, how "Adam[']s sin was enough to damn the whole human Race, without any actual Crimes committed by any of them." The penalty of this crime is worse than nonexistence, yet according to the doctrine of total depravity, no one since Adam had acted in any voluntary way to incur this penalty. Believing this is to believe that God is unjust. And this Adams could not do. Instead he believed that "we are equally obliged to the Supream Being for the information he has given us of our Duty, whether by the Constitution of our Minds and Bodies or by a supernatural Revelation." This duty was the practice of a virtue that included submission to the higher will of God as well as active striving after positive morality.[44]

Within a week after this insight, Adams signed a contract to study law for the next two years under James Putnam, who happened to hold the "Opinion that the Apostles were a Company of Enthusiasts" on the grounds that no supplementary primary source exists to corroborate their miraculous claims. Adams recorded this observation after a day that began with breakfast at Maccarty's, included a visit to "an excentric character" who lived on a farm and kept a shop and some strong opinions, and ended with evening conversation at Putnam's. After two years in this provincial milieu in which a diversity of Reformation Christian convictions peaceably contested one another, Adams had finally resolved his own opinion. He was ready to live out a conviction forged early on in his Worcester experience, on a day when he had heard Maccarty preach twice and dined with another minister:

> Honesty, Sincerity and openness, I esteem essential marks of a good mind. I am therefore of opinion, that men ought, (after they have examined with unbiassed Judgments, every System of Religion, and chosen one System on their own Authority, for themselves) to avow their Opinions and defend them with boldness.[45]

BOSTON RELIGION

Adams turned to legal studies with gusto, quickly mastering a wide enough body of law to impress senior attorneys when he moved to Boston. His range of intellectual exposures multiplied manifold. The Christian poetry of John Milton and Alexander Pope joined his devotional toolkit, so after upbraiding himself for how his attention wandered he now admonished, "I have to smooth and harmonise my Mind, teach every Thought within its Bounds, to roll, and keep the equal Measure of the Soul." His moral striving produced self-restraint when he was sorely tempted to marry before his career was established, and gratification when Abigail Smith—the daughter of a minister—responded favorably to a courtship that included such sweet talk as, "Learn to conquer your Appetites and Passions! Know thyself." When he was invited into the Soladitas Club, a fellowship of lawyers who read and debated together, Adams seized the chance to enact his moral convictions in the theater of law.[46]

The Stamp Act had just pushed Boston into a state of political uproar. Inspired by the moment, but not directly responding to the colonial crisis, Adams drafted an essay out of thoughts he had initially formulated while Abigail was in confinement with their first child, thoughts that connected his religious convictions to his ideas about America. Published in the *Boston Gazette* in installments that ran from August to October 1765, the essay was titled *A Dissertation on the Canon and Feudal Law* when it appeared in the *London Chronicle* in November and December. Part Mayhew, part *Independent Whig*, part New England provincial, the voice of the essay was emphatically John Adams at his most forthright, seeking to press the cause of liberty by the rules of right reasoning. Opening with a line from John Tillotson, the essay rooted American character in the character of the Puritans: "sensible," "intelligent" "men of sense and learning" who migrated to New England because they prized "their knowledge and their freedom of inquiry and examination." Adams imagined Puritans who established a government that provided for public education because they believed in "the dignity of human nature." Now Americans must persevere in this long-established commitment to "knowledge and civility among the common people" by resisting the usurpations of governments or ecclesiastical bodies that overreached their authority. A free press is a necessary part of a liberty-loving society, Adams argued, making the implications of the Stamp Act far graver than its economic impact. Most fundamentally, "liberty must at all hazards be supported. We have a right to it, derived from our Maker."[47]

In many ways this was the Boston religion, perhaps even the religion of New England, because it was a religion that said nothing about creeds and everything about mental independence. Maccarty and Mayhew were both patriots, although Mayhew died in 1766; so was Chauncy, but Gay was not. Adams became such an integral part of the American founding not only because he was exceptional in some respects but also because he was representative in others. He spoke the language of the American Reformation, and increasingly translated it into legal and political terms as he learned his craft and his cause.

Adams brought his Boston religion with him to Philadelphia, where his comfort in dispute made him central in all resolutions. When the rough draft of the Declaration held "these truths to be sacred & undeniable; that all men are created equal & independant," the formulation came in part from Adams's understanding independence to mean the sacred freedom to operate as a moral agent. This was the understanding that infused his extemporaneous speech on the floor of the Continental Congress in response to John Dickinson's argument against independence. Witnesses credited the Adams speech with carrying the day. As one delegate testified, "The man to whom the country is most indebted for the great measure of independence is Mr. John Adams . . . the Atlas of American independence. He it was who sustained the debate, and by the force of his reasoning demonstrated not only the justice, but the expediency, of the measure."[48]

By the time the Declaration of Independence was signed, Adams had acquired a reputation for mastery of the international context in which the new United States aimed for nationhood. A colleague in Congress observed that Adams had "more fully considered and better digested the subject of foreign connections than any other man we have ever heard speak on the subject." So it made sense to send him to join Benjamin Franklin in Paris in 1778. France had already committed itself as an ally by the time Adams arrived, but diplomacy remained a vital tool in the ongoing war. Franklin appeared too fearful of offending his hosts and too fond of their hospitality to prioritize American interests. Not so Adams. He focused unwaveringly on the military situation in North America, recognizing that while the fate of the United States hinged on the course of the war at home, American allies—France, and soon Spain—were far too likely to expend their military assistance trying to settle old scores with England on and around the European continent. He convinced France to increase its North American naval commitment and to send thousands more troops to fight on the ground, but by 1780 he suspected that the Comte de Vergennes wanted the United States to become dependent on France rather than independent of the British. "Keep us poor," Adams wrote in his journal. "Depress Us. Keep Us weak. Make Us feel our Obligations. Impress our Minds with a Sense of Gratitude." He had such a nose for threats to independence because of its value in the American Reformation, and he was right to suspect the French. Although his indiscretion, tactlessness, and outbursts of candor may be counted faults of his diplomatic mission—they inspired Vergennes to denounce him, Franklin to betray him, and Congress to add four more diplomats, including Jefferson, to his peace delegation—those very faults reflected his core commitment to moral agency. His years in France taught Adams that this commitment was not universal even among his fellow patriots.[49]

At the end of the decade, when Adams went in print defending the Constitution, he read the record of human efforts to practice republican and democratic forms of government through the lens of the American Reformation. His approach to federalism reflected his realism about untrained human nature and his democratic faith that government might become an instrument of virtue, for the people's good. "The best republics will be virtuous," he observed based on his historical review of them, "but we may hazard a conjecture, that the virtues have been the effect of the well-ordered constitution, rather than the cause." He had read his Voltaire and Montesquieu, Rousseau and Burlamaqui, but his democratic thought did not validate the popular will as such. Instead it was concerned with the essential liberty of the people, which government must preserve rather than usurp, never extending into the people's divine right of private judgment. Hence Adams stood out from other defenders of the Constitution in not being seduced by utopias, Greek, French, or otherwise. Criticizing the Spartan form of republic where ethics were legislated, he declared such legal binding a form of liberty "little better than that of a man chained in a dungeon—a liberty to rest as he is." For him, government must accept humans as they are while providing scope and structure for them to grow into what they could be.[50]

Adams was not a good politician. He could not curry favor, or make small talk, or flirt. For all his realism about human nature, intrigue and machinations appalled him, and the necessity to be sensitive to public perceptions clashed with his commitment to candor. His presidency was painful. Losing the election of 1800 to Jefferson was more painful still. Adams had not expected to be betrayed by Alexander Hamilton—who published a critical attack on him the month before the election—although he had long been aware of his divergence from his fellow Federalist, who ran against him in 1796. Hamilton then led a group of Federalists in trying to exploit the quarrel with France to impose a militaristic, repressive regime on the country, legislated through the Alien and Sedition Acts, new taxes, and an expansion of the federal government. Adams did not consider France a realistic threat no matter how critical he was of its pretense to republican governance, but he got caught in the middle of a growing political polarization in the last two years of his administration, and he handled it very poorly. Then he was engulfed by some of electoral democracy's first image peddling. Adams himself despised plutocracy as much as any Jeffersonian Republican, but the solidifying Federalist Party of which he was the chief national symbol seemed to link government to the interests of the rich, Republican electioneering painted the Federalists as elitists, Adams a snob, and Jefferson a modest man of the people. Jefferson of Monticello, lover of luxury, exploiter of enslaved humans, and as close to an aristocrat as an American could get, won the mantle of the presidency with the common man's vote The election of 1800 was the first rhetorical contest to expose American democracy's fundamental divide. Claiming to want to liberate individuals from government, Jefferson took over the government from Adams, who wanted the people to use the government to foster the greater good.[51]

Retiring from public life allowed Adams to follow the course of his own nature. He returned to reading, a much more extensive range of reading than was available to him back in Worcester days. He read the Romantics Johann Wolfgang von Goethe and Robert Southey, the women's rights advocate Mary Wollstonecraft, the new biblical criticism and even newer reports on the religious systems in India and elsewhere, histories and works of moral philosophy and theology. He amassed such a large library that his niece Hannah relied on it for the later editions of her groundbreaking *A Dictionary of All Religions* (1784–1817), widely read among New England Congregationalists and praised for its "impartiality." She became the kind of scholar he in his own generation and cultural context never could, but that his American Reformation in part made possible. Although Adams read so much and so energetically, he believed "that there is [not] now, never will be, and never was but one being who can understand the universe," as he wrote to Jefferson in later years. "And that it is not only vain, but wicked, for insects to pretend to comprehend it." Yet trying to comprehend the universe without pretending that one did was an act of piety. His letters to Jefferson seethe with his effort to make sense of his reading, their shared history, the prospects of America, the universe. His voice remained that of the driven inquirer, interrogatory and declarative, bold and implacable, logical and ruthless. He was still no smooth operator.[52]

Adams did not die a Calvinist. To the end, the nexus of religion, morality, and politics remained the great preoccupation and guiding force of his life, the "Objects of my anxious Attention for more than Three Score Years," he told Jefferson (over and over again). His own creed he felt to be singular, his alone, at the very same time he found hearty points of agreement with Jefferson, other friends, and authors. He still never hesitated to disagree, either. When the American Reformation matured enough to produce a crop of Bostonians calling themselves "liberal Christians" in conversation with English dissenters, Adams felt no more hope for their cause than he had for the French Revolution. "I would trust these liberal Christians in London and in Boston with power just as soon as I would Calvin or Cardinal Lorrain; just as soon as I would the Quakers of Pennsylvania"—and off he launched into one of his swashbuckling lists that simultaneously showcased his learning and lumped together the breadth of human experience into one untrustworthy mass. "Checks and Balances, Jefferson, however you and your Party may have ridiculed them, are our only security for the progress of Mind, as well as security of body," the old man argued with his old comrade and opponent. "Know thyself, human nature!" (For all that, Adams did not hesitate to introduce two liberal Christian ministers, friends of his, to Jefferson.) He continued to think for himself:

I drop into myself and acknowledge myself to be a fool. No mind but One can see through the immeasurable system. It would be presumption and impiety in me to dogmatize on such subjects. My duties in my little infinitesimal circle I can understand and feel. The duties of a son, brother, a father, a neighbor, a citizen, I can see and feel. But, I trust the Ruler with the skies.[53]

For Adams and Jefferson both to die on the country's fiftieth Independence Day proves that fiction cannot outdo history. Adams died just in his Christian faith, believing that he had lived the best life he could but concerned about the nation he and Jefferson had helped create. Much as he would have liked to believe that they had established permanent institutions capable of safeguarding liberty and fostering virtue, he worried about laws like some in Massachusetts that legislated matters of belief. "We think ourselves possessed, or at least boast that we are so," he wrote to Jefferson, "of liberty of conscience on all subjects and of the right of free inquiry and private judgment in all cases, and yet how far are we from these exalted privileges in fact." Bringing together the ideals of American democracy with the reality of American society would be the continuing work of the ongoing American Reformation. And it was the liberal Christians of Boston who carried it on.[54]

Mary Moody Emerson, Natural Christian

THE CULTURE OF LIVED VIRTUE AND THE FIGHT AGAINST BIGOTRY

In 1826, a fifty-two-year-old maiden living in Maine wrote a letter to her reverend stepfather about the recent breakaway of neo-Calvinists from his congregation in Concord, Massachusetts. She mentioned her distaste for her own town's Congregationalist minister and confessed that she had started attending Methodist worship in the woods, where the quality of the preaching overcame the ideas she had formerly held against "the groaning religionists." She quoted a seventeenth-century Anglican divine by way of criticizing the "exclusive salvation" of the "narrow minded christians" with whom she and her stepfather disagreed. Then again, she disagreed on some points with her stepfather too, but these she left to the side as she remembered something she had meant to write: "I was going to speake of the singular coincidences of event on the glorious 4th! It was indeed an auspicious day [for] our pious Adams—to be released from earth and care and exhausted powers— and to have such a memory!" The death of John Adams brought to mind her "native state" of Massachusetts, but she had to admit an ignorance that speaks to its cultural distance from Virginia. "Of Jefferson, I know nothing—but respect for his talents & scholarship. What was his prevailing character? If he was not a good patriot & man I would throw up all the rest."[1]

She would indeed. Mary Moody Emerson cared about nothing more than virtue, unless it was for God himself, who gave moral agency to humanity. In these respects and in many others she was very like her admired Adams, whose American Reformation shaped the world of the Emerson family as profoundly as his Revolution did. By the time of the Revolution—in which Mary Moody Emerson's father, then Concord's minister, played a notable role—the architects of the American Reformation had grafted theology from the British Enlightenment onto the New England tradition. Holding fast to the traditional Reformation Christian conviction in the divine right of private judgment, this cluster of theologians in and around Boston devised new rules of right reasoning for arriving at such judgment. Behind these rules lay a definition of religion as the active relationship between divine perfection and human imperfection, which made the growth of moral virtue a proof of religion for the emerging nonevangelical, post-Calvinist wing of the established Congregational Church, which threw its weight behind the patriot cause. Neither this Boston religion of Mayhew and Adams nor the new evangelical Calvinism of their critics were strong enough at the time of the American Revolution to disrupt the denomination, in which all the diversity of beliefs Adams witnessed in the provinces temporarily cohered around the Reformation Christian liberty threatened by the British. Patriot ministers like Rev. William Emerson of Concord preached on "ye Principle of Freedom & Liberty" even before the Stamp Act, urging first parishioners and then soldiers to pursue virtue relentlessly as moral agents possessing a human dignity conferred by their likeness to God. When the war came, it put British tyranny on a par with Romish usurpation of the sacred right of conscience, allowing the Puritan tradition to be mobilized for political ends. The moral agency of the American Reformation thus became, in the memory of greater Boston at least, the meaning of the independence of the American Revolution. As an old minister told Mary Moody Emerson while recollecting her father's character, "[T]he love of our revolution was the love of God & liberty and humanity."[2]

After the Revolution, the new republic in which Mary Moody Emerson grew up looked very different from the various perspectives of the nation's diverse regions, stations, and political statuses. In her greater Boston—where a highly literate, overwhelmingly pious, ethnically homogeneous, relatively prosperous population dominated the local and state governments as well as the established church—the American Reformation continued, now partly in the service of a nationhood understood along Federalist principles. More British dissenting theology entered through Boston, heightening the importance of moral agency and elevating reason as a divinely implanted human faculty for the pursuit of virtue. Church establishment persisted in the new state of Massachusetts, intended to foster virtue among a people now responsible for making good on the American experiment in self-governance and to support clergymen, shielding them from mercenary motivations so that their ministerial work nurturing the people's virtue and their scholarly work pursuing the growth of knowledge could be, at least ideally, free of self-interest.

Knowledge itself, including the new scientific knowledge emanating from Europe, was far from secular in the ongoing American Reformation. The growth of the human mind in the direction of divine perfection necessarily involved the growth of human understanding in the direction of truth, which Harvard's motto of *Veritas* had long enshrined as a perpetual pursuit. Since God was the author of nature, investigating nature meant learning more about God, making Christianity itself natural in a culture where the identity of nature's God with that of the Christian Bible was automatic. For these reasons, learned societies and other voluntary associations for the cultivation of knowledge exploded among the Harvard-educated in the early republic, attracting men like Mary Moody Emerson's stepfather and her brother—another William Emerson, another Congregationalist minister—to participate in the development of a culture of lived virtue.[3]

Mary Moody Emerson could no more join a learned society than she could vote. As a female, she never faced the choice between public service as a minister or an official, and she attended neither Harvard nor any other formal educational institution. Yet she was a full participant in the culture of lived virtue, and indeed one of its very best exemplars. In fact, Emerson exemplified the culture of lived virtue with the very characteristics that feminists like Virginia Woolf and Tillie Olsen later found so appealing about her as they pushed back against the patriarchal norms of their own cultures. Emerson was quarrelsome and unsentimental, as apt to appear at a relative's home alone at the reins of a horse and chaise as to refuse to visit at all, an avid follower of ecclesiastical disputes and intellectual discoveries, a critic of public figures, an intensive reader of all the European literature she could get, four feet and some odd inches of willful integrity, always ready to speak her mind. But M. M. Emerson, as she took to signing herself as an adult, was no feminist, and she acted with rather than against her culture of lived virtue when she behaved independent-mindedly. (Her nephew Waldo got his taste for nonconformity from her.) Thinking for oneself was how a moral agent both got in touch with the divinity within and strained toward the divinity above. "Take from me oh my Father health, knowledge good[s] & home friendship & reputation," she prayed in her diary, "only leave me in the full possession of advancing virtue—conformity to Thee."[4]

This was what the Protestant moral ethic of John Adams produced. The culture of lived virtue focused on mind training at least as much as outward conduct. In social practice, the inner mental and outer behavioral dimensions of the culture of lived virtue made the disputatiousness of M. M. Emerson a form of virtue, too, because interaction between moral agents produced collective insight. Although the culture of lived virtue continued to prize the traditional Christian behaviors that added up to moral conduct—chastity, temperance, frugality, and the like—above such private virtues ranked the mental habits most conducive to moral agency, chief among them being candor and humility. As articulated by the architects of the American Reformation in the rules of right reasoning, humility reflected the awareness of how far short of divine moral perfection human striving inevitably fell. Candor paired this awareness with the commitment to strive nonetheless, since that is why God gave his creatures free will in the first place.

In the early republic the social practices of candor and humility made the culture of lived virtue a culture of inquiry, and of mutual criticism. Being forthright about one's views invited correction. Participating in any Christian fellowship devoted to lived virtue meant paying attention to what others say and how they behave, and challenging them by one's own best lights for the sake of collective moral progress. In the pages of the *Monthly Anthology and Boston Review* (1804–11), co-edited by William Emerson and occasionally contributed to by M. M. Emerson, mutual criticism was mild and genteel, informed by the classical tradition, congenial, literary, and civilized. In the letters M. M. Emerson wrote, in the critiques of sermons and books she composed in her diary, and in conversation, criticism was both delivered and requested with fearless directness. This is why the novelist Henry James described M. M. Emerson as "a spirit that would have dared the devil." After all, she once gave his own father a moral upbraiding during a dinner party at Waldo Emerson's house. No one awed M. M. Emerson but God— God and his gift of truly lived virtue, Christ.[5]

A Christ of lived virtue helped fracture the Reformation Christian tradition in New England. The evangelical kernel of that tradition—in which Jesus Christ symbolized the divine forgiveness of human sin by his innocent death and triumphant resurrection—followed the neo-Calvinists out of Harvard and the other institutions overseen by the rising virtue-driven wing, for whom Christ symbolized the perfection of virtue, as voiced in his Sermon on the Mount. For M. M. Emerson, Christ embodied not the atonement but "moral and intellect[ual] grandeur," as she put it in a letter to Waldo. These different understandings of Christ fed the split in the Congregational Church that led to the creation of the Unitarian sect, but that was much bigger than a denominational spat. True, Christians who ultimately adopted the Unitarian label no longer believed in what M. M. Emerson called "tritheism," nor in some of the other doctrines associated with Calvinism and increasingly deemed, by the virtue-driven Congregationalists, to be man-made. But it is equally true that the neo-Calvinists, in order to make the evangelical kernel the new center of the Christianity they now successfully claimed to be ancestral and hence "orthodox," had to abandon other aspects of the Reformation Christian tradition. This opened a divide in American intellectual culture that steadily widened over the nineteenth and twentieth centuries. The orthodox claimed already to know the truth and aimed therefore to legislate in light of it. Liberals aimed instead to pursue truth through study and dialogue. Free inquiry, private judgment, and liberty of conscience largely went with the virtue-driven wing of the Reformation Christian tradition. Liberals started defining themselves by inclusivity and open-mindedness against what they called the prejudice and bigotry of the neo-Calvinists who presumed to judge who was or was not Christian.[6]

M. M. Emerson displayed plenty of prejudice herself, as did many other Unitarians. Her assumption of the natural truth of Christianity was so complete, she sounded like a Crusader when decrying "Mahometanism," for example, about which she knew nothing, and she scorned the pretensions of women, whom she placed below men. She hated slavery but never reckoned with her father's having been a slaveholder himself, and all the gradations of hierarchy based on wealth and power in New England escaped her notice. But when she saw the beauty in Hindu poetry, worshipped with evangelicals, investigated biblical criticism, or contested the arguments of David Hume, she embodied what she called "the publick mind," the impartial recognition of universal moral agency that ultimately led her famous nephew beyond the Christianity that forever remained her ground and sky. Beneath the inequalities that M. M. Emerson tolerated lay a basic Christian and therefore human equality fought for in the war that, as she put it, "gave my fellow men liberty."[7]

STANDING ORDER ON ITS FEET

The littlest Emerson in Concord had probably only been sleeping through the night reliably for a few months when the church bell suddenly pealed hours before dawn on April 19, 1775. Men must have run from their houses, clapping hats and wigs to ungroomed heads, to hear the news from young Samuel Prescott, a native son of Concord who had rendezvoused with Paul Revere during the night, escaped an armed guard, and taken advantage of both the nearly full moon and his knowledge of the adjoining farms' walls and fences to urge his steed home: the British regulars were coming. Eight hundred of them.[8]

Phebe Bliss Emerson likely nursed Mary back to sleep—no doubt calling first for her indentured English servant, Ruth, to check the baby's diaper—while her husband joined the men. Rev. William Emerson was not about to become a soldier, but he was more than a pastor in the New England town. From the founding of the Massachusetts Bay Colony on, ministers exerted an unusual degree of public authority in society while declining to take public offices, although "authority" may not be the right word for it. In "the Congregational Way," as its leading historian describes it, ministers had no more authority per se than anyone else in the church, whose members gathered together and freely chose which minister to "hear" just as freeholders gathered in town meetings to deliberate public business. Hearing did not require heeding, and when congregations disliked what their ministers had to say for long enough and with enough consensus, they dismissed them. This never happened to Emerson. At one point early on in his ministry at Concord, a critic of his became vocal enough that the congregation called a council to consider the matter, but Emerson stood his ground so firmly and with such evident "consciousness of integrity," according to the later recollection of a fellow minister, that he not only maintained his pulpit but emerged from the crisis more respected than ever. Emerson's congregation listened to him, and sought his counsel. This is why Emerson rushed to join Concord's patriots at that dark hour.[9]

Emerson was a patriot himself. He had been outspoken against British oppression since the 1760s, and in the 1770s he and his brother, also a minister, defiantly abstained from drinking tea. The relationship between Emerson's theology and his patriotism was seamless. During the war, his sermons voiced the same covenant theology and public Christianity that Congregationalists across New England used to support the American rebels in the Revolutionary era. Exhorting soldiers to avoid sin in order to keep God on the side of Americans—who enjoyed a special providence they had to work to keep—was a sort of preaching Emerson did particularly well, perhaps, conscious as he was of preaching in a line of New England ministers that began with the Great Migration, but it was not a theology destined to survive the war intact. After independence was won, providence remained central to nationhood, but throughout most of the new United States, religion atomized as evangelical revivals focused on individual conversions and won them. Many evangelicals depicted society, including politics, as antithetical to true religion and its promise of a heavenly afterlife. In greater Boston, however, the relationship between religion and the new republic looked different. There the moral agency preached by ministers like Emerson even before the war became linked to the independence fought for in the Revolution.[10]

For all the distinction he earned in the Revolution, Emerson was not a particularly distinguished minister. Concord was only one of many modest villages within a day's ride of Boston, which was where the prominent pulpits were, the ones whose ministers really stood at the top of the Standing Order. The best-positioned ministers benefited from the privileges of church establishment, had the richest parishioners to sponsor the publication of their most scholarly sermons, and commanded large audiences on fast days and thanksgivings and the like. Emerson owned fewer than a dozen books and did not get to Boston much. He managed to arrange pulpit exchanges so rarely that few of his sermons were even fully written out, much less developed, but by the 1760s he enjoyed solid relationships with several other ministers who invited him to be heard by their flocks at other towns near Boston, like Malden and Cape Ann. This expanded his sphere of influence, put him in conversation with a broader range of Christian opinions, and gave him the chance to formalize some of his religious ideas.[11]

The doctrine Emerson preached bore the marks of the American Reformation without the polemical force of a Briant or deliberate pioneering of a Mayhew. Instead, Emerson sounded like a good Reformation Christian who read the Bible closely and addressed his hearers in the classic Puritan plain style. Moral agency was central to his theology. He believed that God's creation of humankind "after his own Immage, & Likeness" conferred upon every individual a special "Dignity, & Excellency." (It is worth noting that Emerson appeared to try to be inclusive across genders in his preaching. In one sermon draft, he crossed out "him" and "his," in reference to the Christian, upon revision.) This dignified human nature, which fed into political understandings of self-sovereignty and natural rights once the Declaration of Independence was written, had a transcendent rather than earthly meaning prior to the crisis with Britain. Emerson used this idea of innate—because divinely fashioned—human dignity as logical proof to demonstrate the reality of good old-fashioned Christian immortality. Against worldliness, he drew Christian consciousness up to the empyrean. "Surely we were made for a more noble end yn this!"[12]

Emerson rarely sounded like a good Calvinist, however. When he spoke of Christ he spoke of following the "Lamb whethersoever he goes," not of the blood of the lamb. Moreover, he evidently did not take what was called the "necessitarian" line on free will as established by Jonathan Edwards (1703–1758), who was dismissed by his western Massachusetts congregation after his evangelical reformulation of Calvinism. In Edwards's interpretation—which contributed more to the growth of neo-Calvinism after his death than to Congregationalism when he was alive—a formal, scholastic definition of free will gave humans just enough responsibility for their sins to need the saving grace of Christ. As M. M. Emerson put it when she read Edwards's *Freedom of the Will* (1754) in her thirties, Edwards made "the will of a being with a moral capacity" into "nothing more than an instrument of the divine govt of the most misterious kind." She and her father believed, on the contrary, in free will as the inborn divine power of the moral agent. Free will formed an essential part of the dignity of the soul, indicating a human capacity for moral action that, along with the endowment of liberty and the other inborn mental powers, pointed first to the reality of the soul's immortality and then, just as vitally, to the means of its advancement toward God's likeness. Rev. Emerson wanted his flock to follow the example and teachings of Jesus, and his Jesus wanted Christians to follow him of their "own free will, & Choice, & upo' mature Deliberation." The will was a "Faculty of ye human Soul," like understanding and conscience, all of which Emerson marveled over as "God-like," "noble, and even angelical" powers that gave humans dominion over the rest of God's creation and required them to hold sin in check. Using only his own close readings of selected biblical passages but apparently drinking from the same intellectual waters as the Boston architects of the American Reformation, Emerson quietly amplified the Reformation Christian common ground of moral agency without directly challenging the Calvinist doctrines he chose not to teach.[13]

It is an open question whether Emerson's theology would eventually have gotten him in trouble with his congregation if he had survived the war, but the seriousness of his Christian commitment is beyond doubt. Emerson preached a gospel of self-denial, especially of "Sensual Gratifications, & Comforts, & Enjoyments," which was certainly consistent with Puritan piety as taught from the seventeenth century. In his sermon notes, he used a telling symbol to represent the world: a circle with a dot in the middle. This graphic representation of the modesty of each individual within the immensity of God's creation invoked the Christian paradox wherein each individual is but a speck in the infinite, yet a speck under God's watchful eye, a speck for whom God has designated ultimate purpose. To serve this divine purpose, Emerson reminded his congregation of the importance of Christian meditation, the "daily putting in mind" of God's justice and of one's own conduct relative thereto. Listening to God by listening to "ye Voice of his own Conscience," the good Christian knows that he is subject to the "Sentence of ye Law" if that divine voice within is "not feared as with an hot iron." The mental powers of which Emerson spoke so earnestly, in such faith in the potential of the human mind, were far from earthly in their use. Human insatiability itself, as for ever greater knowledge, only proved to Emerson as it had to Adams that human destiny lay beyond this world.[14]

Within this world, however, the modesty of human potential relative to its immortal scope suggested one final aspect of Emerson's prewar theology that deserves emphasis, for it survived the war in the virtue-driven wing of the Congregational Church and became central to that wing's critique of the neo-Calvinists. Emerson preached against intolerance. A spirit of humility is the appropriate fruit of reflection on one's inborn mental powers, not pride, and not any exalted sense of what humans can do on their own. Keeping in mind the truly exalted—God's moral perfection, and the glory of his design—the faithful Christian must strive to extend toward other creatures of God not only forbearance of faults but also active interest in their interests, and active recognition of their own hidden inner sparks of the divine. On one December Sunday in the early 1770s, for example, Emerson drew the attention of those who would hold themselves above their fellows to the verse in Luke in which Jesus is transformed during the act of prayer so that "the fashion of his countenance was altered, and his raiment was white and glistening." As it had been in the 1640s for Roger Williams, for Emerson the spotless glory of Christ always indicted human pride, making folly of human claims to ultimate knowledge. This particular sermon of Emerson's was composed hastily enough that the notes merely outlined his arguments leading up to his main point: "intolerant Spirit" was set off from the rest of his script on the last page with a bold rectangle inked vividly around it. Emerson must have thought deeply enough about the dangers of intolerance to trust his reflections to bear forth in eloquence at this climax of his discourse for the day. That elaboration is lost to history, but Emerson's message of Christian unity in human diversity became an important development in the American Reformation.[15]

Intolerant spirit divided, setting Christian against Christian, when God's own love would have them united—but the British went too far, acting in ways the patriots designated "intolerable," so the townspeople of Concord drew a circle of Christian unity against the British. Emerson helped forge the new American unity by linking the patriot cause to New Englanders' Puritan heritage and damning the British with the sin of worldliness. The fight to come was a holy fight in defense of Christian liberty, which Emerson called "our glorious Birthright" in a discourse of March 1775, delivered to patriot volunteers assembled in rows on the town green after a review of arms. The British were "hungry Courtiers and greedy Placemen," in Emerson's words, eager to tear into patriotic flesh with "bloody fangs." By remembering their "worthy Ancestors," New England patriots could "put on the whole armor of God" in resisting these worldly oppressors, who sought to entice Americans into "Edomitish prophanity." For Emerson, to capitulate to British aggression would be to rebel against God, who gave these descendants of Puritans the natural right of Christian liberty. If they gave up this right by submitting to the British, they were no better than Esau trading his birthright for a fleeting meal, unworthy of what Emerson in a later sermon called this new "American Israel," updating the new Jerusalem planted at the start of the colony. With a sacred sense of his society's exceptionalism and divine purpose, Emerson helped shape "The Character of the Christian Soldier," as he titled his address to the troops in the cold early spring of 1775. By then, the long work of readying for war was complete.[16]

The people of Concord and their neighbors had stockpiled enough food and munitions to supply fifteen thousand soldiers, secreting the supplies in the ample storerooms of yeoman farmers, in the cellars of the town's most important families, and even under the tilled earth of their surrounding fields. By that late night in April when the minister's wife rocked baby Mary by the window while her husband conferred with the townsmen, the patriots had set up a system for vigilance of Boston Harbor and military intelligence between Boston and its perimeter towns, having decided to conceal Boston firebrands John Hancock and Samuel Adams in Concord's neighboring Lexington. The whereabouts of Hancock, Adams, and the patriots' storehouses were immediately leaked to the British, which was why the army rode first for these two New England towns among the many ringed around Boston. But no matter. The rebels were ready for the invasion.[17]

It came with the rosy dawn, which brought the first contingent of redcoats to Lexington. A Concord scout saw the first shots and hurried home with the news. Concord's patriots gathered at the Manse, the new parsonage built for Emerson and his growing family—a modest building later made famous by Nathaniel Hawthorne, brother-in-law of the chief disciple of William Ellery Channing, the last major voice of the American Reformation. At the Manse, the men planned how to meet the British invasion. They then decamped to Wright Tavern and, after further excited strategizing and confirmation of arms, split into two groups, with the youngest patriots advancing to a hill a mile east of the town center. Soon they saw, according to one eyewitness, the invaders' "noble appearance in their red coats and glistening arms."

Then the British infantry turned decisively toward the minutemen, who rushed away to join their elders back in town on a different hill, high above the meetinghouse near the liberty pole, flag flying. They hesitated. Rev. Emerson cried, "Let us stand our ground. If we die, let us die here!" But the patriots retreated out of town across the North Bridge all the way to Punkatasset Hill overlooking Concord. Minutemen from surrounding towns steadily joined them while the British searched Concord. Finally the British came to the bridge and the patriots streamed down from the hill in formation. Soon, without orders, the British fired first.[18]

During the battle Emerson, weaponless, used his pulpit-trained voice of exhortation and uplift to give courage to farmboys frozen in the terror of their first battle. "Stand your ground, Harry," Emerson urged an eighteen-year-old stricken with panic. "Your cause is just and God will bless you!" The minister had preached providence so long and tied it so securely to the cord of Puritan heritage that his words awakened the young man from his trance. Harry surged to join the rest in a vigorous fight that routed the British decisively. Emerson's role in the battle was so memorable that after the war a Concord soldier named one of his sons William and another Emerson.[19]

Emerson's ministry to the troops continued after the battle begun by "the shot heard round the world," as his grandson later memorialized it. Two days after the battle, Emerson held a prayer service, leading seven hundred volunteer soldiers in pursuit of liberty. He went on from there to minister to soldiers at Malden, and then Cambridge. Once Boston came under siege, Emerson helped evacuate the faculty of Harvard College, escorting them to Concord and preaching to them on such gospel as Galatians 5:1, "Be ye not again entangled in ye Yoke of Bondage." When the new Continental Congress at Philadelphia proclaimed the first Continental Fast for July 20, 1775, Emerson preached a fast-day sermon for national unity. Drawing from Isaiah, he reassured the troops of their covenant with God and urged them to pray, "for they shall cry unto the lord because of their oppressors, and he shall send them a

Saviour, and a great one, and he shall deliver them." (In Philadelphia, John Adams had just appointed the new commander of the new Continental Army, George Washington, whom William Ellery Channing's uncle, Francis Dana, later served at Valley Forge.) Emerson made the Revolution a holy fight for divinely sanctioned freedom.[20]

By the one-year anniversary of the Concord battle, Emerson was hailing "America as the Glory of all lands," and the Declaration of Independence had not even been written yet. Plenty of Puritan notes continued to ring in his theology, including natural Christian hierarchy in an echo of John Winthrop's "City on a Hill" oration. "The high and the low, rich and poor, bond and free" are so "by the wise and sovereign Disposition and Permission of Providence," Emerson reminded his audience of patriots, not yet democrats. In order to keep their covenant with this sole sovereign, Christian patriots must not fall prey to public sins like "Neglect of Family Government," which Emerson preached against and resisted himself.[21]

After becoming an army chaplain in August 1776, Emerson joined the camp at Fort Ticonderoga. From there he wrote home to his "little commonwealth," instructing everyone in the family in their duties according to Christian rules of hierarchy, submission, and piety. He enforced proper family order even from afar. Billy and little Phebe must keep up their reading, their father admonished, and six-year-old Hannah and the servant Ruth must keep up their manners ("be careful, active, and *complying*," Emerson bade the latter). Emerson had liberated his indentured servant into service for the Continental Army, but he told Frank the slave to "cutt up the Wood," "take care of the Hay in the Barn, and the Flax on the Grass and the Corn in the Field." (Instead, Frank absconded to join the British for the emancipation they promised, since the concept of American liberty had not yet been applied to the institution of slavery.) In his own place, Emerson instructed his eldest son and namesake, age seven, to read the Bible aloud to the family "every Morning, except when there is somebody else can do it better." There would be no slackening of Christian piety in Emerson's absence.[22]

Emerson's most tender advice in the letter was reserved for his wife, whom he urged to exercise Christian fortitude. He charged Phebe "never to distrust a kind and watchful Providence for herself," to "strive for Patience," and to "let not a murmuring Thought, and sure not a murmuring Word drop from your Lips. Pray against anxiety—don't distrust God's making Provision for you." The hallmark of Christian piety for Emerson was not Calvinist doctrine but the more basic Christian submission of self-will to God's will. He wanted his wife to exchange the self-interest that would lead to murmuring complaints for the ultimate interest in the wider good that belongs to God. She should trust in the wisdom and benevolence of God's perfect will.[23]

Emerson himself exhibited such trust in a way that might well have made Phebe murmur. Within two months of his arrival at the fort, he contracted camp fever. He was sick long enough to request a discharge from his duties, an act of Christian honor that meant no pension for his wife and their children, the fifth of whom he never met. He died on his way home. M. M. Emerson, now a precocious toddler who answered to Polly, was about to get farmed out to relatives. But she would never forget the Emersons' "noble & heroick Ancestor," as she reminded Waldo decades later, when he seemed to disdain the heritage for which she would keep a candle burning her entire independent life.[24]

THE ORDER OF REASON ESTABLISHED

Phebe Bliss Emerson, the daughter of a Concord minister and now the widow of one, had to take in boarders while the war raged on. Even then she had trouble making ends meet. She had the use of her mother's slave, Phillis, who rocked Mary's new little sister as well as her own baby, but Phebe was forced to apply for succor to the town of Concord, asking her community to "in some way or manner Grant her relief." She was in such "Difficult Circumstances" that she even boarded British prisoners of war. Although her husband had left her almost two hundred pounds after his debts were subtracted, with five children who needed "Boarding Cloathing Schooling Doctoring and Nursing," as she specified in an estate record, the burden was overwhelming.

Two-year-old Mary had already been sent to Malden, where her twice-widowed aunt reared her in a relatively quiet life of shabby gentility. There, the provincial tedium was interrupted only when the sheriff came looking for spoons from the family silver, hoarded while there were debts to pay, or when her grandmother was accused of illegally stockpiling wool and linen. In such crises, the patriot minister Peter Thacher helped out. Back in Concord, the town looked after the rest of the Emerson family.[25]

Soon Phebe found a new form of support. She married her final boarder in 1780. She was thirty-nine years old and Ezra Ripley a decade younger. He had come to Concord to take her husband's pulpit, soon won her hand, but apparently never took full possession of her heart—Phebe often secretly wept over a casket of letters from her first husband, and on her deathbed she asked that Ripley not be called on the excuse that "his boots squeak so, Mr. Emerson used to step so softly, his boots never squeaked." She bore three more children to Ripley, who made life comfortable enough and treated his stepchildren graciously enough that they all treated him with filial respect. He held his Concord pulpit the rest of his life, sustaining the departure of the neo-Calvinists and bringing the most current British dissent into the American Reformation.[26]

It may be that Ezra Ripley walked noisily because he was the son of a farmer and therefore not to the manor born—or to the Manse born, as the case may be—but what he lacked in polish he made up in character. His stepgrandson Waldo Emerson remembered Ripley as "a natural gentleman . . . courtly, hospitable, manly and public-spirited; his nature social, his house open to all men." Since Ripley's father did not have enough land to divide among his many sons—his mother bore nineteen children in all—Ripley traded his manual labor for sufficient education to become a schoolteacher in his teens. He then found himself suited enough to scholarly life to go on with income from tutoring and farmwork to Harvard at the relatively ripe age, especially for the time, of twenty-one. His was the class of 1776. From Harvard it was just one more step to the ministry. Ripley followed a path from field to pulpit that the learned and original Theodore Parker later traveled, although their careers were very different. Ripley, certainly an ancestor on Parker's intellectual genealogy, added only a few volumes to Emerson's spare shelf. And most of what he added to Emerson's theology came from Harvard, where the library had burned to the ground in 1764 and been rebuilt, and restocked, with an eye toward greatness.[27]

The Harvard of the 1770s was a denominational college for a doctrinally heterogeneous denomination, the leadership of which mattered greatly because both the college and its Congregationalism reigned virtually uncontested for religious and therefore cultural power in Revolutionary-era New England. (The Baptists were on the rise, and Methodists too, but both remained minorities in New England, outside the protection of the establishment.) Yale was then just beginning its ascent toward academic parity with Harvard, and in fact achieved this partly by entrenching its Calvinism in light of the polarization still developing during Ripley's college years.[28]

Already by the mid-eighteenth century, the American Reformation had influenced enough of Harvard's curriculum that when the famous revivalist George Whitefield visited from England, he complained that Harvard trained its students' minds at the expense of their hearts. Bostonians did not like this. Whitefield's complaint reflected a new, evangelical identification of religion with the heart's simple acceptance of Christ, which said more about Whitefield's complicated relationship to his own church's often highly scholastic establishment than about the American scene. In the Anglican Church, the Thirty-Nine Articles of Faith had long projected an image of doctrinal unity that enabled those who confessed them to adopt distinct creeds of their own and to develop clusters of like-minded theologians covered by the formal orthodoxy of the establishment. The most important of these clusters had arisen in the seventeenth century at the Puritan Cambridge University, where churchmen known as latitudinarians and neo-Platonists believed that the mental endowment of reason was crucial to religious life—that reason was, as one of them put it, "the very Voice of God." Cambridge was the source for the understanding of reason held by John Locke, whose eighteenth-century political influence was so immense; Cambridge was also the most important source for reason's growing centrality in the American Reformation. Meanwhile, the new evangelicals conflated the reason of dissenters and liberals with the rationalism of the French Enlightenment to depict reason as decidedly nonreligious, a view as powerful culturally as Locke's reason was politically.[29]

The two Cambridges differed in one important respect, however. The Cambridge of England fostered dissent that ran afoul of the Anglican establishment, dissent that entered the Harvard curriculum and was prized and promulgated by its graduates. Hence at Harvard and at the many law offices and pulpits it supplied, especially in greater Boston, what was dissent in England gradually became the establishment in New England.

The theologian who penned the line about reason being the voice of God fell victim to the Anglican establishment during his lifetime and became a significant contributor to the American Reformation in the century after his death. Benjamin Whichcote (1609–1683) stayed at Cambridge after earning his degree under Puritan tutors at Emmanuel, considered the most Puritan of Cambridge's colleges. He eventually rose to become provost at King's College, where he enjoyed Christian fellowship with scholars like Ralph Cudworth, John Wilkins, and John Worthington, but he was deprived of his seat by a special order of King Charles II in 1660. This setback did not stop Whichcote from becoming one of the most influential and underrated theologians in the history of Reformation Christianity. After his dismissal from Cambridge, he preached largely extemporaneous sermons in parishes around England before becoming a vicar in London, where his pious character contributed as much to his reputation as his morally vigorous creed. His funeral sermon was preached by John Tillotson, whose sermons the young John Adams transcribed with such admiration. In the eighteenth century the third Earl of Shaftesbury (1671–1713)—whose theological writings were widely read into the last third of the nineteenth century—put together one of the earliest editions of Whichcote's writings, declaring that Whichcote "may be justly called THE PREACHER OF GOOD-NATURE." Samuel Clarke (1675–1729), one of the theologians Mayhew and Chauncy read and Lemuel Briant's congregation deemed doctrinally dubious, also came out with an edition based on Whichcote's sermon notes. Clarke, whom M. M. Emerson considered a devotional touchstone, found with Whichcote that religion always agreed with "Right Reason" and required "the Liberty of Humane Actions." Yet all attempts to publicize the theology of Whichcote were hampered by the scanty nature of his papers, ultimately lost, and the marginal relationship his admirers bore to the Anglican establishment.[30]

Finally by 1753 the climate in the Church of England had changed. That year Rev. Samuel Salter of Yarmouth issued a revised edition of Whichcote's aphorisms, pared down from the five thousand then in circulation to twelve hundred pithy declarations of what religion is and what it demands of its practitioners. This slender volume reflected Whichcote's arguments with the churchmen of his time, which Salter happily contrasted to his own time, "in which such a generous freedom of thinking, chastened and tempered . . . by the most sound and exact Judgement, in Religion and all Learning . . . meets-with the esteem and applause, it so well deserves." Now that the Anglican establishment faced the challenge of evangelical revivalism, Whichcote's arguments for the role of reason in religion were newly useful. Salter contested "the narrow systematical pretenders to Religion" of the mid-eighteenth century with Whichcote's arguments from the seventeenth century. Such pretenders were wrong to think that they "advance Religion; while they but draw it down to bodily acts, or carry it up into I know not what of mystical, symbolical, emblematical, &c: whereas the Christian Religion is . . . uncloathed, unbodied, intellectual, rational, spiritual."[31]

Clearly, Whitefield's distinction between the training of minds and the feeding of hearts would have made no sense to Whichcote. Renowned for his devotion to "liberty of conscience," according to a younger contemporary who became a bishop, he testified, "I have always found in myself that such preaching of others hath most commended my heart which hath most illuminated my head." Both were natural, for Whichcote, both therefore divine, and both worked for religion only insofar as they yielded moral virtue in inner as well as outer practice. For Whichcote and his eighteenth-century admirers, "real Religion" was a holistic endeavor, an entire training of human might in the direction of God's goodness. As he expressed it in Aphorism 956:

Religion doth possess and affect the *whole* man: in the Understanding, it is Knowledge; in the Life, it is Obedience; in the Affections, it is Delight in God; in our Carriage and Behaviour, it is Modesty, Calmness, Gentleness, Quietness, Candor, Ingenuity; in our Dealings, it is Uprightness, Integrity, Correspondence with the Rule of Righteousness: Religion makes men *Virtuous*, in all Instances.

In other words—in the words of Aphorism 966—religion "doth not deserve that Sacred Name, if it does us no Good." Religion works on the entirety of each individual because its truths, sacred and eternal, are sewn into nature together with the humanity whose nature includes the capacity to grow toward God's likeness. Reason and conscience are means that God provides, also in nature, for the moral agent's progress in understanding and action.[32]

For evangelicals and neo-Calvinists, this natural religion of Whichcote's and his devotees in the American Reformation appeared to be a religion of mere morality. For the British dissenters and their Bostonian talking partners, however, morality was not something to be taken lightly. Moral conduct was the path toward God whose way was shown by Christ. He died in order to establish the moral lessons of the Sermon on the Mount as "his Testament," in Whichcote's words, and he "rose-again, to be his own Executor of it." Jesus completed revelation by embodying "*God* in conjunction with humane Nature," pointing the way toward union with God by personal illustration. Yet to be a neo-Platonist Christian was to believe that there was truth and goodness in the world even before Jesus lived, to believe that revelation was everywhere. Whichcote and his Cambridge colleagues spent years poring over the writings of Plato, Plotinus, and Tully, using their God-given reason and holding all observations against the premise of God's moral perfection. They found in the ancient texts moral standards and truth-claims that were good rules for Christian life. This made sense because God, infinite and eternal, fashioned humanity in his likeness, with the seeds of perfect righteousness within, and gave all individuals tools for cultivating those seeds. The work of such cultivation is religion, making moral action the common ground of all religions. As Whichcote explained, "Religion has different Denominations and *Names*, from different Actions, and Circumstances; but it is One *Thing, viz.* Universal Righteousness: accordingly it had place, at *all* times; before the Law of *Moses*, under it, and since."[33]

Whichcote went well beyond the latitudinarian standard of religious tolerance as a prudent policy such as one hears in Locke's *Letter Concerning Toleration* (1689), which became part of the intellectual justification for American religious freedom, while Whichcote's more comprehensive universalism fed into the American Reformation. Both agreed that religious diversity was a fact of human culture. "It is not the diversity of opinions (which cannot be avoided)," Locke wrote, "but the refusal of toleration to those that are of different opinions (which might have been granted) that has produced all the bustles and wars that have been in the Christian world." This is tolerance as prudence, not justice. Since peace is desirable and prudence promotes peace, Locke's approach says that it is better to choose toleration and include than to choose orthodoxy and exclude. For Whichcote, and for his late-eighteenth-century readers in greater Boston, a much more radical conception of religious pluralism was planted in the idea that religious conceptions necessarily differ but religion itself seeks the universal moral good, so justice demands inclusion. In practice, then, friendly engagement across lines of doctrinal difference rather than cool tolerance of those lines fulfills a religious truth deeper than such differences, because religion "consisteth in a profound Humility, and an universal Charity." Humility reflects human weakness and sin, the awareness of how partial human truths are and how far short of divine moral perfection human conduct falls, while charity is the law of God, who is good. Tolerance is not only a reasonable policy, then; it is an active practice of Christian fellowship in the common pursuit of moral virtue based on a combination of insight into one's own sinfulness and acknowledgment of everyone else's inherent divinity. "Our Fallibility and the Shortness of our Knowledge should make us peaceable and gentle," Whichcote explained. Given that "I *may* be Mistaken, I *must* not be dogmatical and confident, peremptory and imperious." The humble seeker after goodness and truth "*will* not break the certain Laws of Charity, for a doubtful Doctrine or of uncertain Truth."[34]

Christian charity is about how one holds one's truths, not only what those truths are. Trying to live as God loves means trading viewpoints with one's fellow creatures, all of whom are understood to be equally beloved by God as oneself. In seeking to "be *righteous* and *equal*," as Whichcote put it, the Christian should "see, with his Neighbour's eyes, in his own case; and with his own eyes, in his Neighbour's case." This central teaching of Whichcote's, derived from Jesus's command to love your neighbor as yourself, is why M. M. Emerson used him in her letter to her stepfather criticizing the neo-Calvinists who departed from his church. They had created a schism on the basis of differing beliefs, out of pride in their own beliefs' correctness, each of them seeming to claim that "the ch[urc]h I belong to is the only true one," as Emerson saw it. In contrast, Emerson offered Whichcote's position that "the only seperation between the world and the church is that which is made by innocence and virtue," making all churches one insofar as they help sinners pull toward heaven by fostering moral growth. Emerson qualified her own criticism by adding a postscript in which she clarified that she meant "no disrespect to any sect," acknowledging that the "trinitarian might be right," and paying homage to "the good genuine calvinists of which were our fathers."[35]

The fact that Emerson did not see the neo-Calvinists as "genuine" devotees of their ancestral faith is significant enough, for this is an argument her side of the Congregational Church soon lost. Even more significant, though, is her taking on the posture of uncertainty in expressing her beliefs. Emerson could sound plenty dogmatic and imperious as she boldly attested to her convictions, but part of her Christian practice was remembering to ask the other person's point of view and to acknowledge that she could very well be wrong. In a letter to her uncle Rev. John Emerson, for example, with whose theology she knew she disagreed, she wrote a long paragraph describing her reservations about trinitarian doctrine in tones at once respectful and persuasive. Then she explained, "I have ventured to suggest these observations hoping they would draw from your pen something to edify and enlighten." More casually, to one of her nephews she closed a sabbath letter with a request: "If my letter displease—be frank & manly enow to say it." Her gestures of open-mindedness exhibited Christian charity à la Whichcote.[36]

M. M. Emerson had a nickname for her stepfather, one that was friendly and critical at the same time. She called him "Dr. Reason." Ripley evidently took what Whichcote said about the use of reason in religion quite seriously. As he came to theological maturity in Concord, the doctrines Ripley preached both reflected and helped shape the emerging debate over the future of the Standing Order. In all matters of creed, he considered the practical effect on Christian behavior of holding one belief or another. His only starting premise seemed to be the goodness of God and the reasonableness of God's design of humanity and the rest of nature. Liberty and moral agency were necessary to the religious life, so Ripley challenged any doctrines expressed in such a manner as to force the Christian to accept them or to imply the impossibility of moral growth. In other words, Ripley did not dodge the conflict with neo-Calvinists. By the late eighteenth century, although most of the clashes between ministers, congregations, and townsmen over what theology pulpits and taxes ought to support still lay in the future, the long-standing theological diversity of the Congregational Church was starting to crystallize into two distinct positions. Ripley did his part to argue the reasonableness of his side in terms increasingly common in the culture of lived virtue.[37]

Ordination sermons were always good occasions for ministers to clarify their positions. These sermons were often published as pamphlets by state printers, so the guarantee of their circulation inspired extra care on the part of the ministers performing the ordination. Because such sermons were instructing new ministers in the sober duties of their profession, they also framed the outlines of the Christian faith clergymen were to profess. When Ripley delivered the ordination sermon for his stepson William Emerson at a church thirty miles outside of Boston, he aimed to instruct both his charge and the assembled congregation in the essence of a Christianity stemming from a single given claim: "God is infinitely diffusive of good, infinitely removed from self-ishness." The Christian life, then, is a life of growth toward goodness. Such growth is God's purpose, for which "he not only sent his Son, Jesus Christ, in the nature and as the surety of man," but also "hath employed men as instruments and 'workers together with him.'" Ripley used the line from Paul's letter to the Corinthians to tie his theology to the early Christians and to emphasize the active nature of Christian practice in direct challenge to all doctrines that "diminish a sense of moral agency and final accountableness."[38]

The Calvinist doctrine of innate total depravity was a direct target for Ripley and other ministers in the rising virtue-driven wing of the church. This is not to say that such liberals did not believe in sin—far from it, since the fight against sin was central to their understanding of the work of religion. They just did not believe that the doctrine of total depravity either helped in this fight or made sense in light of God's goodness. Since "men discern between right and wrong, and in their sober hours approve the former," Ripley argued, the workings of their reason and conscience prove that depravity is not total. It is, however, universal. All humans are subject to sin, which makes what ministers teach about sin and sinners so important. Ministers must take especial care not "to weaken the reason and force of moral motives," because believing that the sinner cannot improve amounts to throwing away the key to the shackles of sin. The Christian state is instead "a state of 'glorious liberty,'" Ripley used Romans 8:21 to propose, "a freedom from the power of sin and Satan." The feeling of freedom is itself potent, because when "men feel themselves free" they are able to "hear with attention, receive with application and practice with conscience." Ministers help expand this freedom by teaching "that religion consisteth in love to God and love to man."[39]

Considerations of the moral utility of religious doctrines extended all the way to the afterlife, a speculation particularly outrageous to the neo-Calvinist sensibility. Ripley had apparently spent some time poring over Whichcote's Aphorism 100, which depicted heaven and hell as practical rather than supernatural states. Both "have their Foundation *within* Us," Whichcote argued, with heaven consisting of "a refined Temper" and "an internal Reconciliation to the Nature of God, and to the Rule of Righteousness." Hell, then, is an "*inward* state" of guilt and sin that begins on earth, a miserable condition of "Enmity to Righteousness." Ripley considered the moral effect of this idea in his advice that it "may be useful to represent" heaven and hell as essentially "found in the mind . . . inseparable from moral character." This teaching leaves out the atonement but does not preclude the actual existence of the states of heaven and hell beyond earth—in fact, the doctrine of immortality remained vital in the American Reformation all the way through to its post-Christian shoots—but the new interpretation of heaven and hell as inner states does help convince sinners of the reason and righteousness of divine judgment, which then appears to be "impartial."[40]

The impartiality of God in loving as well as judging humanity became an important standard for human social conduct in the development of the culture of lived virtue. By the time of Emerson's 1792 ordination, this culture was increasingly supported by both governmental and voluntary means; the outlook for post-Calvinist Congregationalists was much brighter than it had been for the young John Adams, whose political skills worked better at the state level during and after the Revolution than they would at the national level during his presidency. Adams helped craft the Massachusetts state constitution of 1780, which contained three important provisions for institutionalizing the American Reformation. The first two were in the Declaration of Rights and seem contradictory, making sense only in the context of the American Reformation. Article 2 established religious freedom, stating that "it is the right as well as the Duty of all" to follow the "Dictates of his own conscience." Article 3 established Reformation Christianity as state law, providing public funds to support "public protestant teachers of piety, religion and morality" and making attendance compulsory. The right of private judgment was guaranteed by the same law that provided state funding for ministers to shape that free conscience in the direction of virtue.[41]

The voice of Adams can be heard in these clauses, and his handiwork is even more directly seen in the third constitutional allotment of state means for virtuous ends, when the legislature chartered the American Academy of Arts and Sciences as decreed by the state constitution. The promotion of the advancement of knowledge in the new United

States was necessary, in the words of the charter, "to advance the interest, honor, dignity, and happiness of a free, independent, and virtuous people." Founding members included John Adams and fellow revolutionaries Samuel Adams, John Hancock, and Francis Dana; Boston ministers Charles Chauncy and his successor at First Church, the equally post-Calvinist John Clark; as well as the son of Cotton Mather, a number of state officials, Harvard presidents and faculty, and members of the gentry. There was nothing explicit about religion in the charter, but freedom, independence, and virtue were all concepts with deeply religious valences in late-eighteenth-century Massachusetts, as were dignity and the pursuit of knowledge. At this point in the American Reformation, these concepts remained pan-Congregationalist values in a state establishment as united as the patriots' then-ongoing quest for independence. The American Academy, establishing the cultivation of knowledge as a founding principle of Massachusetts, aimed to provide a setting for continued cooperation on the common Reformation Christian basis of independence and virtue, but the post-Calvinist wing developed increasing power through the academy and the voluntary associations established for similar purposes after the Revolution. In 1791, Rev. Jeremy Belknap, Rev. Peter Thacher, and Boston's first outright unitarian, Rev. James Freeman, founded the Massachusetts Historical Society in order to preserve documents and publish titles in American history. In 1807, another group of Boston ministers and gentry established the Boston Athenaeum, an independent institution intended to serve as both a lending library and a collection of great works. Together, such organizations institutionalized the culture of lived virtue.[42]

The group that created the Athenaeum went by the name of the Anthology Society, and William Emerson was one of its founding members. He had not stayed in his provincial pulpit very long—just long enough to take a bride, the polished and pious Ruth Haskins of New-buryport, where Mary Moody moved when she was seventeen in time to assist at the birth of their sister's first child, and where she listened to post-Calvinist Christian doctrine at the First Religious Society. William Emerson approved of this. He also passed on appropriate readings for his fiancée and sister, British dissenters like Stephen Foster, who warned against "the danger & folly of building devotion on superstitious errors," as Mary wrote to Ruth after moving back to Concord.[43]

In 1799, William Emerson was called to the First Church of Boston. Emerson was so proud of the appointment, he named one son after Charles Chauncy and another after John Clark. Emerson had started to build the institutional memory of the liberal wing of the Congregational Church, going so far as to write a history of First Church in which Chauncy starred as a champion of reason against disorder. Emerson also wrote for the *Palladium* and *Polyanthos* newspapers of Boston, joined the Massachusetts Historical Society and the new Society for the Study of Natural History, and was soon elected to the American Academy. So were several other Anthology Society members: the minister at Brattle Street Church, Joseph Buckminster; the president of Harvard, Rev. John T. Kirkland; and the Massachusetts Supreme Court's chief justice, Theophilus Parsons. These men were all lovers of God—all Federalists, all Harvard graduates, all Congregationalists, and all conscientious about the leadership responsibilities their lives of privilege conferred. Yet there was enough disagreement among them that when the Anthology Society met to discuss what would go in the next issue of their journal, the rules of discourse they developed for airing those disagreements were as important as the common front they increasingly presented in opposition to neo-Calvinism. Emerson claimed to teach his congregants to "preserve unchanged the same correct feelings of liberty, the same purity of manners, the same principles of wisdom and piety . . . which immortalize the memory of your ancestors," as he said in his Independence Day oration for 1802, printed by the state. Yet the practices of mutual criticism he for all his conservatism helped inaugurate were as revolutionary in their way as the event he was commemorating that day.[44]

NATURE'S GOD

"I know not why smoking a social segar should be severely blamed," complained an anonymous writer in an 1805 issue of the *Monthly Anthology and Boston Review*, the journal that shaped the reading practices, theological opinions, politics, memory, manners, and taste of the Boston elite in the early republic. "*Valet auctoritas doctissimorum hominum*" (Let the authority of the most learned men speak forth). On the question of the morality of tobacco use, the learned men presented to testify for its blamelessness included obvious English choices—the imperialist Sir Walter Raleigh, for example, and Samuel Johnson, whose writings M. M. Emerson ruled "favourable to virtue" elsewhere in the journal. An international selection was also levied for consensus. The "Lapland woodcutter," "Turkish bashaw," "Hindoo," and "*mi Caballero Castellano*" all agreed that temperate, social use of this gift of nature was unobjectionable. The author rested his case on "the similar practice of widely distant nations, and the authority of wit, virtue, and erudition."[45]

A light and humorous piece in a journal whose topics ranged from reports of scientific experiments to biographical sketches of theologians and statesmen, this defense of the social cigar says a great deal about the culture of lived virtue. That a pleasure was acceptable only if social rather than solitary reflected the importance of fellowship, which liberals viewed as a duty as well as a good. Both the existence of the Latin phrase and its meaning speak as eloquently. Latin learning remained the mark of the scholar in the early republic, suggesting a male author and a male audience, although this journal was both read and contributed to by women—and the generation just being born included the first daughters who would be educated the same as their brothers. Listening to the authority of learned men was an old standard in New England culture, but noteworthy at this juncture is that men considered learned were no longer necessarily ministers. Rather than a mark of secularization, this broadening of intellectual authority in the culture of lived virtue grew naturally out of a church whose members had always been robust in expressing their divine right of private judgment. More voices were now considered worth hearing in greater Boston, where the Federalist understanding of the nation as a republic held decided sway. A healthy republic needed all the learned opinion it could get, which expanded power differently—more selectively—from how the rhetorical and procedural move to a democracy of the "common man" soon did.[46]

The selection of assorted international tobacco lovers in the "social cigar" piece, however crude and condescending, indicates a new, landmark cross-cultural human universalism in the culture of lived virtue. Christianity was understood to be the only complete religion, adding the revealed word of God through the Christian Bible to the divine law found in nature, but since non-Christians lived under the same law of nature—the "transcript of divine perfection," in Ezra Ripley's phrase—there is overlap across human cultures where truth lies. So the Turkish general has some authority worth listening to, even though the *Monthly Anthology* writer stereotyped him as full of "angry passions," and even though his religion was so bad, in M. M. Emerson's view at least, that when the Greeks were fighting for independence from Ottoman rule in the 1820s, she advocated American involvement for the goal of "destroy-ing Islamism" even while considering the Orthodox Christianity of the Greeks "no better now than Mahometanism." Yet not many years later, her nephew Waldo became so familiar with the new translations of de-votional and mystical writings from the East then trickling across the Atlantic that he published a groundbreaking essay, "Persian Poetry," and sprinkled quotations from the Quran and the poet Hāfez across his journals and lectures. To call his work merely literary would be to miss the point. Waldo Emerson worked out of a new canon with tools fash-ioned in the early American Reformation and refined by his aunt's generation. Among these new Boston liberals of the early republic, the social values of impartiality, candor, humility, and right reasoning resulted in practices of taking diverse viewpoints, including those of non-Christians, seriously. The associated practice of mutual criticism—candidly offered and humbly received—emerged at the same time that the new Eastern translations and the higher criticism of the Bible arrived in Boston, which destabilized the singularity of Christian revelation. In the culture of lived virtue, Christianity's unique status remained unques-tioned until the antebellum era, but the rest of nature bore divine truths to be prized as well, creating a receptive approach to diversity just as immigration and economics were diversifying the young and rapidly growing United States.[47]

Among the issues dividing the Congregational Church in the early republic, biblical criticism was not the only one to grace the pages of the *Monthly Anthology*. There the doctrine of predestination was refuted, the prejudice of neo-Calvinists in Fitchburg decried, and the election of the post-Calvinist Henry Ware Sr.—Ebenezer Gay's successor at Hingham—to the Hollis chair of divinity at Harvard triumphantly praised. The Ware appointment was the last straw for Jedidiah Morse, a member of the American Academy and a "New Divinity" man still stinging from a negative review of his *American Geography* (1789) by James Freeman, whose theology Morse detested. Morse started *The Panoplist* (1805–10) in order to counter the *Monthly Anthology*'s voice. The preface to the first issue mounted a call to the defense of the "Doctrines of the Reformation" and "the religious faith of our venerable forefathers." Morse devoted substantial articles in each of the first five issues to the character of the late David Tappan, whose death vacated the chair now filled by the dangerous Ware. Morse used the term "evangelical" to describe Tappan—used it copiously—in strategic contradistinction to the language of the Tappan obituary that appeared in the *Monthly Anthology* in two parts. In the latter, the values of the American Reformation led the eulogizer to acknowledge only that Tappan "dwelt frequently on what he deemed the peculiar doctrines of revelation" while insisting that Tappan "ever sought to represent them as instruments of moral goodness."[48]

With the passing of Tappan, the former diversity of the Congregationalist establishment polarized into two distinct wings well represented in these warring obituaries. The Yale-educated Morse and the Harvard men of the Anthology Society disagreed on the core matter of what made a Christian faithful to the Reformation tradition. As Henry Ware saw it, the neo-Calvinists adopted "the *peculiar opinions*" of the first Reformation Christians "instead of asserting the great *principles* of the Reformation. They have only changed one human master for another, instead of all authority, but that of our common master, the great head of the church."[49]

Jedidiah Morse put the disagreement rather differently, of course, but it is more interesting how much the two positions shared. Their common ground indicates how even after the schism in the Congregational Church, the American Reformation continued to pour into trinitarian Christian institutions such as Yale and the Andover Seminary that Morse soon helped found. Jedidiah Morse proclaimed an antisectarian, impartial ideal in his inaugural editorial preface, in which he opposed "prejudice," praised "christian candour," and upheld the goal of Christians "to promote general happiness, to do good to the souls of their fellowmen." Tappan himself exhibited "candour of judgment," in the pan-Congregationalist language of the American Reformation, treating all viewpoints impartially. Morse said Tappan was a model Reformation Christian who "knew too much of the constitution of the human mind, and the causes of diversity of opinion . . . had too much regard for the right of private judgment, and the use of free inquiry . . . was too wise, too modest, and too just to indulge in himself, or to encourage in others, a dogmatical, intolerant spirit." No liberal Christian—as some of the rising Unitarians were starting to call themselves—could have said it better. The only difference is that Morse thought that impartial inquiry confirmed that his evangelical faith was the true Christianity, while the liberals believed that Christianity proved itself in moral and intellectual growth rather than a fixed system of dogma.[50]

For a time, though, the two wings of the Congregational Church continued to share the principles of private judgment and free inquiry as well as an overlapping canon. Both sides favored Philip Doddridge (1702–1751), for example, whose mother was the daughter of a Lutheran minister and who never conformed to the Anglican Church. Mary Moody Emerson said of Doddridge's *Rise and Progress of Religion in the Soul* (1744), a devotional manual that circulated widely in America in both pamphlet and bound forms, that "there is no religious tract of more importance to me." She advised every Christian to read its chapter twenty-six regularly. This is where Doddridge modeled how a Christian should meditate in order to grow humility and charity. He pitched a series of questions the Christian could use to guide self-interrogation:

"Do you find your heart overflow with undissembled and unrestrained benevolence?" "Do all the unfriendly passions die and wither in your soul, while the kind, social affections grow and strengthen?" "Do you think of yourself only as one of a great number, whose particular interests and concerns are of little importance when compared with those of the community, and ought, by all means, on all occasions, to be sacrificed to them?" "How does your mind stand affected toward those who differ from you in their religious sentiments and practices?" Such a rigorous piety of self-denial and charity bore pan-Christian appeal in the American Reformation.[51]

By the time Mary Moody Emerson meditated on Doddridge, she was thirty years old and knew she would never marry. She discerned in her character that she was "not destined to please." She was never exactly a spinster, because, as Waldo said, her thimble pressed more wax seals than needles, and because she inherited a modest property from her aunt. M. M. Emerson herself described her condition as a "blessed state of single-blessedness." She believed her solitude gave her a better share of the mental independence that was of chief aid to the Christian life, as well as to civic life, and she declared to Waldo that "the old maid can realize the publick spirit of Plato's republick." Her efforts at such realization consisted of constantly seeking out the opinions and characters of others and just as constantly offering them her own views, which she refined in the pages of her "Almanacks" made of loose sheets bought by the quire, thickly covered with her ungraceful handwriting, and stitched together. (Waldo borrowed them regularly, copying her insights and turns of phrase into his own journals and repurposing them in his sermons and, later, his addresses as America's first public intellectual.) Instead of being bound to husband and children, M. M. Emerson was only bound to God. "I love thee I know it," she professed in her Almanack, "and yet I am not every thing I s[houl]d be." Self-examination, sermon notes, prayer, literary observations, and philosophical arguments flowed in breathless succession over her pages.[52]

In the early years of the *Monthly Anthology*, Emerson contributed a few pieces under the pseudonym "Constance," someone who knew a little about botany and a little about English literature and a lot about Christ, the supreme moral agent, "he who feels himself respectable amidst the obloquies of the crowd, rich amidst losses, prosperous in sickness, and living in death." She read intensively, spending two years on Bishop Joseph Butler's *Analogy of Religion* (1736) and excerpting for the *Monthly Anthology* from Richard Price, a British dissenter who cheered for the Americans in their war for independence, made the acquaintance of John Adams in London, imprinted the theology of Channing, and delighted the book-starved sister of Benjamin Franklin. For the *Monthly Anthology*, Emerson selected a passage from Price on how only voluntary actions qualify as virtue, which is "universal, calm, and dispassionate benevolence." She learned the ritual gestures of mutual criticism from the periodical, which often bore, on the *Boston Review* section's title page, the epigraph "By fair discussion truths immortal find." And she practiced criticism constantly in her own social and religious life.[53]

"You appear in fine health and spirits," M. M. Emerson wrote to her brother William in 1810, "and as usual are pleased to profess a devotion to the pres[e]nt world, and an ignorance of the future." She thought his Christianity was too worldly. As the new Unitarian party developed, she criticized it for being too "polished & plausible" as heartily as she criticized how "calvinist dogmas" contradict reason. Reason is the tool of natural religion, she explained to Waldo, being "what makes man capable of revelation . . . reason the all glorious cause of receiving revelation—what makes man an agent—an immortal being—relates him to God & rendered him worthy of redemption by the divine man—the Son of God." M. M. Emerson never settled under any system and as a moral agent never stopped seeking revelation. In 1810 she worshipped with Baptists, who were friendly enough with the new Unitarians that Aaron Bancroft let them share his meetinghouse in Worcester. The next year she buried her brother, judging him harshly for how he had resisted the death from consumption that came horribly and too soon. She thought that if his faith had been more robust and deeply rooted he would have welcomed death—she herself longed for it, for the sight of God.[54]

In 1812, Joseph Buckminster died, also tragically young, and Emerson attended the funeral sermon, delivered by Kirkland on a text from Job, "Thou destroyest the hope of man." Buckminster awed Emerson as her brother never could, which illustrates the diversity of theological opinion even in the tight Anthology Society. Buckminster seemed constantly to be *"engaged in prayer to God,"* Kirkland had observed, exemplifying learning and piety. Once M. M. Emerson took charge of little Charles Chauncy Emerson, she promised her brother's widow to give him a daily impression of the virtues Buckminster was said to exhibit, "humility, kindness & disinterestedness."[55]

Hence even among the small elite then building a new denomination out of the American Reformation's Boston religion, the practice of virtue—which included inquiry and criticism—remained the glue holding a range of theological tastes and opinions together. Throughout the 1810s and 1820s, M. M. Emerson continued to migrate around New England hearing what preaching she could, reading what she could, and skimming what she could off her nephews' modern educations. As biblical criticism became an ever more controversial field of study, she trotted off one week to hear the liberal Nathaniel Frothingham preach in Boston that the Christian Bible was not divinely inspired, and another to the rooms of Moses Stuart, the neo-Calvinist biblical scholar at Andover. She liked Stuart because, as she told Waldo in disapproval of his decision to attend seminary at Harvard, Stuart "makes mouths at the heartless strainings of kindnesses w'h tickel, not benefit the weak world." (Kindnesses that tickle the senses of the sinful only stimulate the craving for pleasure.) When a different nephew—another William Emerson, studying in Germany in preparation for his own career in the ministry—started taking courses with the eminent biblical scholar David Eichhorn, M. M. Emerson pressed him with questions, all leading up to the money question of what authority the Bible still had. If the Bible is just a story and there are no proofs of Jesus's miracles, "what is the value of the story?"[56]

Young William was shaken enough by what he learned in Germany that he decided not to become a minister, a decision his aunt approved. Her own faith adjusted to any degree of uncertainty because of her deep inner conviction in God's existence and perfection and love for her, "an everlasting love with loving kindness" despite her being "unholy, minute fallibly & often unhappy." This conviction meant that even the brilliant skeptic David Hume did nothing to weaken her faith. "What *did* he *know* or *prove* to vanquish my universals," she asked Waldo. Hume could not pull the rug out from under M. M. Emerson's faith because her understanding included not understanding everything—included awe, the vivid internal sense of both ongoing revelation and sin. "Surrounded by nature, which I was capable of studying and loving," she continued to her favorite nephew ("yours with too much partiality," she signed some letters), "yet it was filled with phenomena—with mystery—with some that spoke of terror & pain."[57]

Praise is a form of criticism too. M. M. Emerson adored Adam Smith

("I shall love him forever," she wrote in her Almanack), Hindu poetry ("sublime devotion," she told Waldo), and the writings of Madame de Staël (Waldo transcribed the entire letter his aunt wrote about that "glorious Auther" into his journal, and copied some of it into his senior essay at Harvard). Admiring good character and good sense in someone else meant recognizing the fruits of religion in them, helping to activate the good in oneself as well.[58]

M. M. Emerson appreciated aspects of Calvinism, crediting what she found good in the theology of rising star William Ellery Channing—whose vestry meetings she participated in whenever she was in Boston in the 1820s—to his having "early embued his mind with a severer theology than prevails at present" (a perspicacious observation that Channing himself voiced to his protégée Elizabeth Palmer Peabody). Emerson did not like everything about Channing, wishing that he thought more "of the pure & spiritual worship of the high & heroic virtues of the trinitarian, rather than of the possible conclusions of their system." But she loved his Providence sermon, "Likeness to God" (1828), and with good reason. It was delivered after the adoption of the Unitarian label and after two decades of intense theological controversy carried out in print and pulpits in New England, so it more than any other text—and Channing more than any other minister—stated the essence and aim of Christian practice from the liberal perspective. Channing's text was from Ephesians, "Be ye therefore followers of God, as dear children," and its message was simple: "[T]rue religion consists in proposing as our great end a growing likeness to the Supreme Being." This was the refined core of the American Reformation. It was M. M. Emerson's father's religion, although Channing's "view of human nature" was polished "too bright for truth," in her opinion. "Never was a more *glorious* sermon," she also thought. Ever the moral agent, she did not forget to ask her nephew to send her a review of the sermon, to report the opinion of a mutual friend on it, and "to know if unitarians do not like Channing's P. Sermon?"[59]

Mary Moody Emerson lived decades longer than she wanted to. She lived long enough to befriend Henry David Thoreau, Margaret Fuller, Elizabeth Palmer Peabody, and other liberals of Waldo's generation, many of whom turned altogether post-Christian by the same light of universal inner divinity in which she believed. Of Waldo's writings she sorrowfully commented, "It seemed there was no other world than this." But she lived for that other world. M. M. Emerson wanted to die for so long that she acquired a reputation for sleeping in a coffin and wearing a death shroud in order to be ready when the Lord came for her; Waldo said she wore out multiple shrouds waiting, but her biographer says there was only one, and that it was only the lining from a robe torn out for use as an outergarment. It showed how little she cared for earthly appearances. When she lived with a niece in her feeble years, she fell in with some Millerites, the precursors to the Seventh-day Adventist denomination who awaited Christ's second coming in 1842, and then again in 1844. About that time Emerson noted in the margin of an old Almanack, "Picked up these written at distant times & as I still live may read them Alas what constant efforts of the same kind & no progress sad sad." She did not even give herself credit for having grown in humility over the years.[60]

Emerson lived to learn of the Emancipation Proclamation being signed into law. She told her nieces and nephews to bury her anywhere there was "no dust of a friend to slavery." Her grave is at Sleepy Hollow Cemetery in Concord, her epitaph drawn from Waldo's memorial address for her: "She gave high counsels—It was the privilege of certain boys to have this immeasurably high standard indicated to their childhood, a blessing which nothing else in education could supply."

Drawn partly from a rich religious "imajanation"—as she often described personal revelation to Waldo and as the next generation of the American Reformation was to expand—those high counsels constituted her legacy. The doggedness with which she tried to follow an immeasurably high standard herself embodied her fidelity to those who came before her.[61]

3.

WILLIAM ELLERY CHANNING, PRACTICAL CHRISTIAN

UNIVERSAL INNER DIVINITY AND SELF-CULTURE

Points have we all of us within our souls,
Where all stand single . . . and make
Breathings for incommunicable powers.
Yet each man is a memory to himself,
And, therefore . . .
I am not heartless; for there's not a man
That lives who hath not had his godlike hours,
And knows not what majestic sway we have,
As natural beings in the strength of nature.

—WILLIAM WORDSWORTH, *The Prelude* (1805),
BOOK III, LINES 186–94

In May 1822, William Ellery Channing and his wife sailed for Europe so that he could take a sabbatical year away from the duties of the pulpit. From the perspective of his adoring—and wealthy—congregation on Boston's Federal Street, he had earned it. Few American Christians were better known at home or abroad at this point than Channing, whose 1819 ordination sermon for Jared Sparks in Baltimore made "Unitarian Christianity" the name for the postevangelical wing of the rapidly splitting Congregational Church. Channing's sermon circulated as far as India and set off the so-called Woods 'n Ware pamphlet war in which Leonard Woods of Andover and Henry Ware of Harvard argued over the Christian principles at the heart of the controversy, an argument followed so closely in New England that Mary Moody Emerson referred to it in a letter to young Waldo with a tone of utter assurance that he understood the debate as well as she did. Yet although Channing helped solidify the long-growing polarization of New England Reformation Christianity, and although he contributed to the split with the Baltimore sermon and later discourses such as "Unitarian Christianity Most Favorable to Piety" (1826), he never stopped thinking of himself as a Congregationalist, a name that described Christian fellowship rather than Calvinism. Channing sincerely felt himself to be no more of a sectarian than M. M. Emerson because he believed as fervently in the divine gift of a moral agency that required liberty for its exercise. He developed a Christianity that was both practical and pluralist—practical in demanding that beliefs manifest in moral action, and pluralist in allowing for "divers gifts and divers ways of presenting the truth," as he once explained his defense of Waldo Emerson's theology, deemed heretical by many. The character and reach of Channing's ideas in his time means that his historical legacy is better understood in terms of the flowering and spreading of the American Reformation than its production of the new Unitarian sect.[1]

When the Channings reached England in midsummer of that sabbatical year, they headed straight to the Lake District, seat of the English Romantic literature then quickly being absorbed into the American Reformation. Channing wanted to meet William Wordsworth, whose poetry confirmed for Channing a spiritual sense he had first formed in youth. Channing and Wordsworth both believed that meditation in and of the natural world brought human nature in touch with the divine nature that dwelt both above and within. Although undoubtedly the English Romantics and later the continental Romantics had immense impact on the last stage of the American Reformation, Channing also might usefully be considered a cocreator with Wordsworth and Samuel Taylor Coleridge of the Romantic turn in Christian thought. By the time the Lake poets added vocabulary, style, and continental sources to the American Reformation, Channing and other liberal Christians centered in Boston had already made the freedom and independence of the individual mind essential factors in spiritual growth, just as Wordsworth and Coleridge did. The English Romantics and the Boston liberals shared the same canon of British dissent, reacted against similar Calvinisms and evangelical currents, and prized the same potential for a republican form of government to foster human progress while fearing the same dangers of demagoguery and popular ignorance. They spoke the same language in more ways than one.[2]

Once Channing and Wordsworth met by Lake Windermere that summer, the ten-year age difference and ocean between them evaporated as they fell to talking with such affinity and enthusiasm that they often interrupted each other. Both Channing and Wordsworth defined the goal of human life as growth toward divine perfection, which Wordsworth called love and Channing called disinterested benevolence, but which meant in either case the impartial benign regard of all of God's creatures. For both, reason and conscience were active powers implanted within for moving in the direction of divine perfection, and imagination was another power for feeding the good and weakening the mental grip of the bad. Both believed above all that these powers were manifestations of an inner divinity that everyone bore inside themselves, a universal quality in which all were equal but all were different too, as reflections of the manifold face of the infinite divine.

During their time together, Channing and Wordsworth discovered much that they had in common. Wordsworth would always remember how Channing rhapsodized by the shores of the shimmering lake that Christianity suited human progress because it neither checked the free "activity of the human mind" nor compelled it "to tread always in a beaten path." Wordsworth agreed, but one of the most dramatic outcomes of the Romantic turn in Christian thought was the path it opened beyond Christianity, a path Channing did not take but some of his followers did.[3]

As Wordsworth and Channing descended into Grasmere by horse-cart that day—for Channing, though younger, was too feeble to walk more than half a mile—Wordsworth felt so inspired by their conversation that he decided to recite part of the long poem he kept in manuscript, thirteen books of blank verse he had already been working on for more than twenty years and would continue to rework for almost thirty years more before dying with instructions for its publication. *The Prelude or, Growth of a Poet's Mind* (1805–50) represents Wordsworth's best attempt to "make / Breathings for incommunicable powers," to express his own inner divinity and to convince himself and his spiritual friend, Coleridge, that he was enough in tune with the divine in a nature that included humankind to add his voice to the artistic chorus.[4]

What portion of the *Prelude* Wordsworth selected for Channing is not known, but his aside to Coleridge in Book III succinctly describes the concept of universal inner divinity that proved so important in both the Romantic movement in literature and the overlapping American Reformation. "Points have we all of us within our souls," Wordsworth said, "Where all stand single," unique, inimitable chips off the infinite divine. Recognizing this in oneself and others is the mark of "genius"—to use the Romantic word later adopted by Waldo Emerson—the necessary inspiration for literary endeavor because imagination is required for recognizing universal inner divinity, given how "each man is a memory to himself," walled off from others by the limitations of sense. "As natural beings in the strength of nature," individuals bear divine potential and exert their "majestic sway" every time they act sovereign rather than conformist, in obedience to their higher nature rather than their lower. This concept of universal inner divinity, received into the culture of lived virtue, provided an ongoing bridge between Christian and post-Christian thought while feeding the literary current associated with Transcendentalism as well as the reformist current in which slaves and laborers became equal moral agents with the elite.

This is where the American Reformation begins to end and the religion of democracy begins to grow. After Channing returned to Boston—having also visited the opium-inflamed Coleridge, who filled Channing's ears with a stream of the ideas that were about to cross the Atlantic in print—there were some years of Unitarian controversy ahead, and with them the fall of the Standing Order. Although Channing supported the growth of the liberal movement, his primary work lay in expressing and applying the religious understanding he had formed for himself by the light of the American Reformation while, unbeknownst to him, Wordsworth and Coleridge were publishing their first poems. Channing reached his height of influence right when the English Romantics reached a wide American audience, their works echoing and amplifying the richest and ripest voice in the American Reformation. The goal of Christian life was "awakening Mind," in Channing's phrase. The goal of human life was growing in "Likeness to God," a sermon title he borrowed from Coleridge, who borrowed it from Plato, from whom Whichcote had borrowed it in between. How to pursue this growth? By practicing the method of moral and intellectual and therefore spiritual development that Channing named "Self-Culture" in an address to work-ingmen that won him fans among the new working class all the way to Liverpool, a method in which ideals serve as practical guides to action. But by the time he delivered this address, the American Reformation was bursting in a thousand directions.[5]

It was 1838. That year the ex-minister Waldo Emerson, who revered Channing and Wordsworth, addressed the graduating class of the Harvard Divinity School with a prayer not to God but to moral perfection: "Virtue, I am thine; save me; use me; thee will I serve, day and night, in great, in small, that I may be not virtuous, but virtue." The same year, Channing's chief disciple, Elizabeth Palmer Peabody, published a review of Emerson's *Nature* (1836), taking the sort of criticism Mary Moody Emerson did privately into the public sphere as a work of Christian service, like the educational endeavors from which Peabody earned a slim living. In 1838 Peabody also introduced her brother-in-law Nathaniel Hawthorne to her future brother-in-law Horace Mann, who was busy that year opening a state university, establishing *The Common School Journal* to boost the goal of universal public education, and helping the Massachusetts state legislature pass the nation's first temperance law— since bondage to drink barred the cultivation of moral agency just like subjection to a master did, or ignorance—with a heavy assist in the last endeavor from the new evangelicals, among whom the choice to convert was framed in terms of moral agency. In 1838, the first American edition of Alexis de Tocqueville's *Democracy in America* appeared; a substantial portion of the French visitor's material for the international best seller came from Boston liberals, especially Jared Sparks, Channing, and the leader of the Unitarian ministry to the poor, Joseph Tuckerman. Also published that year was the first volume in a series called *Specimens of Foreign Literature*, edited by George Ripley, who brought American readers the continental Romantics, German biblical criticism, and more before abandoning his Unitarian pulpit for an experiment in Christian democracy called Brook Farm. Texts from Persia, India, and the Catholic and Buddhist traditions were also newly available and finding newly curious readers among religious liberals, both Christian and post-Christian. The American Reformation had exploded into what Elizabeth Palmer Peabody called "the religion of the Independents," which included as many creedal varieties as voices, yet voices all harmonized around the idea that humanity is equal in its endowments, its obligation to cultivate them, and its right to liberty in this sacred work.[6]

One more noteworthy intellectual production took place in 1838. A tall young lawyer from Springfield, Illinois, mounted the podium at the local lyceum, a voluntary educational institution established by migrants from New England. Abraham Lincoln was not a churchgoer, but he loved Channing's works. The echo of the American Reformation could be heard in Lincoln's praise of how the American Revolutionary generation took the essential "principles of our nature" and made them into "active agents" in advancing "the noblest of causes." Lincoln called on his audience to turn "civil and religious liberty" into "the political religion of our nation."[7]

Certainly a great many more factors went into the making of northern ideology in the antebellum period than the exportation of the American Reformation. Bostonians had a habit of overestimating their national influence. Nevertheless, liberal religion and intellectual culture traveled along with westward migration and the growth of the educational enterprises Lincoln praised in that address. One of the most striking features of the American Civil War is how little it changed the course of the intellectual culture surging out of Boston, because of how profoundly it seemed to confirm the central claim of the American Reformation that the most vital factor in human progress is the freedom of each equal mind.

AWAKENING MIND

John Adams, who never believed in social leveling as a possible or even desirable effect of American democracy, wrote to Jefferson about the rule of privileged families in New England in a letter of 1813. As was typical in these letters of his dotage, Adams recalled a story from his youth, from "57 or 58 years ago," when he read the returns of the Rhode Island elections to one of his Worcester mentors, Judge Chandler, who noted the surnames of the winners and commented that "the most ancient families" ever proved most popular. "To this day," Adams declared to Jefferson, "when any of these Tribes and We may Add Ellerys, Channings Champlins etc are pleased to fall in with the popular current, they are sure to carry all before them."[8]

Adams was right. Although today a historian would add the Adams name to any list of influential American families, William Ellery Channing (1780–1842) was as wellborn as they come. Wealth, honor, piety, and patriotism covered both sides of his family tree, which included not only Ellerys and Channings but also ties to the Cabot, Lee, Jackson, Lowell, Gibbs, Dana, and Allston clans. Adams may have homed in on the Ellery and Channing names because of a letter he received while ambassador to France about the needs of a Newport church that was destroyed in the Revolution; two of the four signatories were Channing's grandfathers. The irony in the fulfillment of Adams's prediction, however, is that Channing was decidedly not "pleased to fall in with the popular current," because his principal familial inheritance was independent-mindedness, a value that happened to align perfectly with the growing mood of his moment and milieu. Since the chief manifestation of Channing's privilege was his lifelong assumption that his voice was worth listening to, he turned out to be an ideal man of his time who used his popularity and magniloquence to urge his audiences to transcend the social, moral, and intellectual limitations of their time. Given this, and given that he enjoyed every advantage of education, opportunity, and personal attractiveness, he did indeed carry all before him. Even—though they did not know it—his enemies.[9]

One of Channing's critical advantages in life was the grandfather after whom he was named. William Ellery lived until Channing was forty, a regular source of wise counsel, high expectations, and penetrating questions. Ellery cut a distinguished figure in Newport society. He joined the Sons of Liberty in 1770 and rose to such a high profile in the movement for independence that he was chosen as a delegate to the Continental Congress. He signed the Declaration of Independence. He also served as a member of the new U.S. Congress for the better part of a decade, where he won "universal confidence for his prudent, straightforward, practical view of affairs, and for his consistent, independent, decided conduct," according to his own recollection late in life, which suggests that he never suffered from low self-esteem. Upon returning to Newport, Ellery served alternately as a judge, a customs collector, and a leading member of his rebuilt church.[10]

Ellery quit frequenting the tavern relatively early in his married life, and as he aged his Reformation Christian convictions became increasingly central to how he understood himself and his place in the world. These convictions included Calvinist articles of faith as well as principles of the American Reformation, especially the divine right of private judgment, which he bestowed with wit and precision on everyone in earshot. Ellery was gregarious and liked company, having a particular fondness for ecclesiastical debate that his grandson later criticized as excessively logical but that must have been a great education for the sensitive boy who seems always to have longed above all else to be good. Ellery was good, or thought himself so, anyway—he claimed that his "character bore the marks of habitual self-inspection and self-resistance"—and he appears to have been a great deal like John Adams in not only living into his nineties but living with a firm sense that some uncertainties must be abided because the whole can be known only by God and that meanwhile what mattered most was honesty, fair-mindedness, and just treatment of others, especially the young, to whom Ellery was affectionately drawn. Channing treasured their relationship and once wrote to him appreciatively, "You have hardly a grandchild who cannot trace back some of his sentiments and principles to your instructive and condescending conversation."[11]

William Ellery and his wife raised a pious daughter who chose for her husband William Channing, a graduate of Princeton. There Channing had been instructed by the Scottish immigrant Rev. John Witherspoon, indirect successor of Jonathan Edwards as president of the college, the only clergyman to sign the Declaration and a mediator between the Calvinism of the American Presbyterian Church and the natural theology of Scottish Common Sense, which penetrated deep into the American Reformation. Channing was pious too, but pious in the manner of a popular lawyer involved in politics and fond of hospitality. He was successful enough that he simultaneously served as the state's attorney general and the local district attorney at one point, possessing a mellifluous style in court and a great number of friends among clergy and laity alike. Understanding this aspect of Channing's character points to a new understanding of the story most commonly retold about his son's childhood.[12]

It is a simple story. Channing took his son to church one day when a famous visiting minister was in the pulpit. The itinerant was a neo-Calvinist who believed in total depravity and the utility of stimulating his listeners' emotions, particularly their fears, which he apparently did quite skillfully. Nine-year-old William Ellery Channing listened intently to a sermon that vividly painted the dangers of hell, the horror of evil, the suffering that Jesus had incurred on behalf of sinning humanity, and the slimness of human chances to evade the wrath of God. Already prone to self-reflection and the grim conviction of his own sins, Channing rode home with his father in a fright made all the deeper after his father pronounced the doctrine of the sermon to be sound, and then fell into silence. But soon his father began to whistle, and at home he stretched his feet before the fireplace and picked up a newspaper to relax. The boy suddenly saw that "his father did not believe it; people did not believe it!" For if they truly did, they could never act so lightly.[13]

The story is generally taken to indicate young Channing's early distaste for Calvinist doctrine, although one scholar perceptively calls it a sign of his incipient pragmatism, since Channing clearly held that the meaning of beliefs is practically demonstrated in action. These interpretations are not untrue, but a fuller interpretation rests on the context in which Channing's father spoke. They were on their way out of the church when someone greeted the father, and to this person papa Channing said, "Sound doctrine, sir." It was a social remark by a politically sensitive churchgoer, far above the head of an earnest young boy. What a parishioner gestures to in public may be different from those beliefs, some of them half formed, held privately.[14]

Especially in a town like Newport. With two Congregational churches broadcasting a range of doctrinal opinion—from the future president of Yale, Ezra Stiles, in whom a devotion to the divine right of private judgment ran as strong as a belief in the trinity, to Samuel Hopkins, the arch-Calvinist disciple of Edwards—parishioners like the elder Channing may have appeared to agree with different positions that were logically incompatible. His own brother was a minister of liberal views, to which Channing had so little objection that he sent William to him for two years of tutoring in preparation for college. Rather than being imprinted by his father's Christianity or his grandfather's, then, young Channing was exposed to a diversity of Christians, including the Baptists then taking up residence in Newport, which means that there was no one orthodoxy against which he later rebelled because there was no orthodox Christianity he was ever taught.[15]

The social exposures of Channing's youth were as important as the religious exposures. At home the Channings had George Washington to dine, as well as Ezra Stiles, John Jay, and other eminent guests, which means that William Ellery Channing was taught the manners appropriate to such company. Celebrating the ratification of the Constitution was one of his earliest memories. Although Newport was a sailors' town, where southerners summered and French impieties ran strong, Channing never once uttered a profane word, another sign of the social tailoring of the family's piety. The Channings owned slaves until the Revolution, at which point they emancipated them and kept them on as servants, which means that no Channing ever emptied a chamber pot, or leapt up from the table to check the stove, or worried about clean linens. An African-born servant carried Channing to school in his arms. Another servant was an ardent Baptist who instructed him almost as closely as his own mother did. Channing's recollection of these relationships was warm and respectful, which suggests that among the lessons learned from this privileged experience was one of common humanity.[16]

Channing's father died when the boy was thirteen, the same age as Wordsworth when his own father died. Apparently the senior Channing's success as a lawyer was not accompanied by success as a financial planner, which made the situation precarious for his widow and ten children, but the event did not prevent Channing's matriculation at Harvard two years later. There he flourished: first in class, prizewinning orator, outstanding scholar in the classical languages as well as modern literature and history, dazzling in composition, and invited member of all the clubs then springing up in the college—but frequenter only of the virtuous ones. He lived with another uncle, Francis Dana, who had served with Washington at Valley Forge and been ambassador to Russia before settling in Cambridge, where he became a judge. Dana's grand house sat on spacious grounds a short walk from Harvard Yard near the northern shore of the Charles River; it was the same house in which the Transcendentalist intellectual Margaret Fuller later grew up. Channing liked to study outside when the weather was fine, to read while walking slowly under a stand of willow trees that afforded an unbroken sightline to the Brookline hills across the river. In this favorite study spot he had his first significant spiritual experience, an epiphany that remained a touchstone for the rest of his life.[17]

He was reading Francis Hutcheson (1694–1746). Writing in the train of Locke and the third Earl of Shaftesbury, Hutcheson and his school of Common Sense had already entered Americans' intellectual sphere through the Revolutionary generation, contributing to the thinking behind the founding documents. Hutcheson's ideal of "disinterested affection," as he explained in a 1725 text, was an attribute of divine character that pointed to the presence of a *"universal determination* to *benevolence* in mankind,*"* an inner moral sense—alongside the propensity to sin— that was held in common by all, hence "Common Sense." John Adams was among those who linked such Common Sense ideas about religion to American ideas about government when he wrote in a letter:

"Sovereigns possess the intellectual liberty to act for the public good or not. Being men, they have all what Dr. Rush calls a *moral faculty*; Dr. Hutcheson a *moral sense*; and the Bible and the generality of the world, *a conscience*. They are all, therefore, under moral obligation to do unto others as they would have others *do to them*; to consider themselves born, authorized, empowered for the good of society as well as their own good."

The letter aptly illustrates how the languages and theories of Christianity, republicanism, and liberalism mixed together in the American founding and the early republic. Liberty is intended for moral action in the service of the common good. Hutcheson gave the founders an argument that the moral sense necessary to republican virtue was naturally found in humankind.[18]

For Channing Hutcheson did somewhat different work, since Hutcheson's oeuvre was substantial and varied, with elements of utilitarianism and aesthetic theory lodged alongside moral and religious arguments. There is no record of exactly which text of Hutcheson's Channing was reading that day, but based on his remarks about it, *An Essay on the Nature and Conduct of the Passions and Affections* (1728) is a strong possibility. In this midcareer book, Hutcheson argued that self-love, motivations of reward, or the pursuit of personal happiness were not satisfying reasons for virtuous actions. Nor can merely focusing on what is good for those one loves or even on the "public Good" completely fulfill what is right, the way pointed to by one's innate moral sense. Instead, focusing on what is good about God will naturally yield good conduct toward others because God's goodness is devoid of self-love, full of truly universal love. This is disinterested benevolence, a human understanding of a divine characteristic that translates into a practical ideal for action. As Hutcheson said and those who followed Channing ever after believed, virtue is not the absence of harm but the presence and preponderance of "*positive Services* to Mankind," which grow in proportion to "*Positive Virtue* toward the DEITY." This is a causal relationship, Hutcheson claimed, because "our *Love to the* DEITY will directly excite us to all manner of *beneficent Actions*." The activity of adoring the divine quality of universal love, moreover, involves an imagination of who God is generated by meditative awareness of such a love's potential in oneself. "In our Conceptions of the DEITY," Hutcheson described, "we are continually led to imagine a Resemblance to what we feel in ourselves." This active process of divine adoration and human service is moral, intellectual, spiritual; progressive, melioristic, and joyful; fitted to human capacities because reflective of the maker's handiwork and wishes.[19]

Channing's elation increased the more he read the book. He later described the experience as providing "the fountain light of all his day, the master light of all his seeing," language he borrowed from Wordsworth retrospectively. The use of imagination in conjuring and adoring an infinitely loving God, whose goodness human beings are capable of emulating in active, concrete service to one another, came clear to him that day, and he "felt as if heaven alone could give room for the exercise of such emotions." The faith in disinterested benevolence as a guiding ideal became a cornerstone of Channing's religious thought, which is to say, of his life. "The Knowledge and Love of the Deity, the *universal* Mind," he read in Hutcheson, "is as *natural* a Perfection to such a Being as Man, as any Accomplishment to which we arrive by cultivating our natural Dispositions; nor is that Mind come to the *proper State* and *Vigor* of its kind, where *Religion* is not the main *Exercise* and *Delight*."[20]

God understood as the universal mind and human perfection as a process of approaching such a mind became essential to Channing's work, as seen even in the very last series of sermons he delivered, near the end of his life. Eventually published by his nephew, the Transcendentalist Unitarian minister William Henry Channing, under a title drawn from one of the sermons, *The Perfect Life* (1873) described the goal of Christianity, one only fully realizable after death but incrementally manifested in the daily internal work of mental discipline. A half century after reading Hutcheson, Channing still praised "disinterested benevolence," declaring that "Religion is the great spring of elevation in Character" grown by "our veneration and love, and perpetual intercourse" with "a Being whose Character comprehends all venerable and lovely attributes; who reveals to us within Himself, without spot or limit, that very Perfection of Goodness, after which our moral nature impels us to aspire." Channing's text for the first sermon in this series was from the Gospel according to Mark: "love the Lord thy God with all thy heart, and with all thy soul, and with all thy mind, and with all thy strength." His listeners could supply the following verse that bade them to love their neighbors as themselves.[21]

It took more than Hutcheson to get Channing to his mature theology, of course, and there was also more than Hutcheson involved in that seminal experience by the Charles. Hutcheson gave Channing a tidy definition of the divine ideal as universal love as well as two important mental powers, intuition and imagination, for his Christian practice. But something else happened to Channing that day, and the beauty of nature had something to do with it, beauty that filled him with energy. Overwhelmed with the heady ecstasy of his experience, he returned to his desk and wrote a letter to the woman he would later marry, a letter he never sent to a girl he had idealized since their grade-school days. Channing, just a teenager, felt desire. He channeled it into a lofty theory about female nature being closer to the disinterested ideal, a theory softly replicated by his early biographers, who were steeped in Victorian notions of pure womanhood, but underneath those theories lies a simpler explanation about a different aspect of human nature from that of the moral sense. Desire—awareness of incompletion, of unfulfillment, of need—was a key element in what may be called Channing's Romantic awakening.[22]

He felt it most keenly in Virginia. Channing needed to find a paying situation after his college graduation. An opportunity arose when he encountered in Newport a Virginian who was so impressed with Channing's moral and intellectual character—and, no doubt, his breeding—that he offered him a job on the spot. Channing moved to Richmond in

1798 to teach a school of twelve pupils, work that required only the first half of each weekday. He lodged with one of Richmond's leading families, the Randolphs, who entertained such guests as John Marshall, the future chief justice of the U.S. Supreme Court, with lavish hospitality. Overall Channing found southern manners, orations, and largesse quite pleasing. Best of all, he had plenty of opportunity to prepare for entering the ministry, "a retired room" to study in, and "a lonely plain to walk in," as he wrote to his best friend from college, William Smith Shaw, who was in Philadelphia serving as private secretary to the president of the United States, his uncle John Adams. In fact, though, Channing was terribly lonely without the company of the family and friends who had surrounded him in New England, away from home for the first time, with no one he could really talk to.[23]

He was also profoundly alienated by southern culture. His cultural isolation in a slaveholding society turned out to be crucial in the making of his spiritual crisis. In "Jacobin" Richmond, he complained, "a licentious and intemperate city," infidelity abounded "among the higher classes" who provided his social companionship. Some of his new acquaintances audibly "wondered how [he] could embrace such an *unprofitable* profession as the ministry," he reported miserably to his uncle. Yet Channing did not waver from his sense of calling because he had his lodestar in the American Reformation ideal of independent-mindedness. He told Shaw that he lifted himself from his surroundings by reading and writing. "Above all things," he advised his friend, "cultivate this independence. You know it is my idol."[24]

Channing's mental independence meant that his immersion in a slaveholding culture sharpened his opposition to the practice rather than softening it. He discussed the topic in Richmond society and had a substantial amount of contact with the slaves themselves, distributing their weekly rations in the quarters on occasion and taking entire charge of the Randolph establishment during one spell when he was left alone there. The result of this experience was the germ of an antislavery conviction that ripened in him over the decades to come, in step with his culture and just a shade in advance of it, a conviction representative of the moderate antislavery middle ground from which abolitionists, immediatists, and ultraists extended their more radical positions. In Virginia, Channing came to feel that slavery was bad for both races, for the nation, for the cause of religious progress, and most of all for humanity itself. "Language cannot express my detestation of it," he wrote home. "Man, when forced to substitute the will of another for his own, ceases to be a moral agent," which makes slavery "degrading to humanity." Enslavement violates "the right of exerting the powers which nature has given us in the pursuit of any and of every good which we can obtain without doing injury to others." Here he expressed the most basic liberal sense of natural rights, applying them to the enslaved. He also prefigured the mature arguments he came to make against slavery more than three decades later, when the violence of an anti-abolitionist mob in Boston inspired him to devote a pamphlet to the subject. The violation of the slave's moral nature remained Channing's most fundamental antislavery argument, while the language of the Virginia letter as well as of Mayhew continues to echo in the 1835 *Slavery*. Everyone is "a Rational, Moral, Immortal Being," he wrote there. "The sacrifice of such a being to another's will . . . is the greatest violence which can be offered to any creature of God. It is to degrade him from his rank in the universe."[25]

Channing's stand on the moral high ground did not bring about his Virginia crisis, though. It was more like a fall from grace. He had always distinguished himself among his peers as an example of upright conduct. One story about his childhood aptly illustrates his penchant for morality. His teacher, exasperated with a misbehaving classmate, allegedly exclaimed, "I wish in my heart you were like William Channing." The unfortunate boy replied, "I can't be like him; it is not half so hard for him to be good as it is for me." Apocryphal or not, the characterization appears valid. Channing did not struggle against vice in college but easily turned to his books and his lofty-minded companions, whose conversations he so missed in Virginia. There, inspired in part by the Stoics—his favorite reading in those days aside from Hutcheson, and the political theorist Adam Ferguson—he strove to embody the ideal Christian character. His efforts of the period reflect the developing culture of lived virtue. According to his nephew, in Virginia Channing habitually studied until the middle of the night, slept on the bare floor (for the purpose of "overcoming effeminacy"), neglected exercise, restricted his diet, and spent his money on books rather than clothing, leaving himself exposed "during the whole winter without an overcoat, except when sometimes he borrowed one to attend church." Hagiography, to be sure, but quite illustrative hagiography reflecting the values of a shared culture, which held that the ideal Christian sacrificed pleasure for spiritual profit won by industry, humility, self-sacrifice, and the pursuit of knowledge. Whether Channing actually ever even temporarily achieved a substantial measure of this ideal is an open question, but without doubt he wanted to, and aimed to, and strove to do so with every fiber of his will.[26]

But then spring came. Nature, which had been a refuge for Channing since childhood, became a snare. He ambled by the James River now, aimless and dreaming, and he could not make himself sit still and study. He complained to Shaw of "a universal languor" that had settled upon him, keeping him from his rigorous commitments. His concern was anguished and deep as he confessed to having "lost every energy of soul" until "the only relic of your friend is a sickly imagination, a fevered sensibility. I cannot study," he groaned. He could not control his will, and ended up misusing his time in a sin that Reformation Christians going back at least to John Adams had struggled to resist, and which M. M. Emerson lamented in her diary: "I groan with ennui. I am not well and my mind cannot operate." But Channing wanted to be a minister, expected to be an example as well as a shepherd, and his behavior was even indicted by its contrast with the advice of a Catholic, the French archbishop François Fénelon (1651–1715), who said that a good minister "preaches to *save men's souls*, and not to *show himself*," a sentiment Channing quoted with noteworthy admiration given how anti-Catholic his culture remained. Fénelon's devotion to self-sacrifice inspired Channing to resolve to "throw away those ridiculous ecstasies" and to form himself "to habits of piety and benevolence." Instead, the lure of nature and indolence conquered him. "I walk and muse till I can walk no longer."[27]

Channing's loneliness only exacerbated the problem, but his attempt to relieve it ultimately brought the crisis to a head. There was a young lady in the neighborhood, "universally esteemed for her benevolence," and evidently she had attracted Channing's interest. He decided to share with her a poem he loved, a sonnet by Robert Southey, the first English Romantic whose work crossed the Atlantic. Perhaps Southey's ode to his hearth fire—"And I would wish, like thee, to shine serene, / Like thee, within mine influence, all to cheer"—the verse struck such a chord in Channing that it "wrung tears" from him. And the promising young lady? "'It is pretty,' said she, with a smile," Channing reported to Shaw with disappointment. "'Pretty!'" He could not understand her sensibility, and she could not understand his. As he reflected on the incident, though, he came to indict himself for want of action rather than her for want of feeling. "I blushed when I thought more on the subject," he confessed. He realized that however much compassion he felt for suffering humanity while reading a novel or "a tale of human woe," he was "still deficient in *active* benevolence." In old-fashioned Reformation Christian self-interrogation, he pursued his own shortcomings, asking himself, "'do I ever relieve the distressed? Have I ever lightened the load of affliction?' My cheeks reddened at the question; a cloud of error burst from my mind. I found that virtue did not consist in feeling, but in *acting from a sense of duty*."[28]

He blushed. A cloud of error burst. He found. The language shows how closely Channing attended to his mental processes in a practice of Christian meditation that held those mental states against the divine ideal without, this time, condemning others. The last component—levying a recognition of his shortcomings into a spring for action—was the crucial element in his Romantic turn. His discovery relates closely to the role that nature came to play in his thought and in the religion of democracy that came after him. So much is made of the starry-eyed hopefulness in both Romantic and Unitarian thought that they and the liberal religion they coproduced are treated as though they left out sin. In fact it was the conviction and abhorrence of sin that anchored the entire progressive structure of the postevangelical Christian program. Channing could not will himself into Christian sainthood. He now found that he had been blind to his own sin, the sin of enjoying the pleasure of nature only for feeling rather than for moral action and the deeper sin of holding himself above others.

In his alienation from Virginia society, Channing had been like the man who sat in the bower of a yew tree in a Wordsworth poem that had yet to circulate in America at that time but became one of liberal religion's core texts. "Lines Left upon a Seat in a Yew-Tree" (1795) tells the tragic tale of a man who withdrew from a world where he had expected to distinguish himself, just as Channing had withdrawn from Virginia society. He chooses intoxication in nature, whose purity he finds exquisite and in whose remove from the disappointing realm of human society he exults. Full of "visionary views," the proud man never bears fruit. Wordsworth warns against what Channing also found: "The man whose eye / Is ever on himself doth look on one, / The least of Nature's works," and "he, who feels contempt / For any living thing, hath faculties / Which he has never used; that thought with him / Is in its infancy." The growth of mind is toward universal benevolence because "true knowledge leads to love," Wordsworth wrote. The mechanism of this movement involves both acknowledgment of sin and aspiration toward virtue. "True dignity"—the objective of moral agency—"abides with him alone, / Who, in the silent hour of inward thought, / Can still suspect, and still revere himself, / In lowliness of heart."[29]

Channing did not encounter Wordsworth's work until he was already back in New England and well established as a minister, but when he did, the poems of *Lyrical Ballads* (1798) resonated strongly with him, especially this one, which was among those he read aloud to Elizabeth Palmer Peabody in the 1820s with the summary observation, "Self-pity becomes a weakening egotism." (She chose its last stanza—with two small mistakes in it, suggesting how long she had mentally fingered the poem—to characterize Channing's essence in her memoir of him sixty years later.) There in Virginia Channing had hit upon the essential Romantic motion described in the poem of discovering the divine within and knowing it to be in others, suspecting the sin within and knowing it to keep one from loving others, all while aspiring to the "lowliness of heart" modeled by Christ.[30]

Channing claimed to have known nothing of Christ up until this point, but after this cathartic spring he studied the Gospel thoroughly, especially the Sermon on the Mount. He concocted ambitious schemes for saving humanity based on a conviction in universal moral nature and an opposition to "the idea that private interest is distinct from the public." His friends back home laughed at his ambitions, recommending he come back to the standbys of British dissent such as Joseph Butler and Richard Price. One teased that Channing wanted to execute the "imaginary republic of Coleridge and Southey," referring to the utopian pantisocracy they devised on egalitarian principles.[31]

But Channing did no such thing. He went home to New England and undertook the schooling of his younger siblings and the training to become a minister. He was ordained the week Waldo Emerson was born.

LIKENESS TO GOD

Channing was by no means a Unitarian when he got back to New England. He was simply an ardent Reformation Christian, and his critique of Calvinism was slow to develop. In fact the minister with whom he had the deepest connection while in Newport was the doctrinaire Calvinist Samuel Hopkins, who shared Channing's enthusiasm for Hutcheson and apparently lived by the ideal of disinterested benevolence to a remarkable degree. Hopkins distinguished himself, in Channing's eyes, by his brave opposition to slavery, his personal generosity with his modest resources, his scholarly industry, his nonconformity to society, and his complete ignorance of fashion. Since Channing already believed that the meaning of religion was found in its moral fruits, his esteem for the Christian character of Hopkins only grew even as he came to find the theology Hopkins preached to be gloomy, severe, and excessively abstract, "utterly irreconcilable with human freedom." Insensitive to his audience, Hopkins preached in an "untunable" voice whose "tones approached those of a cracked bell," Channing recalled. Nevertheless, Channing listened to those sermons regularly and attentively. He engaged in long conversations with Hopkins about the elder minister's life and theological opinions, supplied his pulpit, attended his deathbed, and spoke well of his piety and morality ever after. By all evidence, Channing's association with Hopkins did more to deepen his appreciation of disinterested benevolence than to repel him from Calvinist or trinitarian doctrines. To Hopkins he credited "liberality," a devotion to free inquiry, and a strong dedication to the "idea of entire self-surrender to the general good." Channing was so visibly devoted to Hopkins that his widow gave Channing one of her late husband's manuscripts on morality. Channing's moral seriousness was the most obvious thing about him at the time.[32]

His uplifting comportment in the pulpit was the next most obvious thing about him. His very first sermon—on the text "Silver and gold have I none, but such as I have give I thee" (Acts 3:6)—won him immediate competing offers from the two most powerful congregations in Boston at the time of his debut: Brattle Street, where prominent patriot families congregated; and Federal Street, smaller and less prestigious but wealthier, whose congregation soon multiplied in size under Channing's draw. Such was Channing's attractiveness as a candidate and the status of a minister for a church of high caliber that he negotiated quite generous terms of settlement at Federal Street. The offer letter noted "what profound reflection and laborious inquiry the sacred office requires" together with the intention to ensure that "the mind devoted to such high engagements should . . . be undisturbed by solicitudes and embarrassment from the cares of life." To Channing's comfortable salary was soon added a parsonage, then an associate minister, and at some point a sabbatical every summer, so that his preaching was ultimately reduced to once per week at most and laity overtook his ministries to the poor and feeble.[33]

He never fulfilled expectations for his scholarly productivity, a shortcoming attributed to his fragile health, which was itself attributed to his moral zeal. The success of his ministry thus primarily consisted of his success as a religious teacher, from the pulpit and the invited podium and in meetings with laity held in the church vestry and elsewhere. Right in this moment when the status of the New England minister was still at its zenith, the first shoots of that role's replacement by the more specialized functions of the theologian, scholar, public intellectual, and educator are visible in the career of this favored son. Although Channing's material comfort was bolstered by his congregation's wealth, it was guaranteed by the law of church establishment, after all, an establishment that gradually disappeared over his career. Yet as Congregationalism's star fell, the power of Channing's culture of lived virtue rose. State-supported ministry came to be replaced by state-supported education that sought the same ends as Channing's work, namely the ability of every individual to apprehend and serve the widest possible good.[34]

At the time of Channing's 1803 ordination, neither the demise of the Congregationalist establishment nor that of its institutional unity was in sight, although both were imminent. Channing himself clearly expected that the unity of Christian fellowship should withstand variations in the uniformity of Christian doctrine, for although during his years of training for the ministry he found he could not follow the trinitarian view of Jesus held by the otherwise admirable Doddridge—the devotional thinker to whom M. M. Emerson declared such indebtedness—Channing joined the First Church of Cambridge, then headed by a moderate Calvinist. Even more suggestively, he picked another Calvinist, David Tappan, to deliver his ordination sermon. Channing and Tappan had developed a warm relationship of mutual admiration while Channing was still in training, years during which he served as regent at the college, where Tappan was Hollis Professor of Divinity. Tappan was remembered by a fellow faculty member as "impartial a divine as I ever knew, extremely cautious not to prepossess the minds of his pupils, and always exhorting them to judge for themselves," a reflection of how the American Reformation could still coexist with Calvinist beliefs at the turn of the nineteenth century. But soon after Channing's installment at Federal Street, Tappan died. He was replaced by the liberal Henry Ware, and his religious character and proper legacy became agenda-driven topics of debate in the pages of the *Monthly Anthology and Boston Review* and *The Panoplist*. The fledgling minister found himself learning his trade in the heat of this new polarization.[35]

There is no telling exactly how Channing's theology would have developed if his grandfather were not still alive, active, engaged, and intellectually vigorous in these years. Ellery did not approve of the new liberal movement, to which Channing soon belonged self-consciously enough that in their correspondence Channing used the pronouns "we" and "our" in reference to it. In the years following the Ware appointment, Ellery questioned Channing about liberal Christianity and took the trouble to spell out his objections in letters to his grandson. Channing esteemed his grandfather so genuinely that his responses to Ellery's criticism forced him to crystallize and sharpen his opinions, to express them clearly and succinctly, and to formulate them in light of real respect for his grandfather's beliefs. Representing his religious opinions to his grandfather enabled him to tune them to be heard by more Christians than simply the like-minded.[36]

Ellery complained that liberal Christianity was not "particular" enough, hitting on precisely the most important point about it. Channing explained to his grandfather that "modern divinity," as he called it—liberal Christianity allied itself with progress from the beginning—aimed to "harmonize" with as great a "variety of sentiments" as possible because of how many questions of Christian theology were open questions, lacking concrete evidence to lift positions on them above the "speculative." Given the partiality of doctrinal knowledge and the certainty of human fallibility, liberals used a minimal standard for adjudging beliefs, a practical rule evaluating whether a belief moved the heart toward God. "Practical righteousness is all in all," Channing wrote Ellery. "*Love* is the fulfilling of the law and of the gospel. All truth is designed to excite this temper, and to form the habits which flow from it, and this is the only test which we fallible mortals can apply to doctrines." This is Christian pragmatism. A doctrine's truth-value depends on whether its results be good, and with the jury out on so many articles of the truth, the course of wisdom lies in keeping a fellowship as wide as possible in order to debate those speculative articles of belief among a wide range of viewpoints while coming to consensus on whatever articles can satisfy different parties' requirements for belief. The liberal attitude, for Channing, is intellectual humility born of introspection combined with respect rather than scorn for those who disagree with one's beliefs. "Taught by experience to know my own blindness, shall I speak as if I could not err," he proposed to his grandfather, "and as if they might not in some disputed points be more enlightened than myself?"[37]

Within a year Channing had Ellery agreeing "that the great effect proposed by God, in the revelation he has made, is the *sanctification of the hearts of mankind*, that a certain *state of heart* is the end for which God exhibits certain objects to our view." The two continued to have serious discussions over how to interpret the biblical scripture on which both were relying, discussions that were going on all over and with equal vigor across New England. Moses Stuart at Andover, who called Unitarianism a halfway house to infidelity, argued over the interpretation of the new biblical criticism coming out of Germany against the position of Nathaniel Frothingham, from whom M. M. Emerson heard that "the old bible was not inspired," and against Andrews Norton, possibly the shrillest voice in the liberal movement. Words like Arian,

Arminian, and Socinian were thrown about, and not only did Unitarians argue against the biblical grounding of Calvinist dogmas, they argued against one another's opinions on issues like whether Jesus was born free of sin or became sinless over time, whether his miracles were supernatural, and whether the Bible has anything meaningful to say about the afterlife.[38]

Channing did not engage scholastically with these debates. He kept his own biblical interpretation simple, tied to his foundation in practical Christianity. When a parishioner asked him whether there was internal evidence in the biblical account of Jesus's baptism for the miraculous signs accompanying the event, for example, he translated the symbols of that passage into the practical precepts of the Romantic turn: the suspicion of sin and the reverence of inner divinity. Water symbolized "repentance and reformation," he said, and fire "the transformation of life by love of truth and good." This was the bottom line for Channing, and the Bible was open to interpretation in light of the premise of God's goodness. "The Scriptures are not themselves revelation," he told the participants in the vestry meeting where this conversation took place, "but the *records* of revelation made to men who reported the truths revealed." Channing accepted the historicity of the Bible while restricting his speculations to the barest common denominator—the broadest common ground—of God's universal love. "We reason about the Bible" with an eye to practice, he said later, "precisely as civilians do about the constitution under which we live."[39]

Before long it was Channing's turn to be honored with delivering the ordination sermon for a new minister, John Codman in Dorchester, just south of Boston. The sermon brought him his first widespread public attention, both because it was published and because it was given highly favorable notice in the pages of the *Boston Review* section of the *Monthly Anthology* for February 1809. The sermon itself is remarkable mainly for how neatly it expressed Channing's practical Christianity, his concern for the fallibility of humans and the partiality of doctrinal truth, and his warning in those early years of the Unitarian controversy against party spirit. "Divine truth is infinite and can never be exhausted," he observed, which ought to breed a spirit of humility in those who preach. Ministers should maintain open minds, resist systems, and commit to perpetual self-improvement, "to *do* as well as to *will*."[40]

The review, on the other hand, is remarkable not only for its fulsome praise of Channing's substance and style—his sermon reflected "a mind, elevated by the contemplation of gospel truth, and a heart, warmed by the pure glow of christian love"—but also because it represents the first trickle of what soon became a river of printed support for Channing and his liberal Christian colleagues, a river fed by parochial networks of well-funded friends and intermarried families who broadcast their opinions in the impartial terms of the culture of lived virtue. Both the literary production of liberal clergymen and their stimulating effect in the broader intellectual culture of the nineteenth century brought the American Reformation into its final stage of diffusing its principles and seeding new movements beyond the church.[41]

"None, surely, can refuse to agree with us," boasted the anonymous reviewer of Channing's Codman sermon, "that the spirit of this sermon is the true spirit of the gospel." This objective declaration may well have been penned by William Smith Shaw, now a lawyer. He had returned to Boston after the Adams presidency and cofounded the Anthology Society with William Emerson and Rev. Joseph Buckminster, the brilliant Christian prodigy who took the spot at Brattle Street that Channing had declined. A few years after this review, Emerson and Buckminster were dead, the *Monthly Anthology* folded, but in the burgeoning culture of print many new vehicles for spreading the American Reformation appeared. The most important of these was the *North American*

Review, initially edited by Channing's brother and their cousin, later by Jared Sparks, and proclaiming the scope of its ambition in its title. The next most important was the *Christian Examiner*, whose founding in New York in 1829 signaled the first success of that ambition, the spread of the American Reformation and its liberal Christianity beyond Boston. Evangelicals and neo-Calvinists had their organs too—one Baptist editor in these years called print "the lever which moves the moral world"—but no other sect could mobilize the wealth and cultural capital of the liberals, who had practically the entire merchant class of Boston behind them. One of the striking features of liberal media in this period is illustrated by the titles of these two examples, by what the *North American Review* and the *Christian Examiner* effectively claimed to represent; some print outlets covered the liberalism of their religion with claims to general Christianity, while others covered the religious cast of their liberal thought with claims to general intellectual culture. Together such publications were a potent force in the spread of liberal Christianity and its production of a religion of democracy that was both sacred and secular.[42]

The flood of print was swelling on both sides of the Atlantic, of course, while the passage of print across the Atlantic steadily increased, and so it was that the decade between Channing's ordination of Codman and his ordination of Sparks saw the first significant impact of the English Romantics on literary America, an impact that became seismic after Channing's European sabbatical. Wordsworth's popularity among liberal Christians would be hard to overstate. M. M. Emerson incorporated extracts from his poetry into her correspondence; Waldo Emerson read and reread his *Excursion* (1814) until it became part of his consciousness; Channing's cousin Richard Henry Dana made his literary debut in the *North American Review* praising Wordsworth at the expense of Alexander Pope; when Jared Sparks visited London, he received Wordsworth as a guest three times in one week. Boston liberals were the first Americans to appreciate Wordsworth.[43]

Although the line between literature and religion cannot be made bright in the history of antebellum intellectual life, the principal impact of Wordsworth may have been the positive practical effect of focusing on the possibilities of virtue rather than the frights of sin, which assisted the young Unitarians in their arguments against Calvinism. Rather than fixing the gaze downward like the Calvinist preoccupation with innate depravity did, liberal Christians followed Wordsworth in believing that beholding divine moral perfection in the imagination wrought beneficial effects. The penultimate stanza of "To My Sister" (1795), which Channing read aloud to Peabody in the 1820s, carried a practical prescription:

And from the blessed power that rolls
About, below, above,
We'll frame the measure of our souls:
They shall be tuned to love.

Beliefs like this got Romantics and Unitarians their reputation for overestimating human nature, but they thought their belief in human dignity helped create the potential for its realization in practice.[44]

As the century wore on, Wordsworth's poetry spread far beyond the Unitarian camp, carrying with it the spirit of the American Reformation. By the turn of the twentieth century, Catholics and Methodists were among those who praised the religious effects of Wordsworth's poetry, especially for how it helped Christians revere the natural world that was created by God. "Wordsworth we cannot over-laud," wrote one Methodist in 1904, "who were helped by him to love the things he so truly loved."[45]

Wordsworth was known in America mainly for his poetry, although some of his prose came to American readers tucked in the eclectic pages of Coleridge's literary productions. Coleridge was known for his genius. His singular style and singularly dazzling display of knowledge appeared in poems like the popular *Christabel* (1816) and plays like *Remorse* (1813), a passage of which Channing once read aloud to Peabody—"with an infinite pathos in his voice, and his large tender eyes constantly seeking the repose of mine," she remembered—but Coleridge's greater impact on the last stage of the American Reformation came through his lengthy collages of aphorisms, anecdotes, snatches of verse, bursts of criticism, flights of history, fictional epistolary exchanges, and sermonizing. These works, especially *Biographia Literaria* (1817) and the high-circulating *Aids to Reflection* (1825), were read and discussed among American liberals in the antebellum period but did not initially become part of Coleridge's posthumous literary reputation, when *The Rime of the Ancient Mariner* (1817) and *Kubla Khan* (1816) marked him for the field of literary studies as a poet rather than a religious thinker despite the fact that Christianity was the motivation behind his experiments in verse. There was no separating religion from literature or either from philosophy in his time, and Coleridge was particularly apt to defy conventions and explode categories, which he did with zest and panache and more than a whiff of the midnight laudanum vial. (Channing and his wife expressed the "tenderest interest" in Coleridge's "fearful struggle" against this "weakness," Peabody said.)[46]

Coleridge borrowed and credited other people's voices freely, even convincing Wordsworth to allow a small piece of *The Prelude* to appear in Coleridge's serial *The Friend* (1809–10), which came to American readers in an 1831 edition after a bound volume appeared in London in 1818. Preparatory to instructing his reader in the mental discipline necessary for understanding morals and religion, Coleridge placed

Wordsworth's ode from Book I in which the "grandeur in the beatings of the heart" invoked the central Romantic belief in inner divinity. Coleridge also looked well into the past for divine inspiration from other men's breasts, as well as across the Channel, giving contemporary expression to a cosmopolitan array of thinkers. The autodidact's canon started with Plato and Plotinus and ran through the eighteenth-century Cambridge Platonists, the new German idealists, the early Christians, and a broad idiosyncratic swath of medieval and early modern Christian thinkers including Thomas à Kempis (1380–1471), who wrote a manual for *The Imitation of Christ*; Nicholas of Cusa (1401–1464), whose platonic conception of God as the "Maximum" underpinned Coleridge's never-completed magnum opus; Giordano Bruno (1548–1600), a Dominican monk, Aristotelian, and defender of Copernicus burned at the stake for heresy; and especially Archbishop of Glasgow Robert Leighton (*bap.* 1612–*d.* 1684), prone to fasting and anonymous acts of charity, who wrote an essay on "The Right of Conscience" and left behind fifteen hundred heavily annotated books and a pile of unpublished manuscripts at his death, which he had wished would occur at an inn to symbolize how this world of sense is but a stage en route to union with the divine. (Coleridge's edited anthology of Leighton's work served as Channing's introduction to both Coleridge and Leighton, whom he recommended to a friend in the early 1800s.) Coleridge may be known among scholars today as a host for the ideas of Immanuel Kant (1724–1804), which he brought into English for the first time and which is important enough. He was also a host for a much more diverse Christian smorgasbord than American readers had known before, a feast he digested to purposes he claimed to be orthodox but that whetted his American audience's appetite for more diversity still.[47]

Coleridge himself was not aiming for diversity, and certainly not for the post-Christian religious liberalism that many of his American admirers developed. He was, among other things, a Christian bigot, not only dubious of the possibility that divine truth might be found in any other tradition but certain it could not. At about the same time that M. M. Emerson was suggesting to Waldo that Unitarians should have the "ingenuity to recall the antient philosophy of the Hindoos" and Channing was hoping to meet Rammohun Roy—who had reviewed his "Unitarian Christianity" in Calcutta, and invented Hindu monotheism—Coleridge was calling Hindus civilized but uncultivated "slaves of superstition." He considered himself an orthodox Christian, seeking to reform the Anglican Church from within as the Puritans had tried to do two centuries before. Although in England he was "in bad odor for his liberality," according to Peabody, he did not advocate the liberal receptivity to varied opinions that Channing did. "Toleration is an Herb of spontaneous growth in the soil of Indifference," he complained, a "Weed" with "none of the Virtues of the Medicinal Plant, reared by Humility in the Garden of Zeal." Religious opinions could only be a matter of personal taste if they lacked a spirit of conviction, the zeal that nurtured genuine religious curiosity. Coleridge thus held the same negative opinion of ecumenism that religious conservatives for the rest of the nineteenth and across the twentieth century echoed, a judgment based on the concern that beliefs could only be relative if no one cared much about them. For Coleridge, who cared deeply and exclusively for Christian truth, Christianity was "the perfection of human intelligence," the single ultimate truth toward which the cultivation of human reason tended. Like M. M. Emerson, he was a natural Christian in the sense that he assumed Christianity was the divine truth reflected in nature. Yet through his criticisms of natural theology—the line of Locke and Paley and rational dissent, which had seduced him enough in his youth that he named a son after the founder of associational psychology, David Hartley—he updated the rules of right reasoning that the Boston liberals and their intellectual progeny then used to build the foundation of modern religious pluralism.[48]

Reason had been a key word in the American Reformation since the eighteenth century, an inborn mental faculty Christians could use to hear the voice of God. Together with conscience, reason was the germ of the Romantic concept of universal inner divinity, but among some American Unitarians and British rational dissenters, the heat of argumentation against Calvinists and evangelicals clarified their conception of reason down to the mental function of weighing the evidence of the senses, that which is knowable, provable, demonstrable, and certain. This is the understanding of reason that came to be associated with Locke, producing the empirical tradition in English philosophy that ultimately spawned the psychology pioneered by Hartley, which Jeremy Bentham and James Mill developed into utilitarianism. One word for the type of knowledge accessible by this narrow understanding of reason is "phenomenal," that which can be sensed. In the field of religion, a strictly phenomenal view of reality bred a stern moral science that treated the will as an instrument of control and all human problems as soluble through the exercise of reason and simple resolve. This is the kind of Unitarianism Waldo Emerson called "corpse-cold," a religion of "pale negations" that Martin Luther would have cut off his right hand to avoid, the kind his aunt thought had turned Harvard into "but a garnished sepulcher where may be found some relics of the *body* of Jesus" in need of rescue by "master spirits" like "the consecrated Channing," who had real "faith & lofty devotion." This type of reason was earthly rather than lofty, and that is the problem Coleridge aimed to fix.[49]

He started out by renaming that kind of reason. He called it "understanding." It was useful for investigating nature, and necessary for the lower type of morality Coleridge called prudence, but those who thought it adequate for real religion were gravely mistaken. The pursuit of mere understanding put would-be Christians on the road to "disbe-lief, materialism, and (more pernicious still) epicurean morality." The real function of reason was more purely religious for Coleridge, was in fact "spiritual religion" rather than merely natural. This reason sought after what Kant called the "noumenal" realm, the invisible great beyond that Kant distinguished from the phenomenal. As impossible as it is ever to reach it, the noumenal is where real truth and justice resides—so it is up to every individual to try to live by it even though it cannot be sensed. Reason, for Coleridge, was a transcendent faculty in which individuals use the data of personal experience to bend the arc of the phenomenal toward the noumenal.[50]

Coleridge gave practical advice for how to cultivate this higher rea-son, first by reflecting on "our inward being" where it is housed, linking us to the great divine. He detailed this process of reflection in an apho-rism: "In order to learn, we must *attend*: in order to profit by what we have learnt, we must *think*—i.e., to reflect. He only thinks who *reflects*." This is an active process in what Coleridge called an "*experimentative faith*" through which the Christian builds a "manly character," a con-cept important enough to him that he put it in the subtitle to the book that launched his distinction between reason and understanding, *Aids to Reflection, in the Formation of a Manly Character, on the Several Grounds of Prudence, Morality, and Religion*. To be manly meant to be independent, to shun "the idols of preconceived opinion." But where for Reformation Christians such manliness had once meant resisting reli-gious dogmas others were trying to impose from without, now it also meant resisting the mere evidence of the senses. Coleridge's Christian vision had Jesus coming to earth "to *take captivity captive*," to free sin-ners from the bondage of their own flesh, "to rouse and emancipate the soul from this debasing slavery to the outward senses, to awaken the mind to the true *criteria* of reality," which lies beyond the reach of the senses. Ultimate reality also, as Wordsworth put it, "lies far hidden from the reach of words," but words and senses, experience and action are the tools reason has for transforming understanding into true knowledge.[51]

Coleridge poured some of these ideas into Channing during his 1822 visit, a visit that led him to tell a mutual friend what an excellent conversationalist Channing was, which made Channing laugh because Coleridge had done all the talking. Channing also went out of his way that trip to see Robert Southey, who in his time as poet laureate had sunk "back so far into ecclesiasticism" that meeting him was a disappointment. Channing meant by this something very similar to John Adams's complaint against ecclesiastical tribunals from the eighteenth century, and something important for how Channing's Romantic turn differed from that of the English poets. For all of Channing's reputation as a leader of the Unitarian revolt, he was not trying to reform the Congregational Church as such with his ministry, and he never joined the American Unitarian Association (AUA), formed in 1825. Indeed, Channing later criticized the AUA for its tendency to inhibit what he saw as the core of Reformation Christianity: "individual action, personal independence, private judgment, free self-originated effort." Here he added to the traditional articles of the American Reformation the Romantic element of individual action freely generated from within. He made this update out of his newly expanded sense of universal inner divinity, which made mental independence the cornerstone of his ministry. Unlike Coleridge, who believed that the active process of experimental religion would naturally lead to the doctrines he himself held true—the trinity, atonement, original sin, and so on—Channing believed that "Christian truth is infinite" and that creeds were only "means of fastening chains on men's minds," which his ministry sought to set free. He saw his parishioners as too willing to be led, too eager to be fed a dogma they could then unthinkingly adopt, which is why in his sermons and his vestry meetings he continually struck the note of mental independence, claiming that the first religious duty of the Christian is not to "give up our characters to be moulded by others; for we are individuals, and have duties arising from our peculiar constitution of mind, degree of sensibility," and individual character. "Every whisper of the divine voice in the soul should be heard," he urged.[52]

This idea of human individuality and diversity within the great unity of God's infinite goodness—his "self-forgetting, self-emptying bounty"—allowed Channing to continue to credit Calvinists with real piety even while criticizing their doctrines, to praise the Quaker idea of inner light, to admire the robust faith of the evangelical "sailors' preacher" of Boston, Father Taylor, who admired Channing too, and to continue to support the Transcendentalist renegades Waldo Emerson and Theodore Parker even while privately criticizing the "ego-theism" of the former and the interpretive excesses of the latter. Channing counted that faith real that made a real difference in the believer's life. He thought that the relationship between the specifics of a belief and its moral difference for the believer varied as much as believers did in their makeup from one another. He explained this perspectival view of religious truth in one conversation with the German immigrant abolitionist Charles Follen:

Some persons are not capable of entering into views which are necessary to the salvation of others. *I* may see a doctrine in the Scriptures which is a perfect dead-letter to another man; his mind, at least at present, does not need that doctrine. It would be criminal, however, for *me* to reject it; I should be punished by being of less use to others, misleading them perhaps, and by feeling my character weaker than it would be if it had been fortified by that truth. It is impossible for any one of us to judge for another as to what quantity of truth would save him from sinning. We may judge a man by the effects of his actions, but not by a perception of *his ideas*, still less by hearing the words of his creed.[53]

Beliefs are relative to the individual minds that live by them. This particular conversation occurred after Channing had made the most basic statement of his own creed in "Likeness to God," the sermon that appeared just a year before the first American edition of Coleridge's *Aids to Reflection* (1829). This sermon, more than any other of Channing's or anyone else's, helped quicken not only the Unitarian movement but also the Transcendentalist temperament that shot from it and the new "orthodox" Protestantism that reacted against both. Although the main message of "Likeness" was universal inner divinity—that "the great work of religion is, to conform ourselves to God, or to unfold the divine likeness within us"—Channing's interest in accommodating human diversity is equally on evidence in the sermon. "All men," he said, "of whatever name, or sect or opinion, will meet me on this ground." And, bombastic though this proclamation was, to an important extent they did.[54]

SELF-CULTURE

By the 1830s, the Brookline hills to which Channing had lifted his eyes while high on Hutcheson had been carted away by the shovelful, their dirt filling in the marshes on the Charles River's southern shore to create the Back Bay neighborhood of pricey real estate. Boston was booming. Not booming as much as Philadelphia or New York—Boston never fully recovered its economic stature after the War of 1812—but booming nonetheless from the rise of industrial capitalism, which created a ring of mills and factories around the city and a concentration of wealthy merchants, the majority of whom were Unitarians, within it.[55]

Yet those merchants and the middle class that industrialism also helped grow were not entirely at their ease. Their Federalist Party had been done in by the long reign of the Virginia dynasty and subsequent rise of the new Democratic Party, the country's first nationwide political party and the instrument of universal white male suffrage, which gave civic power to workers like those who carted away the Brookline hills. Church establishment in Massachusetts was done in too, after the Dedham Case of 1821, in which a Unitarian-dominated state supreme court ruled in favor of the liberal Christians in the parish against the neo-Calvinist members of the First Congregational Church. Congregationalist opinion now joined with minority Baptists and Methodists to oppose state establishment. With the Religious Liberties Act of 1824 and the 1833 ratification of the Eleventh Amendment to the state constitution, all church support and participation became voluntary. Now the ministerial association of Cambridge spoke for many in the American Reformation in expressing the fear, in language strongly resonant of Channing's argument against slavery and Mayhew's against tyranny, that disestablishment "would hold forth to the citizens a license to degrade themselves from the dignity of rational beings to a level with the brute animals, among whom no other law or order prevails than that which the stronger impose upon the weaker."[56]

To make up for its lost economic prominence, Boston reestablished itself on grounds of moral and intellectual prominence as the new American Athens, and to make up for their lost ability to legislate the moral guarantees of republican governance, liberal Bostonians established a host of voluntary associations for social uplift and reform. Among these were the Franklin Lectures, named after Boston's native-born personification of American success, Benjamin Franklin, and offered to Boston's workingmen starting in 1831. The series was initiated by Edward Everett, who would eventually be best known as the long-winded orator upstaged by Lincoln at Gettysburg but in the 1830s was a cerebral young member of Congress, already retired from two earlier careers as a professor of Greek literature at Harvard and a Unitarian minister. The "spell binding Everett," as M. M. Emerson called him—not approvingly—was also the first American to earn a PhD, acquired from a university in Germany, which for most of the nineteenth century was where American scholars went for the highest academic training. A high percentage of these scholars were liberal Christians; the next after Everett was the historian George Bancroft, who said in an 1835 speech that the cause of the world's progress was "the culture of the moral and intellectual powers of the people," that "the duty of the individual" is "to strive after a perfection like the perfection of God," and that the "common mind is . . . fit to be wrought into likeness to a God." The echo of Channing, so obvious here, reverberated in the antebellum decades beyond the Boston elite into an egalitarian doctrine quite different from that of the Democratic Party, to which Bancroft alone of the liberal Christian crowd belonged. Boston liberals did not think the masses were good to govern as they were and did not celebrate the "common man" as a slogan for equality as though it already existed. Instead, liberals sought to develop the "common mind" as an instrument for an equality not yet achieved.[57]

The innovation of the Boston liberals and their intellectual descendants consisted of applying the concept of universal inner divinity across lines of culture, class, race, ethnicity, and gender in these decades, bringing every individual formally into the same high potential for character growth and the same moral necessity for growing that character. Their high-minded rhetoric came to sound both fusty and condescending by the time the Victorian era was over, but the crudity of their pluralism should not obscure its novelty. They did not want the working classes to become tools for the agendas of party elites but to become agents for their own moral beings and full participants in an interdependent American society. Liberals applied their moral theory to slaves, women, Native Americans, children, the imprisoned, poor, and insane as well as workers, but because in the antebellum era the only new group to get the vote was the (white) working class, it is there that the transformation of the American Reformation into a nascent religion of democracy is most visible.

"I belong rightfully to the great fraternity of working men," declared Channing near the beginning of his Franklin Lecture, "Self-Culture," destined to become the most famous and influential of the entire series. There was not a drop of irony in this statement, oblivious in obvious ways but purposefully antihierarchical. Channing's Codman sermon had focused on the importance of earnestness in the Christian minister, and now he spoke earnestly in exhorting his audience to practice self-culture by claiming, with all his privilege, to be brothers with laborers; candor was the medium of address between moral agents. He and they were each "a being of free spiritual powers" invested with the right and duty of growing toward the "Impartial, Disinterested, Universal" infinite good with which all are linked because the way humans differ from "brutes" is that "a portion of the same divine fire is given to all," making them ends to themselves rather than means to any other human being's end.[58]

Self-culture involved moral, intellectual, and religious practices, which Channing detailed in programs of moral cultivation and self-education. He praised the efforts of Horace Mann in establishing common schools, urged the value of good newspapers for educating the broad public, and recommended the mental company of great thinkers through books, but self-culture is a self-directed process by necessity because it is about the growth of moral agency, the independent-mindedness as necessary for democracy as for spiritual growth. All occupations are of equal value to a society, Channing said. All individuals are endowed with equal potential. All must respect their own and one another's "peculiar gifts or biases by which nature has distinguished him from others." Channing's universal pluralism worked against class bias and aimed to teach workers how to exert "real influence" in a democratic society rather than remaining "the tools of designing politicians" or falling in with the party spirit, which had the same negative tendency to subvert self-culture as the recitation of a creed or the joining of an association, mostly by giving an incentive to turn a deaf ear to contrary views. Self-culture is an individual and social process that operates by the mechanism of the Romantic turn, by concentrating one's powers on both "self-searching" and "self-forming," exhibiting both a "child-like teachableness" before others and a "manly resistance" to anything that violates one's own individual share of "the common lights of reason, and conscience, and love." Self-culture describes the practical application of universal inner divinity.[59]

A couple of elements in Channing's "Self-Culture" are worth drawing out. First, the voluntariness of this liberal Christian method of mental and moral training—so intimately linked to the long-standing Reformation Christian ideal of moral agency—meant that Channing proposed no great social scheme for correcting either the inequality of wealth or the practical subjection of workers to their employers' control over wages and other terms of employment. He did believe that social progress could be measured by how much of a society's resources were held in common, but he assumed that communal growth would naturally follow the gradual accession of light in the consciousnesses of those who practiced self-culture. He followed Wordsworth in lauding the "dignity" of all forms of labor and the possibly superior morality of workers who were motivated to toil diligently and honestly by the higher purpose of disinterested benevolence. He also despised artificial manners and the propensity of the wealthy to pamper their senses with luxuries, so the potential wholesomeness of laboring-class life drew his pointed praise. But even his modest call for adequate material resources for all—a far cry from economic justice—did not carry with it the request that any body in particular guarantee this adequacy. Channing expected employers to practice self-culture too, which would inevitably lead them to consider workers' interests equally with their own. In the meantime, he expected workers to practice their self-culture on Sundays. To the problem of their limited access to books, he pointed out how delightfully cheap many editions were in that early heyday of print and how, more delightfully still, workers already possessed the best stuff for self-education: the beauty of the nature around them and the divine potential of the individual natures within them. He believed there was no social, material, or political hindrance to the potential of self-culture for wage laborers in the Industrial Revolution. "We can fix our eyes on perfection," he said, confident in his use of the universal pronoun, "and make almost everything speed towards it."[60]

The other noteworthy aspect of Channing's "Self-Culture" somewhat contradicted the first, however, although it would take the rest of the nineteenth century to draw that contradiction out. He was evidently a "classical liberal" in the political sense because he believed that all social improvements should be grounded in voluntary initiative rather than governmental imposition. Yet he defended the new Massachusetts temperance law, which restricted the sales of hard liquor, on the grounds that government is not only to protect liberty by staying out of people's lives, but to protect it positively as well by safeguarding their welfare. In an address redolent with American exceptionalism—Channing believed America immune from European inequalities of wealth and opportunity, and believed, like John Adams, that its origins lay in the Puritan migration "to found here the freest and most equal State on earth"—he framed the unique purpose of American governance in terms that he intended to apply only to the temperance law, but that later liberals departed from the classical tradition to use for the protection of workers' rights and the guarantee of social welfare. "Let it never be forgotten," he said, "that the great end of Government, its highest function, is . . . to prevent or repress Crimes against individual rights and social order." Channing might rightly be accused of paternalism in advocating the social control mechanism of legally restricting alcohol consumption. He knew that the temperance law was unpopular with the workers he was addressing, but he also knew that those workers were part of the body of governors as well as the governed now. As citizens with rights, they were now learning in "the people's University," the republic itself, and even he did not know where such an education might lead.[61]

Channing's "Self-Culture" drew both national and international recognition and praise, but the only instance that caught his attention was a letter of thanks from a society of workingmen in England. "This is *fame*," he told Elizabeth Palmer Peabody with pleasure. However little he kept track of his domestic reputation among the American middle and upper classes, though, it was in the expanding American Reformation through those strata that his practical Christianity achieved the influence of institutionalization, particularly in the common school movement he had praised in "Self-Culture." The movement's leader, Horace Mann (1796–1859), had lost his Calvinism at age fourteen, the day his minister preached a funeral sermon full of damnation for Mann's nine-year-old brother, who had drowned while swimming on the sabbath, a sermon devoid of consoling words for the grieving family. Although it was a number of years before Mann developed a liberal

Christian conviction, the lesson of that grim day seems to have been similar to that experienced by Waldo Emerson sitting in church during a snowstorm while Rev. Barzillai Frost droned on about an architecturally perfect reason that had nothing to do with reality. This disjunction provided the point in Emerson's Divinity School Address when he criticized a ministry that would keep doctrine and "experience" separate, a very Coleridgean critique. The conviction that real religion consists of the moral actions that flow from individual moral sentiment drove Emerson in a post-Christian direction, but the same conviction drove other liberals, like Frederic Henry Hedge—cofounder of the Transcendentalist Club, which went by the nickname "Hedge's Club" because it convened whenever Hedge made it down to Boston from his parish all the way up in Bangor, Maine—in a broadly inclusive Christian direction. Hedge wrote an influential critical review of Coleridge's works in an 1833 *Christian Examiner*, where he found Coleridge lacking on the scholarly grounds of "unity and completeness" and declared their age one "which is peculiarly prone to try every man by his works," not only his apparent gifts. "The test of a true spirit," Hedge once wrote, "is its productiveness," a practical Christian standard that he believed should be the basic unifying standard of a church that not only tolerated a range of beliefs but actively included them. Mann became a liberal Christian in the broad vein of Hedge and Channing, but through his work in the common school movement he broadened this liberal Christianity still further to appear as the general Protestantism of American consensus.[62]

The first issue of the *Common School Journal* included two excerpts from Channing's "Self-Culture." The other items in the issue also voiced the practical Christian conviction in the universality of inner divinity and the incumbent right of liberty and duty of progress. The social and moral implications of the new standard of universal (white, male) suffrage occupied much of the issue, evincing a combination of anxiety over the dangers of an ignorant public and enthusiasm for the prospect of an interdependent society working together for mutual amelioration. Those who are taught "to live less in the region of the senses and appetites, and more in the serener and happier sphere of intellect, of morals, and religion" will make an important discovery for a democratic society when "they find their own best welfare dependent upon the common good." Every man in Mann's America was capable of becoming a philosopher, that is, of achieving "an understanding of one's duty and destination" and a devotion to their pursuit. Now the time had come to give them all means for this pursuit. "That intelligence and virtue are the only support and stability of free institutions," Mann allowed, "was a truism long ago." Yet it was a truism that had up to now only won "the readiest assent of the reason," without quickening "that effect upon the feelings which gives birth to action." Clearly, Mann had read his Channing and Coleridge too. So had "a Lady" who contributed to the issue a piece on motherly duty in which she decreed that "mere knowledge, however perfect, is barren and fruitless till it is practically acted upon." The common school movement amounted to social action on the basis of universal inner divinity, and although in its implementation Mann found he had numerous blind spots when it came to Catholics and Moravians who wanted to keep their own religions and African Americans who claimed their citizenship rights too, making the practical working of the common schools a complex social affair, he genuinely believed in 1838 that the religious understanding behind the movement was as broad and universal as an understanding could be. He thought he was accommodating America's variety of religions with the most simple "Protestant liberty" consisting of the basic religious principle of disinterested benevolence, "love to God and love to man," as he put it in the journal. And although Mann was in fact blinkered by his liberal Christian culture, his formula for a more general Christian American culture that was covertly liberal spread both with and beyond the common school movement.[63]

Alexis de Tocqueville (1805–1859) did not intend to help the liberal Christian cause along when he wrote *Democracy in America* in two of the most important volumes ever to appear on the subject. He meant to help his own country along on its rocky transition from monarchy to republic when he and his friend Gustave de Beaumont crossed the Atlantic in early 1831 on the pretext of studying American penal systems. Yet so much of Tocqueville's time in America was spent in the company of Boston liberals—the Frenchmen lodged for a month at the Tremont Hotel, overlooking Boston Common—and his experience of Boston society so outclassed his experiences in other parts of the country that his description and analysis of American democracy not only conveyed liberal Christian values, understandings, and biases, it covered them with labels like "American," "Christian," and, most important, "democracy" itself. Tocqueville helped teach Americans to call their society democratic—indeed, the first volume of the *United States Magazine, and Democratic Review* (1837–51) included a piece from Tocqueville on "European Views of American Democracy" as well as a review of Waldo Emerson's *Nature* and the argument that "Democracy is the cause of Humanity" because it "has faith in human nature" and believes in humanity's "essential equality and fundamental goodness" while aiming "to emancipate the mind of the mass of men from the degrading and disheartening fetters of social distinctions and advantages." Tocqueville did not work alone in the slow transformation of the American Reformation into a religion of democracy, but he helped naturalize both the liberal Christian understanding of the relationship between individuals and society and the use of the term democracy for that relationship.[64]

Tocqueville's chief informant in Boston was a born bastard. Jared Sparks (1789–1866) was still a baby when his mother married the man who was probably his father, but they remained poor. The story of Sparks's rise to the Unitarian ministry, the chaplaincy of the U.S. Congress, and ultimately the presidency of Harvard is one of merit rewarded by the kindly interest of local ministers, scholarships funded by benevolent donors, and the prevalence of opportunity in an America where the elitism of Boston liberals was porous, open to newcomers like Sparks. All of this activity was voluntary, like the voluntary associations that Tocqueville highlighted in his book as one of the critical supports of a democratic society. His view on these associations came not only from Sparks, who wrote a substantial document on New England history and culture for Tocqueville's use, but also from Joseph Tuckerman (1778–1840), one of Channing's best friends. Tuckerman was in charge of Boston's Unitarian ministries to the poor and believed that social conditions should be improved not by governmental fiat—by "any artificial system," in Tuckerman's phrase—"but alone by the advancement of high moral and religious principle and character throughout society." In *Democracy in America*, Tocqueville argued that this sort of voluntary association and moral culture was necessary for preventing the chief danger to the health of a democracy, the tyranny of the majority, the same danger Channing had already warned his public against the year before Tocqueville's visit. "Civil liberty is not enough," Channing argued. "There may be a tyranny of the multitude, of opinion, over the individual. . . . Popularity enslaves." Naturally the only defense against tyranny of the majority from a liberal Christian viewpoint is self-culture in the service of moral agency, religion itself understood in the terms of the American Reformation. This is the view of religion Tocqueville conveyed in a book in which the character and hold of American Christianity was one of his chief astonishments.[65]

Tocqueville observed the relationship between American political ideals of equality and liberty and American religious ideals of a practical, lived faith. He believed this made American religion a crucial factor in the health of American democracy. Catholics in France "had established the government of the skilful or aristocracy in Religion," Tocqueville told Channing during one of their private conversations, but "you have introduced Democracy." The contrast was one of practice. In his book, Tocqueville criticized that "barren, traditionary faith which seems to vegetate rather than to live in the soul" and praised how "Americans combine the notions of Christianity and of liberty so intimately." He noticed how "religious zeal is perpetually warmed in the United States by the fires of patriotism," which reflected not the enthusiasm of a Christian identity for a Christian America, which would be a much later cultural development, but instead the association within the American Reformation of civil with religious liberty. As Channing said of the new Unitarian missionaries heading west in those years, their mission was to "give a Christian significance to the motto of our nationality,—E pluribus unum; the first nationality the world has ever seen generous enough in its scope and tendency to admit of a free development of Christ's love within it." These were the missionaries Tocqueville wrote about with wonder over their willingness to sacrifice their comfort and homes for migration, these "wealthy New-Englanders" who left home "to lay the foundations of Christianity and of freedom" in western territories out of the deep conviction that "the new States should be religious, in order that they may permit us to remain free." At a time when evangelical Christians were intent on revivals that pitted the Christian afterlife against the profane present, it was Christians in the tradition of the American Reformation who continued to believe that the religious culture of independent-mindedness was necessary to the life of American democracy.[66]

THE RELIGION OF
THE INDEPENDENTS

In June 1842, Orestes Brownson wrote a letter to William Ellery Channing, his "spiritual father" in the Christian faith, whose writings—especially "Likeness to God," which a friend had read aloud to him—had succeeded "in raising me from the darkness of doubt to the warm sunlight of a living faith in God," Brownson gratefully confessed. But he was writing Channing that summer to criticize the tendencies of Channing's theology, particularly the post-Christian infidelities quite visible by that time in the movement that came to be called Transcendentalism. In a brave act of moral agency, Brownson respectfully disagreed with his mentor's creed and put forth a careful, earnest creed of his own. "I think I see wherein my past faith was defective," the acolyte confessed, as careful with his introspection as with his candor. Now he was able "to point out the ground on which both Unitarians and Trinitarians may unite as brothers." That ground was Christ as mediator between earthly and unearthly—a view with which Channing would have entirely agreed, but a view that had indeed been abandoned by the post-Christian liberals.[67]

Channing did not have a chance to respond to this letter. Two months after Brownson wrote it, Channing was dead, leaving behind a host of spiritual children who took his legacy in a variety of directions, shoots springing from their common root in his pluralistic style of practical Christianity. Brownson's letter was published as a pamphlet, and he became a Roman Catholic with strong socialist leanings, the only abolitionist northerner to concede that wage labor was potentially as unfree, spiritually, as slave labor. Brownson's social convictions linked to a theological conviction that opened one of the doors out of the

Unitarian Church. Waldo Emerson, whose apostasy Brownson implicitly criticized in that letter, opened another. He had already gotten so immersed in non-Christian religious traditions that, although he erred in calling the Bhagavad Gita that "much renowned book of Buddhism," he knew about karma and he called god by various names and he followed the example of one of his favorite Persian poets vis-à-vis the Unitarian Church that had nurtured him:

Myself when young did eagerly frequent
Doctor and Saint, and heard great argument
About it and about: but evermore
Came out by the same door as in I went.

—OMAR KHAYYÁM, *The Rubàiyàt*, VERSE XXVII
(TRANS. EDWARD FITZGERALD)

Although Elizabeth Palmer Peabody remained a Christian Unitarian, she opened another door when she translated a Buddhist text, the *Lotus Sutra*, from the French for *The Dial* in 1844. Because this first appearance of Buddhist scripture in America was published anonymously, when the history of the liberal movement developed thirty years later, credit for her translation was mistakenly bestowed upon Henry David Thoreau. He had followed his moral nature away from consumer-driven society in his experiment at Walden, while Theodore Parker, who estimated Channing as the most influential writer in the English language at the time of his death, followed his own faith away from miracles and into passionate abolitionism. The support of Thomas Wentworth Higginson and Frank Sanborn for the evangelical John Brown may be attributed to a practical Christianity, as can Elizabeth Palmer Peabody's futile attempt to save Brown's codefendants. George Ripley, who had become a Unitarian minister because of Channing, stepped away from the ministry in 1840 in fidelity to his devotion to the "essential principles of liberal Christianity," he said, in which religion consisted "not in any speculative doctrine, but in a divine life," as he put it in his resignation letter to his congregation. He went on to try to forge that life at Brook Farm, in which the social distinction between laborer and elite was supposed to disappear in the living spirit of Christ. All of these radical experiments in Christian and post-Christian moral life belong alongside the staid moralism of a Unitarian like Francis Bowen, who taught moral science at Harvard and brought out a new edition of Tocqueville's *Democracy in America* in between treatises on how to think.[68]

They also all belong alongside the trinitarian Congregationalists, one of whom brought out that 1829 edition of Coleridge's *Aids to Reflection*. Several more Congregationalists thinking of themselves as orthodox against the Unitarians' apostasy organized the *New Englander* periodical to defend their Calvinist faith. In one issue they criticized the softness of Channing's creed and the impiety of his legacy in the same article wherein they praised Coleridge and Leighton, called for more "practical" demonstrations of their Christian faith, and identified real religion with the "growth of . . . universal love of a sublime *godlikeness*." This article came out in 1849, one year after the first mention of a "*social* gospel" appeared in a periodical, where it was attributed to liberal churches and urged upon all others. As the social reforms of the antebellum era accelerated, practical Christianity became a pan-Protestant ideal.[69]

The following year was the compromise in Congress that produced the Fugitive Slave Law, among other outrages. Boston became a quivering antislavery mass. The ranges of opinion on ideology and tactics between hard-core abolitionists and appeasement-minded colonizationists still mattered, but in the decade leading up to the Civil War the decided majority of Bostonians—and northerners—in the tradition of the American Reformation backed the Republican Party, free-labor ideology, and ultimately Lincoln's war. Of all the American Protestant denominations, only the Congregationalists and Unitarians remained united across the Civil War, which obscured the doctrinal differences that had bedeviled them before and brought them all together behind the battle cry written by the Unitarian Julia Ward Howe, "As He died to make men holy, let us die to make men free."[70]

WILLIAM JAMES, PRACTICAL IDEALIST

THE MAN OF THE WORLD
AND THE METHOD OF NATURE

Just about every summer of his adult life, William James traveled to Keene Valley in the Adirondack mountains of New York. After his bachelor days of solitary rambles and rousing talks by the campfire, he honeymooned there, and year after year while his wife was tied to children and home he returned there alone, to meet others and to loaf, to give and hear lectures at nearby summer schools, to restore his nerves by light reading and to stimulate them by hikes. He spent so much time sitting on a stone ledge above one camp that it was named after him.[1]

One July late in the 1890s, when James had become as famous for his defense of religious faith as for his groundbreaking psychology, he trekked with a coed group of budding philosophers and social activists half his age to a camp at Panther Gorge in the valley. The moon was high that night and James, always prone to insomnia, found himself in "a state of spiritual alertness of the most vital description," as he wrote home to his wife later. Yet he could not quite describe it. Thoughts of his family, hiking companions, and work "all fermented within me," he told her, "till it became a regular Walpurgis nacht. I spent a good deal of it in the woods, where the streaming moonlight lit up things in a magical checkered play, and it seemed as if the gods of all the nature-mythologies were holding an indescribable meeting in my breast with the moral gods of the inner life."[2]

James had been thinking about the relationship between nature, morality, and ultimate truth all his life. Now, while his professional energies were focused on making sense of what the many varieties of human religious experience said about nature and the divine—he was preparing for the Gifford Lectures he had promised to deliver in Edinburgh, Scotland, two years hence—his own inner life ripened into the most intense spiritual experience he would ever have. The event bore an "intense *significance*" that he struggled to verbalize for his wife, one of "everlasting freshness" as well as "immemorial antiquity and decay," of "utter americanism, and every sort of patriotic suggestiveness," all intermingled with his personal relations "so that memory and sensation all whirled inexplicably together." From this peak experience he came to "understand now what a poet is. He is a person who can feel the immense complexity of influences that I felt and make some partial tracks for them in verbal statement." James discovered that he himself could not "find a single word for all that significance, & don't know what it was significant of, so there it remains, a mere boulder of *impression*. Doubtless in more ways than one though, things in the Edinboro lectures will be traceable to it."[3]

He was right about that, although the mystical event did not appear as such in *The Varieties of Religious Experience* (1902), the book that came out of the Edinburgh lectures, even while other personal experiences of James's did. Instead, the meaningful reality of religious experience—whatever its source or cause—became an unshakable conviction for him that night because he had finally felt it himself after three decades of intellectual work on how scientific standards for claims to truth could be used to justify beliefs unsubstantiated by physical evidence. His answer, rehearsed in his popular addresses of the 1890s for international debut in *Varieties*, was that the truth of religious faith was found neither in the origins of religion nor in its articles of belief but in its "*fruits for life*," which made his approach to religion an entirely practical one. The value of such spiritual practice, though, James tied to a conception of the good that had been almost fully unhitched from its Christian origins in the American Reformation. Now practice was to be guided by a universal ideal that escaped language almost as much as James's *Walpurgisnacht* had, and which he tried to explain as "the mystery of democracy, or sentiment of the equality before God of all his creatures." Such a sentiment he felt to be as impossible to fully realize as ultimate reality was to be fully understood by the finite, partial, limited individual human mind. James conceived of this mind and its limitations in scientific terms that paralleled the Christian terms that his progenitors in the American Reformation had used to describe the same barriers to realizing the same sentiment of equality. Yet to strain toward universal human equality was to act religiously, which is to say, to act in reference to the infinite rather than the particular, the ultimate rather than the conventional, the divine rather than the merely natural. And the religious act involved both believing in one's own cosmic significance, because such a belief aids moral effort, and imagining the equal inner divinity of others. Then one must act on the basis of this creative imagination.[4]

The dawn after James's epiphany in the woods, his companions rose fresh and together they planned an ambitious hike leading first up the Adirondacks' highest peak, Mount Marcy, and then up and down several smaller mountains for a day that would add up to more than ten hours of straight exertion. James had hired a guide, in part to haul some of his provisions, but in an act of misguided chivalry he directed the guide that morning to carry some of the possessions of his female hiking companions instead, taking on himself, in his heavily fatigued state, a burdensome load for a long day that began with their embarkation from camp at 6 a.m. The young women were demonstrably more robust than James, who had been vulnerable to physical collapse since his early twenties and was now pushing sixty, but he insisted and got his way and arrived at the lodge that night with the first symptoms of the heart ailment that killed him a dozen years later. His wife forevermore resented the young women for their usurpation of the guide's services, especially nettled by the one on whom James was overtly sweet, but no one but James was to blame—except maybe patriarchy, a web of social assumptions too thick for most anyone caught in its grip to untangle. James was no exception, except that he did try to untangle it, rejoicing that the "girls" wore hiking trousers rather than skirts, taking female professionals seriously, and attempting—particularly in his essay "On a Certain Blindness in Human Beings" (1899), which he mailed to that nettlesome hiking companion, Pauline Goldmark—to pry apart culture and nature from inner divinity so that the irreducible particularity of human individuals could stand out as vividly as their varieties of religious experience.[5]

The more diverse viewpoints on reality were respected and taken into consideration, James argued, the more the bounds of cultural hides might burst by attention to difference rather than mere tolerance. The more all individuals are seen as fellow strivers after the divine bearing their own hidden chips of the divine, the more social progress is possible because the more reality is comprehended. In a crude but pathbreaking way, James attempted to teach his fellow Anglo-Protestant members of the American educated elite to view laborers, the Chinese, women, African Americans, Filipinos, and immigrants from the universal perspective of the eternal rather than the limited perspective of their own cultural particular, for in this way "the world does get more humane." This pluralism, with invisible roots in that of Channing and visible shoots in twentieth-century social thought, James developed over his career without ever feeling he had mastered it. He called it "the religion of democracy." It was the principal thing of which the "americanism" he had felt in the woods consisted.[6]

The only summers James did not visit Keene Valley were those he spent in Europe, where he eventually became such a celebrity that one clerk at a conference in Italy almost fainted when he gave his name. The European education he spottily received in his youth, the European intellectual community he fostered over his adulthood, and the European audience that received and propagated his ideas were all important factors in the cosmopolitan universalism of his thought, but rather than distinguishing him from others in his American milieu, they were consistent with the values and practices of his most formative intellectual context, American liberal religion. James did not go to Germany for study by chance, nor was he the first American religious liberal to do so. He did not frequent Keene Valley by chance either; hordes of social thinkers reared on the precepts of the American Reformation convened in the valley all the summers of the late nineteenth century and into the twentieth. James made his first attempts at intellectual production in the pages of the *North American Review* and the lecture hall of the Concord School of Philosophy, a post–Civil War institution inspired largely by Emerson, whose massive literary body lay between the post-Christian religious liberalism of James and his associates and their common ancestors in the American Reformation. Liberals viewed Darwin and the rest of modern science with sanguine hope. They were interested in the religions of India and the philosophies of Germany. They read Romantic poetry and French literature and they traveled to Europe for study, culture, and health whenever their finances and leisure allowed. "Freedom and fellowship" and "deed not creed" were their watchwords, and although James was never a card-carrying member of anything, he absorbed from the arenas of amateur liberal thought the meliorism that looked to the future, and to progress as the measurement of success, as well as the faith that ideals could be used as practical guides for action. James was not alone in making ideals practical, and in coloring them democratically, despite being one of a kind.[7]

The last time James went to the Adirondacks was in 1907, the year he published *Pragmatism: A New Name for Some Old Ways of Thinking*, which formalized the philosophy he had named pragmatism in an address at the University of California at Berkeley, in 1898. In the book's dedication, James claimed that it was from the English liberal thinker John Stuart Mill that he had "first learned the pragmatic openness of mind." Pragmatism was an international hit, but it was also a coproduction of the English and American sprouts from the liberal line of Reformation Christianity after the Romantic turn. Mill and James—neither ever Christians—both claimed a sort of divine right of private judgment, married to an ideal recognition of others' equal rights of so judging. Pragmatism really was an old way of thinking, made post-Christian and as adaptive to different cultural lenses and mental diversities as James could make it, as well as a new one, bubbled up from the American intellectual scene but instantly sparking fire in other countries. "Pragmatism" itself became a line in professional philosophy, which was international because it was academic, and which developed in increasingly specialized and technical ways so that by 1905 James's wife could no longer understand his philosophy. But the practical idealism of which pragmatism was one distinctive variety remained popular during James's lifetime, international because it was pluralist, and serving as the guiding orientation of liberal religion headquartered in American intellectual centers but increasingly practiced abroad as well. Hence when James wrote home to his wife from the lodge in Keene Valley for the last time, he described the wonderful traveling companion he had happened to meet on the train, "a splendid Roumanian jew named Mascowitz" on his way to a conference on ethics at the Keene Valley summer school begun by a late friend of James's. Mascowitz was reading a book by a British pragmatist—a correspondent of James's—and he worked for the same organization of ethical religion that employed James's brother-in-law. James "found that he was an ardent pragmatist . . . and one of the best human types I ever saw."[8]

THE DILEMMA OF DETERMINISM

William James was born the year William Ellery Channing died, 1842. He was the firstborn child of Mary and Henry James, who lived on inherited wealth in New York City at the time. Henry James had not yet begun writing the articles and books that would make him a minor celebrity in mid-nineteenth-century America, but he had already started exploring the great questions of society and the cosmos current in the day. When the baby was two months old, Henry James headed out to the New York Society Library to hear a visitor give a lecture on "The Times." The visitor was Waldo Emerson. Henry James immediately struck up acquaintance, which bloomed into friendship, and when William was about eight months old Emerson visited the unbaptized babe in his crib and blessed him.

Late Transcendentalism is part of the story of why William James became the most important American thinker of the late nineteenth century, and of what his thought means. In the 1840s the Transcendentalist mood was still growing. A bold and learned cast of characters experimented with social arrangements and social reforms, writing styles, lifestyles, continental philosophies, religions from Near East and Far, print organs, and politics. Their chant was newness, their only exclusion that of close-mindedness. Most of them came out of Unitarianism; many of them remained Christian; all of them believed in the American Reformation ideals of inborn divinity, moral agency, and the incumbency upon each individual to strive toward perfection. They had no leader—equality was their faith as much as freedom—but they had leading voices, and around midcentury many of these started dying off. Brook Farm had already failed; so had *The Dial*. Margaret Fuller had been abroad for some years, sending the voice of republican Italy home in the pages of the *New York Tribune*, but she, her new husband, their son, and her manuscript on the 1848 Italian revolution all died at sea within sight of the American shore in 1850. That was the year of the Compromise in Congress that made ending slavery far and away the most pressing of the social changes northern reformers sought. Theodore Parker led the Transcendentalist chorus in an abolitionist movement that included evangelical Christian and Quaker voices as well as those who might best be called republican Christians, especially Frederick Douglass; the antislavery crusade so dominated the period that even Waldo Emerson, who criticized how reforms "mix the fire of the moral sentiment with personal and party heats" in the lecture Henry James heard, got involved. Parker was the most eloquent and passionate of liberal Christian abolitionists and became a hero to many in that crucial decade of the 1850s. Then in 1860 he died. Lincoln and his war came, and in 1862 Thoreau—who stood for moral agency if anyone did—succumbed to tuberculosis. What remained of the Transcendentalist movement on the other side of the Civil War was carried on by a diverse body of liberals committed to what Elizabeth Palmer Peabody called, in a letter written around the end of the war, *the great family interest of mankind.*" That, and Emerson.[9]

Yet although Emerson mattered a great deal to the intellectual life of William James, his was not the greatest impact on James's youth. True, the Emerson children became playmates for the James kids, of whom there were five, and after Henry moved the family to New England, the Emersons reported home with great delight on the fun that could be had at the James dinner table. But William himself, sharpening his logic and wit on the mystical dogmatisms of his father, may have been the most brilliant performer there. His younger brother Henry was already practicing the great powers of observation that made him a writer "on whom nothing is lost," while their younger sister, Alice, inescapably responded to the actions of the elder males in their Victorian home rather than initiating sallies herself, and the two younger brothers had trouble getting themselves heard at all. (Of Mary James almost no record survives.)[10]

A good window onto the family's connectedness to the Boston liberal scene comes in a letter William wrote to Alice in 1867 reporting that "Barbara Channing & Mrs Follen Cabot are giggling & chirping in the next room while Father is plying them with candy." By this point, William James was getting accustomed to "thinking of myself as an exceptional being," as he later admitted in a letter to his future wife. He fit no track he could see laid out before him, so he laid his own tracks through ambitious reading lists, sketching and painting, instruction in art and science, travel, and intimate correspondence with family and friends. He joined the pseudoscientific expedition to Brazil of Louis Agassiz, a racist bigot who resisted Darwin's claims later than most biologists and hoped to prove polygenesis with his fieldwork. James disagreed with Agassiz but went along anyway, contracting a bad case of fever and an important cultural exposure to aboriginals along the way.

Vaguely spiritual or cosmic talk did not interest him much at the time, and his father's Swedenborgian enthusiasms got a lot of pushback from the intellectually nimble young man. Yet however much Henry James Sr. and William James disagreed with one another over the character of the universe or the wisdom of pursuing a career as a painter—which William made a modest attempt to do—they agreed on which star on their era's intellectual horizon burned brightest: science.[11]

Darwin's theory of biological evolution through natural selection hit print when James was seventeen years old, but by then he had already gotten the principle of *"amelioration in nature"* from Emerson—if not from Emerson's essay "The Young American" (1845), where the phrase appeared, then from the wider liberal culture that supported Emerson's idea that the world's population "is a conditional population; these are not the best, but the best that could live in the existing state of soils, gases, animals, and morals; the best that could *yet* live." (James marked this passage in his own copy of Emerson's collected essays, but there is no way to know just when he did so.) Religious liberals believed in the malleability of human character for a hundred years before Darwin came along, so rather than destabilizing their sense of cosmic order, the theory of natural selection gave them a language and a logic for progressive change, providing reason to hope that given how far human beings had advanced from their primate origins, there was no telling how much further they could yet progress. These were liberals who had already discarded the idea that the Christian Bible bore any unique revelation, and who had long since revolted against Christian doctrines that laid claim to orthodoxy, so they cherished no six-day creation timetable and no springing of womankind from the side of Adam anyway. Praise for Darwin's intellectual bravery and appropriation of his findings for social purposes ran high in the social circles of James's early manhood.[12]

James was as unperturbed by Darwin's theory as anyone around him, but he was too good a scientific thinker himself to misconceive evolution as somehow progressive. While so many liberals around him assumed that onward meant upward—a common misinterpretation of Darwinian evolution called Lamarckianism, after a discredited French biologist—James saw that Darwin's theory was merely "descriptive or historical," as he put it in a review of one of Darwin's later books. The theory of natural selection generally explained the changes that had gotten species to the present but provided no specific understanding of the mechanics behind those changes and no road map for the future. Indeed, far from assuming that natural selection guaranteed progress or even augured it, James thought that evolution tended in no direction and was governed by no law other than "that of Caprice—caprice in inheriting, caprice in transmitting, caprice everywhere, in turn." This came from an unsigned article for an 1868 issue of the *North American Review* and was among the first things he ever published, but it contains one of his abiding preoccupations in its caution that there may be no law at all, natural or divine, governing the course of affairs. Given the primitive state of science, which James also noted in the review and on which he also abidingly insisted, the discovery of any law other than caprice was not impending. In light of the massive scope of natural explanations even for human, even for social behavior, he soon came to wonder, what place was there for human will?[13]

When this review came out, James was in Germany, whence he had traveled both to take the cure—the beginning of a lifelong quest for relief from a variety of physical and mental ailments—and to study in an exciting new field of mental science, physiological psychology. He did not succeed at entering the circle of acolytes around Hermann von Helmholtz and Wilhelm Wundt, Germany's two leading practitioners of the new science (nor, to be sure, at getting cured), but he did begin to clarify what troubled him and to identify ways to manage the crippling depression that had set in during the winter of 1866–67 and would continue another five years. He developed an introspective familiarity with his moods and found some mental rejoinders for combating the gloomy ones. As he advised his friend Tom Ward, who had been part of the Brazil expedition and who also struggled with depression, the experience of mental anguish should not be indulged. Instead, James proposed to "regard it as something as external to you as possible, like the curl of your hair," and then willfully bring into mind something uplifting, like sunlight sparkling on the surface of the Amazon. He said that he found himself clinging to "the thought of my having a will, and of my belonging to a brotherhood of men possessed of a capacity for pleasure & pain of different kinds." In the absence of a belief in God, he still drew courage from "the divine enthusiasm of moral culture (Channing & c)" by grafting it onto a utilitarian faith that "we can by our will make the enjoyment of our brothers stand us in the stead of a final cause." Human service required self-culture, although James described the process of reforming one's character in more Emersonian language. "Grapple to your soul with hooks of steel all the good points," he told Ward, "and with patience and enduring courage gradually mould & forge the rest into harmony with them. Thus is nought wasted in the world."[14]

For all his ability to preach a "Gospel of cheer" to Ward, though, James was deeply worried that he would never find a way to contribute to humanity's lot. At twenty-six, he had yet to earn a penny at anything, despite having studied at the University of Berlin, the Lawrence Scientific School, and Harvard Medical School. He had long been torn between his interests in art and science, and long avoided making up his mind by engaging in deeper and more extensive readings in mental science, the ancient Vedic hymns of India, their modern reinterpretations in the works of Goethe and Schiller, and the wider world of German idealism, including Kant. A letter of introduction from Waldo Emerson to Herman Grimm, the art historian and son of the folklorist, and a dinner party at Grimm's, where the philosopher Wilhelm Dilthey held forth on the history of Buddhism and the natural forms of early religion, helped James prolong his wavering. Could his readings in psychology turn into practical work? What sort of social role could a man like James play? Should modern thinkers tell "the public" that "God is dead, or at least irrelevant," he wondered in a letter to Wendell Holmes, if empirical principles are borne out in experience—if, that is, the facts turn out to mean that "we must . . . interpret this rich and delicate overgrowth of ideas, moral, artistic, religious & social, as a mere mask, a tissue spun in happy hours by creative individuals and adopted by other men in the interests of their sensations?"[15]

What James called in a diary entry his "contemplative Grubelei," the stuff his mind kept worrying over, amounted to nothing less than the meaning of human life itself. He hardly considered himself fit for such speculations, yet he could not leave them off, and ruminating on them made him feel very dark, alienated by human society, and tempted by suicide. "My old trouble," he noted to himself in 1869, "and the root of antinomianism in general seems to be a dissatisfaction with any thing less than grace." The echo of the Reformation Christians behind James is audible.[16]

James wrote this reflection amid lengthy praise of an essay by the German Romantic Friedrich Schiller (1759–1805). In the essay "On Grace and Dignity," Schiller said that grace involves "voluntary movements" that "express some sentiment of the moral order," a definition that shows how deeply the thinkers of Germany were enmeshed in the same set of issues that engaged the thinkers of the American Reformation. The question of voluntary moral action lay at the heart of James's dilemma. He could neither make himself act, so hemmed in was he by indecision and faulty confidence, nor find any intellectual justification for voluntary action at all. The old American Reformation ideal of moral agency, which rested on the exercise of free will, was in peril before the explanatory sweep of modern science, which implied a moral system as closed as the doctrine of total depravity once had. In 1869, James admired on the one hand how John Stuart Mill advocated women's rights as part of the "democratic flood" of their time, and despaired on the other over the implication of the empirical philosophy of Mill and others that "we are Nature, through and through, that we are *wholly* conditioned, that not a wiggle of our will happens save as the result of physical laws." How could human culture move toward the universal equality championed by Mill if individuals and society are governed by large material forces? More personally, how could James contribute anything to such a society, how could he make himself act at all, if the future were predetermined, not by a Calvinist deity this time, but by a biological power blind to justice? Indeed, biological force seemed to master him at every turn, his eyes too weak for reading, his back too weak for sitting, his nerves too weak for socializing. By this point he had even resolved never to marry in order to avoid passing such weakness on to the next generation.[17]

The next year, 1870, marked both James's lowest point and the beginning of his way out of what he later called "The Dilemma of Determinism." First his beautiful cousin Minnie, with whom he shared a strong mental affinity and enormous personal affection, died at age twenty-four after a long fight against tuberculosis. During her decline, she wrote James a number of letters describing her disaffection with a liberal Christianity that was all moral striving after an ever remote perfection. In one letter, of which only a fragment survives, she testified to what became her dying belief and an essential piece of James's living faith when she described imaginary music coming "like a divine voice to tell me to be true to my whole nature—to stick to my key-note & have faith that my life would so, in some way or other, if faithfully lived, swell the entire harmony." This letter arrived soon after James had seriously weighed abandoning his preoccupation with "the moral interest" but decided instead to pursue it, "and it alone, making everything else merely stuff for it." The moral interest was his keynote, and soon, although it took years to develop, he converted Minnie's idea about the contribution such a life could make to the invisible whole into a solution to the problem of nature versus reason, or might versus right, or the real versus the ideal, too. The solution involved faith, a faith made real by lacking any guarantee that it would ever be shown to be right.[18]

In order to reach this solution, James had to find a way to conceive of human life in both material and ideal terms. In those days of warfare between science and religion, as some would call it, there were three available approaches, all of which he found unsatisfactory. The materialists believed that empirical or phenomenal reality was all the reality that existed, denying the existence of any spiritual realm at all. James called this approach "pessimistic" because it left no room for human will. The person with this attitude he knew best was Chauncey Wright, a brilliant member of the Metaphysical Club that met on and off in Cambridge, although the English scientists Herbert Spencer, T. H. Huxley, John Tyndall, and W. K. Clifford became targets for James as well. "*Fiat justitia, peribit mundus,*" James wrote in his diary to characterize their attitude. Power justifies itself, let the world perish.[19]

The idealists, who represented the second approach to the conflict between science and religion, were horrified by this view. They followed Kant in acknowledging the reality of phenomena while insisting that the reality that counted was the invisible Absolute in which all material swam. James called this approach "optimistic." He associated it with the popular president of Princeton, James McCosh, although later

James's friend and colleague Josiah Royce exemplified the absolute idealist for James, and most Christians, Vedantists, and Hegelians also qualified.

Finally there were spiritualists—a term James used to designate not the psychics in whom he was genuinely scientifically interested from the 1870s until his death but instead to describe those who depicted separate territories of reality for the material and the ideal, marking off a preserve for religion into which science could not reach. James thought this approach was silly. His own conviction was that human beings and the rest of the universe are somehow made of both nature and the divine, but he could not conceptualize this. Meanwhile he was bowled over by the explanatory power of empirical philosophy. He called it his "pessimistic crisis."[20]

For two years he produced nothing but diary entries and letters, a drought after several years of publishing anonymous reviews. He had finished a medical degree with little enthusiasm, no determination to make use of it, and a final oral exam during which one professor asked for news of his family. It was the only degree he ever earned. But he read a lot in his four hours of good vision per day, so he encountered two important thinkers—an idealist and an empiricist—who gave him the tools he needed to begin to create room for free will in a world of sensations. First, the French neo-Kantian Charles Renouvier posed a definition of free will James soon adopted: "the sustaining of a thought *because I choose to*." So James chose to sustain the thought that free will was true. When he wrote in his diary in 1870 that his "first act of free will shall be to believe in free will," he meant that just as he had been testing the validity of empirical principles in his own experience, now he would test the validity of a faith in the reality of his ability to make choices. The second tool pertained to habit, which James in his *Principles of Psychology* (1890) called "the enormous fly-wheel of society" because it controls so much of human behavior. Yet habit is indubitably malleable. Alexander Bain, a psychologist of the British associational school of empiricism, provided James with a concrete method for acquiring new habits by following a dramatic initiative with steady order. James decided to use this method to acquire the habit of sustaining the belief in free will. Leaving off speculation over the either big picture or the ultimate ground of things, he resolved to suspend his logical objections and to see how life went when lived according to the belief that "in accumulated *acts* of thought lies salvation."[21]

Salvation was not imminent, and James suffered setbacks—one of them severe enough that it reappeared in disguise in *Varieties*—but his "voluntary faith," as he started calling this approach, gradually began to buoy him. He got help from Wordsworth, whose *Excursion* he read hungrily, finding in it the argument that the way to correct despondency was faith in immortality and the reality of divinity. Wordsworth taught James that it is "well to trust / Imagination's light when reason's fails." Finally, in 1873, James started pulling free enough of pessimism to call it "ludicrous." His method was working.[22]

He called it "the method of nature" in his diary, and the individual who follows it "the man of the world." The man of the world does not flinch from facts of any kind—from sensations, empirical findings, truths—whether pleasant or unpleasant, but observes them from some sober remove in which his inability to grasp the whole is part of the reality being uncovered day by day. A liberal who does not fear the truth, the man of the world is not an optimist, who needs to select from phenomena those suitable to an interpretation of the universe in which good governs and justice prevails. Nor is he a pessimist, who accepts the evil in the universe as the price paid for rule by mere might. The man of the world is instead a meliorist who never loses sight of the ideal but "flanks" it, dealing with phenomena as they arise and nudging what he finds he can control toward that ideal. Mental experience, James now believed, is made up of which facts are attended to. By always keeping the ideal in mind—"the potential . . . in comparison with the actual"—while accepting whatever arises, the man of nature attends to both what is and what should be, all while "smiling" and in no "despair at postponing a solution." This is the kind of man James aimed to be, bad back, weak eyes, jumpy nerves and all. It is a post-Christian version of Ebenezer Gay's definition of religion as the human actions required relative to the perfections of God, and of the humility and resignation of John Adams before an inscrutable universe.[23]

Now in his thirties, James was better able to engage in active moral life because he finally had a job, teaching anatomy at Harvard. He would rather have been teaching mental science, and he complained a lot about how his new responsibilities taxed his delicate system, but interacting with students, choosing textbooks, preparing lectures and exams, even grading all forced him to act and thereby raised his sense of his own capabilities. He now lived by what he called religion, which he defined as "the affirmation that all is *not* vanity." He was finding that his voluntary faith imparted "a whole character" to his experience, he wrote in his diary during that first year of teaching, because this belief is "a truth of orientation, serving not to define an end, but to determine a direction." Evil exists, but it stands the chance of being mitigated only "on the condition: *if* we assist by faith and act."[24]

Even so, James still had trouble getting himself to act. After his first semester of teaching at Harvard, he requested a year's leave from President Charles Eliot so that he could go to Europe to try to resolve what might in the twentieth century have invited a diagnosis of manic depression or bipolar disorder but in the nineteenth went under the name neurasthenia. As he described his condition to his brother Henry, he alternated between periods of "the most extreme languor & depression," during which he slept well, and "fits of equally uneven duration of great exhilaration of spirits, restlessness, comparative bodily & mental activity—coupled however with wakefulness of the most distressing sort that makes me absolutely sick." But the good news was that "my ideas, my plans of study are all straightened out." Now he just needed to fix his health. Concerned that their now-married brothers needed their father's surplus income, James borrowed a thousand dollars from their aunt to fund the voyage.[25]

He initially considered getting his way to Europe paid by offering himself as a tutor to a teenage boy, such as family friend George Bancroft had done for Frederic Henry Hedge forty years before. James decided against this tack, resolving instead to continue his career at Harvard, but becoming a professor was by no means the default mode at the time for supporting a vocation in the study of the mind such as he was now determined to do. Charles Eliot had just begun the process of remaking Harvard into a modern research university, and almost none of the thinkers James admired made their living as academics. Not Charles Renouvier, not Charles Peirce or Chauncey Wright, and not John Stuart Mill, who earned his bread pushing paper for the East India Company. James himself had more fallen into teaching at Harvard than sought it out as a career, and he did not regard the teaching of human anatomy to be closely related to his life's work. But college life suited James, who quickly attracted increasing numbers of students. When he returned to Cambridge from his European sojourn of 1873–74—where he socialized, appreciated art, and got sick from a new fever rather than well—he took up his responsibilities in earnest, soon opening the first psychological laboratory in the United States. In 1876 he was appointed assistant professor of physiology. He was thirty-four years old.[26]

And then he fell in love. James had gone to a couple of meetings of the Radical Club, a much more prestigious scene than the casual Metaphysical Club that met in Cambridge and brought him into conversation with other men interested in big questions. The Radical Club met at a home on Beacon Hill belonging to a Unitarian minister, John Sargent. His wife, Mary, invited aging Transcendentalists, ministers, visiting scientists, social reformers, and writers on the third Monday of every month between 1867 and 1880 for "the freest investigation of all forms of religious thought and inquiry," according to her memoir of the club. It inspired copycats in most major cities in the United States and its proceedings were regularly reported in the *New York Tribune* and other newspapers as far west as Chicago. Liberals like William Henry Channing, Julia Ward Howe, and Thomas Wentworth Higginson headlined at Radical Club meetings, where the propriety of extending suffrage to women was generally approved, the goal of disinterestedness applauded, and the aim of a "larger liberty of faith, fellowship, and communion" achieved. Attendance ranged from thirty to two hundred of Boston's better sort, and among these in early 1876 was William James, who complained to his brother that the evening amounted to little more than an "esthetic tea." He only went because Mary Sargent had been pestering him to attend, and he reported that the evening consisted of some individuals who "read poetry, whilst others sat and longed for them to stop so that they might begin to talk." Droll though his tone was, James himself had very much enjoyed his talk that night with a teacher at a girls' school, Alice Howe Gibbens, a twenty-seven-year-old maiden of good breeding and modest means.[27]

Within two months he had invited her for a boat ride and explained to her his theory about how unhealthy persons should not marry, since doing so would violate "the outward order that keeps the world so sweet," as he explained in a follow-up letter. He had now devised an exception to this rule, however. In some rare cases, when the individuals involved make an "appeal to some metaphysical world 'behind the veil,'" the unhealthy person may be so benefited by the union that the healthy partner chooses to violate the conventional moral code as a sort of "tragic duty." James and Gibbens spent the next two years debating whether theirs was such a case.[28]

Unfortunately for history, the Gibbens voice in that discussion is lost. James destroyed all of her letters from their courtship. He viewed his documentary record with an eye to posterity—after they were married, he sometimes referred to the "family archive" in letters he wrote from his travels—and such sentiment and passion as Alice Howe Gibbens expressed did not belong in public view, not in a highly gendered Victorian era with a fierce regard for privacy. James eventually regretted the destruction, but another purge was later performed by their son, so that of all the letters Alice wrote James before and during their long marriage, almost all of the scant survivors are those she penned five years into their marriage during the weeks Henry James Sr. lay dying while James was on another of his European trips to palliate his nerves. In other words, her status was completely derived from men, her voice in the surviving letters considered worth preserving only because it contained record of the last mental states of a public figure, Henry James Sr. Otherwise she was strictly an entity of the private sphere.[29]

Evidently this was just the sort of marriage James wanted, even during the years he planned to forgo intimacy and family life altogether. In his review of Mill's *On the Subjection of Women* (1869), he skillfully criticized the writing and argumentation of the other book under review—written by Horace Bushnell, a Congregationalist clergyman who had taken the Romantic turn while insisting, in *Women's Suffrage: The Reform Against Nature*, that women be kept in their place—but James did not follow Mill all the way to social equality and complete independence. For an American male, whose erasure of women in the institution of marriage had astonished Tocqueville, "the wife his heart more or less subtly craves is at bottom a dependent being," James wrote. He sounded the ideology of separate spheres in his elaboration in the review on how the man toils out in the precarious world, from which he returns to the "one tranquil spot where he shall be valid absolutely and once for all." The public male's feelings of private "security and repose" require a wife who relies "on him to be her mediator with the external world" and is essentially enveloped by him, "his activity overlapping hers and surrounding it on almost every side, so that he makes as it were the atmosphere in which she lives." This was the Anglo-American Victorian ideal of the middle to upper classes; it was the sort of marriage James's parents had; it was the recipe for complete acceptance and recognition that he desired for himself, and ultimately found with Alice. As he told her once during an upswing in their tumultuous courtship, he believed that "the mission of your sex is not to originate but to judge." For someone with such intelligence and refinement as she had to judge him so favorably gratified James immensely. He begged her to "stand by me & advise me & be my soul & my conscience, my good angel."[30]

No wonder John Stuart Mill stood out to James as a paragon of open-mindedness. Several decades older than James, Mill was more forward-thinking on this topic than James ever became. Mill's mother had been no more of a personality than Mary James, but he got a radical social education from his father, James Mill, cofounder with Jeremy Bentham of the utilitarian school of thought in which there was no God. Then John Stuart Mill had his own mental crisis. Like James, Mill discovered with alarm that purely empirical philosophy did not satisfy his conception of the good, that "the pleasure of sympathy with human beings," as he put it in his autobiography, was not sufficient for happiness. Like James, Mill gradually alleviated his distress by reading Wordsworth. He came to believe that feelings mattered even though they could not be explained by the associational theory he had learned from

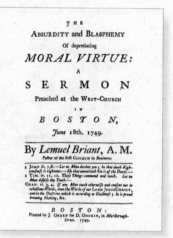

Rev. Jonathan Mayhew by Giovanni Battista Cipriani, line engraving on laid paper, 1767. The Boston minister acquired an international reputation after composing a sermon that the young John Adams read and reread "till the Substance of it was incorporated into my Nature and indelibly engraved on my Memory," he later told Thomas Jefferson. | *Collection of the Massachusetts Historical Society*

Title page for Lemuel Briant, "The Absurdity and Blasphemy of Depretiating Moral Virtue," 1749. John Adams was away at college when his hometown minister delivered this controversial sermon from Mayhew's pulpit. The ecclesiastical debates that erupted upon its publication involved ministers and laity from across the Boston area, beginning the American Reformation.

| *Early American Imprints, Series I: Evans, 1639–1800*

Portrait of John Adams, pastel on paper by Benjamin Blyth, circa 1766. After deciding against the ministry, Adams became a lawyer and moved to Boston, where he sat for this portrait soon after publishing an article against the Stamp Act, which brought him his first transatlantic fame.

| *Collection of the Massachusetts Historical Society*

One of the only surviving images of Mary Moody Emerson, the pious, independent-thinking aunt of Ralph Waldo Emerson, who borrowed some of his best lines from her diary. She read intensively and prayed to God, "I love thee I know it—and yet I am not every thing I s[houl]d be."
| *Courtesy Concord Free Public Library*

Wax portrait of Rev. William Emerson (1770–1811), Mary Moody's older brother and Ralph Waldo's father, who combined Enlightenment ideals with the principles of Reformation Christianity. He participated in a developing liberal intellectual culture of lived virtue through fellowships like the Massachusetts Historical Society and the American Academy of Arts and Sciences. Emerson coedited *The Monthly Anthology and Boston Review*, whose motto ran "through fair discussion truths immortal find."
| *Courtesy Concord Free Public Library*

Ralph Waldo Emerson carried the principles of the American Reformation beyond Christianity—and New England—to a wider American public, having left the ministry in fidelity to his conscience. His aunt did not approve of the worldly cast of his mature thought. | *Courtesy Concord Free Public Library*

Mary Moody Emerson meditated on death all her life, longing for union with God. When she died in Brooklyn in 1863, her surviving kin commissioned this ferrotype of her. | *MS Am 2982 (84), Houghton Library, Harvard University*

As she requested, she was buried where there was "no dust of a friend to slavery," at Sleepy Hollow Cemetery in Concord. Her favorite nephew—Ralph Waldo—wrote the epitaph. "She gave high counsels—It was the privilege of certain boys to have this immeasurably high standard indicated to their childhood, a blessing which nothing else in education could supply."

| *Photograph by Cherrie A. Corey*

William Ellery Channing, D.D., engraving on tissue by Wm. Hoogland from a picture painted by Chester Harding. Channing sat for this portrait soon after taking the pulpit at the Federal Street Church in Boston in 1803. He was already the golden voice of the liberal movement in the Congregational Church, then the established church of Massachusetts. | *Collection of the Massachusetts Historical Society*

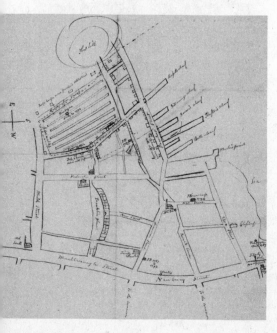

The patriot minister Jeremy Belknap sketched this map of Boston for a friend and mailed it on September 20, 1794, indicating the Federal Street Church as a landmark and "JB" where he had lived. As the neo-Calvinists began to break away from the liberals in the church, the liberals became Unitarians who took over Harvard, the state government, and the most affluent congregations—yet Channing became an international hero because he argued for the divine potential of workingmen and slaves.

| *Collection of the Massachusetts Historical Society*

In 1866, the future philosopher William James drew this self-portrait while considering a career as an artist. He was just beginning to descend into his "pessimistic crisis," as he called the period of personal anguish that lasted into the 1870s.

| *MS Am 1092.2 (54), Houghton Library, Harvard University*

HERE I AM₁D SORROW SIT

James was so distressed over how modern science threatened moral agency—the ability of the individual to make choices—that suicide became an obsessive temptation. | *MS Am 1092.2 (55), Houghton Library, Harvard University*

The Foreboding Meeting
or
The Artist's Fate.
Drama
Dram. Personæ.
Sage of Concord
W. J.
Scene
Parkars boots blacking
establishment

Enter W. J.
W. J. I say, boy, just give my boots
a lick.
× × × ×
Enter. S of C.

This twentieth-century postcard memorializes the Concord Summer School of Philosophy, which offered morning and afternoon lectures in the spirit of liberal open-mindedness from 1879 to 1888. William James spoke here before an audience of aging Transcendentalists and young social scientists. | *Courtesy of the author*

"The Foreboding Meeting, or the Artist's Fate," undated, but likely also during the crisis years. The "Sage of Concord" is clearly Ralph Waldo Emerson, a family friend and a sizable influence on James and every other liberal in his generation. Here he imagines himself—"W.J."—striking up conversation with the preeminent symbol of intellectual integrity in America.

| *MS Am 1092.1 (172), Houghton Library, Harvard University*

William James (standing, far left) with his company at Putnam Camp in Keene Valley, the Adirondack Mountains of New York, in 1896. James visited the camp almost every year of his adult life; it was his favorite place on earth. His friend, Dr. James Jackson Putnam (standing with arms crossed in doorway), hosted Sigmund Freud and Carl Jung at the camp in 1909.

| *Courtesy of Putnam Camp, Keene Valley*

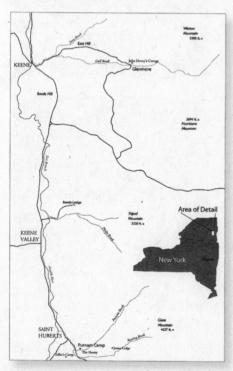

Thomas Davidson, aged thirty-one, in Hastings, England, August 22, 1871, about the time he befriended William James. Born in Scotland, by this point Davidson had moved around Great Britain and across the Atlantic numerous times, living in Toronto, Boston, and for a long time, St. Louis, where he and Joseph Pulitzer became lovers. | *Thomas Davidson Papers (MS 169). Manuscripts and Archives, Yale University Library*

Putnam Camp was only one of several vital intellectual communities in Keene Valley in the decades around the turn of the twentieth century. This map shows the most important of these communities along with the surrounding mountains, where James experienced "every sort of patriotic suggestiveness." | *Created by David Kittelstrom*

Davidson with guests at the Glenmore School of the Social Sciences, which he established in Keene Valley in the 1890s with the help of Pulitzer's money. Camping, communal meals, lectures, discussions, and group singing—and bathing—made life at Glenmore "Heaven," according to one visitor.

| *Courtesy of Keene Valley Public Library*

GLENMORE, KEENE NEW YORK, EARLY 1890's

STANDING LEFT TO RIGHT: PROFESSOR JOHN DEWEY, RABBI MARGOLIS
WILLIAM T. HARRIS, A BEDOIN — NAME UNKNOWN
SEATED IN CHAIRS: PROFESSOR MURRAY OF McGILL UNIVERSITY
SEATED ON PORCH: PROFESSOR JOSIAH ROYCE, THOMAS DAVIDSON

Thomas Davidson on the porch of his Glenmore cabin with Percival Chubb, who joined Davidson's "Fellowship of the New Life" in London and followed him to the United States. Chubb became a leader in the Society for Ethical Culture, whose founder, Felix Adler, also summered in Keene Valley. | *Courtesy of Keene Valley Public Library*

Like James, Davidson used the phrase "the religion of democracy" to describe the creed he held, a belief in the sacred equality of every individual and the necessity of freedom in everyone's activity and interaction, in all their infinite diversity.

| *Courtesy of Keene Valley Public Library*

Before his death in 1900, Davidson began the Breadwinners' College of the Lower East Side of Manhattan, a voluntary educational association populated by Jewish immigrants from Eastern Europe. Adler delivered his funeral sermon at Glenmore, where his gravestone quotes Swinburne, "He has bought his Eternity/with a little Hour/And is not dead." | *Photograph by David Kittelstrom*

James wrote and lectured widely on psychology, science, philosophy, and religious belief, becoming so famous that a hotel clerk in Italy once nearly fainted upon hearing his name. | *MS Am 1092 (1185) #71, Houghton Library, Harvard University*

The monument on the Boston Common to Colonel Robert Gould Shaw and the Massachusetts 54th Regiment he commanded during the Civil War. The most famous deployment of African-American soldiers in the Union, the Massachusetts 54th proved the liberal contention that African Americans and Euro-Americans could work together for their common higher democratic interest. William James and Booker T. Washington spoke at the monument's unveiling. | *Photograph by Amy Kittelstrom*

William Mackintire Salter at age eighteen, preparing to enter divinity school to become a minister like his father. Instead he became a post-Christian leader in the Ethical Culture movement, the brother-in-law of William James, defender of the Haymarket anarchists, and author of philosophical writings admired across Europe and all the way to Mahatma Gandhi. | *Special Collections and Archives, Knox College*

Salter with his wife, Mary Gibbens Salter, and their son, John Randall Salter (Frank Gray), at Silver Lake, New Hampshire, August 1911. John was thirteen years old at the time. A Native American—mostly Wabanaki with some Mohawk—he had been a two-year-old ward of the state when the Salters adopted him. Their relationship ultimately broke down, but John went on to the Art Institute of Chicago with aid from the estate of William James. | *Courtesy of Hunter Gray (John R. Salter, Jr.)*

Jane Addams in an undated photograph, probably around the time she opened Hull House in 1889 at age twenty-nine. Rejecting the condescending philanthropy of the Victorian era, Addams and her college friend Ellen Gates Starr wanted to live among the people of Chicago "in reciprocal relation" and find out from them what they needed. | *The Jane Addams Collection, Swarthmore College Peace Collection*

Jane Addams with Mary Rozet Smith, her beloved companion and the biggest financial contributor to Hull House, which became an enormous enterprise of social service, activism, and research. | *The Jane Addams Collection, Swarthmore College Peace Collection*

Jane Addams reading to children at Hull House, in an undated photograph taken probably around 1930. Addams lived to be seventy-five, an international organizer and author, the first American woman to win the Nobel Peace Prize. | *The Jane Addams Collection, Swarthmore College Peace Collection*

his father, who held that all knowledge comes from sensory experience. As he was grafting his new belief onto the strictly rational system he had been taught, he fell in love—with a married woman.[31]

It is not that adultery was unheard of in Victorian England, but it was decidedly frowned upon in the polite circles to which both Mill and Harriet Taylor belonged. Both of them genuinely respected Harriet's husband, "a most upright, brave, and honourable man," according to Mill, "of liberal opinions and good education, but without the intellectual or artistic tastes which would have made him a companion for her, though a steady and affectionate friend." So Mill and Taylor struggled with their feelings for three years before Taylor separated from her husband. They settled into a lofty friendship of mind and spirit that endured over two decades and lots of gossip. Then her husband died, and after a two-year stall they finally married. Their public union lasted seven and a half years—"seven and a-half only!" Mill remembered with anguish—before she died too.[32]

During the platonic phase of their life together, Harriet Taylor referred to John Stuart Mill as her *Seelenfreund*, her soul mate, and he felt just the same about her. His most durable intellectual productions followed their acquaintance. Although he had done some writing and engaged in some social reform activity before they met—indeed, Mill believed that his youthful conviction in human equality and the need for women to be able to represent themselves politically helped attract Taylor to him—their partnership transformed his mental life. Mill credited his soul mate with complete intellectual coproduction of all his major works from *Principles of Political Economy* (1848) through *On Liberty* (1859), particularly *On Liberty*, surely his most widely read work, which he summarized in terms of "the importance, to man and society, of a large variety in types of human character, and of giving full freedom to human nature to expand itself in innumerable and conflicting directions." The book was jointly composed during their marriage. "When two persons have their thoughts and speculations completely in common," Mill explained, "when all subjects of intellectual or moral interest are discussed between them in daily life . . . it is of little consequence in respect to the question of originality, which of them holds the pen." Mill said that he and Harriet went over the manuscript together sentence by sentence through multiple drafts, so that he could not tell which part was whose, and in the writing of which and thinking about which "she benefited me as much by keeping me right where I was right, as by leading me to new truths, and ridding me of errors."[33]

Harriet Taylor Mill had flaws, but Mill could not see them. He described her as "a woman of deep and strong feeling, of penetrating and intuitive intelligence," a noble spirit "with whom self-improvement, progress in the highest and in all senses, was a law of her nature," endowed with strong mental "faculties which could not receive an impression or an experience without making it the source or the occasion of an accession of wisdom." When they met he saw how her potential had been thwarted by the gender discrimination of their era, and as they discussed philosophical and social matters he learned from her concretely just how such barriers limited progress by limiting liberty. This recognition inspired *On the Subjection of Women*, in which Mill applied associational philosophy to the problem of gender and called for complete equality in education, opportunity, and civic power. Even more profoundly, though, the experience of deep contact with a mind that fit his like a glove moved Mill legions. He described their "close intellectual communion" as one of overlapping insights, one in which her "genius . . . continually struck out truths far in advance of me" and her originality and unerring "moral character" gave him "a wise scepticism," a bent toward "practicality," and, most important of all, the animation of his theoretical understanding of human liberty into "a living principle."[34]

Alice Howe Gibbens James was no Harriet Taylor Mill, but her importance to the mature mental life of William James was as vital as the intellectual communion between the Mills. James turned to her with his every thought for confirmation, corroboration, correction; she took notes for him, supplied quotations, helped him sound out key phrases; she bundled up examination packets and mailed periodicals and books to him; shielded him from every harassment of needy children and domestic care so that he could travel frequently, restore his nerves, catch up on his sleep, and concentrate on his work with a free conscience. He loved the way she bossed workmen. Most fundamentally, she made the religious convictions he had worked out in his mind live and breathe in his heart so that his faith became vivid and real. Her own religious education had been in the liberal Christian vein, her judgment and piety practical matters of daily life. Hers was the ideal self-sacrificing life of the Victorian woman fashioned for devotion to a man. Thinking about how her narrow experience compared with that of "the attractive, cultivated men and women" James met abroad made Alice "tremble" with anxiety, but she reassured herself that, "as Channing says . . . elevation of soul can be had anywhere, in any calling if we only work for it." The calling she answered and lived by was to love James.[35]

This love transformed him, not least by inspiring him to admire and adore someone besides himself. Early in their courtship he wrote to her with gratitude: "you teach me that certain goods are *real*, and compel me to live so as to merit them, or to die trying to do so." Changing his life was a matter of changing his heart and therefore his most basic self-awareness. "To have you recognize me," James exulted, "to have your truth acquiesce in my better self" made that better self real, reflected in her sweet sight, and it helped him pursue "the only, single use for which my life was given me, namely the *acting* for the deepest, widest, most general good I can see and feel." His practical idealism sprang to life under her loving touch. The idea of the metaphysical world "behind the veil," whose justice the moral actions of humans may serve, became palpable to James through the intensity of love, the living out of which required him to take a moral leap that violated conventional justice as he understood it. (Having approvingly read *The Jukes: A Study in Crime, Pauperism, Disease, and Heredity* of 1878, he helps indicate where the progressive impulse that led to eugenics came from.) He took the leap for the sake of a higher justice, a justice that would not "exact such sacrifices as the violent breaking of such faith and love as ours has been in each other," he wrote his beloved during their courtship. James believed they were helping to create this higher justice, because decisions like theirs "seem acts by which we are *voting* what sort of a universe this shall ultimately be." He even sent his bride part of his diary from the pessimistic crisis to help her see how their love helped fulfill the truth of his religious philosophy. With every incremental step toward the ideal, James confidently declared a few months before their wedding, "I can repeat 'Look to thyself O Universe, Thou art better, not worse!'"[36]

The student of William James may recognize this crow to the universe from his most famous and popular essay, "The Will to Believe" (1896). The line also appeared in an article first published in the *Unitarian Review*, "The Dilemma of Determinism" (1884), where it illustrates his view that "the universe belongs to a plurality of semi-independent forces, each one of which may help or hinder, and be helped or hindered by, the operations of the rest." It was only the first of many of his most potent lines created in the magical heat of trying to express his truest sentiment to the woman he loved, and only the beginning of his productive life.[37]

By the time James married, all the essential ingredients for his mature philosophy were in place. He began at last to hold forth in his own voice. After only ever having published unsigned reviews and two letters to the editor—one of which was signed "Ignoramus"—he shed his reticence and dared to publicize his ideas beginning in the year of their marriage. That year, 1878, he published his first original piece of scholarship under his own byline, taking on the most popular social scientist of his day in direct challenge and concluding with bravado: "Spencer's formula has crumbled into utter worthlessness in our hands." He also published his second original piece—in French—and his third, an article that served as the initial installment in the long work of his monumental *Principles of Psychology*. And he had a fourth in draft. In that draft manuscript, later published as "The Sentiment of Rationality," he testified to his essential faith in an inner divinity in which he would have all believe because such a faith works. "If all men could permanently say," he proposed, "'In my heart there is light,' though they should for ever fail to give an articulate account of it, existence would really be rationalized." The real and the ideal were one. Realities and ideals, many.[38]

MAKING LIFE WORTH LIVING

At Harvard James was collegial, warm, and playful. He enjoyed talking shop. One day in 1881, he got into a conversation about visual perception with his colleague Charles Carroll Everett (1829–1900), a near relation of Edward Everett's who had earned a medical degree from Bowdoin College and a degree in theology from Harvard Divinity School. Everett studied in Berlin, became a minister at the Independent Congregational Church in Bangor, Maine, and then taught modern languages at Bowdoin before publishing *The Science of Thought* in 1869. This treatise on logic won him an appointment in New Testament criticism and interpretation at Harvard, where he taught a course on East

Asiatic religions starting in 1872, the first such course in the United States. Everett liked going to the Radical Club, and he liked thinking about the problem James presented him so much that he went home and tried an experiment James had requested. Inspired, Everett improvised a couple of other experiments as well. First he placed a pea on a table and crossed his fingers in front of his eyes to double the pea, visually, without moving it physically. Then he went outside and turned his head upside down, facing the horizon, so that the ground appeared to be the sky and the sky the ground. As he returned upright, he noticed that the horizon seemed to draw near and the landscape seemed to rise. Then he tried the experiment again from a higher vantage point, finding the results even more impressive. Finally, he wrote a letter to James explaining the results. His postscript to the letter reproduced lines from the Talavakara Upanishad, an early Hindu text: "By him who thinks that Brahma is not comprehended, by him he is comprehended; he who thinks that Brahma is comprehended, does not know him. Brahma is unknown to those that know him, & known to those who do not know him."[39]

Optical illusions, Vedic riddles, and intimations of the divine belonged together in the intellectual culture of American religious liberals in the late nineteenth century. James was not alone in trying to figure out how both the real and the ideal could be true in light of modern science and the instability of biblical revelation. In the early decades of his productive life, he found talking partners among liberals like Everett who shared his vocabulary, his canon, and his concern for the higher life. These were times in which experimental psychologists stimulated decapitated frogs with dabs of acid and concluded from the twitching limbs that something they might call the soul existed independent of the brain. Theologians in those days stood "a better chance of being listened to," according to James, when they "quote Darwin and

Helmholtz" rather than only "Schleiermacher or Coleridge," and scientific findings dispersed into the culture so that "all educated people know what reflex action means."[40]

James made these observations not long after Everett's experiment. He was delivering an address before an audience of Unitarian ministers, an important audience for James despite the fact that neither he nor anyone else in his family had ever been either Unitarian or Congregationalist. (Henry James Sr. had early become an apostate from the family's Presbyterian Calvinism.) Unitarians—or ex-Unitarians—populated so much of the intellectual world in which James lived that he may not have been aware of how much he owed to them. Religious liberals provided him with platforms for launching his most seminal ideas; in pitching those ideas to their reception, he packaged them in the format most likely to become popular with a wider American public educated by the institutions of practical Christianity. James may indeed have been an exceptional being, but he was also representative of his cultural moment and milieu, and perhaps most exceptional in the exquisite ear he had for the language and ideas around him.[41]

This public shaped him too. The resolution of his pessimistic crisis had involved a decision to act as though an ultimate moral order really existed and as if this infinite good could really be served by individual moral action; it had not involved a conception of God. This had changed by the time of his address at the Unitarian Ministers' Institute in 1881. Entitled "Reflex Action and Theism," the talk mounted a defense of faith in God on the grounds that the mind is a teleological mechanism, providing a scientific echo of the old Puritan belief that the end for which we are made is to know God. James agreed, finding grounds in the results of experimental psychology to claim both that the mind is fashioned for an end and that calling this end "God" has such a positive effect that "theism itself, by reason of its practical rationality, is certain to survive all lower creeds." He illustrated this Darwinian defense of religious belief with allusions to the Unitarian revolt against Calvinism, saying that "no fitter body of men than the Unitarian clergy exists" for the job of fighting scientific determinism because Unitarians had departed from "our orthodox ancestral Calvinism" out of a sound moral objection. "A God who gives so little scope to love, a predestination which takes from endeavor all its zest with all its fruit," he said, in a conflation of Calvinism with deterministic science, "are irrational conceptions, because they say to our most cherished powers, There is no object for you."[42]

The God in whom James came to believe was very different from the deterministic deities of Calvinism and "scientism," as he called materialistic determinism. "A power not ourselves," he described the divinity in which he had faith, "which not only makes for righteousness, but means it, and which recognizes us." Invisible, noumenal, but partial and limited in power in order both to be defined as good in a world that contains evil and to be assisted by human moral action, this somewhat Manichean God was a scientifically developed version of the good God of practical Christianity defined by disinterested benevolence, to be served by generous and impartial acts.[43]

James knew his audience. He also meant what he said. Later the lapsed Presbyterian Thomas Davidson read the address in the *Unitarian Review* and criticized James's theism in a letter. James protested that although the idea of God had been abused throughout history, "as an Ideal to attain and make probably, I find myself less and less able to do without him." For him, theism had become an essential element of the middle way between idealism and materialism, so although he never became a Christian—he explained to a Christian correspondent many years after this address that the idea of God's choosing between the saved and the damned was intolerable to him—his ability to say sincerely that "God's being is sacred" enabled him to be heard by Christian audiences.[44]

Yet what got James those audiences in the first place, aside from his social position, was his currency in the latest research in physiological psychology. In fact, the magnitude of his popular success may be attributed in part to his ability to demystify modern science—many ministers in that Unitarian audience may actually have understood little to nothing about reflex action before he spoke—and to combat its conceits. His early work reached, for example, the poet Emma Lazarus, best known to history as the author of the inscription on the Statue of Liberty, whom he met at an 1882 soiree and who told him, as he reported to his wife, that his "works had converted her from pessimism to optimism!" They also won him a spot on the program at a session of the Concord School of Philosophy, a venue for intellectuals so famous that its quaint meeting hall appeared on postcards well into the twentieth century, although the school itself met only from 1879 to 1888. The school had been a half-baked plan of Emerson and Bronson Alcott before the war and finally came to life with the help of people like Frank Sanborn, also a cofounder of the American Social Science Association and the principal of an antebellum private school attended by the two younger James boys.[45]

The biggest names in American religious liberalism headlined at the Concord School: Alcott, Elizabeth Palmer Peabody, Cyrus Bartol, William H. Channing, Julia Ward Howe, Frederic Henry Hedge. German idealism was a regular topic, bringing in William Torrey Harris, who later became U.S. commissioner of education, and George Henry Howison, who started the philosophy department at the University of California at Berkeley, founded the same year as the Concord School. One of the Concord School's biggest draws was Thomas Davidson, a Scottish immigrant, a close friend of James's and widely considered among the most learned and humane thinkers in America. Rowland G. Hazard, who had discussed democracy with William Ellery Channing and exchanged criticism with John Stuart Mill, spoke on the platform at Concord, and so did Charles Peirce as well as James McCosh, who was still using Scottish Common Sense for a moral philosophy in support of a Christian commitment. The activist and writer Ednah Dow Cheney lectured on the religions of India every summer, Emerson and later his widow always attended, and college instructors and students helped fill the seats. Elizabeth Palmer Peabody, about the time she was unwittingly providing the model for a dotty humanitarian character in a Henry James novel, participated every year and wrote to her sister in rapture from the first session, "I never felt so completely *at home* as I do in this School of Philosophy the spirit of which is to listen to & appreciate whatever may be said on the themes whose discussion 'makes the soul.'" The Concord School sought after the whole range of human and divine nature.[46]

When William James appeared on the program in 1883, his name was so little known that the advertisements for the session did not feature it in bold, but the ideas he presented there changed the field of psychology forever. He had been developing them for years. James first floated these ideas about the mind and consciousness at a philosophical discussion group in London in the spring. In the weeks before the Concord session, he got into a genuine writing fever as his critique of all the psychology that had come before him began to coalesce. "On Some Omissions of Introspective Psychology" did not have to take on the old faculty psychology of Scottish Common Sense; that had been dismantled by the associational school of James Mill and Alexander Bain, which treated thoughts as discrete units, individual wholes that add together to form consciousness. Instead, James out-empiricized the empiricists by pointing out how "a little attention" clearly shows that thoughts act in no such way. Thoughts flow into and through one another and include feelings, the intersections between them being as much a part of them as the contrasts between succeeding thoughts. Consciousness, James argued, is therefore better described as a stream, "free water" in which no one ever bathes twice because experience is constantly changing and moving and altering shape, impressing even the structure of the brain itself. He complained about "what immense tracts of our inner life are habitually overlooked and falsified by our most approved psychological authorities." He proposed to begin including in mental reality things that do not fit into neat categories, since "namelessness is compatible with existence" and a more complete psychology comes from the "re-instatement of the vague to its proper place in our mental life."[47]

No one had heard of the stream of consciousness before. No one serious would treat consciousness as consisting of separately whole thoughts again.

Yet James was not entirely original. His critique of introspective psychology was based in part on introspection, his own habitual practice of mental self-observation, a venerable New England tradition. So was his manly posture of inviting others to verify his results, and so, most vitally, was the moral concern that drove his work. The reason he supplied so much scientific proof for the mind's being fashioned for ends that exist outside of it and for its plasticity was to encourage moral effort. In his important work on habit, he echoed the Virginia insight of Channing when he complained of "the nerveless sentimentalist and dreamer, who spends his life in a weltering sea of sensibility and emotion, but who never does a manly concrete deed." James believed that individuals could become "saints in the moral" sphere by acting and working and exerting the will in the self-fashioning of character. One of the best tools for this, he held, was giving the will "*a little gratuitous exercise every day*" by regular acts of self-denial and service, by doing "every day or two something for no other reason than that you would rather not do it." The will was as much a muscle to be exercised for James as it had been for Channing. "Let me every day give away something," Channing prayed early in his ministry, "and daily deny myself something, that I may have more to give."[48]

After his Concord School appearance, James published some of his late father's work and then spent the rest of the decade on the *Principles of Psychology*, which appeared in two volumes adding up to fourteen hundred pages in 1890. Then he spent much of the next decade condensing and popularizing his findings in various formats and venues. He came out with a textbook version of the *Psychology* in 1892, lectured on the topic to schoolteachers in Cambridge, drew on it for his presidential address before the newly formed American Association of Psychologists, and compressed it down still further for talks he gave to audiences of teachers—whose "earnest and helpless" minds and twangy voices he condescendingly described in letters to his wife—in Boston, New York State, and Colorado Springs. He got a great deal of professional mileage out of this opening body of research, and with it the freedom to follow his mind where it led.[49]

When James was invited to speak before the Young Men's Christian Association of Harvard in 1895, he decided to try to cure his audience of the same sort of struggle of the will he had undergone as a young man. In doing so, he brought Christianity into a wider frame of religious belief on an equal plane with all other faiths, an action that defined Christianity in a way incompatible with exclusivity. He titled the address "Is Life Worth Living?" His answer was yes. Drawing on popular literature to illustrate the mood that tempts the desperate toward suicide, James voiced his doctrine of interdependence by claiming that "we are of one substance with these suicides," and he revealed his developing

pluralism by describing reality as a "moral multiverse." He acknowledged that his "final appeal" was to "religious faith," but not to the
natural religion of yore, which he considered bankrupt, and therefore
not to a religion that centered on a single omnipotent, omnipresent
deity. In this address he started filing such conceptions of the divine
under the label "monistic superstition." Such an all-encompassing entity
as idealists believed in worked no better for James than the morally
blind determinism of science. What is scary about the world is that it is
unfinished and there is no all-powerful, all-good Being in charge, he
allowed, but that is also what is good about it. Even without a plan laid
by God, everyone in an interdependent multiverse has real power of
some indeterminate degree, so each is morally obliged to "wait and see
his part of the battle out." Defining religion in terms of supernaturalism—
what stands above and beyond the natural—James said that "we have a
right to believe the physical order to be only a partial order" even without proof and "a right to supplement it by an unseen spiritual order
which we assume on trust, if only thereby life may seem to us better
worth living again."[50]

The practical effect of faith in one's individual life is reason
enough to believe. Against the magnitude of what science has not yet
discovered—"our science is a drop," James said, "our ignorance a sea"—
there is no real reason not to believe, and he provided reasons, even
Darwinian reasons, to do so. "For such a half-wild, half-saved universe
our nature is adapted," he argued. Our thoughts and feelings are part of
nature too, part of what creates the future of our interdependent whole.
"Believe that life *is* worth living," he advised, "and your belief will help
create the fact."[51]

Often overshadowed in James studies by "The Will to Believe,"
which he delivered the following year and in which he introduced the
important concepts of live beliefs and momentous, forced decisions, "Is

Life Worth Living?" is as important for its reception in its moment as for its intellectual content. Delivered to Christians, it was first published in the *International Journal of Ethics*, a forerunner to the professional philosophical journal of record *Ethics* still published out of the University of Chicago. The "Int. J. of E.," as James referred to it in notes, began in 1890 when the momentum of liberal religion in the United States had merged enough into the European conversation to bring about a transatlantic platform for "the Advancement of Ethical Knowledge and Practice," as the subtitle announced. The journal was run by an editorial board comprised of thinkers both academic and amateur from Prague to Manchester, New York to Paris. This must be where Fanny Morse, James's friend since childhood, read the piece, and the fact that she did so highlights how conversations on ethics took place both within and beyond academia throughout the nineteenth century.[52]

Fanny Morse's enthusiasm for the article also provides a witness for the development of religious pluralism to its next stage beyond Channing. "Your article justifies me in the sympathy I feel with various beliefs that I do not share," wrote Morse. She specified "the Evangelical Christians" with whom she cooperated in social reform activity; the Social Gospel was developing rapidly during these years, an ecumenical movement. The evangelicals' zeal for the work impressed her without overcoming her skepticism about their creed. "They *believe* they can jump the chasm, & they can . . . it is their faith rather than their formula which carries them over." On this common vector of faith—and aim—those of differing beliefs could find the common ground necessary for collective moral action.[53]

Morse was so moved by the article that she offered to pay for its republication as a pamphlet, but plans for that were already under way through the Society for Ethical Culture, three leaders of which served on the board for the *International Journal of Ethics*, and another leader of which was James's brother-in-law William Mackintire Salter, ministering to the ethical flock in Philadelphia at the time. Ethical Culture was the society whose motto was "deed not creed." It stood for the very sort of pluralism James's essay helped Morse embrace. James quoted Salter prominently in the essay, right before the concluding paragraph—"as the essence of courage is to stake one's life on a possibility, so the essence of faith is to believe that the possibility exists"—which states the essence of practical idealism perhaps as neatly as possible. When the ethical culturists decided to publish the pamphlet, they hitched their wagon to the rising star of William James. It became one of their most popular publications.[54]

James had arrived as a public intellectual. The next year he published a collection of essays under the title *The Will to Believe* (1896), with a preface calling for "the freest competition of the various faiths with one another," an adaptation of Mill's marketplace of ideas made vital through "the active faiths of individuals . . . freely expressing themselves in life." That summer, before his pilgrimage to Keene Valley, James gave a series of talks out of his *Psychology* in Buffalo and at the Chautauqua Institute, as middle American a place as late-nineteenth-century America got. The Chautauqua movement had grown out of the camp meetings of Methodists who, as the nineteenth century wore on, got less enthusiastic in the expression of their spirituality and more interested in a general Protestant orientation that included leisure, civics, progress, and moral uplift in the institute built by the shores of Lake Chautauqua in western New York.[55]

At Chautauqua James surprised himself by staying on after his paid work was done. He learned the Delsartean technique of dance, baked a loaf of bran bread, heard a lecture by his soon-to-be comrade in pragmatism, the young John Dewey, and was astonished by "the charmless goodness and seriousness of the place," a judgment that soon spurred a new development of his pluralism. But he was even more astonished when he ate breakfast with a family he had met and found out what sort of popular reputation he had acquired. "The wife said she had my portrait in her bedroom with the words written under it 'I want to bring a balm to human lives'!!!!! Supposed to be a quotation from me!!!"[56]

James was confounded, but the event makes sense. What he actually wrote that year, in answer to one correspondent's response to the "Is Life Worth Living?" pamphlet, gives a better indication of how he understood his audience and his message: "I take it that no man is educated who has never dallied with the thought of suicide." He was no Pollyanna, and he did not imagine his ideas reaching middle-class housewives, but he did try to offer others the medicine that had alleviated his own distress. He promoted the voluntary path of individual social contribution with a keen awareness of the ancient problem of evil and the education in reality it provides to those who reckon with it. James as public figure fulfilled a role once reserved for ministers, apparently a profitable enough role that someone could make money pirating his picture with a bogus line on it—and inspiring enough that a devotee could gain strength from it. He had become successful thanks partly to his connections in the privileged social world of Boston liberals; now he had a constituency in a wider American public ready to hear what religious liberals had to say. He never became comfortable with that public, but for the rest of the century he assumed the voice of a general American "we" in order to urge this public to a higher realization of its own democratic ideals.[57]

OUR AMERICAN RELIGION

At the northeast corner of Boston Common stands a bronze-and-granite monument crafted by Augustus Saint-Gaudens, a sculptor previously commissioned by the grieving great-grandson of John Adams, Henry Adams, for a memorial in the image of a Buddhist bodhisattva at the grave of his wife, Clover, a suicide. For the monument on the common, Saint-Gaudens was hired by the parents of the slain Civil War colonel Robert Gould Shaw to depict the enlisted men of the 54th Massachusetts Volunteer Regiment—the Union's most famous military deployment of former slaves and descendants of slaves—along with their son the officer. The Shaws' decision was consistent with their insistence that their son's corpse be left in a common grave with his men in South Carolina rather than receiving a hero's burial back in Boston. This resolve makes the Shaws and the monument to the 54th outliers on the landscape of Civil War memory. Once federal enforcement of Reconstruction ended with the withdrawal of troops from the South in 1877, most of the country agreed to act as though the Civil War had not been fought for emancipation and indeed had little to do with slavery, a collective amnesia reflected in how the majority of Civil War monuments depict only the classic heroic soldier, Confederate or Union, often mounted and always brave. The monument for Shaw and the 54th is one of the few that include African Americans at all, and the others mostly picture slaves kneeling in supplication as standing soldiers bestow freedom upon their passive, often semi-naked figures. Not so the Saint-Gaudens. There the soldiers march with round-cheeked, resolute faces, each set of features unique. Their postures are proud and erect, their guns smartly shouldered, their packs neatly rolled, their strides united not behind but alongside the mounted figure of Colonel Shaw, a relation of John Adams's wife and William Ellery Channing's college friend. The inscription emphasizes that not only was the end of slavery the meaning of the war, it was something "THE WHITE OFFICERS" and "THE BLACK RANK AND FILE" accomplished "TOGETHER." These volunteers "gave to the nation and the world undying proof that Americans of African descent possess the pride courage and devotion of the patriot soldier." The monument, as well as the liberal culture that made it possible, strenuously affirmed that the Civil War was indeed about slavery, about the denial of human rights to human beings, and about fulfilling the promise of American freedom.[58]

The monument to Shaw and the 54th was unveiled on Memorial Day 1897, with the remaining survivors of the regiment present in places of honor. Afterward, the crowds moved down the road to the Music Hall, where Theodore Parker had once delivered sermons in support of the theology of human rights now illustrated in the monument. There were two speakers at the commemoration and three thousand spectators in the audience. One speaker was Booker T. Washington, the most prominent former slave in the country; Frederick Douglass had died in 1895, the same year Washington gave an address at the exposition in Atlanta in which he promised to accommodate Jim Crow. Washington had risen "up from slavery," as the title to his autobiography put it, with the help of white philanthropists whom he followed in believing that if African Americans worked hard and got the skills industrial America needed, discrimination would not be a barrier to their advancement. In Boston the line of Washington's that drew the most applause shows what a great politician he was, alert to the sensitivities of a society devoted to self-culture: "The white man who retards his own development by opposing a black man is but half free." One witness said he uplifted everyone's heart.[59]

The other speaker that day was William James. Why was he chosen? He had already taught as a student and hosted as a dinner guest the man about to grow into Washington's chief antagonist—W. E. B. DuBois— but James was chosen to speak that day in part for his public reputation and in part because one of his younger brothers had served in the 54th, suffering grave wounds in the battle where Shaw and so many men died.

James wrote to Washington that spring in advance of the event, using carefully respectful language, offering a draft of his address, inviting Washington's "critical suggestions," and acknowledging Washington's "proved powers" in oratory. In letters to his wife and brother, however, he referred to Washington as a "darkey." The casual slur marked Washington as an outsider to liberal culture, invisibly coded Anglo-Protestant there at the end of the nineteenth century. The distance between the liberal belief in universal freedom and equality and liberals' cultural practice of homogeneity and hierarchy was large. It is hard not to see Washington as a mascot for liberal inclusivity and the wild praise for his speech—which promised that African Americans would cause no trouble and asked only that their efforts meet no opposition—as vocal displays of a racial egalitarianism that did not exist. But the event and the ideas it fostered became the basis for a future liberal culture in which practice came closer to theory, in which beliefs in equality helped a society pursue its realization.[60]

Writing the speech forced James to specify what he took the meaning of America and its Civil War to be. Undoubtedly his was an emancipationist understanding of the Civil War, what he called in the speech "the profounder meaning of the Union cause." That was inherited from his liberal context. So indeed may have been his way of talking about "our American religion," the faith in freedom and in "common people" working together for "their salvation." Yet because the occasion compelled him to think deeply about the meaning of the American creed and about what "Shaw and his comrades stand for and show us," James brought his philosophical thinking about pluralism and the purpose ideals give a life into his awareness of the wider social world around him.[61]

James had always been an ambivalent American at best, in love with German culture when he was in Germany and with American mountains when he was in them, allergic to American-accented English and eager to be liked by the American farmers who lived around his summer home in New Hampshire, cosmopolitan in his taste in contemporary thought and irrepressibly iconoclastic in his affection for cranks, eccentrics, and originals in multiple walks of life, the diversity he found in the United States. Designated to speak on behalf of liberal culture at the monument's commemoration, he started thinking about the country in terms of cooperation across difference, and he started representing America as an ideal of equality that could shape behavior as powerfully as religious ideals shaped an indeterminate life. The heroism of Shaw and the 54th demonstrates the practical possibility of lived equality. "Americans of all complexions and conditions can go forth like brothers," James said, "and meet death cheerfully if need be, in order that this religion of our native land shall not become a failure on earth." He used a line contributed by his wife, alluding to the Puritan idea of the New Jerusalem that would be like a city upon a hill. "So may our ransomed country," James prayed, "like the city of the promise, lie four-square under Heaven, and the ways of all the nations be lit up by its light." His uplifting message carried with it a warning, though. "Democracy is still upon its trial." No one can rest on the accomplishments of the past. The sacrifice of Shaw and his soldiers would be in vain unless today's Americans have the courage to live by the same civic vision for which those men died.[62]

The language of Americanism was so young then. The Puritans had started it unwittingly when they bequeathed a sense of exceptionalism and divinely sanctioned purpose as a sort of aura around the nation's founding ideals, built with the help of deliberate myth-making by people like John Adams. Right away three distinct strains of Americanism appeared. One used providence to create Manifest Destiny, which justified the dispossession of Native Americans and the expediency of slavery on behalf of a glorious American progress that had more to do with liberty—and a selectively applied liberty at that—than equality. This strain of Americanism soon absorbed the symbol of "the common man" as the personification of American greatness. The second strain appeared in the complaints of steadily increasing numbers of voices over the early republic and antebellum era as disfranchised groups and their sympathizers levied America's stated ideals against American practices. From the first petition by slaves through David Walker's "Appeal to the Coloured Citizens of the World" (1829) and the resistance to Cherokee removal on through William Lloyd Garrison's burning of the Constitution and the "Declaration of Sentiments" at Seneca Falls, Americans called on their country to heed its own universal principles by applying them consistently and seeing that the people being discriminated against were some of the best potential citizens possible. Frederick Douglass was a genius at this.[63]

The third strain of Americanism overlapped with both of the others, forming a middle way between them, and was embodied in the American Reformation and its commitment to moral agency. John Adams believed America was great, even exceptionally great for its novelty in enacting lofty ideals, but he did not believe it lived up to them, was never optimistic that it ever would, and was convinced that constitutional restrictions on popular liberty and a steady expansion of education were necessary for the health of a republic ever dependent on the judgment and values of its electorate. Mary Moody Emerson also thought America was great for its gift of liberty, but she saw what a stain on its glory slavery was and believed that the cultivation of mental independence was the only appropriate use of that gift. William Ellery Channing declared himself "always young for liberty" while believing that most people had no more business voting than his ten-year-old.

In this tradition of Americanism, freedom was always ripe for a "new birth," in Lincoln's phrase, because it had never reached fruition and probably never could.

James inherited this middle-way Americanism, coming into it late in life and at an interesting historical moment in the discourse on the American idea. On one side of him was the new labor movement, skilled in the use of republican language for protesting against how modern industrialism robbed workers of liberty, the right of self-determination, and the opportunity to cultivate the virtue necessary to sustain society. Modern wealth worked against the traditional commonwealth in this line of reasoning; the seemingly triumphant American goal of constant progress actually bred poverty rather than prosperity; and so laborers and their champions called for a return to preindustrial values in which hard work and merit paid.[64]

On the other side of James was Walt Whitman, the poet of democracy, who loved America so much that as a young man he had backed the Mexican-American War on the logic that American expansion was inherently justifiable: the more America, the better. Whitman was a great egalitarian who, when he sang the body electric, sang free of prejudice and full of love for slaves and women and sailors and stevedores. James enjoyed Whitman's poetry and sampled it in his own writings, treating Whitman as an exemplar of healthy-mindedness and optimism. What Whitman did not have was room in his expansive all-inclusivity for the problem of evil. He was a monist, from James's perspective, his optimism positively Hegelian in its faith that all would not only be made good in the end, it was good already.[65]

James could not agree. For him, a worker out of work who resorted to death by carbolic acid rather than watch his family starve was a grim fact of reality that could not be abstracted into an airy illusion. At the same time he knew that the ancient metaphor of never stepping in the same river twice applied to history too.[66]

At the tail end of the nineteenth century, James brought what he knew of the facts of modern industrial America into both his understanding of "our American religion" and his philosophical convictions in pluralism, interdependence, and the role of voluntary faith in producing practical action. He is not known as much of a political thinker, particularly not in comparison with his fellow pragmatist John Dewey, and with good reason: he did not view contemporary politics as his calling. Though he never claimed to want to bring a balm to humanity, he seemed to aspire to a somewhat transcendent role in his work, perhaps best revealed in a letter he wrote to his wife in 1897. "If one could be both poet, philosopher & historian," he proposed, "one could write a pretty bully book." He accomplished this in *The Varieties of Religious Experience*, where he was also a scientist, and he spoke in the sort of voice suggested by this conjunction of forms in popular addresses that made his psychological findings into moral precepts for dealing with human difference.[67]

In these addresses, James spoke on behalf of his audiences and himself in a "we" that was general without being universal. Addressing his public, a public limited by socioeconomic forces, he absorbed their perspectives into his own when he said "us Protestants," or "we of the highly educated classes (so called)," "we of the so-called better classes," and even "our Anglo-Saxon race." He adopted this limited collective "we" for a very particular purpose—to make the implied "them" less foreign, more alive. He came to this purpose through a logical extension of his psychology, where he had objected to the oversight of "immense tracts of our inner life" and pointed out the problem of sense, in which another person's consciousness is opaque to oneself. Now he gently accused his fellow educated elite of being culturally "hidebound," of being "stone-blind"—a term he took from Emerson—to the indubitable but remote importance of "alien lives" and therefore to "the vast world of inner life beyond us."[68]

Educated elites failed even to acknowledge, much less to recognize, that Chinese immigrants, Turks, unlettered workers, Appalachians, Viennese peasant women, and "the Italian and Hungarian laborers in the Subway" had inner lives as significant to them as his and his audience's were to themselves, with the same potential to marry efforts to ideals in the pursuit of lives worth living. One of these essays was in fact a clear social extension of his old "Is Life Worth Living?" address, now reformulated as a declarative statement on "What Makes a Life Significant." It was not education, or wealth, manners, or status. It was "*progress*," and since this can be judged only from within one's private consciousness it may be cultivated in the imaginative apprehension of others' "inner divinity" and measured in the old Reformation Christian virtues of "humility on your own part, and tolerance, reverence, and love for others." Even for "Chinamen." In fact, James's certainty of anti-Chinese prejudice on the part of a Cambridge audience was so thorough, he relied on it to clinch an argument about immortality when he asked his auditors, some fifteen years after the passage of the first Chinese Exclusion Act, how many would see "any fitness" in the eternal lives of the Chinese. "Surely not one of you," he predicted with confidence. This view he then condemned as "a remnant of the old narrow-hearted aristocratic creed" that must yield to the belief that "this is indeed a democratic universe."[69]

In these essays and in his favorite, "On a Certain Blindness in Human Beings," James preached what he now called a religion of democracy that not only included everyone in schemes of immortality beyond and of common good here and now. It also forbade judgment of others' incomprehensible values and ways because in a moral multiverse in which each individual's perspective is partial, each culture is partial too, each position "peculiar," and therefore each angle on reality is needful. Now, James said, "our ancient national doctrine of live and let live" holds a vital living key for the problem of labor in which workers and management do not acknowledge each other's angles on reality. The principle of interdependence calls for intersubjectivity also, for recognizing in the expression of one's own subjectivity the equal sanctity of the subjectivity of the other as well as the progressive value of the third thing created by dialogue between the two.[70]

The method for practicing this religion of democracy involves viewing one another from the plane of the eternal—"*sub specie aeternitatis*," James flourished to an audience that may or may not have known Latin—that is, as if from the disinterested perspective of the impartial divine. Imitating God's perspective is the antidote to human division, Hutcheson's disinterested benevolence applied to social stratification. "What most horrifies me in life," James explained to Pauline Goldmark when he sent her the volume in which two of these essays were included, "is our brutal ignorance of one another."[71]

James did not pretend to solve the problem of labor with this address, which was the beginning and end of his activism on the topic, but in developing his religious pluralism to include individual and cultural difference he went a fair step beyond Channing's extension of the right and duty of self-culture to workingmen. This was an important step that then enabled his student Horace M. Kallen to devise "cultural pluralism," a term Kallen coined in 1915, formally challenging the supremacy of Anglo-American norms for judging the many cultures of the modern United States. Yet Kallen was so uncomfortable with racial difference that he found it "personally repugnant" to take tea in Oxford with the first African-American Rhodes Scholar, and pragmatist, Alain Locke.

Kallen actually left African-American culture out of his argument on *Culture and Democracy in the United States* (1924) even while invoking the Ku Klux Klan as a menace to democracy and promoting his own Jewish culture as vital to the American symphony.[72]

Jamesian pluralism was not a ticket to instant enlightenment. It was instead a method for destabilizing any individual or group's sense of moral or intellectual superiority. In the context of his time and his own culture, that meant that James used liberal values to challenge the authority of the educated Anglo-American elite that had devised those values, thereby challenging the identity of American culture with Anglo-American culture. Kallen's work was succeeded by that of another Jamesian, Randolph Bourne, who argued that American culture was only as great as its immigrants, and only as great as its immigrants' continuing vital ties with their cultures of origin. W. E. B. DuBois argued that African-American culture was the most "American" culture because freedom held such a central place within it. Pluralism begets pluralisms. What tied them together was the universal ideal of freedom for the sake of progress, a freedom for which American democracy stood.

Until American exceptionalism failed. James was among the first to pronounce its demise. The most political he ever got came from his sense of betrayal when the United States took the Philippines as a colonial possession through the Spanish-American War of 1898. He really had been proud of America's difference from the European powers on the matter of colonialism, he found, when suddenly the McKinley administration and its jingoistic supporters induced the nation to "puke up its ancient soul, and the only things that give it eminence among other nations, in five minutes without a wink of squeamishness," he bellowed in a letter. James wrote lots of letters on the subject, speculating to a European correspondent "that the spectacle of our piratical dealings with the poor Filipinos would take out all the pleasure of your thoughts about our country. All Liberals here are in despair over it." He joined with other liberals in leagues and congresses and campaigns of anti-imperialism, disagreeing with fellow anti-imperialists who did not want the Philippines because they did not like Filipinos and disagreeing just as strenuously with "the cant about educating them to freedom etc.," which he found "simply nauseous."[73]

The thing about freedom and its institutions, for James, was that they could not be forced. The opposition to coercion was a long-standing article of the American Reformation, and of course was equally fundamental to the democratic idea. James had no pretensions to understand Filipino culture himself; all he knew was that American imperial policy was sure to violate its own democratic standards in administering its military conquest. Whatever receptivity to American influence the natives of the Philippines may have had before, the violence, divisiveness, and avarice of the American occupation would obliterate it.

By 1903 James had given up, admitting that to most Americans "the word anti-imperialist suggests a thin-haired being just waked up from the day before yesterday, brandishing the Declaration of Independence excitedly, and shrieking after a railroad train thundering toward its destination to turn upon its tracks and come back." James knew the train had gone. The traditional belief "that we were of a different clay from other nations" was a live belief no longer, revealed to be "pure Fourth of July fancy." The United States was just like any other modern country.[74]

But something else happened when American exceptionalism died. It died only for some, for those who saw as James did that imperialism was imperialism whether it flew the stars and stripes or not, for those like James who responded to evidence and reason as well as ideals rather than rhetoric and whitewashing and what he called "cant and humbug." James had inherited the whole train of liberal thought in America from the eighteenth century to the twentieth, and he had uncoupled it from the implied Anglo-normative homogeneity with which it had happened to grow up. Liberals from John Adams through Channing had been intent on using reason and conscience in their own lives to fight against passion and sloth, prejudice and partiality, and they had gradually extended the capacity for reason to ever greater numbers of their fellow human beings, enabling fights against slavery and against discrimination on the basis of gender, class, and ethnicity. Now James socialized the ancient contest of reason versus passion in the context of his nation's fall from grace by elevating a new type distinguished only by its intellectual style, not its ethnicity or status. His language shows a comfort with hierarchy that his own logic would soon date, but it was progressive language for his time to propose an "eternal division inside of each country between the more animal and the more intellectual kind of men, between the tory and the liberal tendencies, the jingoism and animal instinct that would run things by main force and brute possession, and the critical conscience that believes in educational methods and in rational rules of right."[75]

James probably had no idea himself how old these terms were, or how faithful he was to the standard "rules of right reasoning" Lemuel Briant had preached, even though in his youth he had read the same eighteenth-century moral thinkers that John Adams, Mary Moody Emerson, and William Ellery Channing had. But he pronounced a certain break between "the old liberalism and the new liberalism of our country" in the wake of any reason to believe that America was exceptional among nations. The Dreyfus affair in France, in which a Jewish soldier had been unfairly convicted of a crime and *les intellectuels* rose to his defense, had made a big impression on him, helping lead him to pronounce that thinkers had political work to do in America. Now that colonialism in the Philippines could no longer be prevented but merely managed, liberal intellectuals had to produce ideas that would work like habits on public opinion. "Phrases repeated have a way of turning into facts," he promised. "The older liberalism was in office," he observed, rightly, since it had in fact been the establishment, "the new is in opposition." American thinkers had no ethical choice but to follow their consciences into a wider sphere. "The great international and cosmopolitan liberal party, the party of conscience and intelligence the world over," he proposed, would become the new cultural home of those now disabused of the American dream. From this berth, James hoped, they would pursue their "campaign for truth and fair dealing," against falsehood and injustice, "until the end of time."[76]

REASON'S LICENSE

James believed he had work to do. His individual sense of calling was as strong and deep as a Puritan's, even without a personal deity and a pre-ordained cosmic plan, even with his levity and love of wit. The vocation he pursued, which he had described to his bride as service to the widest good he could perceive, was not something he ever felt he achieved or even explained correctly—which makes sense, since it had to do with expressing the inexpressible, with using the crude tools of language to bring unearthly truths to life in life, in a life lived according to a moral vision even the seer can never see in one frame. Cultivating one's individual moral vision and finding words to explain it was a lonely business, but it was also a social business, because in the culture of lived virtue that James inherited, the moral agent speaks with candor and humility to other moral agents who do the same.

It may be that no American thinker whose scholarly output matters as much as James's published so little in comparison to his social output. In addition to his many dinner engagements, camping parties, and social rendezvous, James was a great letter writer who always apologized that he had not written sooner or at more length and whose selected published correspondence dwarfs his entire published oeuvre. Moreover, even in that comparatively modest published body of professional work, he inserted long passages of other people's voices into his texts, letting them speak for him where they agreed and letting them illustrate the best possible version of viewpoints with which he disagreed. James was an elite, but he was not an elitist. The intellectual class he called upon to do persuasive work in the world was not to be elevated above society but embedded within it, actively engaged with contrary viewpoints and receptive to their better points. His philosophy had room for a variety of mental types; his immensely successful *Varieties of Religious Experience* sought to prove how different beliefs work effectively for different kinds of minds; his engagements across philosophical difference were, if anything, more cordial and dignified than those within circles of agreement. His spirit of intellectual charity was a vital part of his religion of democracy.

In such a spirit James traveled to Berkeley, California, in 1898, in response to an invitation from his old sparring partner from the Concord School of Philosophy, George Henry Howison. A public university, the University of California at Berkeley was built by Congregationalists, who by the time of its establishment had so warmed to liberal Christianity that the street named Channing Way cuts a prominent line along the campus. James prepared a talk for the occasion in which he aimed to describe the method of truth-finding that he had been employing these decades into his career, and which he now credited to Charles S. Peirce (1839–1914).[77]

James had already tried to promote Peirce more than once. He had dedicated his *Will to Believe* to him, he had arranged for Peirce to give lectures at a salon in Cambridge, he had given him personal funds and eventually took up a collection to provide the indigent philosopher an annuity. No doubt James felt he owed Peirce a personal intellectual debt, but he also felt that Peirce, who by the end of the 1870s had become incapable of expressing his ideas in anything but technical, abstruse language, was a genuinely original thinker who deserved more exposure in an intellectual culture in which original thought was always in short supply. So James gave the philosophy he had been calling "practicalism" the name "pragmatism" so that he could allot Peirce credit for it, little suspecting how offended Peirce would be by his misappropriation of the idea. He suspected even less how many admirers would seize the term and make of it a formidable school of professional philosophy in the coming years.

In the address James explained pragmatism in simple, practical terms. "Beliefs . . . are really rules for action," he said he had learned from Peirce, an idea with which Channing agreed and that Peirce got in part from his close reading of Coleridge's *Aids to Reflection*. James used pragmatism to justify his scheme of voluntary faith and to locate the discussion over values and the meaning of truth in the realm of experience and consequences. He later regretted the name as unsuitable for a philosophy meant to be popular. He sometimes followed an English colleague in calling it "humanism," but "pragmatism" stuck, the school took off, and eventually Peirce's reputation did too.[78]

This visit to Berkeley meant that once the Gifford Lectures were delivered, James spent as much time responding to critics as putting forth his original views. Philosophy was becoming a professional academic enterprise in the very same years the school of pragmatism was generating books, articles, reviews, and conferences, so philosophers with newly minted doctorates took to pragmatism—or took after it— with gusto. A. O. Lovejoy soon announced that there were thirteen pragmatisms, all intellectually bankrupt, and before long the arguments were flying back and forth across the Atlantic and between the pages of increasingly refined philosophical journals. This was when James's wife read one of his articles and confessed she could not understand it.[79]

James had to respond to criticisms with increasingly technical language because that is how specialized academics make progress. So with the support of other philosophers in France, Italy, the United States, and Great Britain, he rebutted the accusations that pragmatism was a quick route to relativism—that, as one journalist put it, it was "merely a kind of easy way of convincing yourself that any sort of a system or doctrine is true that you want to believe in. It is a scheme for turning the backbone of all religions into a chocolate éclair." James felt misunderstood. In the last three years of his life, he used increasingly detailed arguments and academic references to explain what he really meant. But to no avail. "The pragmatism that lives inside of me is so different from that of which I succeed in wakening the idea inside of other people," he finally confessed, "that theirs makes me feel like cursing God and dying."[80]

James worried about the social effects of this type of discourse. On the one hand he believed in the value of higher education for the sake of a democratic society, as he explained in "The Social Value of the College-Bred" (1907). On the other, too much higher education became a self-reflexive industry. James published a screed against "The PhD Octopus" (1903) as un-American and artificial, and when a young philosopher with a new PhD named Ettie Stettheimer wrote him an extended criticism of his philosophy, he responded at length. She deliberately misrepresented his views, he objected, confirming his sense "that the whole Ph.d. industry of building up an author's meaning by separate texts leads nowhere, unless you have first grasped his centre of vision, by an act of imagination." An imaginative act is an expression of inner divinity, a leap beyond the reach of reason. James did believe, as he said in one of his late works, that philosophers differ from others in that they must have "reason's license" for claims they make, but reason is insufficient. Something like poetry, which he invoked in his Berkeley address, must still be involved too, because originality is the only gold in thought. He urged Stettheimer—who, in a professionalized academic discipline, had less chance of being heard than Elizabeth Palmer Peabody and Ednah Dow Cheney had been in amateur arenas—to "turn your back on that sort of academic artificiality altogether and devote your great talents to the study of reality in its concreteness." James thought Stettheimer had the making of greatness, and took her seriously.[81]

The democratic frankness with which James took Stettheimer and a host of other intellectual unknowns must finally be accounted as an essential part of how he worked. His promotion of Peirce succeeded because professional academics later started taking Peirce seriously; some of his other promotions did not. Yet those attempts say something important about the intellectual culture of his time. Liberal thought helped incubate modern academic life by pioneering the use of conferences and journals in promoting formal settings for new ideas. Liberal thought also helped empower wide numbers of individuals outside those forums with faith in the validity of their own ideas. James gave as much credit to one such individual as he did to Peirce, although the name Benjamin Paul Blood has never inspired a dissertation. Blood lived in Amsterdam, New York, wrote letters to newspapers and to James, and occasionally worked up a pamphlet. James first came across Blood's work in the 1870s, finding it powerfully illuminating. They began a correspondence. In the 1890s James toyed with the idea of publishing an anthology of Blood's work but found himself too busy. He apologized to Blood in a letter of 1896, but also made a promise. "I shall work for your fame *some* time! Count on W.J.!"[82]

Fourteen years later, James placed an article about Blood in a professional philosophical journal. He called it "A Pluralistic Mystic," explaining that most mystics were monists but here was one who preached pluralism out of what looked like direct experiences of divine revelation that left the universe unfinished. Blood described the "anesthetic revelation" in which the things one cannot even feel become a part of the reality one knows. James especially admired how Blood both checked his insights against reason's license and kept in reality that which reason could not explain. In a line at once Romantic and resonant with the insights of introspective psychology, Blood described how "behind the proudest consciousness that ever reigned, Reason and Wonder blushed face to face." With copious extracts from Blood's work, James praised Blood's thinking, his intellectual bravery, and especially his writing. "Who of us all," he asked, "handles his English vocabulary better than Mr Blood?" James agreed with Blood that however hard one strains to grasp and state the whole, something always escapes verbalization and comprehension. "Let *my* last word, then," James wrote, "be *his* word:—'There is no conclusion. What has concluded, that we might conclude in regard to it? There are no fortunes to be told, and there is no advice to be given.—Farewell!'"[83]

James died the next month.

THOMAS DAVIDSON, LIBERAL

FREEDOM, FELLOWSHIP, AND THE SOCIALIZATION OF SELF-CULTURE

Ha! You old thief!" William James exclaimed when he caught sight of the Scotsman descending Hurricane Mountain, at the north end of Keene Valley, in the green flush of some April in the 1890s.

"Ha! You old blackguard!" Thomas Davidson replied, chuckling, grinning broadly, cheeks rosy, his hand already outstretched while James was still yards away, his dog, a collie named Dante, bounding at his side.

They had already been friends for twenty years when James arrived to help Davidson open up the menagerie of buildings he occupied from spring to late fall every year. Davidson studied there and wrote books and articles, and at the height of summer he hosted friends, students, and visiting scholars for the most important voluntary school of them all, the Glenmore School for the Culture Sciences. James tended to be elsewhere when the school was actually in session, but he visited Davidson at the beginning and end of each season, welcomed him as a houseguest in Cambridge, and debated philosophical points with him energetically and in great good humor—a good humor that was necessary for maintaining a long friendship with Davidson, who had a rather strong personality. Cheerful, friendly, and warm though he generally was, he could also act touchy, particular, opinionated, pushy, intellectually prideful, and scornful not only of convictions that differed from his own but often even of those that basically did not. James abided these foibles affectionately, cherishing Davidson's willingness to go his own way and relishing their "thoroughness of sympathy," as he recalled when Davidson was gone.[1]

There was a reasonable basis for Davidson's intellectual pride. Acclaimed in the *London Spectator* at the time of his death in 1900 as one of the twelve most learned men on the planet—though who the other eleven were, or how this assessment was reached, nobody ever said—Davidson had extraordinary powers of verbal recall as well as an extraordinary mastery of a wide range of texts and a stunning ability with languages; he was equally conversant in French, Italian, German, and English, spoke Latin with the pope himself, was fluent in both modern and ancient Greek, and picked up enough Arabic and Hebrew to study the holy books of those cultures. (His obituary boasted that he also read Spanish and Norse "and was fairly well versed in Czech, Russian, and Magyar," while another source credits him with Sanskrit, but there is no evidence in his papers to corroborate these claims.) Moreover, as a childless bachelor who lived by his pen, Davidson had thought deeply and steadily about his day's social, moral, religious, and philosophical questions in light of all this learning. He had reason to profess his views with conviction.[2]

He had no reason to belittle other people's views. Or did he? As a liberal, Davidson was committed to free inquiry above all, to the open exchange of ideas by equally divine because uniquely gifted individuals with a collectively great potential. By both conscious commitment and explicit declaration, he believed that everyone must work out their own operative truths by careful deliberation, that these truths become meaningful when they manifest in practical action, and that the only rule for common morality is love, treating others as impartially and benevolently as a truly good God would. Davidson shared this liberal commitment with other independent thinkers in the United States, to which he emigrated at the end of the Civil War, as well as in Great Britain, where he returned often enough to maintain significant intellectual ties.

Yet these fellow liberals were the very thinkers Davidson antagonized with his pugnacity. His trouble balancing the strength of his intellectual passions against his formal respect for human differences reflected not only a personal temperament that was by all accounts ardent to the point of perfervidity, it also reflected a central paradox of liberal intellectual culture. Liberals were to grow their moral agency through nonconformity, resisting conventional authority and traditional standards and fixed ideas in several ways: by cultivating their individual understandings as active forces capable of shaping practice; by accepting uncertainty and partial truths as inevitable features of an unfinished, infinite, pluralistic universe; and by expressing their convictions forthrightly, without regard for reputation. Davidson was an exemplary liberal in this respect, denouncing the adoption of "placards" as labels that closed off thought while expounding his positions with patience and care. Yet liberals were also to engage in mutual criticism, which meant listening to contrary views and exercising upon them the same analytical powers and discriminating faculties they used to develop their own views. This often led to more disagreements than agreements, more splintering than unity, and competition between personalities rather than cooperation among them.[3]

Davidson's style was so much that of the intellectual maverick that he often appeared to agree with no one around him. He attacked James's

"Is Life Worth Living?" "Human Immortality," and "The Will to Believe," criticized the efforts of the Free Religious Association to achieve the "freedom and fellowship" to which he himself was devoted, and picked apart the *Ethical Religion* (1889) of William Mackintire Salter even while lecturing to Ethical Culture audiences at the invitation of Salter's mentor Felix Adler, an Adirondack neighbor and a good friend of Davidson's. Focusing more on the gradations of intellectual difference close at hand than on the starker differences between liberals who would change the social order and conservatives who would maintain it was not, however, a habit unique to Davidson. It was part of the paradox of liberal intellectual culture and was actually a marker of what common ground liberals had achieved.[4]

From the beginning of the American Reformation, people like John Adams who did not think of themselves as liberal nonetheless held to the basic liberal premise of open-mindedness and inclusivity. It came from the Reformation Christian commitment to the divine right of private judgment, and it fostered the variety of doctrinal positions in New England Congregationalism in the eighteenth century. That variety persisted at the time of the Revolution, at which point the first parcel of liberal common ground was staked out. To be American meant to be independent, and to hold liberty and equality as supreme values. In other words, the ideal American acted like a moral agent while recognizing the moral agency of others. Within this commitment to moral agency, a range of interpretations of the proper meaning and application of liberty and equality coexisted with a range of opinions on topics from tobacco use to the relative literary merits of different authors, especially among the new liberal Christians of Boston who fostered a culture of lived virtue. They disagreed over biblical interpretation, the wisdom and propriety of different social schemes and educational methods, and the value of current scientific findings, but their practices of mental training and mutual criticism produced the next significant acreage of liberal common ground: a rejection of the doctrines of total depravity and predestination, a stance against slavery, and a commitment to self-culture as the duty of Christians who worship an all-loving God. Liberal Christians and their post-Christian descendants continued to argue about lots of things, but they could take for granted that those who moved in their circles considered it morally wrong to own another human being and morally right to seek progress, especially through education, both formal and voluntary.

By the other side of the Civil War, a liberal intellectual culture was fully established, very nearly synonymous with American intellectual culture, concentrated in the Northeast but increasingly active in the West. Liberal intellectual culture spread with migration, the expansion of public education, the ongoing growth and circulation of print media, and the new opportunities for higher education created when a pair of New Englanders got a land-grant college bill through Congress during the war. In this liberal intellectual culture, the paradox exemplified by the career of Thomas Davidson was on full display. It was at once the broadest mental practice in the country—possibly the world—and the narrowest. This paradox was in part a function of the common ground of values and knowledge achieved by that point. For liberals, a number of possible beliefs were totally "dead," to use the term William James employed for beliefs that were not live options. Some had never been alive simply because they had never been introduced to American circles, or never properly introduced; in his "Will to Believe," James used the impotent hypothesis of believing in the Mahdi—referring to a Sudanese who had recently declared himself the Islamic messiah—to illustrate a dead belief, one that was simply not on the table at the liberal American smorgasbord.

Such cultural selectivity, a circumstantial legacy of the ethnic homogeneity and well-to-do leadership of the liberal movement up to that point, represented one aspect of the narrowness of liberal intellectual culture. But it was actually counteracted by the practice of liberal culture, which pursued knowledge open-mindedly. Liberals traveled, learned languages, and read literature from an increasing variety of cultural origins, exhibiting a cosmopolitan curiosity that swelled over the nineteenth century until Thomas Davidson brought Arabic and Persian culture into a human story that included all literate cultural traditions on an even moral plane in an unprecedented way. At the same time, liberal organizations that had been overwhelmingly privileged and Anglo-Protestant became leavened over the last decades of the nineteenth century by the activism and leadership of women, laborers, and immigrants and their descendants, especially among Jews. Thus the narrow elitism of liberal culture—by its own logic of open-minded inclusivity—gradually broadened into some of the most diverse communities of discourse that could be found anywhere.

There was another sort of dead belief in liberal intellectual culture, no less important. It was any idea that had been so discredited by scientific or other reason-driven analysis that it was effectively finished for liberal thinkers. Liberals had been practicing the rules of right reasoning since the eighteenth century, sacrificing sleep to study, and sharing their findings. This led not only to an accumulation of knowledge but also to the closure of certain questions. By the last third of the nineteenth century, no liberal believed in the inerrancy of the Christian Bible and all of them thought that Darwin was essentially right about biological evolution. This put them in a rather delicate relationship to a wider American culture that was increasingly evangelical Protestant. For the first time, many liberals stopped calling themselves Christian at all, while most insisted that they were still religious, defining religion as Davidson did in terms wholly resonant with the American Reformation: as the love that prompts moral action, "a belief or theory of man's relation to . . . the universe, with action based on that belief or theory," an attitude toward life that calls for what he named "intellectual piety." The liberal pursuit of knowledge and understanding according to the new model of modern scientific inquiry used the old standard of measurement derived from the Romantic turn, that which evaluated practice against the supreme ideal of infinite, perfect, impartial benevolence. Or love. The liberal commitment to intellectual piety meant that the size of the category of liberal thinker was limited to those who got "reason's license" for their beliefs and could therefore agree on the liberal common ground of established knowledge, which is part of why universal education was such an important cause for liberals, who argued only over the details of education, not its necessity.[5]

Here is another face of the liberal paradox. Liberals like Davidson believed that education was "world-building" in two senses: education was the only way to build a better future for the world, and it grew an inner world within the student, the integrity of the moral agent. Liberals thought everyone could and should engage in this world-building. Yet this breadth of inclusivity ran alongside a narrowness produced by liberal consensus on some issues, which moved their conversation to more refined issues on which progress could still be made, alienating people who might have been welcome to join the conversation but had to master a certain amount of knowledge to participate in it, and to give up a certain amount of prejudice. Liberals argued over Hegel and monism, the single-tax proposal of Henry George, and the utility of yoga for modern life; they were often talking to one another rather than to the wider culture.[6]

Davidson believed that by building "Fellowships of the New Life," as he called the groups he founded in London and New York, progress would radiate outward as liberals shed light on social problems and led the way in solving them by the example of their communities' harmony, virtue, and enlightenment. He unabashedly expected that these fellowships would be composed of the more advanced members of the educated elite, whose influence would stir the better natures of the moneyed elite, who would then voluntarily ameliorate the working conditions of laborers—freeing workers, too, to follow the path forged by the fellowships. This was the old city on a hill adapted for modern industrialism.

Along with this trickle-down enlightenment came a new kind of American exceptionalism. Davidson believed that American democracy should be made into a religion, and he boldly dismissed the fitness for modern consciousness of any other creed. If liberty and equality themselves were made into articles of faith—and the only articles of faith—humanity could progress through free individuals freely developing their own potential and sparking the development of other free individuals through interaction and mutual stimulation on the ground of equality and the plane of eternity. William James got his *sub specie aeternitatis* from Davidson, his "religion of democracy" too. In a precursor to the "common faith" of his Adirondack neighbor John Dewey, Davidson proclaimed a gospel of democracy as the ultimate human creed, the only one capable of fostering both individuality and sociality, both the uniqueness of inner divinity and the equality of individuals in the infinite, both the particularity of human experience and the universality of human nature in eternity. Davidson used his knowledge of the history of human civilizations to tell an evolutionary story that led through American democracy and pointed beyond the primitive state of American culture to an ideal future, a fully exportable model of universal human freedom. Anything authoritarian, prejudicial, or dogmatic was a dead belief for Davidson—a dogma he argued with great authority and settled judgment.[7]

One of the things Davidson considered a dead belief was socialism.

He bristled at the very mention of the word. It was not that he was a reactionary, or a conservative, as some of those who eulogized him thought. He certainly wanted to see workers win their fair share of profits. His close-mindedness on the subject came in part from his having considered the socialist system fully when Marx's *Das Kapital* (1867) was first published, and then feeling weary as generation after generation of social reformer newly discovered it. His disdain for socialism also came from a fundamental claim of the liberal faith: that materialism was not the whole of life. He was religious, emphatically religious, like most of his fellow liberals. He thought that the most important part of a person lay deep within, far deeper than material circumstances. He disliked socialism because it was too superficial, aiming to solve the cosmic riddle of human existence by a cheap trick of trading the oppression of economic inequality for a new oppression of ideology.

In fact, Davidson thought socialism did not go far enough. Yes, rectifying the wrongs of economic inequality was a prerequisite for the utopia to come, he believed, but the chief feature of the coming utopia was universal freedom, and this socialism could not secure. He feared its potential for despotism, its requirement that its adherents toe its ideological line, making socialism the placard he despised the most because it had the greatest potential to promise progress while actually delimiting it. Yet socialism was the creed that took Davidson's London Fellowship of the New Life away—it became the Fabian Society—and socialism was also the vision that bedazzled the students of his favorite fellowship of them all, the Breadwinners' College of the Lower East Side, the one that changed his previously fixed idea about the role of the educated elite in producing the religion of the future.

The students of the Breadwinners' College were all working-class Jews, first- and second-generation immigrants in New York at a time when anti-Semitism pervaded American culture. They themselves became quickly alienated from their parents' Old World ways. Davidson loved them. He lectured to them once, and by the power of their response—in beginners' English, in the hungry tones of those exploited by unregulated industrialism and eager to change the world—he instantly promised himself to them for a spontaneous course in moral education.

Davidson had known cultured Reform Jews through the Free Religious Association, societies for Ethical Culture, and the Educational Alliance that sponsored his initial lecture, but these were unlettered Eastern European Jews, unassimilated and unaware of their own divine potentials, he thought. He taught them Plato, Wordsworth, and Tennyson, the philosophy of Goethe's *Faust* and the psychology of James Mark Baldwin, the wisdom of their own Hebrew ancestors, of Darwin, Emerson, Aristotle, Herodotus, and Wundt, ethics, logic, and correct pronunciation and punctuation. They learned quickly, and they taught him that Sundays were not sufficient for education, that the wages of industrial labor could not rent room enough for a quiet corner for study, that books were scarce but intellect was not, and that something needed to change if the change he wanted to see were ever to come about.

Davidson died before he finished his second year with these most beloved students of a lifetime devoted to education. They carried on his work into a Progressive Era in which more structural changes were tried and tested than Davidson himself ever would have advocated, but they did it on the grounds laid by his own ethic of individual self-culture made social through community life. He brought some of them to Glenmore; one of them became the philosopher who resuscitated the professional reputation of Charles S. Peirce. All of them seem to have abandoned socialism and adopted the idea "that the first of all spiritual blessings is freedom," as Davidson wrote them in a letter the summer before his death. The right use of such freedom is devotion to others, he

explained, without condemnation of ways they have that may be different. He illustrated this ethos of devotion to "universal interests" with a
passage from Wordsworth's "Lines Left upon a Seat in a Yew-Tree":

> *The man whose eye*
> *Is ever on himself doth look on one,*
> *The least of Nature's works, one who might move*
> *The wise man to that scorn which wisdom holds*
> *Unlawful, ever.*[8]

INTELLECTUAL PIETY

Born in 1840, Davidson grew up poor in the rural north of Scotland.
Most accounts say his mother was a widow; one says Thomas and his
younger brother were illegitimate; in any case his mother worked hard
on other people's washing in order to send her boys to school, where
Thomas excelled. His skill in Greek and Latin showed early, as did a
natural inclination toward spiritual contemplation. He took "Scotch
orthodoxy" on a child's ready trust, participating in the rituals of church
attendance and prayer and becoming serious enough about his Christian practice that in his early teens he read a book called *Saints' Heavenly Rest*, by a seventeenth-century English Puritan, Richard Baxter.
The experience of reading Baxter's description of saintly life here and
beyond became a touchstone for Davidson, who said that when he read
the book "a divine fire was lighted in my soul which nothing can ever
quench." He felt almost as though he could touch the reality of eternal
life, of a great effulgence that is human destiny. This was the book that
Max Weber used to illustrate the Puritan sense of calling, or vocation,
the earthly purpose laid for each individual by an all-wise, all-good

God as part of his heavenly plan. Davidson's Christianity did not last, but his sense of the reality of divine life and the sacred purpose of earthly life did, and so did his emerging sense of his own calling as an educator. As a "monitor-boarder" at parish school, he started teaching at age fifteen.[9]

As it turned out, Davidson's Christianity did not even last through his teenage years. "Then came what comes to most serious young men of my generation," he recollected decades later, "an eclipse of faith followed by various phases of belief and unbelief." He never explained exactly what eclipsed his Christian faith, only that it ceased to light his way, but the loss was not Darwin's fault; On the Origin of Species (1859) had not been published yet. Both Charles Lyell's geology from the 1830s and Robert Chambers's anonymously published and speculatively evolutionary Vestiges of the Natural History of Creation (1844) circulated among Victorian readers, as did news of biblical criticism, but they were not direct portals to unbelief. Rather, the experience of Davidson and apparently a good number of his peers may best be accessed through an autobiographical novel written by an English contemporary, Samuel Butler, who permitted The Way of All Flesh (1903) to be published only after his death because that was how scandalous apostasy remained in many circles. William James called it a "big truth-telling novel."[10]

Butler's account of his protagonist's loss of evangelical Protestant faith illustrates how the principle of free inquiry, which animated the Boston liberals to turn away from Calvinist doctrines, continued to operate in different times and places, all of which had their own character and therefore their own patterns of orthodoxy and heterodoxy. Only in countries where the church remained established, as in England and Scotland, could there be said to be an "orthodox" Christianity, in fact. When the book's hero, already an ordained minister, reads the gospels of the New Testament with an open mind for the first time at age twenty-four—"trying to find out not that they were all accurate, but whether they were all accurate or no"—the supernatural side of his Christian faith suddenly evaporates and he is left with only the vague sense that "the just shall live by faith" and no sense at all of what the contents of that faith might be. At a somewhat younger age, Davidson found himself in a similar position.[11]

He alighted on his first temporary spiritual resting place when he discovered the philosophy of Johann Fichte (1762–1814), whom Davidson termed a sentimentalist and who is often classed with the larger school of German idealism that includes Kant. Fichte's admirers in the latter part of the nineteenth century included William James's friend and colleague Charles Carroll Everett, who wrote a book on Fichte's science of knowledge. Fichte believed in the free will of moral agents as a practical fact of experience, which gave Davidson a terrific "sense of freedom," yet without a foundation. He soon found himself depressed, spiritually adrift, morally unhealthy, and tempted to revive his Christian commitment, but in a sign of how de-Christianization is not the same as secularization, his "soul revolted against the very thought" of such a return to something that had become a dead idea to him.[12]

He soon discovered the positivist philosophy of August Comte (1798–1857). He found it compelling enough that he considered joining one of the churches of humanity then operative in London, a church such as the one into which a later student of William James—Herbert Croly (1869–1930), author of the "new nationalism" behind the early-twentieth-century Progressive Party—was baptized as an infant, or the one that inspired Jane Addams on a postcollegiate trip abroad. Comte's scientific positivism described progressive stages of human development ordered by their prevailing system of belief. The earliest stage was theological, which depended on supernatural explanations. As a product of the French Enlightenment, with its anticlerical association of religion with superstition and unearned privilege, Comte is one of the sources of the secularization thesis that has associated modernity with a freedom from religious belief—an association always more true in France than elsewhere, but a potent formula. The next highest stage in positivism after the theological was the metaphysical, a stage in which Davidson could easily see himself as having just been in his romance with Fichte. Beyond that lay the promised land of positive philosophy. Knowledge could be scientifically acquired, bit by bit, and laid up with the motivation of benefiting humanity until all the world proceeded on a rational basis. It was a heady vision. Comte and his churches passed away, but positivist explanations of reality lay behind many a secular worldview from here forward. Davidson found it thrilling stuff in his youth, when the evident power of his own mind intoxicated his sense of what it was possible for him to achieve, but after a few years he found that an altruistic motivation was hard to live by without better tools than the scheme Comte provided. He entered a period of "spiritual darkness" that the works of Herbert Spencer—bedeviling William James in the same years—did nothing to relieve.[13]

Then he migrated to North America. He spent an undocumented year or two in Toronto, a cosmopolitan center that later hosted the most important phase of the psychologist James Mark Baldwin's career. Then he spent a short spell in Boston, almost equally undocumented but bringing him into contact with the religious liberals then calling themselves radical as they pushed back against a new Unitarian denominationalism. He moved to St. Louis at the end of 1867. Founded by the French and populated by easterners and German immigrants, the city had become a gateway to the West when Missouri was a flash point of sectional struggle for several decades before the Civil War. Unitarians migrated into the city in the 1830s and 1840s, swiftly founding educational institutions including the Washington University in St. Louis, brainchild of a Unitarian clergyman and his wealthiest parishioner. The slave state of Missouri sent Union recruits into the war, one of whose heroes was a Prussian immigrant named Henry C. Brockmeyer. Loquacious, tireless, with a huge crooked nose, Brockmeyer held forth on abstruse metaphysical concepts while gesturing with both hands, one of which always held a pipe. A colonel in the Union army who had set up a law office in St. Louis by the time Davidson arrived, Brockmeyer later helped draft the state constitution and rose through state politics all the way to governor. On the scene Davidson found William Torrey Harris, who had been enraptured by Bronson Alcott when they met at Yale in the 1850s, and who produced the *Journal of Speculative Philosophy*, in which Davidson—and later William James—placed some early work. At the same time Harris served as superintendent of St. Louis city schools. The very fact that those schools existed was a sign of the success of liberal Christian efforts as led by Horace Mann.[14]

Brockmeyer and Harris welcomed Davidson into their philosophical discussion group. Devoted largely to German idealism, the club included James's friend George Henry Howison, a handful of European immigrants, and an intellectual character named Denton J. Snider who inspired an Association for Universal Culture that lasted until 1930. They read Kant, dipped back into Leibniz, took glancing looks at Spinoza, and settled into a long study of Hegel, whose progressive view of history put Comte to shame by taking in all of mysticism and all of what looked like tragedy too in a hungry dialectic that let no contradiction escape unflattened. Davidson claimed to have already read and dismissed the value of Hegel by the time he arrived in St. Louis, but a philosophical discussion group anywhere was the surest place to find him in whatever city he resided, so there he remained for eight years, arguing against Hegelianism as "the wildest of nonsense" and starting a rival philosophical discussion group devoted to Aristotle. He earned his bread teaching Greek and Latin in the local schools thanks to Harris.[15]

And he enlivened his evenings—and nights—with the company of another newcomer to the Hegel group, a Hungarian Jew named Joseph Pulitzer. Seven years younger than Davidson, Pulitzer had emigrated in time to serve the last year of the war in the Union army before getting into German-language newspaper work and encountering Brockmeyer in a reading room.[16]

Davidson's intimacy with Pulitzer must be where he got his reputation for familiarity with the Magyar language. Historians can only imagine their pillow talk and whatever else their nights together involved—they maintained separate quarters while typically staying together at one place or the other—but the intensity of their connection was such that they remained in regular contact for the rest of Davidson's life. (After Pulitzer came into the fortune with which he transformed American journalism, he funneled some of it to Davidson for purchasing the property at Glenmore.) When Davidson left Pulitzer for Boston in 1874, Pulitzer complained that Davidson was "a cold-blooded heartless chap," declared himself a fool for continuing to cling to him, kept picturing his face, and longed for him to beckon Pulitzer to join him. "Yours forever," Pulitzer still wistfully insisted six weeks after Davidson abandoned him.[17]

Davidson had already behaved passionately with other young men, one of whom wrote him the same year he met Pulitzer, remembering "how queer [he] felt about [his] heart" when Davidson gazed at him fondly once, encircling his neck and snuggling into his bosom, and how it seemed as though Davidson were his "sweet-loving bride." Another said his highest hope had been that Davidson might be his "wife." It appears that William James did protest too much in his reminiscences of Davidson when he attributed Davidson's bachelorhood to the fate of an early romance with a girl who died young, venturing rather obtrusively to call him "one of the purest of human beings." James and his wife were extremely uncomfortable with his sister's apparent intimacy with a female companion and seemed entirely ignorant of his brother's attraction to men, a discomfort and ignorance wholly typical of their Victorian age and set, which makes the obscure intimate life of Thomas Davidson worth considering. The nineteenth century was "homosocial," one historian says, a world in which accepted emotional and physical intimacy among members of the same sex made bed-sharing such as Davidson and Pulitzer enjoyed unremarkable. The category "homosexual" had not yet been created; in fact, one of the members of Davidson's London Fellowship of the New Life, Havelock Ellis, helped found the field of sexology and named same-sex sexual behavior "inversion," the flip side of the heterosexual norm. Walt Whitman seemed more omnisexual than homosexual in his exuberantly loving poetry, but the religious fellowships devoted to his work were among the few places in the late nineteenth century where same-sex attraction could be tentatively acknowledged, somewhat less tentatively in England than in the United States.[18]

Davidson developed several more intense attachments over the next decades, all with males around twenty years old, all ambiguous. Some of his earliest publications were love poems, gender undefined. The fact that he never spoke his love's name shows how the inclusivity of liberal intellectual culture proceeded one case at a time, with sexuality not entering the docket in the nineteenth century. Indeed, the confinement of sexual behavior to marriage was an ethic so taken for granted among liberals that they barely discussed it, although Davidson specified that

"Monogamy is the law" in his code for the London Fellowship of the New Life. For the most part, the moral life by which liberals weighed their beliefs had to do with public actions between social individuals, and on these questions Davidson spoke out openly.[19]

Davidson's positions on the big questions of religious liberalism in the 1870s were scarcely distinguishable from those of most other liberals, however stridently he argued—and he argued so stridently, it seems, that he alienated everyone on the Harvard faculty but James and thereby eliminated any chance that he might get an academic appointment. Arriving in Boston in 1874, he often hosted the philosophical club where his friendship with James began, a club that included Charles Carroll Everett and picked up where the equally informal Metaphysical Club left off. Davidson also attended the Radical Club, where he spoke on individuality and heard comments from respondents including Thomas Wentworth Higginson, Benjamin Peirce, and Felix Adler. It was he who introduced William James to Miss Alice Howe Gibbens in 1876.[20]

During his Boston stint Davidson published two papers on John Tyndall, one of the popularizers of Darwin whose dismissal of religion roused James in those years. Like James, Davidson questioned Tyndall's authority to deny humankind its right to believe. Like a good liberal, he praised Tyndall in the vocabulary of the American Reformation for "his manly and determined opposition to dogma and authority, and . . . his demand for the free and unprejudiced discussion of all questions." The words could have been those of an eighteenth-century Congregationalist, but modern science had changed the context. Then manliness was a matter of listening to the reason within one's own breast and resisting dogmas imposed from without. Now Davidson felt sure that there was "a faculty above reason" and that science could neither explain it nor teach people to live by it. He left the country in search of some key to the higher life he craved.[21]

First he went to Greece. Having ruled out the vitality for modern life of Protestant Christianity, he decided to try Orthodoxy—but found it wanting. In art, though, and in the glorious architecture of Athens, he had his first experiences of sacred truth since reading Baxter. He could neither explain nor describe this sacred truth, but he was convinced that art could be "one expression of the Divine," and he went on to Italy in search of more. (He had brought to Europe a bright Harvard student named Arthur Amson, whom he sent to study in Leipzig, where Amson died suddenly. Davidson later dedicated a book on Greek architecture to Amson, a book headed by a poem he wrote about the Parthenon frieze with a climax in the line "I stand and blindly grope for thy dear hand." It may be that he went to Italy partly to escape the place where he had received the heartbreaking news of Amson's death.)[22]

No liberal since Orestes Brownson exhibited so open a mind toward the Catholic Church as Davidson. He studied the tradition thoroughly, declared himself willing to take orders if it withstood his investigation, and interviewed cardinals, priests, bishops, archbishops, and indeed Pope Leo XIII in his quest for understanding. He found Catholic piety compelling enough that he stayed in Italy for six years, although he returned to New England for the opening session of the Concord School of Philosophy, where he lectured on Greek life and literature. Then he went back to Rome.[23]

Davidson did not become a Catholic, ultimately finding its dogmas dead, "at best mummies of spiritual things that had once been alive." But its "organized life" he found truly admirable, truly divine. For the first time he encountered "men whose lives were full of God, who were never out of the attitude of prayer, whose acts form one long catalogue of self-sacrificing kindnesses." Davidson wanted to learn how to live like these good Catholics despite not sharing their beliefs. He went to Domodossola in the Alps, where a monastic community was organized around the legacy of the priest Antonio Rosmini-Serbati (1797–1855). Davidson came to believe that Rosmini was the greatest thinker of the nineteenth century, and he was voluble enough on the topic to convince James to review his volume on Rosmini's philosophy for *The Nation*. In the review, James prefigured his pragmatism when he called Rosmini heroic for cutting through the dualism between sentimentalism and rationalism by proclaiming the reality of the "world of experience" in which we practically live. For both James and Davidson, Rosmini appeared to have led a contemplative life and to have observed in his own mind grounds enough for faith. In Rosmini's writings, Davidson found a useful relation between the ideal and the real as both contained by the soul, which is "the principle of feeling." If the soul can perceive something to be possible, that possibility exists—it is in fact real, because the soul's perception is itself an existing reality. Rosmini found, in Davidson's words, "a luminous point in thought," an *"ideal being"* needing neither origin nor ground but only faith and practice. The aspiring heart has all the justification it needs simply in the fact of its own aspiration.[24]

Davidson left Italy in 1882 with his sense of his life's purpose firm and clear. He intended to devise "a philosophy justifying the claims of the intelligence which sees God to the supreme place among the human faculties" and to lay "the foundation of an institution for the cultivation of this supreme faculty." He thought that by modifying the insights of Rosmini he could land the philosophy. And to found the institution he went to London.[25]

THE FELLOWSHIPS OF THE NEW LIFE

He lasted maybe two years. Things started well enough. Davidson took rooms in Chelsea and invited sympathetic members of the local literati to join him for discussions of what he then called the "Vita Nuova." With his magnetic personality, his knowledge and cosmopolitanism and exotic experience, his flattering curiosity, and the sheer force of his will, he soon gathered a dozen or so followers and a protégé, Percival Chubb, who later shared his cabin at Glenmore before moving on to become a leader in the Society for Ethical Culture. As a young man in London, Chubb regarded the forty-two-year-old Davidson as a sort of guru, a mentor in shaping Chubb's spiritual development—a role Davidson appeared to like quite a bit, but other participants in their new fellowship did not. They "rather feared being so dominated by him as to have their own personalities dwarfed," one founding member recalled. When Davidson furnished a draft constitution for their "Fellowship of the New Life," the society discarded it in favor of a shorter statement declaring their devotion to the "cultivation of a perfect character in each and all" and the "subordination of material things to spiritual things."[26]

Liberal openness was a letter in the fellowship's law. "Unsparingly to put aside all prejudice" had been a first principle of Davidson's draft constitution, and the members of the fellowship agreed to keep their minds open to input from all ages and peoples and to recognize that "their own mental and moral status, the very conceptions by which they interpret experience," depended on the cultural contexts they had experienced and were therefore not fixed, not permanent, not immutable. (This was at about the time Davidson observed in an article that Christians hold their creed because of "a mere geographic accident" and "would have held a different one, had they been born in India or Turkey.") The constitution included pity for anyone who claimed final knowledge and the declaration that members were neither agnostics nor dogmatists nor skeptics. They were there to grow.[27]

And so they did—they grew apart. Their constitution was finally hammered out in November 1883, and by January 1884 the splinter group that became the Fabian Society had formed. Davidson returned to Rome in exasperation. Chubb's letters to him indicate that a personality conflict with a Dr. Burns Gibson had as much to do with the schism as socialism did, and Burns Gibson got Havelock Ellis, Edward Pease, Maurice Adams, Frank Podmore, and others from the fellowship to join him, soon attracting George Bernard Shaw, Beatrice and Sidney Webb, and Graham Wallas to the organization that helped bring about social democracy and the Labour Party in Great Britain. Chubb stayed behind, keeping the fellowship alive even while his own leanings became more socialistic. Finally he chafed under what he called Davidson's "intellectualism" and complained that his efforts for the "the insignificant & unknown or little esteemed Fellowship" went unappreciated.[28]

Chubb was probably right. Davidson had moved back to the United States, which now became his permanent home base, and moved on from trying to cultivate a community among Britons. (Soon he would be writing about "The Democratization of England" as something that lay in the future, an article in which he praised the Fabian Society but insisted that "the claims of all to the dignity and inheritance of humanity" were not yet sustained by the British state.) He found American intellectual culture much more receptive to his talents. Settling for a few years in Orange, New Jersey, he started a New York version of the Fellowship of the New Life, which lasted at least eight years. He also got back in touch with Frank Sanborn, who fit him onto the Concord School program and linked him up with the American Social Science Association (ASSA), then the most lively place in the country for discussions of political economy and how to shape a just future. He gave an address on art and education at the 1885 ASSA meeting and later became a featured speaker on the question of Henry George's single-tax reform. He campaigned for George in his bid for the mayorship of New York City in 1886, the year Davidson criticized "the political economy of selfishness" in an article, so George's reform in the interest of equity may have seemed likely to attract him—but it did not. Davidson admired George's character while rejecting his solution for modern industrialism, holding reservations on both logical and spiritual grounds that are important indicators of what values religious liberals held dear in the last decades of the nineteenth century. At the same time, Davidson's friendship with George indicates how wide the liberal fellowship in America was becoming.[29]

Henry George (1839–1897) grew up in Philadelphia, turned away from evangelical Christianity, moved to California, and came upon the thesis for his *Progress and Poverty* (1879) while riding on horseback in the hills of Oakland. He paused at a vista overlooking a pasture with cattle grazing upon it and asked a passing teamster what land like that cost. A thousand dollars an acre, the teamster replied. "Like a flash it came upon me that there was a reason for advancing poverty with advancing wealth," George saw, in the closest he ever had to a religious experience. "With the growth of population land grows in value, and the men who work it must pay more for the privilege." His reform aimed at sparing workers that superadded land value and taking it instead for a government that would do more for society. This was George's single tax.[30]

Davidson evaluated this reform on a platform at the ASSA meeting of 1890 along with William Torrey Harris, William Lloyd Garrison Jr., and the progressive economist Professor Edwin Seligman of Columbia, with response by George himself. The debate over the single tax was an important step in the long, uneven transition in American society from classical or laissez-faire liberalism to the modern liberalism in which the state actively guarantees rights. Scholarly use of these terms diverges from how historical figures spoke of themselves and their times. Late-nineteenth-century thinkers like Davidson and James called themselves "liberals" to signify their commitment to the moral and intellectual approach examined in this book; scholars have tended to follow the twentieth-century sociologist Louis Hartz in speaking of a secular political "liberal tradition in America" in which everyone basically participated, allegedly explaining why there never was a significant socialist movement in the country. Now, at the end of the nineteenth century, the religious liberalism that had been behind the extension of the state into education got tangled up with the new progressive liberalism that pushed the more expansive extension of the state in the reforms of the twentieth century, which ultimately manifested in the New Deal. This tangle produces altogether too many liberalisms. Even the noun "liberal"—as James used it in speaking of his type of anti-imperialist, or as "A Liberal" wrote into a journal in 1888 naming Davidson among a few others as liberals, "names which command the instant attention of every intelligent man in the country"—becomes troublesomely difficult to use accurately. Still, the ideas that lie behind the term remain important, and 1890 is an optimal year for looking at them. The conflict of the facts of modern industrial life with the promises of American ideals was acute, and proposals for the resolution of this conflict tried to balance liberty and equality. Edward Bellamy, in *Looking Backward: 2000–1887* (1888), imagined a sort of state socialism in which freedom and self-determination were sacrificed to material equality. George maintained only the "shell" of property ownership in his single tax, taking the "kernel" for the state. Davidson believed that the function of the state was the protection of individual rights and freedom, and since these are the grounds on which modern liberalism actually advanced in the United States, his argument is worth examining.[31]

Davidson agreed with George that the current system of private property was exploitative and in need of reform; he did not agree that abolishing it, through either the single tax or socialism or any of the

various anarchistic approaches then in the air, would bring about justice. He thought the single-tax approach took "a low and unspiritual
view of man, of the State, and of the relations between the two," because
it rendered human rights equivalent to animal rights and the state a
mechanistic convenience. Interestingly, for Davidson any form of socialism made too little of society and too much of the individual by attribut-
ing all value to solitary labor, a misreading of Marx, for whom the social
value of labor was critically important. Davidson wanted to increase the
value of the state beyond what these proposed reforms would do by con-
ceiving of human nature in terms of interdependence, citizenship, and
statehood. The state reflected not merely a Lockean compact for the protection of property but naturally arose, in Davidson's telling, through
the interactions of social beings for their mutual development. Individuals find their "true being" in community, the highest form of which is
the state, he said, reflecting his knowledge of the ancient Greeks rather
than anticipating any totalitarian ethos. He did not pretend to have a
reform to propose in place of the single tax, but he did have a question
whose answer would point to that reform, a question about how to
develop "the political virtues" through the state. "How shall all citizens
be best helped to realize their political nature," he asked, "with all that
that implies in the way of intelligence, sympathy, and helpfulness?"[32]

Davidson did not offer a strictly voluntary answer to that question,
as liberals before him had. He saw injustice in the distribution of property as a guarantee of widespread social injustice; therefore, he wanted
the state to get involved in regulating capital and property. As he said in
a different address before the ASSA, "if any community allows its land
to become the property of a portion of its members, these will have it in
their power to sterilize the labor of all the rest, and so reduce them
either to beggary or slavery." Since he believed that reaching for perfection was the goal of human life and that the state exists "for no other

purpose but to put a stop to the action of the sub-human, Darwinian law of the survival of the strongest and the tyranny of the most cunning," he believed state intervention was justified. He argued that it is not only a right but a duty "incumbent upon every community to regulate carefully, by stringent laws, the amount of capital which any man may employ in production" in order to maintain the fundamental "privilege of making an independent living," a privilege that should be protected for all as an American, nay a human, birthright. Specifics for the workings of such a state he did not pretend to have. But coming up with such specifics he called "the religious task of the immediate future."[33]

The ASSA was only one of many venues in which Davidson presented his ideas upon his return to the United States. An even more natural fit for him was the Free Religious Association (FRA), formed in Boston in 1867 after the first national Unitarian conference resulted in the adoption of a Christian platform for the denomination with an objectionable commitment to "the Lord Jesus Christ" in the preamble. The move may be seen as a sign of the larger cultural shift toward formal organization, which one historian calls a "search for order" growing out of a "bureaucratic ethos," and which also fed the rise of the ASSA. It was also consistent with the liberal paradox. Those who led the American Unitarian Association felt that they had established an explicitly Christian orientation as part of the common ground of liberal intellectual culture. Calling Jesus "Lord" is very different from calling him "Savior," as an evangelical Christian would, and learned Unitarians like Frederic Henry Hedge certainly believed that Christ's Sermon on the Mount stood up to objective scrutiny and comparative analysis vis-à-vis any other moral code on the planet, so he and other leaders of the denominational declaration may have been surprised by the objections raised by their fellow Unitarians. Yet both sides of this divide thought they were being true to the liberal spirit—much as both sides of the Congregationalist split earlier in the century thought they were being true to the spirit of the Reformation.[34]

Both sides had reason to think so. On the Unitarian side, since William Ellery Channing himself was a Christian and the authors of the platform thought of what they wrote as "Channing Unitarianism," the creedal statement seemed simply to spell out what they thought obvious to most Unitarians by that point, a verbal formulation of the liberal Christianity they had been practicing and refining since the dawn of the century. Hedge was deeply committed to liberal inclusivity, but he thought the line of Christian fellowship had to be drawn somewhere—had to be drawn at Christ. Hedge must have been aware of Channing's esteem for his ministry, given that when Channing needed his pulpit supplied toward the end of his life, he told Elizabeth Palmer Peabody he wanted Hedge to be the one to fill in. Peabody included this detail in her reminiscences of Channing, written a decade after the FRA founding; the controversy shaped some of Peabody's tone and selection of evidence in the capacious but not exhaustive memoir. Channing had a much more profound view of truth, Peabody said, than "the audacious thinkers who suppose all that is most sacredly true is yet to be evolved!" Peabody defended the liberal inclusivity of Channing by saying that "there is no modern free religionist who was more glad to accept the inspirations of eastern theosophists than he," citing as proof his correspondence with Rammohun Roy and his interest in a new history of Mohammed, but the key word there is "inspirations." Reading in non-Christian traditions was no different from reading in pre-Christian Plato for the common divine truth in which all share, but that only Christ expressed in a truly universal way, Unitarians like Peabody thought. This aspect of the newly formal Unitarian creed made it akin to the contemporary expressions of Protestant Christianity that one historian calls "modernist," in which earthly virtue took on a new importance over doctrinal correctness, a modernism that arose in the Presbyterian and Congregational churches and became linked with the Social Gospel, which also inspired Methodist and Baptist leadership. At the same time, Christian Unitarians like Peabody and Hedge were plenty radical in terms of their relationship to the status quo of American society—Peabody in particular crusaded constantly for humanitarian reforms and contributed to publications like *The Radical*, a serial dedicated to free thought on the cutting edge in which Davidson also published—symbolizing the important historical truth that Transcendentalism always included more Christians eager for social and intellectual change than post-Christians.[35]

The Unitarian creedalizers were trying to stanch the oozing of young Unitarians toward post-Christianity, so in that sense the Christian platform was conservative; they wanted to preserve liberal Christian truth. But they thought this was a truth that was all about freedom because it served moral agency. Peabody complained that "our modern free religionists . . . seem to themselves and some others to be a higher order of the Unitarian sect than Dr. Channing" when they depict "Jesus Christ as resting his claim of *authority* upon the correspondence of the circumstances and facts of his life to the expressed hopes of the old Hebrew prophets, or as setting up an *autocratic* church whose idea was to sacrifice the present life, and skip all its duties and possible achievements, in order passively to receive a reward for professions of allegiance to him." This, Peabody objected, was far from the Christianity of Channing, "and even of those Unitarians who most differed from Dr. Channing." She thought the free religionists completely misunderstood the Unitarian tradition from which they had so noisily broken.[36]

Of course, the free religionists thought the Unitarians had misunderstood their tradition, which many of the upstarts were extremely well positioned for evaluating. Octavius Brooks Frothingham illustrates this better than anyone; his father was the Nathaniel Frothingham whose lectures on biblical criticism Mary Moody Emerson used to hear, his brother Paul Revere Frothingham among Channing's first biographers, and now he advocated a "secular religion" engaged with "practical affairs." The founding members of the FRA were almost all Unitarian ministers who became incensed at the national Unitarian conference when the imposition of allegiance to Christ violated their divine right of private judgment. Even though most of them did in fact remain Christ-centered in orientation—at least up until that point—the simple fact of requiring Unitarians to sign on the dotted line of formal Christianity went against what they understood liberal religion to be. These liberals requested that the Unitarian declaration of faith be emended to attest that "perfect freedom of thought is at once the right and duty of every human being" and that religious fellowship was about "unity of spirit rather than uniformity of belief." This was the spirit of Channing and the American Reformation too, as even Orville Dewey—once Channing's assistant minister at Federal Street, and a defender of the sacrament of communion as well as the Christian preamble—admitted at the conference.[37]

In the long run the Unitarians reabsorbed their dissenters. The Western Unitarian Conference, founded in 1852, kept a looser liberal incarnation active throughout the late nineteenth century, while publications from both Unitarians and free religionists describing "our liberal movement in theology" over the centuries created a common history for the split groups. After the World's Parliament of Religions at Chicago in 1893, an inclusive approach to non-Christian orientations no longer seemed radical, so in 1894 the American Unitarian Association dropped the creed and took the FRA's "freedom and fellowship" as its new tagline—and took most of the former dissenters back with it. But in the short run the FRA played an important role in American intellectual

life. During the twenty or so years of its existence, it kept an open conduit to the liberal Christians through their overlapping participation in
the Radical Club, joint commentary on a common canon, and shared
audiences in the wider literate American public. The FRA may have
been small in membership—five thousand subscribed to its periodical—
but it played a vital and vocal role in American intellectual life not only
in providing a place for independent intellectuals like Thomas Davidson to air their views, not only in providing an American platform for
Indian voices like the representatives of the Brahmo Samaj theistic
church founded by Rammohun Roy, not only in promoting a lived inclusivity that drew the active participation and leadership of Jews as important as Rabbi Isaac M. Wise, the lion of the Reform movement in the
United States, but perhaps most importantly in articulating the liberal
universalism that underlay such inclusivity.[38]

It may be unfortunate that this articulation often sounded stridently
anti-Christian, but it was a very different sort of stridency from that of
Robert Ingersoll, America's first professional atheist, and a very different sort of rejection of Christianity. Liberals rejected exclusivity and
therefore actually included Christ—as equal to Buddha. Free religionists distinguished their pursuit of "positive virtues," in Davidson's
phrase, from the shallow negativity of Ingersoll, and they promoted
their liberalism as "a liberalism of earnestness," one in which the goal of
truly universal equality and freedom was ever kept in view. So while
free religionists certainly defended free thought—Davidson explicitly
called for "free-thought education" (which brought him an invitation to
head "The Freethought University" of thirty-six students)—their reason for defending freedom of thought was the larger goal of spiritual
development, and therefore social development, not mere freedom.[39]

The social mission of the FRA may have been preached more than
it was practiced, as Davidson argued in an 1887 address at an FRA

conference. Accomplishments like the FRA vice presidency of Frederick Douglass—who does not appear to have been more than a titular leader—may have been hyped as symbols of postracial inclusivity, but there were few other organizations in the 1870s and 1880s where such values were even recognized as worth pursuing. Both Frothingham and Thomas Wentworth Higginson, who led a "colored" regiment during the war and now advocated women's rights and edited the *Atlantic Monthly*, chose the FRA to vocalize their liberal vision on the platform and in publications like Frothingham's history of Transcendentalism and Higginson's widely circulated "Sympathy of Religions" (1873). A lot of other former abolitionists and social activists also participated in the FRA, believing that what they were doing there together, united only by a common aspiration toward the highest human development and a common commitment to liberal inclusivity, was historically novel and socially vital. "For the first time in religious history," claimed one FRA leader in 1868, "not only representatives of different Christian sects, but people of all religious names and of no religious name, are invited to come together as equal brothers, and confer with one another on the highest interests of mankind." Religious pluralism was the basis of racial and ethnic inclusivity. Where else could "our Hebrew friend" and "our India brother" find such a welcome?[40]

The most vocal and most stridently post-Christian free religionist must have been Francis Ellingwood Abbot (1836–1903). Abbot served for many years as the editor and chief writer for *The Index*, the FRA's periodical, where FRA addresses were reprinted, Brahmo Samaj letters appeared, busts of Emerson were advertised, quotations from Romantics and the Buddha were sprinkled throughout, and Abbot's "Fifty Affirmations" of religious liberalism began with the definition of religion as "Man's effort to perfect himself." Free religion was consistent in this definition with the post-Christian religion in Davidson's London fellowship, but there was more real religious diversity in the American scene, and no single orthodoxy. Also, where Davidson and his fellows had left Christianity and then groped toward some new life that could animate their residual religious longings, Abbot had been in the middle of composing a sermon on the religious necessity of submission to Christ at the time of the Unitarian conference, which exposed for him the exclusivity inherent in the framing of religion as "Christian." His free religion then pushed back so hard against a strictly Christian frame that it became shrill. Clearly, Elizabeth Palmer Peabody was reacting against these affirmations of Abbot's when she emphasized his unjustified use of the words "autocratic" and "authority" in her defense of Channing's Christianity. But Abbot's affirmations spelled out a newly pluralistic understanding of religion worth considering. He said that all religions were historically conditioned and therefore plural, but all rooted in human nature, and therefore one. Praising the "muscular Parseeism" he observed as part of the free religious movement in India, he suggested that the new prominence of "the universal elements of religion" pre-saged the imminent "consummation of religious unity in the actual rec-ognition of human equality and brotherhood." Free religion became, then, the recognition of universal human rights based on something sacred about human beings no matter what they believed. This univer-salism formed the basis of Abbot's protest against Christianity, his source for this very idea.[41]

Years before the Unitarian conference, when Abbot was a newly ordained minister with a stammer, he told a friend in a letter, "I would die, and be damned too, before I would mortgage my tongue." With this he voiced the central cry of the American Reformation, the defense of moral agency. He did not expect then that it would take him in a post-Christian direction, but first through the FRA and then through his opposition to an 1872 movement that sought to amend the U.S.

Constitution to declare the country a Christian nation, he became a spokesman for independent thinking, leading what he called "The New Reformation." He helped found "Liberal Leagues" across the United States and then was surprised when the freethinking elements within them spouted Ingersollian tones of amorality. He wrote a book called *Scientific Theism* (1885) and then was surprised when people like William James could "not digest a word of it," as James divulged to an English correspondent before telling Abbot of his "great disappointment at its contents." He wrote another book called *The Way Out of Agnosticism* (1890), and when Josiah Royce reviewed it sharply, Abbot went after Royce and Harvard too, finding himself defeated and humiliated in the end. Finally, he laid out his complete philosophy in an impossibly dense book that he got into manuscript in time for the tenth anniversary of his wife's death, upon which he drank poison and lay down on her grave. Everyone understood.[42]

Davidson was also dead by then, but while they were both living, Davidson provided Abbot some solace when he described the real "intellectual piety" in *Scientific Theism*. "That utters the soul of my philosophy," replied the gratified Abbot. Other liberal connections of Davidson's did not necessarily thrive. After a number of years lecturing at the Concord School of Philosophy every summer, Davidson got annoyed by how William Torrey Harris seemed to pander to the fawningly attentive young women in the audience, so he struck out to start his own summer school. In 1888 Davidson opened his first course in the "Culture Sciences"—by which he meant the systematic acquisition of the tools necessary for cultivating the higher life—at Farmington, Connecticut. The following year the property in the Adirondacks was purchased, the Concord School folded, and the experiment at Glenmore began.[43]

If you were an independent young woman in the last decade of the nineteenth century and you liked to read and think and write, or a man whose occupation provided leisure in the summertime and mental space for big ideas, and perhaps you had read Thomas Davidson's writings in one of the periodicals that reached you or you had stumbled into a meeting of his New York fellowship, you might have carved out time for a stay at Glenmore one summer, and returned the next and the next. You could take a boat up the Hudson River and then catch a train at Albany, getting off at Westport on the edge of glittering Lake Champlain. A coach would take you another twenty miles into the town of Keene, past the camp at St. Hubert's with Felix Adler and his crowd of ethical culturists and social reformers, past William James's beloved Putnam Camp too. Then one of Davidson's neighbors—sheep farmers, most of them, the foothills of Mount Hurricane being largely deforested in those years and reforested only over the twentieth century—would take you by wagon past Beede's boardinghouse where James sometimes stayed, past the Willey House, a grand country hotel that closed its doors to Jews in the 1890s and got boycotted by James thereafter, up a winding road past John Dewey's cottage and into the 160 acres that made up the Glenmore compound. In early years you could stay in the old farmhouse or pitch a tent nearby. In later years many students had built cottages and together had erected an impressive lecture hall with a massive fireplace and a wall plaque inscribed in Greek: "Without friends no one would choose to live, even with all other good things." (One year this hall burned to the ground and Davidson watched the fire with neither rage nor despair.) In a stream running through the property, bathing was done in sex-segregated shifts in a basin that had been deepened by cooperative student shovels year after year. A dining hall was built above the lecture hall; a horn sounded at seven-thirty each morning so all could gather for breakfasts of local dairy and eggs at eight. A path between the two halls was marked with signs: "Ascent of Man" at the bottom, "Descent of Man" at top. Lectures by a roster of thinkers and reformers were at ten, one, and eight; while the speakers held forth, some students sewed pillows stuffed with balsam needles. There were dramas, masquerades, and Davidson's Scottish ballads in the evenings, and sometimes a dram of whiskey. There were hikes and hammocks and expeditions to John Brown's grave. Davidson's library was open for borrowing, his porch for conversation, and his mind for questions.[44]

The purpose of Glenmore was neither to replace the Concord School nor to compete with the summer school of ethics that Felix Adler started at Plymouth, Massachusetts, in 1891. It was to create an earthly outpost of "The Kingdom of Heaven," as Davidson titled one Glenmore lecture, later published in the weekly journal *Christian Union* in the same issue to carry Lyman Abbott, the liberal Congregationalist minister, and a poem by Oliver Wendell Holmes Sr. Invoking Jesus's Gospel that the kingdom of God is within everyone and rhapsodizing on the power of nature's beauty to arouse inner divinity, Davidson painted his Glenmore as a vision of individual and social goodness based on moral agency. "What can we do in common," he asked, "in order to show our love to each other, in order to elevate the whole community, and make it as healthy and beautiful as the surroundings?" Glenmore was his best attempt yet to cultivate the spiritual qualities of political virtue in a fellowship in which each individual could grow partly through interaction with other individuals.[45]

Davidson wanted everyone to behave according to "The Ethics of an Eternal Being," the title of a piece he published in the *International Journal of Ethics* during his Glenmore years. In this article, he elaborated on his idea of the kingdom of heaven with pointed reference to the era's social problems and proposed solutions. If everyone measures their actions by the scale of eternal perfection, which is to say complete, impartial benevolence, they will create a society that is "a kingdom of holiness." Instead, today's members of the "industrial state" measure their actions only by material worth, pursuing the puny goal of accumulating "the goods of the temporal world" and aiming only "at the greatest possible amount of possession . . . without being called upon to exercise generosity or self-sacrifice toward any being." In Davidson's democratic utopia, in which citizens act as though they and everyone else are immortal, "each subject will claim property only in what he *is*, holding all that he *has* as a mere temporary trust, to be used as intelligence and love shall dictate." He wanted a society "which will correlate itself naturally with a civic state aiming at external freedom and justice, and offering the widest field for the attainment and exercise of every virtue." Freedom and justice would live in harmony at last, as they seemed to sometimes at Glenmore.[46]

Of course criticism was always on open tap at Glenmore, where James did a trial run of his memorial address for Shaw and the 54th. The speech "fell *very* flat on all concerned," he reported worriedly to his wife. Davidson declared that "it is no oration at all but an essay." James had some weeks left to improve matters; Goethe was not so lucky. Davidson knew Goethe's *Faust* (1808–32) so well that he could recite large parts of it in German without consulting the text, having read it and Dante's *Divine Comedy* (1472) at least fifty times each, he claimed. Yet he pronounced *Faust* "a distinct failure" on moral as well as aesthetic grounds. Believing like James that "true poetry may contain all the content of philosophy and much of that of religion" as well as of history, he used his analysis of *Faust*—in lectures he refined over a number of years by delivering them at Concord, Glenmore, New York City, and Cambridge—to explicate his own philosophy as much as to engage with that of Goethe. In fact, reviews of the book eventually generated from these lectures, like reviews of Davidson's books on Tennyson and Rousseau, charged him with errors of both fact and interpretation as well as a general tendency to make grand pronouncements far beyond the reach of his evidence. That was probably fair. Davidson forever offered the most debatable opinions in the most certain tones, but those opinions were important more for what they said about Davidson's synthesis of liberal religion than for any light they shed on Goethe.[47]

Davidson depicted Goethe's moral struggle as a contest between the universal spirit of the divine and the individual spirit of Mephistopheles. Goethe's demon was not wholly evil but only "partial," unable to see beyond the "empirical" realm of the "phenomenal" and therefore logic-bound, grossly material. Blind to the value of the ideal realm himself, Mephistopheles lures his victims toward disintegration and differentiation until individuals are separated from one another like "atoms." Similar to what James did in his pragmatism, Davidson sought—by bringing together the empirical and ideal—to preserve the distinctness of individuality without collapsing into so many possessive individualisms. For him, the ideal was to be found in the social realm, where eternality is the invisible characteristic everyone has in common, and where social interaction leads toward the "integration" of differentiated parts. Individuals interacting positively with one another can approach the universal by following the impulse of godly "love" and expressing this love through "humility and charity" as well as "rational, self-determining action."[48]

Davidson had absorbed the spirit of the American Reformation and made it into a global story, able to be read in the Rig-Veda, according to his sources, in the ancient Greeks, modern Germans, and American idea as well. In Davidson's religion of democracy, human beings do indeed "rise to likeness with God" through a kind of "evolution" in which diverse individuals interact to produce a higher collective social good. Each individual contains "a true moral self," is a sacred being "in whose heart sits God in the form of a right will." By expressing and acting upon this inner divine, individuals become free and rise to "universality," treating one another as equally free and equally sacred. Davidson used *Faust* to describe the arc of human history as one of the "emancipation of the individual from institutionalism," repeating John Adams's central claim in his *Dissertation on the Canon and Feudal Law* and updating it to solve the problem of modern life. Bringing together the individual and the social leads human beings to realize their inner divinity and actualize in the world of sense the ethics of the eternal. "This is the new gospel of deed," said Davidson, "the gospel of modern life, and it is a noble one."[49]

One of the most interesting aspects of the liberal paradox on display in Davidson is how this noble vision of his was at one and the same time notably cosmopolitan—global in the evidence it drew upon, universal in scope—and unapologetically Americanist. The global side can be seen in the use he made of Islamic materials in his histories of human civilizations. He spent time in Cairo at least twice in the 1890s, ostensibly to learn Arabic, though there is little documentation of his time there and little concrete evidence that he used Arabic in his research. Instead he used mostly German scholarship to examine "The Creed of the Sultan," as he titled one article, and to learn about the eleventh-century Egyptian movement "The Brothers of Sincerity," as he titled another, in order to build an understanding of how Muslim education fit into the wider human story of how peoples were to be instructed, and with what purpose. Davidson's standard for judgment was clear and consistent: Are the members of any given society "educated for subordination and function," he wanted to know, or "for freedom"? Do individuals in a given society rise to "moral freedom," "critical reflection," and "action determined by reflection and contract," or are laws to be "obeyed rather as authorities than as embodiments of reason"?[50]

In Islam Davidson found both the ideal of submission to authority—the word Islam itself means submission, he noted—and the impulse of freedom. Arabs "set the example of opening institutions of learning for all the world," providing not only a template for "Christian Europe" but also concrete materials so that when the medieval universities of Europe followed the great Muslim universities, it showed that Europeans "had not sat at the feet of the Muslims in vain." Including chapters on Muslim education and education in China and India distinguished Davidson's history from previous histories of education, although he minced no words about what Islam needed: "rational enlightenment." Until Muslims have "learned the lesson of toleration," he wanted the sultan "dethroned, and all political power taken out of the hands of the Muslim." (By whom, he did not say.) Meanwhile, using the universal standard of freedom, he called Islam "the principle of Judaism carried to its logical conclusion, plus primitive Christianity untouched by Hellenism," and gave the Muslim faith credit for many social improvements. "It checked the very common practice of burying female children alive," he said, "it effectually proscribed drunkenness; it lightened the yoke of slavery; it enjoined kindliness to women and gave many laws in their favor."[51]

The standard of gender equality was possibly the most important parcel of liberal common ground. If the root of modern feminism can be traced to the rational dissenter Mary Wollstonecraft in England, the root of American feminist culture can be traced to her first readers in New England. John Adams was one such reader, Mary Moody Emerson another. Channing—another—went against the practice of *femme couverte* by insisting that his wife keep her property after their marriage. Although liberals differed on specific social questions related to gender, they agreed that women were full moral agents, deserving of education and opportunity and independence. The post-Christian Boston liberal Margaret Fuller was the first thinker to develop the principle of moral agency into a considered argument about the infinite possible range of intellectual attainments of which women are capable and the dependence of males' freedom and scope for self-culture on the liberty and progress of females. In the Free Religious Association, the only reservations voiced against the Brahmo Samaj targeted the relatively primitive state of women's rights in India and the Brahmo Samaj leader Keshub Chunder Sen's possible maltreatment of his wife. Many suffrage leaders appeared at meetings of the Radical Club, where Julia Ward Howe once sighed that "there is something very divine about a caucus" and William Henry Channing said that granting the vote to women will be "the next step towards getting the voice of humanity as a whole."[52]

Davidson marched right in step with this ethic of gender equality. One of the women who attended Glenmore remembered him as "the only teacher I ever had who did not condescend to the alleged incapacity of a woman's mind," and he was careful to use gender-inclusive language in much of his work. Feminism was by no means a major focus of his thinking, but it was a fundamental article of his democratic faith. He simply extended the principles of freedom and equality to the case of women in society and included the question of how family relations might be changed to boost social development. He thought the patriarchal nuclear family belonged to "an obsolete, inhumane, and un-American order of things, against which the apartment house and the family hotel are clear protests." He wanted to see child care and meal preparation collectivized, an idea he may have taken from the pioneering feminist Charlotte Perkins Gilman—or may have given to her. In 1896 she too came to Keene Valley, where she heard a lecture by "that impressive man of learning, Professor Thomas Davidson," on which she took plentiful notes at "great gain for my head," she recorded in her diary. Davidson said in an 1899 address that the man "whose labor and thought are expended altogether on his family is only one step above the man who labors and plans only for himself." And Gilman, in her *Women and Economics* of the same year, said something very Davidsonian:

> Work the object of which is merely to serve one's self is the lowest. Work the object of which is merely to serve one's family is the next lowest. Work the object of which is to serve more and more people, in widening range, till it approximates the divine spirit that cares for all the world, is social service in the fullest sense, and the highest form of service that we can reach.

From the liberal point of view, the emancipation of women from the constrictions of nuclear family life was a positive social good, one on which human development depended.[53]

A higher scope for the development of women was far from the only social good to which the principle of equality pointed. Gender equality was linked in Davidson's mind with what was distinctive about America, namely its exceptional devotion to the universal ideal. Criticizing Goethe's weak, submissive, naïve, and narrow Gretchen—the best the benighted German could come up with for a heroine—Davidson crowed that "in the history of woman 'ante-American' means 'antediluvian.'" In a similar vein to that of William James in "The Gospel of Relaxation" (1899), Davidson claimed that "only in America" has society "come fully to appreciate that for women, as well as for every one else, life swimming is best learnt in the stream of life." He never tired of linking female emancipation to American greatness in his work, in which the American religion James thought threatened by American imperialism was alive and well and just different enough from a patriotic American creed of exceptionalism to bear scrutiny. Davidson was more optimistic than James about the prospects of American society given its relatively milder form of imperialism, he thought, but he did not attribute American greatness to Anglo-Saxonism, industrial might, natural resources, or even its history. The most important aspect of Davidson's Americanism was its ethic of universal rights, which made it impossible for him to claim that the United States had already manifested the high potential he would take as a practical ideal. As he put it, Americanism is the noblest religion because it "best insures the realization of the highest manhood and womanhood, and points them to the highest goal,—a goal which it is their task throughout eternity to approach without reaching." In other words, the meaning of Americanism for Davidson was not American at all, but human and therefore divine.[54]

This then was his message for the world. To treat "American Democracy as a Religion," he explained in an 1899 article, was to recognize that the "world must be fundamentally a democracy" made up of "essentially individual" human consciousnesses whose "progress towards well-being is entirely due to social interaction, and is greater as that deepens and widens." The more diverse and broad a society's webs of association, the more that society progresses toward realizing divine consciousness. Davidson wanted his audience to "discover a religion in the principles upon which our civic life rests" and to live by the equal autonomy and freedom of everyone else even though we are separated from one another by the problem of sense and therefore "we are hypotheses to each other." By developing relationships of active, mutually respectful interactions, individuals "have larger worlds."[55]

Davidson anticipated objections to his treatment of a form of government as a religion. He revealed just how select his own mentally diverse world was when he dismissed such objections as "mere prejudice, born of traditional notions." At a time in history when the majority of Americans professed an evangelical Christian faith, Davidson pronounced the transcendent deity a dead article, declaring it a simple matter of fact that "the old external god, an autocratic spirit among spirits, being incompatible with freedom and ethical life, finds no justification for continued existence as a factor in thought." Roughly contemporary with Nietzsche—whom Davidson does not appear to have read—but a crucial valence apart, he did declare a God dead, ridiculing the idea of God as "a being reflecting barbaric splendor from a cloudy throne, to awe a race of helpless, cringing sycophants." But he believed he had found real God. "Our American ideal . . . gives us the only God about whom there can be no doubt, the God whom each one of us knows as the deepest impulse in his own soul."[56]

A fellowship that excludes those who worship a God above is a narrow fellowship indeed, yet seemed as wide as the sky to Davidson. His work at Glenmore and elsewhere aimed to impart views of which "the educated classes stood so greatly in need," one of his Glenmore students recalled, and therefore reflected his understanding of their character as well as of truth itself. At the same time, his belief in universal inner divinity made him treat individuals from outside that educated elite as equals with his customary students, and the appeal of Glenmore proved to transcend differences of class and ethnicity. At about the time he published his article on American democracy as a religion, one of the working-class Jews from his Lower East Side college came to Glenmore for the first time and, "writing to friends in the New York home he had temporarily left, dated his letter 'Heaven, Aug. 14th, etc.'"[57]

EDUCATING WAGE EARNERS

"A free life is the only life worthy of a human being." These were the first words Davidson spoke to the audience that, unbeknownst to any of them at the time, included the nucleus of a class he came to cherish so much that he later signed his letters to them with salutations like this: "Yours with a love that will not tire." On this first occasion of their meeting, though, he was wary of an audience he had been warned would include socialists, anarchists, and revolutionaries with the most radical and oppositional attitudes. So he decided "to avoid disputable assertions" in his lectures and only to make truth-claims he considered beyond controversy—only to assert the established common ground of liberal intellectual culture. The sponsors of the lectures were dubious, telling Davidson that working-class immigrants wanted to hear lively talks on current events "profusely illustrated with stereopticon," but Davidson refused. "I don't wish to do at second hand the work of the periodical class," he sniffed. He was committed, he said, to conveying "the highest truth I know in the simplest terms I can find," so this was why he spoke of freedom and human life. "That which is not free is not responsible, and that which is not responsible is not moral. In other words, freedom is the condition of morality. That is simple enough."[58]

Simple enough, since the association of freedom and morality was old news in liberal intellectual culture, but not so simple for someone who is uneducated and therefore cannot help but be "a slave to other people's opinions," Davidson continued. Not so simple, either, in a society rife with the "snobbish, undemocratic notion that the so-called 'lower classes' require no more education than suffices to enable them to earn a livelihood," he observed in a footnote to his self-satisfied memoir of the educational endeavor that grew out of that lecture.[59]

Davidson was far from alone in progressive America in trying to educate the working classes beyond occupational function. The Educational Alliance that hosted his lectures had been formed in 1891 by upscale Jews intent on Americanizing the new immigrants, and it was in good company in urban centers at that peak of both immigration and unregulated industrial capitalism. Indeed, Davidson's lack of uniqueness is exactly what makes his approach so instructive. Brashly though he claimed the singularity of his views and methods, he was actually a sponge for thought and culture, so what he expressed reflected the liberal environment in which he developed his convictions. At the same time, his direct interface with immigrant workers was historic. Channing had lectured to workingmen twice. Emerson had tried dining with his servants and found it awkward. George Ripley had spoken with ostentatious familiarity to unlettered workers at Brook Farm. William James had imagined himself into the viewpoint of workers constructing a skyscraper, chatted with tradesmen in his employ, and read one first-hand account by a Princeton-educated Christian of "tramping" among laborers. Davidson spent the last two years of his life living for immigrant workers. He started with a knot of fifty-six out of the six hundred who came to his opening lecture series.[60]

After forty years of teaching, he found himself facing his first working-class audience, his first audience made up largely of immigrants, his first audience reared in a non-Christian religion. Pitching intellectual culture to them, he started incorporating their viewpoints into his teaching also. His first observation? Something Channingesque in his first lecture was wrong. Davidson had advised that each member of the audience keep a stack of books and a clear surface in "some undisturbed corner" at home so that they could study in their off hours. He soon learned "what ignorance" of the working and living conditions of these tenement dwellers this suggestion showed, and "what bitter irony" his words contained. The students taught him what issues were important to them, and he taught them how to think for themselves so that they could be no one's slave.[61]

At least that was what he wanted to do. He brushed up on his Magyar, picked up some Russian and Czech, and got to work—in English. The class started with weekly meetings, which grew to five classes per week, then to eight with the help of extra instructors. The number of students grew to 150 and the proportion of students who were female also steadily increased. (As described by the writer Anzia Yezierska, peer of these students, education for girls was not necessarily encouraged by parents in this community.) Davidson assigned a rigorous reading list and required recitations and 250-word essays, which he graded scrupulously for comprehension, style, and usage. He flatly "refused to admit to the class any one who could not attend regularly and do all the reading and writing assigned," which resulted in a group so dedicated to the work, they continued it faithfully during the summers Davidson spent away at Glenmore, reporting their progress in weekly letters to him and reading his responses aloud. This achievement represented the fruition of his intention to teach them "faith in individual effort and manly and womanly self-dependence," as he put it in one letter to them, and his resolve "to make *them* do as much of the work as possible," as he explained in his history of the experiment. The dominant tone of his letters to them is pride in their work.[62]

He also took pride in their social position—it proved his theory about universal inner divinity. From the first meeting he noted how most of them spoke in a "very foreign accent," while all of them claimed to be there only out of a desire for knowledge. An essay on Aristotle of such richness that the group discussed it for several evenings was written by "a young woman from southern Russia, who makes her living with her scissors and needle," while an admirable essay on religion was written by "a clerk in a hat factory." Davidson was no more amenable to socialism than ever, insisting that those among them who professed adherence to Marx were not exercising right reasoning, but he believed the emancipation of the working class was coming just as the emancipation of the bourgeois had come in the age of revolutions. Now the workers were to become full moral agents, and as equals with employers who grasped their interdependence, laborers themselves would see to "the safeguarding of moral liberty and its conditions." The only way for this to happen, Davidson thought, was for workers to demand "culture and freedom, and colleges where these may be learned."[63]

So began the Breadwinners' College of the Lower East Side, which continued for several years after Davidson's death and eventually merged into the City University of New York. Some of his followers organized themselves into a group called Rodfe Tsedek—Hebrew for "Seekers after Righteousness"—while others continued Glenmore's programs until at least 1909, and still others organized the Thomas Davidson Society, which ran schools from elementary age through college, organized nature outings, neighborhood clubs, and culture classes, and tried to keep his spirit alive. Central in these efforts was Morris Cohen, who had been a socialist ready to heckle Davidson at that first lecture and who eventually got a PhD in philosophy at Harvard. Other Davidsonians became social reformers, educators, and intellectuals. Yet they did not adhere to any program. Davidson had warned that "universal human well-being does not mean universal leveling," which meant that progress did not tend toward sameness but toward differentiation and interaction. As ham-handed as he could be, the thing he was trying to convince them of was the importance of resisting any fixed program of thought. His liberal spirit was expressed best in one of his last letters, written when he was already quite ill. "Creeds make sects; truth makes men," he summed up the liberal ethos. "I trust, therefore, you will endeavor to arrive at truth and to live it. Above all, cultivate the faculty for truth, the power of seeing things without veil or prejudice."[64]

Toward the discovery of truth, he had a request. "Will those of you who have been, or are, engaged in shops or factories give an account of your experience, in writing? A collection of such accounts would be most valuable, and might be published." Liberal intellectual culture was about to change.[65]

The inclusion of diverse voices was a big part of that change, one that Davidson would not live to see, and one that departed in both tone and content from his certainties of taste and judgment as well as his canon of classics and poetry. His career illustrates how liberal common ground was extended in this period to make this change emerge, as the creation of a pluralistic framework theoretically equalized individuals from whatever background as well as non-Christian religious orientations. Davidson also oversaw the clarification of the liberal commitment to uphold not only the moral agency of individuals but also the social environment in which they live and work for the sake of higher collective progress. Turning Channing's self-culture into a social commitment, Davidson reflected on how far they had come and where they had to go. "Thus far we have mainly sought self-culture," he observed; "in the future we must go out and impart the blessings of culture to others."[66]

Davidson died thinking he knew what that culture was and should be, but the logic of his own intellectual culture questioned such conviction. As liberal thought pulled away from its berth in the American Reformation, it became linked to the concept of democracy as a set of ideals capable of guiding practice, as indeed a kind of religion, and therefore one that depended on the taste and character of all its practitioners.

6.

WILLIAM MACKINTIRE SALTER, NEW LIBERAL

ETHICAL CULTURE AND
SOCIAL PROGRESS

In 1880 William James received a letter from a Unitarian minister serving a congregation in Roxbury, just outside of Boston. William Mackintire Salter, eleven years James's junior, must already have met "Dear Prof. James" when he plied him with technical philosophical questions in this and subsequent letters, receiving in return both an offprint of "The Feeling of Effort," which Salter then publicized in the *Unitarian Review*, and personal servings of James's metaphysical reflections and kindly humor. "But to discuss free-will in a note is ridiculous," James observed at last. Soon the two were arranging visits where more lively conversation could take place.[1]

Both admiration and criticism were mutual. Salter was dissatisfied with how James argued for practical belief in "Rationality, Activity, and Faith" (1882) because for Salter "some ultimate phil[osophical] conviction & on purely phil[osophical] grounds is a matter of life & death." Poor James. "Et tu Brute!" he replied. "I have never received a harder blow than from the discovery that you too were dominated by the passion for possessing truth in a *closed* form." James taught Salter how to hold truths provisionally. Salter taught James how to apply them to social questions.[2]

Soon Salter left the Unitarian Church and joined Felix Adler's Society for Ethical Culture, becoming the leader of its Chicago fellowship. By 1883 it was his turn to send James pamphlets of his own addresses on topics including "The Social Ideal" and "Why Unitarianism Does Not Satisfy Us," work that James praised emphatically. From then on, it appears that each read everything the other wrote.

"Can't you on your way home join us in Keene Valley for a week or so?" James wrote Salter, then in Paris, in the summer of 1884. "Adler I suppose will be there; I, and Mary Gibbens and possibly Thomas Davidson will be at the Putnam's settlement close by." Salter had made it into the Adirondack circle. Soon he made it into the family circle as well, for he and Mary Gibbens—the sister of James's wife, Alice—evidently enjoyed each other's company; they got engaged the following year. James could hardly have been more pleased. He liked Mary very much indeed. When he announced the engagement to a friend, he described Salter as "an uncommonly fine fellow, of great intellectual ability, and beautifully frank & high minded character." By the end of the decade James called him simply "Mack," and in 1897 sold him a lot carved from the property he owned in Chocorua, New Hampshire—sold it to him for a dollar so that the families could have adjacent summer homes. Their friendship was probably the most important in either man's life.[3]

Salter is not only important to history because he married into the James family, although it must have felt that way to him sometimes. Whether he incubated ideas that became central to pragmatism or James conveyed concepts that became part of Ethical Culture is debatable—most likely, given their closeness, both were true—but a more vital question is what the career of William Mackintire Salter says about the fate of liberal intellectual culture in the twentieth century. He may have been the most careful spokesman for practical idealism, a man whose Christian faith gave way before his reason but whose deep religious faith continued, and continued to drive him to search for verbal formulations to crystallize his vague convictions. His call for "a practical religion, not practical and ideal, but practical because ideal," represented the legacy of the American Reformation in as technically true and universally broad a form as he could create, but he concocted it in the middle of Chicago in the 1880s and therefore in the middle of the most intense laboratory for labor activism and progressive reform in the country. Stunned by "The Problem of Poverty," as he titled one of his addresses, he strove to take what he had learned from Emerson above all—"The Culture of the Moral Nature," as he titled another—and bring it to bear on the vexed questions of modern industrial life. What he witnessed in Chicago drove him to demand a "new industrial ethics" and a new extension of the reach of the state into the regulation of wages, hours, and conditions as well as a new logical application of the American idea to include workers as real equals in decision making of all kinds.[4]

Salter called his conviction "The Liberalism Needed To-day," which he articulated with enough clarity and force to influence some of Chicago's most active reformers, especially Henry Demarest Lloyd, who described the necessity for "A New Conscience" (1888) with obvious ties to the very old idea of conscience as the universal voice of God within. Salter defended the Haymarket anarchists and attacked robber barons and Social Darwinists according to a very basic principle he could expect all to share at least rhetorically: a commitment to democratic liberty and equality he wanted society to enact practically. This work changed the way reformers, social thinkers, and philosophers alike talked about radical ideas; James distributed a dozen copies of one such pamphlet himself. It also got Salter removed from Chicago.[5]

The circumstances of Salter's removal are murky, but seem to reflect a difference of social opinion between him and Adler, who did not care for his criticisms of the business class. Within the Ethical Culture movement there was an inherent tension. Ethical culturists wanted to woo liberals away from Unitarianism, free religion, Reform Judaism, and mainstream Protestant denominations, which they criticized for failing to act on the grave social problems of their time. Yet if they criticized Reform Jews and various Protestants too sharply, they risked alienating the very population they needed to grow their movement. This tension drove Salter's reassignment to Philadelphia.

Within Salter too there was a tension between his wish to be of practical service to his community in the present and his unshakable craving to find the ultimate philosophical ground for moral action of which he wrote to James so early in their relationship. This made the Philadelphia appointment unstable too when one member of that fellowship started broadcasting views on free love—inspired by Walt Whitman—with which Salter could not agree. He went back to Chicago, turned his social commentary away from economic matters, and found himself more consciously riven by the liberal paradox than Davidson had ever been. As a leader and essentially a preacher, it was Salter's job to exhort his congregants to moral action and inspire in them visions of the higher life to guide their practice. But as a growing aspirant himself, he felt compelled to continue working on philosophical problems, and some of these were hard to explain from the ethical pulpit to hearers less interested in (or patient with) technical problems. Even as his reputation grew to international proportions, he found his eloquent words about a moral ideal on which everyone in his audience theoretically agreed falling increasingly hollow on his own ears.

Then, at the turn of the twentieth century, Salter went deaf. He was forty-seven years old. Although he could continue to preach, he could not engage in the dialogue on which the liberal culture of mutual criticism relied. Increasingly he wondered about the premises for moral action. He and his wife, who had buried their only child before her second birthday, adopted a toddler, a Native American ward of the state, but despite their best liberal assimilationist intentions the Salters found domestic harmony impossible to achieve. Salter retired from Ethical Culture at fifty-five and spent his days in his study, reading George Bernard Shaw, learning about Buddhist thought and culture, and eventually discovering Friedrich Nietzsche, who confounded his assumption that Christian morality should survive Christian theology. He wrote a study of Nietzsche's thought in which he bravely faced the overturning of Emersonian optimism by Nietzschean skepticism verging on nihilism, a book in which he acknowledged that any moral claims liberals thought they had established may have no foundation. In conclusion, though, Salter considered the possibility that his old search for solid ground to stand on might be the wrong goal, and that there might be a unity between philosophical truth and social morality even so, a unity located in the frustrating elusiveness of anything but provisional understanding. In place of the search for some eternal verity as an ultimate end that could be the basis of universal harmony, the study of Nietzsche led him to think that "in fact there might be end beyond end, the work of organization never being perfect, the completely ordered world remaining forever an ideal. In that case struggle and competition would ever and anon arise afresh."[6]

After writing this, Salter laid down his pen. It was 1917, and although he lived another fourteen years, he made no comment on America's entry into World War I and passage through the tumultuous twenties to the dawn of the Great Depression. Ultimately, the historical record of William Mackintire Salter is a record of the fissure in liberal intellectual culture into activist and academic wings. Salter spent most of his career under the old paradigm in which advancement in ideas about moral and ultimate truth was tied to advancement in social ethics, which brought liberal religion into the world of progressive reform intact. When he left that paradigm for the pursuit of understanding that would answer his own higher nature, though, he left his audience as well. When his hefty volume on Nietzsche was published, it received a couple of favorable reviews in specialized philosophical journals but faded quickly; he had never earned a doctorate and the field of philosophy was rapidly moving in highly technical directions. The book did get a brief notice in a modern version of *The Dial*, a periodical that co-opted the allure of the Transcendentalists to aim at the general reading public. There this defender of the Haymarket anarchists and author of ethical tracts that had gained followers across Europe and as far away as India was identified with one phrase only: "a brother-in-law of the late William James." The book never sold much. By 1923 sales were down to twenty-nine copies for the year.[7]

THE CULTURE OF
THE MORAL NATURE

William Mackintire Salter was the firstborn child of Rev. William Salter and Mary Ann Mackintire Salter, the bride Rev. Salter went back east to fetch in 1846 after securing the pulpit at the Burlington Congregational Church in Iowa. Salter senior had trained at Andover Seminary, a stronghold of neo-Calvinism against the liberal Christianity of the Unitarians. Rev. Salter then joined the "Iowa Band" of eleven new Andover graduates who set out to evangelize the frontier under the sponsorship of the American Home Missionary Society. (Another member of the Iowa Band became the father of Henry Carter Adams, who grew up to become one of Mack Salter's chief allies in Chicago working at the nexus of liberal religion and industrial reform.) Notably, the Iowa Band went west to bring Christianity not to the Native Americans still populous in Iowa Territory but to the Euro-American migrants who were displacing them.[8]

Salter first roamed over the area around the town of Maquoketa, bringing the gospel of sin and salvation by horseback to farmers and entrepreneurs more inclined toward freethinking and Methodism than Congregationalist Calvinism. He boarded with a family who provided him a place to study by hanging a curtain to create a partition. Converts were few. When the Burlington spot opened up, Salter did not hesitate to move to the town on the Mississippi in which business was booming and a railroad hub was built before long. This did not mean that he became any more successful at preaching to Iowans; it meant that his congregation filled with migrant New Englanders.[9]

Life in the West had a curious effect on theology, though. Pretenses to orthodoxy were hard to maintain amid the motley self-government of frontier life. Then the issue of slavery became acute. Salter had arrived in the territory already opposed to slavery, but being adjacent to the slave state of Missouri sharpened and intensified that opposition. He preached in favor of immediate emancipation, and when the war began he assisted fugitive slaves by providing a safe haven and directing them on to points north. Eventually he joined the U.S. Sanitary Commission and ministered to soldiers in the field. He also wrote a pamphlet on the conflict for the American Reform Tract and Book Society. By the end of the war, he had brought back to Burlington a theology that was much more about love and service than guilt and damnation. His own service beyond his congregation lay in writing histories and supporting educational institutions. With such a character, no wonder his eldest son wanted to follow in his footsteps.[10]

It is a good indicator of the softening of Rev. Salter's theology that when Mack Salter graduated from Knox College in Illinois and looked east for divinity school, he started at Yale but got the necessary parental blessing to move to Harvard. And it is a good indicator of the character of Harvard Divinity School in the 1870s that Salter arrived in Cambridge a Christian among classmates who also professed a specifically Christian religious commitment. Yet he felt he differed from his peers in the class of '76 in two important respects. On the one hand, he had evidently inherited his father's Congregationalist view of Christ, believing that "in Jesus, God had spoken to the world, and that under God he was the Lord, and Saviour, and Judge of men," as he later expressed it. Surrounded by Unitarians, he sometimes wondered whether their resistance to thinking of Christ as an authority "was not doing more to dissipate Christianity, than to build it up." On the other hand, he thought his peers took their faith on trust, which he could not do, needing like the Reformation Christians of his heritage "to test, examine, and conclude for myself," he recalled.[11]

He found himself spiritually at sea. "The question was, where could I find a point to start from; not what was the whole truth, but what was the truth I could be immediately sure of . . . light that I could not question?" He sought it in the record of biblical revelation, noting that "if there was any sure ground for the Christian believer, it was to be found in Christ himself." He thought Unitarians ignored Jesus's own words when they declined to confess in his name. This line of inquiry brought him to the question of Christianity's exclusive claim to ultimate truth. "Was it exactly natural," he considered, "that divine light and guidance and forgiveness should be thus present, as it were, on earth for a few years, and then become entirely a matter of history and antiquarian research?" If all Christians based their claim of ultimate truth on the same book, moreover, he wondered how that book could provide "the basis to the Presbyterian creed, to the Methodist creed, to, one might say, a hundred creeds, even including the slender one of Unitarians." Facing the fact of doctrinal diversity even within Christianity, he found himself struggling both at Harvard and during a fellowship year at the University of Göttingen, aching to satisfy his reason, which he defined as "the demand for a set of views that should be harmonious and consistent."[12]

He found some light to guide his way—not the light of certainty, but light nonetheless—in the writings of the most influential English convert to Catholicism, Cardinal John Henry Newman (1801–1890). Salter first read Newman's work while still at Cambridge, most likely the 1870 *Essay in Aid of a Grammar of Assent* that made it into the hands of William James around the same time. In Newman, both Salter and James found a way of thinking about religious belief that, far from diverging from the principles of the American Reformation, breathed fresh life into the ideal of moral agency. Salter thought that Newman "opened the windows of his mind, instead of keeping them shut; that he set out on living a life of reason instead of one of prejudice," and that he exhibited an open-ended devotion to religious inquiry, being "determined to seek out and follow the truth on whatever shores that quest should land him." Newman's key word of "assent" became a tool in James's brief for voluntary belief, although James agreed with Salter that some questions were never open for Newman and used him in "The Will to Believe" as an example of a type of human mind for whom the Catholic system was "an organic need and delight." In other words, Newman's work helped Salter and James appreciate how a religious approach they themselves never adopted nonetheless served the primal function of belief for someone like Newman, who made an important distinction between "a dogmatic creed and a vital religion" in a passage James underlined. Catholic religion was a live religion that worked for Newman, who "had faced the problems of religion for himself," Salter said, and who taught the doubting divinity student how to think about belief. In an 1891 article that James later echoed in his description of the "faith-ladder," Salter explained how Newman's idea of "certitude" related to practical action, and how this could be used to justify religious beliefs even without solid evidence underlying them. "We are mentally sure almost every day of many things which could not be demonstratively proved," he pointed out; "we are practically as sure of them as if they could be proved; we are ready to act on the basis of them, and that is the test of practical certitude." He was on the search for beliefs on which he could act.[13]

His quest led him to a place historians cannot follow. He went to Colorado, where he worked as a shepherd for two years without leaving a documentary trail. There is no available evidence detailing where in Colorado he lived, for whom he herded sheep, nor what his living conditions might have been, so imagination is required to picture the young Salter packing for the sojourn and deciding what few books to bring. Emerson's essays seem the most likely choice. For one thing, Emerson's works sold more widely in the last third of the nineteenth century than ever before, especially among religious liberals, who referred to his genius and quoted his memorable lines so often, the love of Emerson was practically a calling card of American liberal culture. More specifically, Salter drew on Emerson's thought and language in nearly every essay and address he produced, starting with the book he wrote in Colorado. The 1879 *On a Foundation for Religion*, a copy of which Francis Ellingwood Abbot owned, was a small volume in which Salter considered how an awareness of interdependence and a practice of gratitude and submission could add up to a faith that survived the loss of a biblical conception of God. "In your metaphysics you have denied personality to the Deity," Emerson said again on Salter's page, "yet when the devout motions of the soul come, yield to them heart and life, though they should clothe God with shape and color." By 1884 Salter could historicize Emerson as "the finest flower of New England culture" and confess, "I know not what true thought of mine you may not find, stripped of its imperfections of statement, in him." Wavering in his Christian faith, skeptical of the Unitarian solution, he found in Emerson a prescription for pursuing the higher life he sought. Emerson taught Salter to accept "the consolation, the hope, the grandeur that come alone out of the culture of the moral nature."[14]

The American Reformation ideal of moral agency appeared clarified of Christian dross in Emerson, for whom the moral guidance of one's inner light reigned in sole supremacy, giving Salter and many of his peers a guidepost for their journey into post-Christian religious liberalism. Salter took from "Self-Reliance" Emerson's assurance that "conforming to usages that have become dead to you" is unwise, helping him to leave a uniquely divine Christ behind. And Emerson's firmness in believing that real religion survived the death of the old forms bolstered Salter's confidence to proceed even without biblical revelation nor any other ground beneath his feet. "I see that sensible men and conscientious men all over the world were of one religion," he quoted Emerson in an early address, "the religion of well-doing and daring, men of sturdy truth, men of integrity and feeling for others. My inference is that there is a statement of religion possible which makes all skepticism absurd." Emerson was not afraid of newness. Far from it. "There will be a new church," Salter used Emerson's words to decree, "founded on moral science . . . the church of men to come." He wanted to make this prophecy come true.[15]

So this is how Salter joined the Society for Ethical Culture. After his return from Colorado, he spent only a year in the Unitarian pulpit before moving to New York as a new convert to ethical religion. There he found an attempt to live out the "enthusiasm of humanity" stirringly described by Sir John Seeley in the book *Ecce Homo* (1866), which Salter had read as a divinity student. Ethical Culture was a young organization when Salter met his mentor in Felix Adler (1851–1933). Like Salter, Adler had intended to follow in the footsteps of his father, the rabbi of the Reform Temple Emanu-El in New York. He pursued his rabbinical studies at the University of Heidelberg with faithful zeal but encountered first the philosophy of Immanuel Kant, which destabilized his sense that religion needed to operate within a traditional theology, and then the relatively radical thoughts on labor circulating in Germany at the time, which destabilized his sense that the work of religion was separate from the work of society. He came home in 1873 and delivered his first—and only—sabbath sermon at his father's temple. "The Judaism of the Future" proclaimed that the good thing about Jewish religion was the prominence of moral law as the measurement of practice. The bad thing about Judaism was the idea that Jews are the special chosen people of God, making the faith exclusive rather than universal. What was needed, Adler said, was a religion that permeated society and put its "greatest stress not on the believing but the acting out. A religion such as Judaism ever claimed to be—not of the creed but of the deed." This he wanted to see, and he wanted to "discard the narrow spirit of exclusion, and loudly proclaim that Judaism was not given to the Jews alone, but that its destiny is to embrace in one great moral state the whole family of men."[16]

Adler had read his Emerson too. The spirit of the American Reformation breathed in the Society for Ethical Culture from its inception, which came just a few years after Adler's sermon when a group of a hundred Jews from his father's congregation gathered signatures and donations to start the New York society in May 1876. Naturally Adler also frequented the Free Religious Association, in which he served as an officer until 1882. At the FRA, he encountered rabbis Isaac M. Wise and Max Lilienthal, who both thought that Reform Judaism still had reason to exist as an independent entity despite their overlap in philosophical agreement with Adler's point of view. Reform Judaism, after all, was essentially Enlightenment Judaism, born in Germany but almost hegemonic among American Jews until the late nineteenth century, when Eastern European Jews started arriving and the American Jewish establishment started institutionalizing partly in order to teach Enlightenment Judaism to the immigrants. Far from thinking that the Boston liberals and their spawn had an original perspective on moral agency and practical religion, Wise thought that free religion and Unitarianism were both essentially Judaism. He wanted liberals to admit that they had arrived late to a Jewish religion of humanity rather than that Jews should follow Adler in discarding their Jewish commitment in favor of what could appear an assimilationist form of religious practice. But although the composition of the New York Society for Ethical Culture was predominantly Jewish and the later congregations gathered at Chicago, Philadelphia, and St. Louis were disproportionately so, the ethical movement never became large enough to pose a significant threat to the vitality of American Reform Judaism, which remained in active conversation and social cooperation with liberal religion, both Christian and post-Christian, across the turn of the twentieth century. Rabbi Stephen Wise, for example, traded podiums with Davidson and corresponded with him about Zionism. In other words, being a Reform Jew practically meant being a liberal, a term prominent leaders like Morris Cohen and Rabbi Emil G. Hirsch explicitly adopted. After the Pittsburgh Platform of 1885 made social justice central to the definition of the American Jewish tradition, reform-minded Jews found plenty of work to do through their temples, which also engaged them in rituals that connected them to their ancestors and marked the ceremonial passages of major life transitions.[17]

The Society for Ethical Culture also developed rituals and ceremonies, but because the movement always aimed to speak in universal terms for a diverse humanity rather than in the name of any specific tradition, these functions tended to appear vaguely Judeo-Christian with a smattering of Hindu and Buddhist touches rather than coherently symbolic. The ceremonies were explained largely in terms of their uplifting and energizing effect on the moral striver. Ethical symbols evoked universal meaning rather than marking a shared past. Salter defended the celebration of Christmas, which the New York society commemorated with a pageant, because whether any of the stories of Jesus's nativity were true or not, there was only one question that mattered. "Have streams of influence for good gone out from him," Salter asked, "has he helped our world, does the remembrance of him give us courage and hope?" Salter's Christian frame of reference remained solid enough that the value of the figure of Christ endured, as it did among Unitarians and most other liberals.[18]

For both Salter and Adler, as well as later leaders like Stanton Coit and Percival Chubb from England and Anna Garlin Spencer and Horace Bridges from the United States, ethical religion was indeed intended to perform the functions of a church or temple, minus the need for unity of creed. Therefore the Sunday service remained the cornerstone in the life of a society, a service tied to a theme like "Brotherhood of Man," for example. The structured event began with a lead-in motivation, often a quotation from a sacred text like the Talmud or something from Channing, included the singing of hymns, reached its climax in the delivery of the leader's address, and closed with a dedication, also often a quotation. The hymns were meant to inspire moral conduct, and they reflected the Protestant tradition of hymnody with the ethical demystification of symbols. "I believe in human kindness," began one such hymn, leading the congregation to profess Reformation Christian moral values divested of their creedal referents. "I believe in self-denial / And its secret throb of joy; / In the love that lives thro' trial, / Dying not, tho' death destroy." As the post-Christian liberal religion of Ethical Culture gradually filtered into what one historian calls ecumenical Protestantism or Protestant liberalism, by the mid-twentieth century a hymn Adler wrote—"Hail the Glorious Golden City"—appeared in the Congregationalist *Pilgrim Hymnal*.[19]

All of this ritual activity took decades to develop. At the beginning there was Adler and his New York group, and then came Salter, dispatched to Chicago in 1883. He helped Adler crystallize the purpose of the society in a "Statement of Principles" headed by service to the state through the cultivation of individual "well-doing." They defined Ethical Culture practices as favoring rational ideas over dogmatic ones, studying the laws of moral and intellectual life, finding unity in association, and using the methods of lectures, discussions, and schools. Ethical Culture really seemed to its founders to be the organizational fulfillment of Emerson's hope. Salter quite deliberately historicized ethical religion by placing it at the foot of a liberal lineage leading back to Channing, whose words Unitarians had never put into action, Salter said. Above all, adherence to Ethical Culture meant acceptance of a "sacred duty" to help the less fortunate. With this motivation Salter settled in Chicago.[20]

A NEW INDUSTRIAL ETHICS

In his inaugural lecture at Chicago, Salter argued against the "ordinary Liberalism" that tolerated the modern organization of industrial life and only mouthed the old Reformation Christian ideals. He blasted the morality of the present system, "in which self-interest is not only the impulse but the rule, in which we consider men not in their rights or claims, but as to how well and completely they may serve us and contribute to our own gains." Using social statistics, he complained about the widespread use of child labor and the inability of half of Illinois workingmen to provide for their families. Most gravely, "corporate capital" tends "not only to lord it over the labor which feeds it, but to question the sovereignty of the state itself." Salter was only at the beginning of his career, but already he had seized the inner logic of his mature argument for modern liberalism: the idea that corporate capital and the business elite—if they continued to operate by the supposed natural law of self-interested individualism rather than the moral law of liberty, equality, and the common good—posed the real threats to democracy, not the agitation of workers deprived of their birthright of civic participation.[21]

Salter claimed Ethical Culture to be a fresh departure from older religions, which he pointedly criticized, but in fact his approach bore all the hallmarks of American liberal religion, particularly in the role of conscience, the repudiation of self-interest, the guiding faith in a higher law beyond the reach of the senses, and the underlying concern for moral agency. The cure for the industrial problem, according to Salter, involved acting upon the principles of the American Reformation. Like any sin, this industrial system arouses "the conscience," which he called "the utterance of the God in us," just as though he were in the eighteenth century. Conscience is the "inward monitor" that "signifies that we are part and parcel of another order of things than that which we can see and handle." Salter's ethical religion was a sacred religion through this tie to the infinite and eternal, the incomprehensible. It was also a practical religion because "social questions are fundamentally moral questions" involving "what the relation between man and man should be." This fundamental question had not yet been solved. The reluctance of Judaism and liberal Christianity to address it, according to Salter, made those religions unsatisfactory and demanded a religion in which ethical ideals were made into practical laws for individual and social behavior.[22]

It is not surprising that Salter arrived in Chicago with a fire in his belly. He had already published a piece in the FRA organ in which he answered the question "Do the Ethics of Jesus Satisfy the Needs of Our Time?" with a resounding no. The problems of poverty, work, and citizenship could neither remain in the private sphere nor be remanded to mystical justice in a life ever after, he declared. In a religious critique of Christian charity that mounted a political critique of the nineteenth-century state, he charged that a moral people could no longer "commend the poor and unfortunate to the care of the 'heavenly Father'; nor can we assent to the cool indifference and practical materialism of *laissez-faire doctrinaires.*" His argument copied how James likened the materialist Chauncey Wright to the idealist James McCosh for a similar critique of how both sides accept an earthly life by fiat. But moral agency is about action. Since the idea of a commonwealth is "to secure the ends needful for all," Americans need "a new industrial ethics" of cooperation and "fair profit" involving a "new reverence for the State." Salter wanted to know whether the government really could be for the people as well as of them. "Shall the common, universal good be secured, and no individual freedom or rights be allowed, which tend to the destruction of the freedom and rights of others?" In other words, Salter wanted Mill's principle of liberty to be implemented at the state level so that everyone's exercise of rights was balanced against their interference with the liberty of others.[23]

What Salter found in Chicago was a city in which government appeared to him to work for the prosperous few at the expense of the liberty of the impoverished many. Destroyed by the Great Fire of 1871,

Chicago had rebuilt at an opportune moment to lead the second wave of industrialization in America, taking advantage of the young transcontinental railroad and plentiful immigrant labor to connect farmers with markets and manufacturers with consumers, constructing factories, plants, and mills, all fueled by the stockyards on the South Side. When business boomed, as it did between 1879 and 1881, food prices rose by as much as 100 percent while wages remained stagnant. When business slowed, especially during Chicago's grim winters, wages and hours were decreased and workers were laid off. Salter arrived in the middle of an economic downturn that forced the average industrial worker to be idle three months a year.[24]

There is a reason why Chicago became emblematic for poets and novelists trying to represent the essence of modern American life. Edward Bellamy's contrast between the dystopia of unregulated capitalism and the utopia of state socialism in *Looking Backward* was set there. Upton Sinclair's attempt to illustrate the essential unfreedom of even the most honest, industrious immigrant laborers in the meatpacking industry, *The Jungle* (1906), made the Chicago stenches of offal, booze, and corruption all too vivid, and Theodore Dreiser's *Sister Carrie* (1900) came fresh from the farm to face the temptations and opportunities of the modern city in the shops and seducers of Chicago. William T. Stead tried to imagine what would happen *If Christ Came to Chicago* (1894); surely Jesus would do something about the brothels, saloons, gambling dens, and theaters that blanketed the slums. For the radical poet Carl Sandburg, most sensitively, Chicago's "big shoulders" had grown that way in order to carry all the contradictions of the industrial powerhouse, from the poverty marking the faces of women and children to the bounty shipped to the nation from its depots. The city could be observed

Under the smoke, dust all over his mouth, laughing with
white teeth,
Under the terrible burden of destiny laughing as a young
man laughs,
Laughing even as an ignorant fighter laughs who has
never lost a battle,
Bragging and laughing that under his wrist is the pulse,
and under his ribs the heart of the people,
Laughing!

The influence of Whitman is obvious here, but Emerson was just as important to Sandburg, a second-generation Swedish American who grew up by the light of an American dream betrayed by the industrial city. And of all American cities, nowhere were those contradictions visible in more dramatic relief than Chicago.[25]

As much as Chicago personified opportunity and oppression, it also contained a host of reformers intent on correcting the course of modern life. Some of these came from within the ranks of workers, often carrying radical ideas from their native countries, defiant of an American system that robbed them of their just share of the profit from their toil. The Knights of Labor appeared in Chicago in 1877 and, while carefully distant from socialist ideology, encouraged the city's laborers to think of themselves as a distinct working class and to organize, even to boycott, in order to exercise power against unscrupulous employers. On the other end of the spectrum were benevolent businessmen like George Pullman, who invested part of the profits from his luxury railcar company to start another profit-making venture, the model town he named after himself. Pullman filled the town with his own workers, who enjoyed every advantage of middle-class life there except the democratic right of civic participation, as the economist Richard T. Ely observed in 1885. Between these two poles—and essentially connecting them— were the liberals and their colleagues in progressive reform.[26]

Chicago was home to a number of important figures and institutions in the broad, diverse, and perhaps too often invoked social movement that has gone by the name of progressivism since the twentieth century. The University of Chicago, founded in 1892, functioned as an engine of social reform thanks not only to its research-driven faculty working in philosophy and the social sciences around a common set of questions about justice and democracy but also to the social laboratory that was Hull House, founded by Jane Addams in 1889, which produced data, connected professors with a nonacademic public, and gave college students and graduates training in the field. Chicago hosted the pulpit of the liberal Presbyterian minister David Swing, one of the early voices for what came to be called the Social Gospel, in which the mission of Christ required social ministry. The city was also the home of Rabbi Emil G. Hirsch, who headed the Sinai Congregation from 1880 to 1920 and called for a "new social adjustment" in light of the fundamental human "right of self-determination." The Unitarian minister Jenkin Lloyd Jones got to Chicago just a few years before Salter, founding an "All Souls Church" intended to be "a free congress of independent souls" and taking over the Western Unitarian Conference, launching the journal *Unity*, and forming Mutual Improvement Clubs. His church eventually founded a community outreach center named after Lincoln. Working outside the institutions of liberal religion, figures like Henry Demarest Lloyd and Henry Carter Adams were also active in Chicago advocating for economic justice and writing for the press to spread a "religion of altruism." Historians often divide progressive reformers into secular and religious camps, the former driven by science and the latter by Protestant morality. Seen by the light of the American

Reformation, though, all of these middle-class reformers were engaged in a common enterprise and a common conversation. Science was a tool developed from the divine faculty of reason, and conscience was to be the driver of change. Salter was far from alone in Chicago in actively seeking a new industrial ethics.[27]

The work of Salter and others in Chicago reveals the confluence of liberal religion and radical politics in America. Incidentally, while "radical" came in the twentieth century to signify a commitment to some variant of Marxian socialism, in the nineteenth century the first Americans to call themselves "radical" were the religious liberals who chafed under the Unitarian yoke, such as the founders of the journal *The Radical*, and those behind *The Radical Review*, which printed a pamphlet of one of Salter's early sermons for Ethical Culture, "The Problem of Poverty" (1884). More substantively, the religious version of radicalism meant an unwavering commitment to moral agency, one's own and that of others. This root commitment drove an engagement with social questions to the point where religious liberals on the radical edge like Salter wanted to see a restructuring of American governance in light of the new inequality bred by industrialism.[28]

Modern liberalism, in which the government acts on behalf of the collective popular good, was a radical goal in the late nineteenth century. Salter asked, "[W]here shall the limit be set of government interference in behalf of the weak as against the strong?" His answer was the positive liberty of modern liberalism. Government should "strive to give opportunity . . . for every life to become a positive blessing, both to itself and others." He sought a social and therefore public recognition of "the universal rights of man." He wanted to change the system from one that favored individualism to one that supported individuality, an important distinction found in Davidson's thought as well. In individualism people pursue what they think is good for themselves and willingly use others as means to their ends, which is sinful by any vantage point that takes the eternal seriously, according to the logic of the American Reformation. Individuality, though, is the unique development of each individual's moral agency and interior perspective on the divine—which poverty effectively prohibits. In a tenement, where a large family is crowded into one or two rooms, Salter questioned, "what sanctity of person can there be? And yet the individuality of every one should be sacred from the earliest years upwards, body and mind." This old idea of universal inner divinity powered his critique of his day's conservatives.[29]

To the dominant notion of some iron law of wages that free markets magically manifest, Salter retorted that there is no such law but only the rule of human selfishness, which government is obligated to rein in. Taking on the conservative economist William Graham Sumner by name—Sumner, who has been called a Social Darwinist, adamantly scorned any initiatives to interfere with competition—Salter scoffed at the idea that laws like supply and demand are any sort of "ultimate force or fact," an idea that underestimates human agency and treats economics as supernatural. "Hypocritical mysticism," he called laissez-faire doctrine, which he criticized with the help of lengthy quotations from a new British book on economics by the father of John Maynard Keynes. "A new morality is needed."[30]

The alliance between liberal religion and radical politics appeared not only in pulpits and pamphlets but also in social service and political action. The Chicago Ethical Society's social outreach began when Salter became involved in the movement for the eight-hour workday early in his ministry. Announced in Chicago by the Federation of Organized Trades and Labor Unions to begin on May Day 1884, the Eight-Hour campaign arose in part as an answer to unemployment; more workers would have work if businesses had to calibrate their productivity to a restricted workday. The campaign also featured a slogan pitched to appeal to liberal sensibilities. "Eight hours for work, eight hours for rest, eight hours for what we will" called for moderation, a moderation in the service of moral agency. Workers needed to be able to exercise choice in their use of time before they could practice self-culture.[31]

Salter became active enough in the eight-hour movement that he started speaking at rallies for the cause. By 1886 his skills and dedication had earned him a spot as one of seven speakers at an event that drew seven thousand workers to the hall, with fourteen thousand more outside. Salter must have felt they were on the verge of victory.[32]

Then, at another rally a few days later, a bomb went off in Haymarket Square. To this day no one knows exactly who was responsible, but the bomb itself did less damage than the reaction of the police officers on the scene. One had been killed by the bomb, several others wounded; their stunned comrades opened fire, striking a number of civilians and inflicting casualties among themselves so that in the end, sixty-seven policemen were either injured or killed. At a point in American labor history when strikers and security forces came to pitched battles so regularly that one historian says the social order was "standing at Armageddon," the violence at Haymarket alarmed and infuriated the defenders of the status quo in the popular press and state government. Reaction was swift and ruthless. In the absence of evidence about the actual bomb thrower, the police seized eight foreign-born anarchists and the court quickly convicted them, sentencing seven of them to death for the murder of the police officer who had been killed by the bomb. The majority of public opinion backed this resolution of the tragedy.[33]

Salter was not in this majority. His initial response to the event was to try to understand the perspective of the workers who were willing to use violence in pursuit of their aims. Although the convicted men were anarchists, which meant that they adhered to no ideology more specific than a loose egalitarian collectivism, Salter had heard enough of Marx in the labor movement that he spent the summer of 1886 reading *Das Kapital* and learning the language of commodity, the social value of labor, and industrial exploitation. This education heightened his existing concern about the tendency in modern industrialism of employers to treat employees as means to their ends rather than ends in themselves. Marx also gave him a new concern about the growing antagonism between the classes. "The property of the wealthy classes is . . . stolen property," Marx taught Salter, so socialists "believe workingmen have a right to reclaim their own," just as anarchists believe that workers should rebel against the injustices imposed by the government and the wealthy. For individuals in America to think of themselves as belonging to classes with warring interests rather than to a humanity with a great collective interest clashed with Salter's deepest convictions about the meaning of American society. As he visited the convicted anarchists in jail—he was the only clergyman they agreed to meet, and he became particularly close to August Spies—he learned the depth of their alienation from American democracy and began to see industrial conflict as a fight not only for social justice but for the integrity of American governance itself.[34]

Salter thought that the conviction of the anarchists and the unwarranted severity of their sentencing damaged America's case for the impartial working of its government, which is to say for its democracy. He led the charge for clemency, joining with other Chicago liberals including Rabbi Emil G. Hirsch and Rev. Jenkin Lloyd Jones as well as the novelist William Dean Howells in circulating a petition to Illinois governor James Oglesby to spare the anarchists because their conviction had been unjust. They won the prominent support of the labor leader Samuel Gompers, the English socialist William Morris, and the activist Voltairine de Cleyre. (William James declined to sign the petition although everyone in his household—even his five-year-old—favored the anarchists.) Taking to the podium at Chicago's Grand Opera House, Salter argued that workers were wrong to think that a democratic government did not work equally for them but that Governor Oglesby and the financier Jay Gould were also wrong because the corruption of the system in favor of the wealthy needed to be checked. Turning the rhetorical tables against an elite complaining that workers wanted government to become an instrument for their own interests, Salter charged "that influences are already at work to revolutionize our government, and make it the tool of a class," the wealthy class. He acknowledged that some of the anarchists on death row could justly have been convicted of some crime—potentially lethal materials were found in the possession of a few of the convicts, one of whom made an incendiary speech just before the bomb was thrown—but none deserved his punishment. Salter begged that the rule of law be impartially administered rather than given over to vengeance. "There is no more sacred thought than that of justice," he claimed, linking the work of religion with the work of society. "The divine institution in the world is not the Church, but civil society," because that is where power may recognize the innate worth of all members of society. If instead the tendency of American society continues to ostracize workers with reasonable complaints and to favor an elite with disproportionate power and wealth, democracy will turn into a plutocracy "that if unchecked, will destroy our government far more surely than the wildest anarchist plot ever concocted."[35]

Salter's petition did not save the anarchists. Two had their sentences reduced and were pardoned by a later governor, but four were executed and one died by suicide. Yet Salter did not stop talking about anarchy and the problem of labor. He tried to address what he saw as the more fundamental problem behind the injustice: the lack of mutual understanding between workers and management, their thinking of themselves as separate and opposing groups. In 1888 he organized six conferences to be held on successive Sunday evenings for conversation between workers and businessmen. The first dialogue drew a full house, so the subsequent five were held at the Madison Street Theatre, packing eight hundred people in every time. Between two-thirds and three-fourths of the audience was made up of workingmen, whose intelligence surprised the businessmen, according to a reporter on the scene. The success of this initiative led to a series of Economic Conferences that ran for several years featuring lectures such as "An American Trade Unionist's View of the Social Question," as well as to the organization of the Sunset Club for discussion of labor/business relations, one of the venues where Jane Addams gave lectures after her arrival in the city.[36]

Within the Society for Ethical Culture, a number of initiatives aimed to put social morality into practice. The first settlement house in the United States was the Neighborhood Guild, founded by ethical culturist Stanton Coit in New York in 1886. Then came Jane Addams, Hull House, and the settlement wave; the Henry Booth House was founded by the Ethical Culture Society in Chicago in 1898. Before that, under Salter's leadership the Chicago society initiated a series of "Relief Works," starting with nurses sent into low-income neighborhoods on the city's North and West sides. Out of the conversations with workingmen had emerged the need for workers to have access to legal representation, so in 1888 an attorney in the Chicago society organized the Bureau of Justice, which was the first initiative in the country to provide legal help to the poor, eventually becoming the Legal Aid Society. Over the decades around the turn of the twentieth century, the Chicago society started a kindergarten, a penny savings bank, a summer baby tent, a milk commission, young people's groups, summer camps, a library, and domestic science classes. Their Women's Union distributed food and medicine, paid visits to juvenile court, and gave sewing jobs to poor women, layettes to poor mothers, and food and milk to a "diet kitchen" on the North Side. Ethical religion had become practical morality.[37]

All of these programs, as for similar programs going on across progressive America, were voluntary enterprises of private initiative. The ethical culturists exercised their own moral agency in acting practically to increase the scope of choice for the working poor of Chicago. Their effort to live out their moral values was consistent with the culture of lived virtue from the beginning of the century, a belief that what was good for individuals would be good for society and that such positive efforts would add up to be good for the state as well. Although Salter as leader called for changes in the scope of American governance, the moral efforts of the society itself were aimed not at the government but at the people society was ill-serving.

After the failure of the petition to Oglesby, Salter never again spoke directly to the government. Instead, he aimed his moral instruction at workers and especially at the subset of the middle class that had the ear of some elites, perhaps, but did not fence itself off from those below them on the socioeconomic ladder. These middle-class liberals were the segment of American society that acted as the most direct—or least indirect—cross-class cultural conduit; even the least socially active representatives of the liberal middle class employed members of the working class as personal staff they were proud to believe they treated as equals while they dined and clubbed with the elite. While some accounts treat the Society for Ethical Culture as uniformly well-heeled and therefore touchy about Salter's solidarity with laborers, the volume of social action done by the Chicago chapter and other parts of the historical record suggests otherwise. When Salter first proposed to Mary Gibbens, William James confided to his wife that Mary might not want to accept given Salter's "poverty and the poor social quality of his congregation."

He was poor by James's standards because the congregation was neither large nor wealthy. Naturally Mary accepted from high-minded ideals of her own—S. Burns Weston, leader of the Philadelphia society, told James that well-bred Mary "would 'draw' others to the society"—and the congregation grew slowly until it reached a relatively comfortable 254 members by the time the Salters moved to Philadelphia once Weston became director of that society's settlement house. During the Salters' Philadelphia years, a friend visiting James told him that when she had mentioned Salter's name to her seamstress, the woman "pricked up her ears" and asked "if he were the Ethical S. That's my religion, she exclaimed." So it was a transclass organization, historically continuous with the antebellum enterprises of Boston liberals like Joseph Tuckerman but more internally heterogeneous.[38]

The thinking behind what Henry Demarest Lloyd called "the religion of labor" was also continuous with the liberal Christianity of the American Reformation. Lloyd (1847–1903) corresponded with Davidson, lectured at the Chicago Ethical Society, and often worked with Salter, whom Lloyd credited with the inspiration behind his stump speech, "The New Conscience, or, Religion of Labor," which he published as a pamphlet in 1888. Universal inner divinity was the underlying premise of Lloyd's post-Christian religion—that, and the moral agency it mandated. "The only religion" worth practicing, he said, is one that "clears off . . . from the face of man the earth-stains that hide the God imprisoned in the flesh." Lloyd spanned the secular-religious divide with ethics, arguing that the only church society needed was one "where science, the revelation of what has been, will never be at war with religion, the revelation of what ought to be." The new conscience would be a "collective conscience," one in which what was good for oneself was deserved by all and the ideal fellowship was "a church in which God will be natural and men supernatural." He had read his

Emerson too; in fact, he got the gift of Davidson's friendly criticism when he wrote an article on Emerson that Davidson considered "none the worse for a little hero-worship." Lloyd's social thought represents the progressive application of American Reformation principles beyond either social control or moral uplift. He wanted to see a civil religion of democracy in which the principles of equality and collective human potential were made into social practice and common law. When he published *Wealth Against Commonwealth* in 1894, he modernized the republican idea of the common good as the goal of government by identifying the commonwealth as a founding American ideal that the accumulation of wealth in the hands of financiers and industrialists was rapidly destroying.[39]

By that point Salter had moved to Philadelphia. He came back to Chicago for the massive Columbian Exposition of 1893, as neat a symbol for Chicago's contradictions as could have been devised. It opened a year late because of labor problems but was the most ambitious, awe-inspiring assemblage of structures and sights the country had ever seen. The flashiest part of the expo—both in the "White City" of buildings devoted overwhelmingly to commerce and industry and in the world's first Midway devoted to exotic entertainment by foreign-born primitives—declared America's success in material terms, exulting in the dazzling glare of Westinghouse's new electric bulbs and the bedazzling splendor of California's oranges stacked in the shape of a Liberty Bell, as well as the Midwest's grain, built into a palace somehow more mechanistic than agrarian. The other part of the expo declared the state of the American field in intellectual terms. The so-called intellectual congresses of the expo met in the White City and brought together representatives of all the areas of study operative in the country. The most famous and groundbreaking of these was the World's Parliament of Religions, convened by liberal Protestants who invited representatives of all the text-based world religions to come to Chicago and peaceably discuss what they believed without attempting to convert one another. The intellectual congresses also included meetings of the new professional associations for various academic disciplines, including the American Historical Association, where the star paper was Frederick Jackson Turner's assessment of the significance of the frontier. Liberal intellectual culture, as nurtured in fellowships, summer schools, clubs, and associations across the nineteenth century, began to coalesce into modern academic forms at the intellectual congresses of the expo.[40]

Among these intellectual congresses was the Labor Congress, where Salter delivered a paper on "Moral Forces in Dealing with the Labor Question," which he later published in the *International Journal of Ethics*. Here he likened the problem of labor in the late nineteenth century to the problem of slavery in the first half of the century, observing that slavery had been absolutely legal, absolutely entrenched in American society, and as much a part of the American norm as unregulated capitalism, but it had been abolished on moral grounds more consistent with the meaning of democracy than arguments for its continuation were. Therefore, labor was not an intractable problem, but one fixable by a change in moral consciousness. "The law is born of the human will and the will can change," Salter said. Taking the classical argument for moral agency from the American Reformation and applying it to the problem of labor, he explained that "the end of life is the development of the total humanity in us." This right is not to be reserved for members of one class, but instead "possibilities are precious in all men," all of whom deserve "dignity and responsibility as human beings" and every chance for "progressively realizing the possibilities of their natures." Rehearsing again all the obstacles operating in society to inhibit this self-culture among workers, Salter called for "the abolition of the spirit of bossism," the idea that employers deserve the rights of autocrats because they give work, as though they were benign despots. That is not what America is supposed to mean, but America is a country that has not realized its own most basic premise, he said. "Until men are democratized at heart, the forms of democracy count for little." This means that workers should not think of their jobs as gifts and employers should think of workers as equals.[41]

But this was the 1890s. Industrial conflict showed no sign of abating. Salter preached before the Philadelphia society on "Bad Wealth: How It Is Sometimes Got," taking the title from Emerson. Then he wound up to the last contribution he had to make on the labor question. Reframing the debate as a choice between different means of living out the American principle of liberty, he cleverly associated "anarchy" with laissez-faire capitalism and "government" with the modern liberal state in *Anarchy or Government?: An Inquiry in Fundamental Politics* (1895). This book argued that the line between public and private was not absolute because of interdependence, a human fact of life with which practice must reckon. American critics of workers' rights were unreasonable both in pretending that government was somehow wholly distinct from society and in limiting workers' freedom to strike and to organize—their liberty—while doing nothing to curtail employers' impositions of power over workers. "To say that . . . employees *may not act as they see fit*," he observed, "and yet *to leave their employers free* to fix wages, hours of labor and other conditions of employment as they like, is simply monstrous. Either hands off,—or hands on impartially!" Hence the choice between anarchy, or liberty, and government, or justice. As expressed by Salter's contemporary Morrison I. Swift—whose work James admiringly used in his own arguments about labor—"The cry of many, and particularly of the wealthy, is, 'Do not increase the functions of the state.' There is an alternative. . . . If individuals, those who have the means at their disposal, will apply the individual initiative they are so fond of talking about, to reform and improvement, the state will not be called upon. Otherwise—."[42]

These were arguments for modern liberalism. Salter grounded his call for a more responsible democratic government not only in the logic of moral agency but deliberately in the lineage of the American Reformation. His book opened with a pair of quotations about how compulsion is contrary to justice, one line from John Stuart Mill's *On Liberty* and one from Channing. "The voice of command is never heard among the spirits of the just," Channing said, giving Salter entrée to point out that where justice failed and self-interest ruled, either workers must be left free to strike or society must ensure that none of its members are imposed upon. Coercion had been the chief foe of liberals since before the Revolution.[43]

The book was reviewed quite favorably in a number of venues whose range exhibits the breadth of penetration of liberal intellectual culture by the turn of the twentieth century. The *International Journal of Ethics* called it "fresh and stimulating," astutely observing that the ethical movement may be "regarded as one of the last manifestations of the individualizing tendency set going by the Reformation." A brief notice appearing in *The Chautauquan* weekly reached a broad, Protestant middle class with its judgment that Salter's arguments for "the necessity" of extending government's functions are "wholesome and sound," an endorsement echoed in stronger terms in the *Philosophical Review*, where the reviewer expressed the "wish that this little book might find its way into the hands of every law student and every judge in the United States." Meanwhile, on the far side of the mainstream, an anarchist journal winningly titled *Liberty (Not the Daughter but the Mother of Order)* carried a running debate over several issues between Salter and an anarchist critic, Victor Yarros, who did not want the cause of good government against untrammeled liberty to win. Salter's arguments helped move the American center toward modern liberalism.[44]

"The voice of command is never heard among the spirits of the just." Channing helped Salter point out that the business class needed justification by faith, to be converted to a democratic way of thinking and therefore acting. This could happen only through the bubbling up of social morality from below until the government above reflected the impartial ideal of American democracy, guaranteeing a positive liberty of universal moral agency. The liberal politics of moral suasion that had been exercised against drink and slavery now targeted the industrial elite as the body in need of reform. The historical impact of Salter's efforts cannot be measured, but both the continuity of those efforts with the project of the American Reformation and the novelty of his case for the modern liberal state demonstrate how the liberal Christianity that fostered a culture of lived virtue grew into a religion of democracy that made liberty and equality into practical ideals.

STRIVING TO BE MAN

During Salter's Philadelphia years, he got embroiled in a controversy that framed the opposition between liberty and justice in rather different terms from those involved in modern industry. The problem was love. Salter, like Adler, never questioned the sanctity of marriage or the suitedness of women to partnership with men, the latter a modern ideal that he was proud to distinguish from the unenlightened notion that a wife should only be the "mere attendant and helpmeet for man." Salter favored the "Real Emancipation of Woman," he said. Like most religious liberals around the turn of the twentieth century, he wanted to see women develop their divine potential, even their civic voice and "economic independence"—without neglecting the home. He thought women were domestic goddesses, although he read Charlotte Perkins Gilman approvingly and thought that hired help might be the best way to free women to pursue great things. And how many mothers could afford hired help?[45]

Salter wore similar blinkers when he read Whitman. Preaching on "The Great Side of Walt Whitman," he applauded Whitman's view that women are equal to men, with equally "high ends of being." But he saw a "Questionable Side of Walt Whitman" too, as he titled a subsequent address. It was that Whitman made no distinction between good and evil. This is the same criticism William James made of Whitman as a monist or absolute idealist. The paragon of healthy-mindedness, Whitman exhibited a wonderful "universal sympathy" but not a truly great moral nature since he did not struggle against sin, either in himself or in society. Salter liked Whitman's democratic mind-set, but because the problem of evil was a real problem for Salter—was in fact the reason for the necessity of religion—he could not agree with Whitman's underlying philosophy.[46]

Salter felt it necessary to explain all of this from the pulpit partly because one of his most active congregants was an avid Whitmanite. Horace Traubel (1858–1919) considered Whitman a religious prophet. He was one of scores of disciples to the great American democrat on either side of the Atlantic. Whitman's followers began their shrines and fellowships devoted to the man and his poetry while Whitman was still alive and continued their spiritual homage after his 1892 death.

Traubel's Whitmanism initially posed no conflict with his membership in the Philadelphia Ethical Society, which after all embraced comers of all faiths and no faith. As Salter put it in an address, "[C]onscientious and diligent seekers after truth must be expected to more or less differ from one another in their conclusions for some time to come," making dialogue, engagement, and respect the rule of ethical societies. The only common ground for Ethical Culture must in fact be ethics, "the pursuit of moral perfection." Salter did not initially see that the definition of moral perfection was then bound to be a matter of dispute, but the drama with Traubel showed that the social understanding of the good is exactly the discussion to which a society of Ethical Culture tends. People simply disagree about which actions are good and which not.[47]

Traubel published the lecture in which Salter made these remarks in pamphlet form. He also published a journal, *The Conservator*, in which he reported on the doings of the Philadelphia Ethical Society, the Ethical Culture movement in general, and all things Whitman. Salter agreed to stock *The Conservator* on the table at the back of the society where pamphlets and programs were available, and he regularly announced new issues from the podium. Traubel served as secretary of the society as well, and evidently was an upright member of the congregation. Even after the controversy Salter respected him and considered him "conscientious . . . of the stuff of which heroes are made."[48]

A hero in the logic of liberal religion was a full moral agent willing to take any consequences for expressing beliefs with candor. Traubel's belief was that "all views must have equal rights" in the movement, in Salter's recollection, and that "free love" was one such view deserving of a fair hearing.[49]

Free love had been debated in liberal circles since the mid-nineteenth century. Henry James Sr., though a monogamous husband himself (insofar as anyone knows), had advocated revocable consent as the basis of heterosexual union. He held a moderate position between Stephen Pearl Andrews, an English defender of free love who opposed any legal binding for couplehood, and Horace Greeley, the antislavery newspaper editor turned reconciliationist running mate to an ex-Confederate, who insisted that marriage be legal and permanent. In the adultery scandal of the century—when the Congregationalist minister Henry Ward Beecher stood trial in 1875 for "alienating the affection" of the wife of a parishioner—free love was wielded as a tarbrush for painting characters black. At the same time, the first female candidate for U.S. president, Victoria Woodhull, used that platform and any other she could reach to proclaim the doctrine of free love as the next step in the advancement of humanity. Free love was to gender and sexuality what free religion was to theology.[50]

Logic may have been on the side of the free lovers, but culture at the time was not. The institution of marriage in the nineteenth century was far from egalitarian, with women losing legal and property rights upon becoming wives and divorce illegal in most states, so even if a man abandoned his family, his wife could not regain her independence. The idea of free love held that the state should get out of the marriage business and that conjugal unions should then be based on mutual consent, altogether removing coercion by either state or spouse from this highest of spiritual bonds. The free love of the late nineteenth century was different from the free love of the 1960s in that it was not supposed to be a ticket to promiscuity, although Woodhull and others rather undermined the lofty claims of their cause with frequent dissolutions and unions. Free love was intended to be about freedom and choice and self-determination, the hallmark concerns of liberal religion. For how could a moral agent fully develop his or her higher nature if trapped in a relation to a partner who stifled spiritual growth?[51]

Traubel took this view, and took it increasingly vocally in *The Conservator*, while Salter disagreed. Salter responded in two ways. First, he started publishing a journal of his own, *The Cause: Devoted to Moral Progress*, so that parishioners could read about ethical matters without encountering free love doctrine. Then he stopped announcing *The Conservator* from the pulpit. Traubel reacted by pressuring the board of trustees to command Salter to announce the paper, a strategy that failed. Soon Traubel proposed a resolution at the annual meeting of the society to the same effect, also failing. Finally he and his couple of dozen followers resigned their memberships. Traubel thought that Salter "had offended against equal freedom," while Salter "held that the Ethical Society's object and reason for being was to favor some things and oppose others, that it could not be non-committal, or 'stand indifferent' à la Walt Whitman." As the leader of the Philadelphia society, Salter felt not only justified in declining to advertise for free love doctrine, he felt bound by duty to uphold what he believed was right. In the case of marriage, it must be freely entered into but then becomes an obligation, "a contract for life," or else "it loses all it has of human dignity."[52]

Human dignity, of course, is acquired through successive acts of moral agency, a right that carries with it a sacred responsibility. This is how Salter defined the good. Hence he got snarled up in another knot in the liberal paradox after joining the Indian Rights Association (IRA) while living in Philadelphia. He had thought before about the relationship between Americans and the indigenous peoples of what became the United States. In an 1883 ethical address on "The Social Ideal," he bespoke a basic Lockean liberalism in his way of thinking about property. He also displayed what one historian calls "unilinear evolutionism" by placing people who do not turn land use into profit behind people who do on a scale of progressive social development. This aspect of liberalism was a sword that cut two ways. On the one hand, Salter believed "that civilization has a perfect right to dispossess barbarism of an exclusive and profitless occupation of the soil," which meant that he saw no injustice in the American conquest of the continent from sea to sea. On the other hand, Native Americans "are human beings" with all "the rights of human beings," which means that government should protect those rights rather than trampling on them. Salter joined the founders of the IRA in seeking to defend Native American rights, but to do so according to a Euro-American conception of what those rights should be. This means that the IRA, founded in 1882, was a progressive organization on the question of what should be done with the (vanishing) Indian, worth considering against those for whom every dead buffalo was a dead Indian. The IRA was more progressive than either domestic imperialists like Theodore Roosevelt or reformers like Carl Schurz—an anti-imperialist like Salter and James—who favored a gradual approach to ameliorating the deplorable poverty and hopelessness of Native Americans unable to maintain their ways of life on reservations and subject to repeated massacres by American troops and vigilantes. IRA members were known as "Friends of the Indian" for a reason. They wanted full citizenship for Native Americans and they wanted it immediately, suffrage included. Then they wanted every Native American to have the forty acres and a mule that had been denied to African Americans after the Civil War—or at least to have some land of their own to improve by hard work and merit. With the means of self-determination at their disposal, Native Americans could become complete moral agents and "take a place in the ranks of civilized people," in Salter's words.[53]

This was the logic behind the Dawes Severalty Act of 1887, strongly backed by the IRA, which allotted plots of land to every Native American in the country. Disastrously. Land speculation, fuzzy conceptions of ownership, mismanagement, and greed produced a rapid loss of land out from under Native Americans. A provision in 1891 allowed the leasing of the lands held in severalty, followed by a 1906 act permitting their sale, which eventually reduced Native landholdings from 156 million acres in 1881 to 53 million in 1933. The goal had been to provide the means for self-sufficiency and civic virtue through the rights of property; the accomplishment was the reverse.[54]

The failure of the Dawes Act's good intentions was still invisible at the time Salter joined the organization in 1894. IRA work continued to pursue the goal of Native American citizenship in the 1890s through education. By extending the means of self-culture to Native American children, benevolent educators believed they were giving them the means of independence and equality. That institutions like the Carlisle School of Pennsylvania cut off the long hair of Native American boys, forbade the use of Native languages, and taught Protestant Christianity along with the three Rs seemed right and proper to these educators, improving acts rather than culturally genocidal measures. The reformers who backed these enterprises thought that the blend of manual education, book learning, hygiene, and manners they were teaching was simply the objectively best means of advancing in a civilized society they firmly believed was the best way of life on earth, a generous sharing of culture rather than a murderous extinction of it. It meant they thought the Native Americans were equals—at least potentially.[55]

Even the emphasis on mechanical or trade skills that W. E. B. DuBois later found so limiting in the educational vision of a Booker T. Washington reflected—in part—a liberal sense of how comprehensive education should be for every child. The ideal of a balanced education that included manual arts goes all the way back to Horace Mann's inclusion of exercise in the school day and on to the twentieth century through John Dewey's "whole idea" of education, which Felix Adler developed independently of Dewey and Thomas Davidson advocated as well. Indeed, when Henry Demarest Lloyd read Davidson's theory of "complete education," in which students would cooperate in everything from bed making to wall building in order to progressively train all their faculties, including their social and moral ones, he thought immediately of the Hampton Institute, where Washington had gotten his start. "That school seems to need only the admission of white boys and girls to be the nearest your ideal of any in the country," he wrote Davidson. "There red and black, the real and ideal in training meet." Lloyd noted the irony that "the best education given on this continent today is given to the children of the Indians and the Negroes whom we have robbed and murdered and enslaved." He wanted Euro-American children to be admitted so that they could enjoy such a quality education too, and so that the school's integration could be complete. He called it "a great injustice" to the Hampton's present students as well as to "*our* children that whites cannot be stirred into the same brew of the future people." Lloyd's comfortable use of "we" to refer to American exploiters is especially interesting given that Davidson's ancestors were in Scotland and therefore not responsible for the pillage on the American continent, but more historic is the noteworthy fact that Lloyd's liberal sensibility deplored the pillage and looked forward to a "future people" that stirs Native Americans, African Americans, and Euro-Americans in together. This is the liberal integrationist dream.[56]

"Assimilation" became a dirty word in some circles in the twentieth century when the unique value of every culture came to be prized in a newly loud and proud way. Yet the "cultural pluralism" that voiced an antiassimilationist critique of cultural homogenization, ethnocentrity, and liberal integrationism actually came from the same place as the conception of universal human rights behind the integrationist dream. Cultural pluralism was formally developed by Horace M. Kallen, a student of William James's who took the pluralism James had illustrated in "On a Certain Blindness in Human Beings" and applied it to cultural groups including Jews, whom Kallen included in the great American symphony in his 1915 argument against the melting pot. What had been an individualist idea in James and other liberals—that everyone bears a hidden inner spark of the infinite divine and that differences reflect divine splendor—became a social idea in Kallen and later cultural pluralists, providing them a way to push back against a monocultural model of taste and value. All of this lay ahead of Salter and his colleagues in the IRA. From the vantage point of the 1890s, the best way they could see of supporting the rights of Native Americans was through including them in society and educating them for citizenship. For this reason the IRA also backed the adoption of Native American children into suitable families.[57]

"I can't help from expressing the feelings which have been besetting me throughout the day," William James wrote his mother-in-law in 1900, "and growing hourly stronger, about the Salters' project of adopting a child." He and Alice thought it was a terrible idea. The Salters were getting on in years. The child would be a financial drag. He would make study impossible for Mack and repose impossible for his wife. They would be unable to travel abroad. And it would interfere with their ethical work, which James considered public service enough. "I simply can't bear to think of Mack's & Mary's arduous public function being so prodigiously interfered with as it would be by such a policy of expansion. It is worse than annexing the Philippine Islands."[58]

The imperial metaphor is the closest James got in the letter to referring to the ethnicity of the child. Frank Gray was a two-year-old Native American, descended from New England Micmac, Abenaki, and Mohawk—Wabanaki for shorthand—who may have been related to one of the servants James and his wife kept at their Chocorua home. The Salters adopted him through the state of New Hampshire, to which he had become a ward, and changed his name to John Randall Salter. James's objections arrived too late. The couple had been heartbroken since the death of their daughter by measles a decade before, their home life bleak, and they badly wanted a child to love.[59]

How well they did so is a private and ultimately irretrievable matter. John Salter appears in a photograph with his adoptive parents in New Hampshire when he would have been thirteen and they were pushing sixty. All are smiling. But in adulthood John Salter voiced such painful memories of his life with the Salters that his own son changed his surname back to Gray. John apparently never knew that Mack Salter had grown deaf, but he remembered him as distant and disapproving. Mary Salter was warm, and summers with the James family were even warmer; John remembered sitting by the lake with James discussing the possibility of frogs having souls. "There was nothing ever even slightly remote about William James," John told his son years later. The children of Mack Salter's brother Sumner, however, treated John with contempt according to stereotype. "Sitting Bull," they called him. Once they accused him of stealing a watch.

John remembered visiting the deathbed of William James that mournful August of 1910. Within a few years after that, life in the Salter home apparently became difficult. When the Salters traveled abroad, they boarded John with a family in Evanston, Illinois. This was not necessarily a telling decision; John Dewey and his wife also left their sons at home when they went to Europe (two died while they were away on separate trips). But John Salter felt neglected, often seeking relatives in the New Hampshire Wabanaki community for company in the summer. His schooling was patchy and he never enrolled in high school, an astounding omission for a family that valued education as much as the Salters did. When he was only fifteen years old, Mack Salter dragged him down to army recruiting headquarters, where he tried to enlist the boy but was abruptly dismissed because John was obviously too young, he later told his son. John left home two years later, hitching a ship out of Boston as a cabin boy. Mack Salter disowned him, but Mary set up a small trust fund for him at the State Street Bank in Boston. When he eventually enrolled in the Art Institute in Chicago—ultimately becoming a successful artist across a range of media—the estate of William James supported his tuition, a fitting legacy from a man who once tried his hand at painting. When John Salter married, he got a gift "from your cousin Alice and me," that is, from William James Jr. and his wife. He kept the complete works of Salter and James as well.[60]

Salter showed no curiosity about his son's Native heritage. In all his research into different religions over the twenty-five years he served as a lecturer for Ethical Culture, he never investigated the spiritual traditions indigenous to the American continent. Yet he was interested in non-Christian thought and culture, particularly in Buddhism. Some knowledge of Buddhism came to him through the FRA and the liberal journal *The Open Court*, published out of LaSalle, Illinois. The journal was edited by a German immigrant named Paul Carus who had found science in conflict with his native Lutheran faith. Science won. Carus made a serious enough study of Buddhism that he published *The Gospel of Buddha* in 1894 and ultimately arranged to have D. T. Suzuki, the most important Zen master in America in the twentieth century, emigrate from Japan.[61]

Salter, like many liberals in their cohort including James, was somewhat allergic to Carus's monistic philosophy, though. Salter pursued his own study of Buddhism through a wide-ranging survey of available knowledge, which was at once limited, biased, and burgeoning. The Western study of Indian and Far Eastern religions had grown over the nineteenth century among German Romantics, European academics, American religious liberals, Oriental enthusiasts, and theosophists so that a substantial volume of material was available by the late nineteenth century. At the same time, although many of the scholars and linguists involved were post-Christian themselves, even the name "Buddhism" was bestowed on the tradition through a Christian frame of reference.

Western understanding of the varieties of Buddhist traditions was both dim and distorted, generally reached through an assumed superiority of Christianity as the usher of the modern religion of humanity.[62]

Buddhism was widely seen as pessimistic, even nihilistic. Thomas Davidson was not atypical in calling it "a degraded idolatry, coupled with doctrines of metempsychosis and nirvana." The Buddha was often portrayed in free religious writings as an ethical teacher analogous to Christ. Most popularly, Sir Edwin Arnold's poem "The Light of Asia" (1879) depicted the Buddha as a mystically wise figure. As invoked by a poetess in the Chicago Ethical Society who managed to get her verse published in *Unity*, seeing a Chinese shrine in a museum could engender vague feelings of spiritual tranquillity: "Stealthy twilight overtakes me as I drowse before the god; / Western idols are abandoned under bland Gautama's nod; / Drenching timelessness enshrouds me with a sense of suave release / As I yield in wise surrender to the Orientals' peace!"[63]

Salter did not appear to have much of a mystical faculty himself. Nor did James, who liked Buddhism for more concrete reasons. He allegedly once called Buddhism the way of the future and confessed in his postscript to *Varieties* that he agreed with "the Buddhistic doctrine of Karma" insofar as he understood it to unite "judgment and execution." He appreciated the practicalism of Buddhism, but he knew very little about it. Some scholars have noticed an affinity between pragmatism, especially Jamesian pragmatism, and Buddhism, but any resemblance is not derivative.[64]

It is tempting to think that Salter and James discussed what they knew of Buddhism during their summers by the lake. Salter's interest appears to have been more sustained than that of James. Salter referred to the tradition in many of his lectures, starting with his first, appreciating Buddhism as an example of nontheistic religion with a high ideal and a rigorous ethical practice. He understood that "Buddha" is not just another name for God. In Salter's inaugural lecture in Chicago he noted that "there is a wider sense of the word religion" than the one denoted by the words God, prayer, and immortality, "one that would give a place to Buddhism" because it fulfills the American Reformation's definition of religion. Buddhism "sets a supreme ideal before the human mind and prescribes a rule for its attainment." Buddhism was a form of practical idealism.[65]

Buddhism's ultimate ideal Salter found to be extremely exalted: the ideal of placing one's own interest behind the interest of collective humanity. Analogous to the understanding of God in the American Reformation, whose impartial, self-forgetting love his creatures are to imitate in service to one another, Salter's Buddhism did away with God and kept the disinterested benevolence. In his description of the moral force necessary to deal with the labor question, he argued that the "consuming thought must be that of brotherhood, of an equal realization by all of the great ends of existence." Universal human brotherhood requires an active commitment to the practice of self-forgetfulness. He then declared that "in the spirit of the holy Buddha, we must learn to say, 'Never will I receive private salvation.'" Salter invoked the Mahayana commitment of the bodhisattva to universal compassion, which he contrasted to what he frankly considered the selfish idea of evangelicals' afterlife.[66]

Moreover, Buddhism not only set forth a high ideal but also inspired a high standard of ethical practice, it seemed. Salter clipped an article in 1887 that purported to have made a comparative examination of crime among adherents of different faiths—or civilizations, or nationalities; the typology of peoples in the piece was inconsistent. The study claimed to have found that there was only one criminal per 3,787 Buddhists, as compared to one in 274 among Europeans, one in 509 among Eurasians, one in 799 among "native Christians," one in 856 among Muslims, and one in 1,361 among Hindus. Salter underlined the article's summary conclusion that the dramatic law-abidingness of Buddhists "is a magnificent tribute to the exalted purity of Buddhism."[67]

Buddhism did somewhat different work in the final phase of Salter's career. He had gone back to Chicago after his replacement, the charismatic M. M. Mangasarian, responded to Adler's censure of his extreme anti-Catholic views by leading half the Chicago Society away to start a splinter group. Salter wrote some powerful pieces against American imperialism in the Philippines and the lynching crisis at the turn of the century. He contrasted the use of force in either case with the historic American commitment to self-determination. Still, he longed to satisfy his old philosophical urges, which he could not do while tuning his message to a general audience.

Salter's formal philosophical career had been launched in 1892 with a well-received little book, *First Steps in Philosophy*, which aimed in a somewhat positivistic way, just like its title said, to venture forth with views he felt solid enough to build upon. His principal argument there was that everything should progress toward its ideal form, that "what should be . . . is the realization of the nature of each particular thing without limitation," a basic liberal principle he tried to establish scientifically. He closed the book with liberal humility: "I will not even say that it is the true theory; I can only say that it is true to me, (with the best exercise of rationality that I have been able to command); whether it is true to others . . . they must themselves decide." The right of private judgment he properly reserved to his readers. And it was in connection to this right of private judgment, now ancient, that an understanding of Buddhism came into play.[68]

Salter retired from the ethical pulpit fed up with himself. He had faced "the subtle temptations of a preacher" and found himself wanting. "One feels so good" in oratory, he explained, "one *is* so good for the time—and one with many speeches may multiply those times, until one has an almost continually swimming consciousness that he is good, while as to the reality he may know nothing." He had met his ignorance in his parenting of a runaway child. Now he went in search of something he might know about reality—sought it in George Bernard Shaw, who punctured the Western faith in progress with which American liberal culture was imbued; sought it in Arthur Schopenhauer, the first serious Western philosopher to incorporate a version of Buddhism deep into his metaphysics; sought it finally in Nietzsche, who took in Schopenhauer and much of the rest of Western thought and gave out something that blew the liberal common ground of morality to bits. It was a radically rationalist individual relativism. Scholars are right to observe an intellectual kinship between the relativist philosophy of Friedrich Nietzsche and the pragmatic philosophy of William James, but Nietzsche's works could never have been written by an American steeped in the liberal religious tradition. Nietzsche had devoured Emerson, but his was a fundamentally different mind from Emerson's. As Salter put it, Nietzsche's joy, such as it was, was "ever a warrior's joy—it is never the easy serenity, the unruffled optimism of Emerson."[69]

Nor was it exactly the pessimism of Schopenhauer, although Nietzsche deeply considered how Schopenhauer took the Western caricature of Buddhism and turned self-annihilation into a positive good. The relativism of Nietzsche was more like the way William James considered religious experience in terms of the varieties of human minds, each temperament requiring a different religious formulation. Taking the diversity of mental natures seriously meant allowing for truths to appear different ways to different observers. Perspectivalism, this is called in pragmatism. In Nietzsche the focus was not on the positive additive possibilities of granting the equal possible validity of different viewpoints as it was in James, though. Nietzsche focused on the absence of ground beneath any law. Salter explained how this operated in Nietzsche's works to make it impossible to declare what is valuable or good. "To a Schopenhauerian or Buddhist," he pointed out, "a strong lusty man, eager for life and power, is not in a state of health at all; while from another point of view, it is the Schopenhauerian or Buddhist, craving for the extinguishment of his individuality, who is sick." There is no universal right if every perspective is sovereign.[70]

This was a shocking place for a liberal like Salter to land. Relativism has been charged to liberal intellectual culture since the neo-Calvinists first worried that reading the Bible historically would lead to infidelity. The liberal answer to the relativist charge had always been that using reason was what God wanted them to do and that they were doing it in order to become more moral, not less. Yet their commitment to the pursuit of moral perfection had always been coupled with liberal open-mindedness in the pursuit of truth. Whether Nietzsche had seized truth or not, he made very clear to Salter a fundamental finding of liberal intellectual culture: "The ideal that mankind may have in common can only be very general and one that for many will perhaps seem far away." Salter did not stop there, though. He had his brother-in-law's version of pluralism to provide a kind of suspension underneath this floating multiplicity of personal truths. "[I]deals are relative to the lives that entertain them," James had said in "What Makes a Life Significant." They are acted out in the theater of humanity, and, each life's being sacred by its invisible glow of inner divinity, that general truth itself provided reason enough to learn from others' ideals while living by one's own. After taking full stock of Nietzsche as a thinker with frequent textual comparisons to Emerson, Salter concluded that progress ought to come after all, and that the goal of progress explained the necessity of struggle in life. Even if Nietzsche were right about the necessity of future wars for

mental conceptions or even about the undesirability of universal brotherhood, "a universal reign of law would seem to be inevitable."[71]

But 1917 was not a good year to try to sell American readers a book
about a German thinker who seemed to think he was some kind of
superman. Salter had become accustomed, in his days as a star of a rising
movement, to better press—and better sales. By the 1890s he had a lecture that was popular in Norway, where ethical societies were springing
up, as they were in London, Vienna, Lausanne, Zurich, Berlin, Amsterdam, Auckland, and Tokyo. His volume of collected addresses, *Ethical
Religion* (1889), had been translated into German and Dutch, had deeply
impressed a professor of moral philosophy at the University of Ghent,
had gotten banned in czarist Russia, and—as explained in a newspaper
article that journeyed from India to Chicago in less than two months in
1925—had found its way into the Yerwada Jail and into the hands of
Mohandas Gandhi, who read it so closely and liked it so much that he
summarized it in his native Gujarati in the book *Nîthi Dharma* (1922).
Salter had lectured in Berlin and been invited to more congresses than
he could remember. Now his work seemed to be done. He came back to
the ethical pulpit just once, in 1924, to define Americanism in old-
fashioned liberal terms rather than those of Henry Ford, or the nativists
behind the National Origins Act of the same year, or the many Babbitts
worshipping the bigger and better, the sleek and the new. "Americanism
is an ideal," Salter insisted. "The Constitution becomes little better than
a scrap of paper if the living conscience and will of the people are not
behind it."[72]

By then even Ethical Culture had institutionalized and fully human-
ized its mission. Salter was not in step with its new therapeutic ethos.
But he had done his work. Even through his reading of Nietzsche, he
had continued to be faithful to Emerson by being faithful to his vision

of a future, perhaps unreachable form. "Striving to be man," Emerson had written in *Nature*, "the worm / Mounts thro' all the spires of form." By the end of his life Salter had come to doubt that those spires were strictly graded or steadily progressive, but he remained a liberal—now a contested term—meaning for him "that whatever creed one may hold none can claim to be infallible, or of exclusive divine authority, and that good men of different creeds should respect and tolerate one another." In fealty to this liberal, anticreedal creed, Salter had defended the Haymarket anarchists and accommodated their points of view without entirely agreeing with them. He had called for a modern liberal state while acknowledging reasonable objections to it. He had disagreed with Horace Traubel while respecting his character. And he had read Nietzsche with an open mind and believed in progress anyway. But he had seen American imperialism triumphant and lived past the cultural expiration date of his Victorian sonority.[73]

7.

JANE ADDAMS, SOCIAL DEMOCRAT

UNIVERSAL NEEDS AND THE COOPERATIVE ROAD TO INTERNATIONAL PEACE

Late in the summer of 1902, William James read a book he soon urged upon a friend—in superior distinction to his own newly published *Varieties of Religious Experience*—as a "*really* great book." To another friend he called it "a very big book," although in size it was really rather small, not much over a hundred pages of simply written prose with few quotations and no footnotes. The book was *Democracy and Social Ethics*, written by Jane Addams, to whom James then wrote a personal "tribute of thanks." Her work appealed to him because she actually practiced the democratic faith he preached. "The religion of democracy," he wrote to her, "needs nothing so much as sympathetic interpretation to one another of the different classes of which Society consists." Addams performed this service "in a masterly manner."[1]

Addams, nearly two decades younger than James, had been running Hull House for more than a dozen years by that point, an enterprise based on the idea that residents of the settlement house and their neighbors in the community serve one another as equals with mutual needs that could be met only through dialogue and cooperation. This experience indeed made her a master of what she called in the book a "social morality" that emerges through real, daily, lived contact with "diversified human experience." By analyzing the many different viewpoints involved in turn-of-the-century American domestic, industrial, and political relations, Addams perceptively conveyed to James and other readers a broad range of American subjectivities and credibly argued for a truly democratic approach to progress: democratic because it included all voices, progressive because it advanced common interests in a way made sustainable by the patient building of consensus. Addams offered "a conception of Democracy not merely as a sentiment which desires the well-being of all men," she wrote, "nor yet as a creed which believes in the essential dignity and equality of all men, but as that which affords a rule of living as well as a test of faith."[2]

Much though Addams spoke James's language here, she does not appear to have read any of his work at this stage of her career, although she may have known of him from Salter, at whose Chicago society she lectured, or from Davidson, who was an early adviser to Hull House—initially a dubious one, and then an enthusiastic one when his Breadwinners' College changed his mind about interclass social progress. But Addams never operated in Boston Unitarian circles, rarely referred to herself as a liberal, and used little of the old Victorian vocabulary for inner divinity and moral nature. In fact, the one criticism James ever made of her pertained to her plain style of writing, a style that both connected her to the Puritan roots of the American Reformation and marked her departure from the older generation of liberals as she sought a universally accessible way to express the essentials of human experience.[3]

Addams grew up affluent but unconnected to the networks of liberals descended from the great Reformation Christians of New England Congregationalism, her father a self-made man who attended church but said little about religion. Yet she moved thick in the flow of religious and social faiths those liberal networks helped produce, and she seems to have been reading from the same playbook as James and his friends when she wrote *Democracy and Social Ethics*, in which certain hallmarks of the American Reformation pointed toward "a new affinity for all men, which probably never existed in the world before." Experience, for Addams as for earlier liberals, was a crucial basis for discovering truth—from which there is nothing to fear—and habit a conservative force susceptible to modification by new convictions. She praised "voluntary morality" over passive virtue and the superiority of devotion to the common welfare over self-interest, especially in light of the social fact of human interdependence. Vividly updating the practical Christianity of Channing's generation, she argued that "action is the sole medium of expression for ethics," which are discoverable "only by tentative and observant practice." The "fallible intelligence" of human beings inevitably produces misunderstandings "due to partial experience" that can be fully overcome only in the ultimate peace and freedom of death. Meanwhile, partial understanding may be ameliorated through the conscious, deliberate acceptance of "Democracy and its manifold experiences." Addams might be the most exemplary product of the American Reformation to shape the twentieth century.[4]

She was a teetotaling virgin who was not a prude, which means she effectively solved the liberal paradox that bedeviled the careers of Davidson and Salter as well as the presidency of John Adams. Maybe she figured it out because having a curved spine forced periods of invalidism in her youth and adulthood, periods in which she examined her soul and found it wanting, which meant she bore a profound humility in all environments together with an immense inner strength and straight-talking manner. Maybe she figured it out because she grew up in a rural village—she often stopped in at the blacksmith's shop and the miller's on her way home from school—and only fully encountered the modern industrial city as an idealistic young adult who found more in common with immigrant peasants than with some urbanites. Maybe because she never showed interest in marriage while girls all around her conformed to the late Victorian ideal of sanctified motherhood, and yet she loved many children and mothers as though they were kin because her most basic belief was in the preciousness of every human being. Or maybe because her father told her "you must always be honest with yourself inside," so she was able to withstand the evangelism of Christians and socialists alike while appreciating their moral qualities and listening to their perspectives. She listened to murderers, thieves, prostitutes, and addicts too.[5]

Addams was as devoutly committed to open-mindedness, in fact, as to what her father called "mental integrity," the other horn of the liberal paradox, which she solved by getting comfortable on the saddle of thin air between the two horns. "The last word on anything is never said," her colleague Lillian Wald remembered Jane Addams as believing. She tended toward "the middle of the road," she herself said, committed to achieving "the best possible" in an evolving present instead of proclaiming—or even pursuing—some new and final religion of the future. Holding clearly and exclusively to the most basic liberal claim that each human individuality matters equally, she devoted herself to the continual reception, interpretation, translation, and coordination of multiple individual perspectives so that common ground emerged in ever-shifting parcels and hillocks, no position final but always contingent on the active, ongoing dialogue and experiment of this liberal middle way. "But just whither the said religion of democracy will lead," wrote James, who had most finely worked out in theory what Addams put into practice, "who knows? Meanwhile there is no other, in human affairs, to follow."[6]

Of course something depends on how one defines "virgin." Addams had intense private attachments to two female companions in particular, one until death. More publicly, she created a social world that was decidedly not male-centered. Hull House churned with representatives of both sexes, all ages, all socioeconomic strata, all lines of work and faith and language and worldview. Thousands of people representing eighteen nationalities came through Hull House every week, rendering Addams rich with experiences, her own and those others related to her. This experiential depth and breadth dispelled the liberal naïveté that had so cheerfully assumed the adequacy of preindustrial virtues for modern America. Unlike many of her fellow progressive reformers, she did not think American society could or should march backward into the old republican model of economic self-sufficiency and local autonomy. Nor did she think there was any exceptional greatness to the American character capable of overcoming the contradiction between the promise of American freedom and the stark facts of social and economic tyranny over industrial workers. She did not pretend those workers were free of vice themselves, but she saw her neighbors' problems with alcohol and delinquency as by-products of what she called the "maladjustment" of the modern city to serve the most "primitive"—and therefore vital—human needs.[7]

With clearer eyes than many of her comrades in social reform and most of her predecessors in the liberal train of the American Reformation, Addams saw that the only modern force catering to the primitive human needs of pleasure, stimulation, and communal joy was the commercial force driven by the motive of profit and therefore unbound by any sense of duty or conscience beyond the dollar. The voluntary activities of Hull House in providing entertainment, knowledge, aesthetic appreciation, and egalitarian sociability were deliberate attempts to serve such primitive human needs alongside the more obvious necessities of health and safety. This work also helped create modern liberalism; Addams and her colleagues pressed the city and the state to step in where so far commercialism held iniquitous reign. Government, the collective will of the people, must provide public services and wholesome opportunities for "the spirit of Youth," as a later book of hers that moved James almost to tears described the human drive for justice and progress as well as adventure and "the fundamental susceptibility of sex." Only then could a democratic society thwart commercialism's ambition to so sensationalize the young that they "early become absorbed in a hand to mouth existence, and so entangled in materialism that there would be no reaction against it."[8]

Addams described the community at Hull House as a "fellowship," one key word of the American Reformation she did retain. Because she experienced this fellowship's diversity as a strength that clarified which differences were incidental to human cultures and what human essentials those cultures served, she then applied the concept of diverse fellowship to the international scene in a serious quest for world peace. As she explained at a conference William James attended in 1904 and in a book he liked so much he sent a copy of this "new political gospel" to George Bernard Shaw, Addams believed that war could be made a relic of barbarism if nations came together and forged agreements on what needs are universal and how they may be cooperatively met. She suggested that "cosmopolitan affection" for all peoples is possible in the whole world exactly as "in the new world, all the immigrants are reduced to the fundamental equalities and universal necessities of human life itself." She meant that urban experience clarifies collective needs and leads immigrants to see past their differences and act in common cause, so their experience should be a lesson to the international community. To an audience that steadily narrowed domestically and widened internationally as World War I developed, Addams argued that nations would not have to go to war for territorial gain if, say, what they really need is access to a seaport that could be supplied by mutual consent. The pluralism that made modern liberalism a tenuous reality in America also made world peace a practical possibility rather than an airy ideal.[9]

Needless to say, the world on which Jane Addams closed her eyes for the last time in 1935 was not a world on the brink of peace. Neither the League of Nations she favored nor the Nobel Peace Prize she won nor the United Nations that materialized after her death succeeded in coordinating the needs and interests of the globe's many peoples. But both her articulation of a logic for world peace and her method of devising it are significant for understanding the American Reformation, the religion of democracy it produced, and the liberal mental practice that guided postevangelical Reformation Christians in New England and their increasingly diffuse Christian and post-Christian descendants. If the chief characteristic of the European Enlightenment is the belief in progress, together with the necessity of reason in its pursuit—a process widely considered to be secular, as in devoid of supernatural constructs—the chief legacy of the American Reformation, which absorbed Enlightenment principles into New England Christianity before spreading with liberal mental culture, may be a practical idealism that holds as its supreme ethic the living out of natural human equality, a progressive goal involving the use of reason as a common denominator of human thought that is secular, as in inclusive of all perspectives, including those informed by supernatural beliefs. Universal human moral agency, a right and duty that requires freedom for its exercise, was rooted in a specific variant of Reformation Christianity from an ethnically homogeneous corner of a society that became more and more diverse as the centuries went by. For Jane Addams, moral agency appeared free of its Christian roots as a basic human right, an empirical finding of a lived

diversity as well as the generator of her ability to withstand losing supporters and comrades in her ongoing pacifism. She based her life's work
on a conviction she shared with John Adams, a faith that Jane Addams
described in 1922 as "the categorical belief that a man's primary allegiance is to his vision of the truth and that he is under obligation to
affirm it."[10]

MENTAL INTEGRITY

It may seem odd that an independent professional woman whose father
advocated the suffrage she lived to exercise nevertheless used such gendered language to express a universal principle she held—but if it is odd
it is not surprising. Ideals, practices, and vocabularies are not born
matching, and Addams had virtually no female role models among her
elders and few among her literary heroes. The Anglo-American canon
of the late nineteenth century was such that Addams read Ralph Waldo
Emerson but not Mary Moody Emerson; Thomas Carlyle but not Margaret Fuller; Wordsworth and Mill and Joseph Butler but not Mary
Wollstonecraft, and not Madame de Staël. At least she had George
Eliot—who, after all, wrote under a male pseudonym—but above all
Jane Addams had her father, John Addams, the leading citizen of their
little Illinois town. He was a founding member of the Republican Party
and for sixteen years a state senator whose vote Lincoln himself cared
for so much that he wrote letters soliciting the opinion of his "dear
Double-D'ed Addams." Lincoln knew, he wrote, that Addams "would
vote according to his conscience," and indeed, action in the service of
what he thought right seemed to be the central motivator of Addams's
life, at least in his daughter's recollection. He harbored a fugitive slave
en route to Canada, sponsored a combat unit of the Union army, funded

a subscription library, and worked to reform prisons, asylums, and schools while steadily serving their village church. His personal dignity and the respect with which he treated others formed the atmosphere in which the motherless Jane Addams grew up.[11]

The adult Addams seems to have sensed that her father was being sly when he told her he was a Hicksite Quaker, as she wrote in her autobiography, but the child to whom he said this did not understand it, nor has many an Addams scholar since. There was no apparent affiliation of anyone in the Addams family with the Quaker sect and no Quaker meetinghouse in their town of Cedarville or its vicinity. A biography of Elias Hicks sat on the family bookshelf, that's all. Quakers had long represented a slim percentage of the American Protestant population and a disproportionately large presence in the reformist community and—especially—imagination. Encouraging his daughter to tell people who asked that he was a Hicksite Quaker was John Addams's way of saying that he heeded the guidance of his own inner light rather than of the conforming hordes, who had no business inquiring into his private conscience. Moreover, he told this to his daughter during the same conversation in which he advised her always to be honest with herself. This was his antidote to the evangelism raging around her, making her uneasy about the fate of her soul. Revivals came through Cedarville, and although John Addams did not allow Jane to attend them, she heard about the rapturous conversions there, as well as the tearful agonies on the anxious bench where the unconverted writhed. Her classmates wanted to know whether she was saved or not, as did she. Her father did not help settle the question. He was quietly content to attend church without joining it and to teach in its Sunday school without professing anything. This example gave Jane Addams the fortitude even as a child to wonder whether a good doctor, newly dead, might be righteous despite never having uttered the words on which salvation was said to hinge. Eleven hundred miles from Boston, then, without a Unitarian church or a sermon by Channing, she learned through her father's character that doctrinal allegiance was not as important as conscientious conduct.[12]

John Addams also taught his daughter devotion for the democratic tradition through reverence for its exemplars. Neither blind devotion nor servile reverence, an attitude of attentive respect for the words and achievements of Lincoln and the Italian revolutionary Giuseppe Mazzini passed from father to daughter and into her work and writing. It is illustrative that these two democratic heroes represented "the greatest American," in Jane's words, "who has cleared the title to our democracy," and a great foreigner who attempted to bring democracy to the disfranchised Italian peasantry. Jane Addams was, on the one hand, a plain midwesterner whose state's martyred leader represented some of America's most cherished myths, especially the idea that from humble origins the truly deserving rise by merit and hard work. Her public admiration for Lincoln was both natural and savvy, sincere and effective, giving her common ground with the many other Americans who viewed Lincoln through the misty light of adulation and providing a ready indicator of the sacrifices that had already been made for the principle of equality.[13]

On the other hand, Addams developed a global consciousness over her career. Her father's interest in Mazzini first taught her, she wrote, about "the genuine relationship which may exist between men who share large hopes and like desires, even though they differ in nationality, language, and creed." Mazzini was only the first of many foreign inspirations for Addams, who helped import European municipal reforms and who advocated a doctrine of conscientious nonresistance she attributed to Tolstoy. Mazzini may be an especially fortuitous example of the cosmopolitan aspect of the democratic faith, however, since he fraternized with Margaret Fuller during the revolutionary 1840s. Words of his that Addams quoted in *Democracy and Social Ethics*—"that 'the consent of men and your own conscience are two wings given you whereby you may rise to God'"—sound more like an emanation of the American Reformation than of Roman Catholicism. One historian calls Addams a "cosmopolitan patriot," a designation that her fondness for these two democratic heroes helps ratify.[14]

The uses to which Addams put Mazzini's words and Lincoln's example exceeded what she absorbed from her father. In the tumult of labor activism and attempts to arbitrate disputes between workers and management, she learned that democratic practice went far beyond the ballot box—and fell far short of the standard of equality for which Lincoln and so many soldiers had died. When she quoted Mazzini in *Democracy and Social Ethics*, she used his lyrical line about conscience and consent to demonstrate how undemocratic a mind-set was exhibited by George Pullman, the owner of the Pullman railcar company and of the model town in which workers had all the material trappings of civilized life but none of the civic power. Mr. Pullman, Addams said, thought he knew what was best for others and so "did not appeal to or obtain the consent of" the workers who lived in his town. When an economic downturn came and he cut their wages without lowering their rent or agreeing to arbitrate, they struck. He was shocked by their ingratitude.

Pullman's shock demonstrated to Addams that he misunderstood the internal attitude of equality and external pursuit of consent necessary in a democratic society. "The man who insists on consent," in contrast, "who moves with the people," learns to look at the ideal outcome in practical terms, to behold both the absolute right and the possible right in the same visionary frame, to pursue "Mr. Lincoln's 'best possible'" and therefore to suffer "a sickening sense of compromise with his best convictions" but nevertheless "to move along with those whom he leads toward a goal that neither he nor they can clearly see till they come to it." Only in this consensual way can progress be made secure, not rapid but "incomparably greater because lateral." The old right of private conscience conjoins with a public process of dialogue and consensus to produce what is democratically sound. Writing eighteen years before she had the right to vote and astutely using only male pronouns, Jane Addams sounds here like the skillful politician her experience was teaching her to become.[15]

Before she could exercise such sagacity in the public sphere, though, Addams spent decades maturing in the private sphere then held to be the rightful dominion and only proper place for elite Anglo-American females. Often she inwardly chafed at this place. In her writing she likened the rarefied cultivation of her domestic environment to the nauseating sensation of eating a sweet confection for breakfast. Something in her strongly recoiled from the class-bound hospitality, ornamental arts, and dilettantish talents taught to her by her stepmother, for whom the Addams wealth was a privilege that carried no public responsibility. Obedient, dutiful, and appreciative of her advantages, Jane Addams served her stepmother's preferences and escorted her abroad. Inwardly, though, that honest voice her father had taught her to heed protested against the channeling of all her intelligence, drive, and education only for this, "the family claim," as she later called it.[16]

Sometimes the clash between her familial obligation and private conscience drove her to collapse, unable to act when the war within waged too violently. Her first major crisis came after her beloved father's sudden death when she was not yet twenty-one. In such times she was treated by S. Weir Mitchell, the same doctor who procured peyote for one of the psychedelic experiments William James tried, and the doctor behind Charlotte Perkins Gilman's "The Yellow Wallpaper" (1899), in which the unhappy mother is separated from her child, forbidden to write, coddled, and confined to a barred room in which she goes slowly mad. Gilman and Addams both underwent the gendered treatment for what was then called neurasthenia. For this nervous condition, doctors like Mitchell prescribed strenuous activity for patients like James, cure by rest for females. On one occasion Addams was "literally bound to a bed" for six months.[17]

At the same time, experiencing a distinctly female dominion proved empowering for her. At Rockford Seminary, the college to which her father determined she should go, she relished the companionship of other earnest young women, who looked to her as a natural leader. The opium episode in which she and her friends forayed onto the mystical path taken by Thomas De Quincey—"no mental reorientation took place," she reported, not even sleepiness—may have been the most colorful event of their college years, but the dominant note of her recollection of the period is intense moral and intellectual conscientiousness. She still remembered De Quincey years later when she saw real poverty for the first time in London's East End, so seriously did she and her classmates take their literary bread and butter at school. As college women, they were proud of their school, especially when it offered a full bachelor's degree for the first time to Addams and three others. She and her friends may have been most proud, however, the day Bronson Alcott came to lecture—proud of their campus, and tellingly more proud that their guest was Emerson's friend than that he was Louisa May Alcott's father. A quarter century later, Addams still remembered "cleaning the clay of the unpaved streets off his heavy cloth overshoes in a state of ecstatic energy."[18]

Rockford was a Christian seminary, though, headed by a scrupulous evangelical. This aspect of her education set Addams on a trajectory that was both genuinely Christian and decidedly universalist. Like an old Reformation Christian, she learned her Greek by studying the New

Testament every Sunday for two years. The "wonderful Life" she learned there contrasted strongly with the emphasis on conversion made by her college's president and faculty, one of whom tried to convince her to become a missionary to Turkey. Nothing doing. Addams listened to her inner voice and experienced the "beauty of holiness" through her private devotional practice while manifesting complete "unresponsiveness to the evangelical appeal."[19]

The origins of her lifelong reverence for "primitive Christianity" may be found here. When she developed a "realization of sorrow as the common lot, of death as the universal experience," she found vital comfort in the example of the early Christians who followed, "with a certain joyous simplicity," Jesus's "command to love all men," as she put it in her first important essay, "The Subjective Necessity for Social Settlements" (1892). Her anchor in this simple Christianity became an important language in her reform work and a critical factor in her leadership. At school "the pressure toward religious profession" increased over her senior year, creating a stress that she met with "passive resistance" by "clinging to an individual conviction," a process she described as "the best moral training I received at Rockford College." It prepared her for later encounters with dogmatic representatives of what she called "the social faiths"—followers of Comte or Henry George, preachy socialists, ardent anarchists—and prepared her to resist their attempts to pressure her into agreement with the same sober courage. She saw that Rockford evangelical Christians were motivated by "genuine zeal and affectionate solicitude," but nevertheless found she had "to stand on my own feet and to select what seemed reasonable from this wilderness of dogma."[20]

In the life and writings of Leo Tolstoy (1828–1910), Addams discovered support for her developing devotion to early Christian principles as well as an example of socially conscious moral courage that both inspired her and—somewhat to her own surprise—ultimately repelled her enough that she crystallized her own convictions more firmly than ever. Over the twentieth century Tolstoy's reputation came largely to be attached to his early literary masterpieces, but in the late nineteenth century he was an international hero for his mature social criticism. William James, for example, thought *War and Peace* "the greatest of human novels," while finding Tolstoy's *My Confession* worth quoting at length in one of his essays on the problem of labor. Tolstoy had learned belief by witnessing its beneficial power in the lives of the "laboring folks" of Russia, a pragmatic approach to religion admired by Ethical Culturists too, particularly as it came at the expense of the aristocratic set. Soon after college Addams read Tolstoy's account of his religious faith, which held that man "must live his life not for himself but for all." When Addams chose to be baptized and received into Cedarville's Presbyterian church at age twenty-five, entirely free of external pressure and lacking the experience of conversion, she described the religion she was adopting in a Tolstoyan manner. She embraced a simple Christian faith "boldly opposed to the accepted moral belief that the well-being of a privileged few might justly be built upon the ignorance and sacrifice of the many."[21]

In a few more years she began Hull House, and at about that time Tolstoy's *What Then Must We Do?* (1886) hit the American progressive scene. His indictment of Russian social inequality was stern, unsparing, and profoundly humane, a deeply reasoned observation that the cause of poverty and exploitation is the dependence of those who enjoy leisure on those who labor for them. Tolstoy offered a Christ-based denunciation of the common human weakness for fine fare and raiment. What we must do, Tolstoy said, was to "serve the welfare of others," to live like bees by toiling happily for others because "man, to say nothing of his reason or innate love of his fellow man, is called on by his very nature to serve others and to serve the common human ends."[22]

Addams—who read and reread everything of Tolstoy's she could—was chosen to write the introduction for a 1928 edition of *What Then Must We Do?* She said that the effect of the book under the conditions of late-nineteenth-century industrial Chicago "was curiously like that formulated by Abraham Lincoln . . . when driven by the existence of slavery to a long meditation on the basic relations between man and man." Lincoln's words harmonized with Tolstoy's approach as well as that of Thorstein Veblen (1857–1929), a maverick economist whom Addams also read and cited in her arguments for economic reform. "As labor is the common burden of our race," she quoted Lincoln to illustrate Tolstoy, "so the effort of some to shift their shares of burden onto the shoulders of others is the great durable curse of the race." Tolstoy had reached the top echelon of Addams's guiding lights.[23]

But she took no faith on trust. When she went abroad for her first real respite after seven years of running Hull House, she was invited to meet Tolstoy in person on his family estate. Naturally, she seized the chance to learn from him directly. Tolstoy had long since abandoned all luxuries and committed himself to regular toil alongside his field laborers, winning the admiration of social reformers across Europe and America as an example of someone "who has had the ability to lift his life to the level of his conscience," in Addams's words, "to translate his theories into action." She wanted to know whether this conscientious life had brought him peace. Could Tolstoy help her discover "a clew to the tangled affairs of city poverty[?]" Not even close. His person was impressive indeed, she found, in his coarse-spun shirt and untrimmed beard. She cringed when he lifted one of the sleeves of her dress, commenting that there was enough fabric there to clothe a child and suggesting she adopt peasant dress in order to connect with those she served. She knew better. The community she served was too diverse for her to be able to choose one folk style to imitate; immigrants adopted

American fashion as soon as they had wages to spend; and her work included fund-raising among the business elite whose sensibilities needed consideration as well.[24]

Then Tolstoy criticized Addams as an absentee landlord. She blanched, but she had already impaled herself on the futile effort to live purely in an impure financial system. She had sold a farm rented to such poor tenant farmers that the children's feet looked like hooves. Then she realized that her renunciation solved no one's problems. The new owner would simply rent it back to the same impoverished farmworkers. Afterward, she determined that the well-being of the community was more important than her own ethical purity. Her conviction withstood Tolstoy's criticism. Addams was still attracted by Tolstoy's "sermon of the deed," as she put it, but through conversation she came to think that "he made too great a distinction between the use of physical force and that moral energy which can override another's differences and scruples with equal ruthlessness." Echoing all unknowingly the criticism of the Great Awakening made by Charles Chauncy on the use of compulsion, she stood by her own conviction, forged with her associates in the early days of Hull House, "that we might live with opposition to no man, with recognition of the good in every man, even the most wretched."[25]

Tolstoy's politics of denunciation and dogmatism did not square with the ideal of universal fellowship held by Addams. Still, she was moved enough by the encounter to resolve to add some physical labor to her days. She decided to contribute a concrete material measure to the life of Hull House by spending two hours a day baking bread, real "bread labor" just as Tolstoy advocated. Then she got back to Chicago. "The half dozen people invariably waiting to see me after breakfast, the piles of letters to be opened and answered, the demand of actual and pressing human wants,—were these all to be pushed aside and asked to wait while I saved my soul by two hours' work at baking bread?"[26]

Addams did not lose her respect for Tolstoy. Nor did she seem to perceive that his disdain for her had any relation with his distinctly anti-modern views on what women should do with their lives, but her mental integrity was firmed up by the encounter. The search for personal righteousness, she had discovered in her agonized twenties, was ineffectual and even selfish in a suffering world that needed saving even by the impure. She did not judge Tolstoy harshly for the ways in which his theory and practice clashed with her own; she attributed the difference to his Russian context of rural poverty and ethnic homogeneity. She went on to use a phrase of Tolstoy's—"the snare of preparation"—to describe what young people, especially young women, experienced after years of education and training to build them up for a vague though lofty purpose that was then subverted by the family claim. She went on further to praise and assist followers of Tolstoy, especially the Doukhobors, admirable exemplars of Christian nonresistance who settled in Canada and then donated half the proceeds from the publication of Tolstoy's last novel to Hull House. And in that introduction to the centenary edition of Tolstoy's *What Then Must We Do?* Addams subtly qualified what Tolstoy had achieved. "It may be no clearer to us than it was to him that a righteous life cannot be lived in a society that is not righteous," she wrote. "It was clearer to him than it has been to any others, save to a small handful of shining souls, that the true man can attempt nothing less and that society can be made righteous in no other way."[27]

DIVERSIFIED HUMAN EXPERIENCE

When William James spent time in Chicago in 1905, the institution of Hull House was so positively renowned that he called his visit to it "inevitable," a must-see for socially aware liberals of his set. A similar reflection of the settlement's fame appears in Paul Revere Frothingham's 1903 biography of William Ellery Channing. Frothingham credited Channing with anticipating the settlement idea all the way back in 1837, when Channing had written at length about what good a man could do

> with his heart in the work, who should live among the uneducated, to spread useful knowledge and quickening truth by conversation and books, by frank and friendly intercourse, by encouraging meetings for improvement, by forming the more teachable into classes, and giving to these the animation of his presence and guidance, by bringing parents to an acquaintance with the principles of physical, intellectual, and moral education, by instructing families in the means and conditions of health, by using, in a word, all the methods which an active, generous mind would discover or invent for awakening intelligence and moral life; one gifted man, so devoted, might impart a new tone and spirit to a considerable circle: and what would be the result, were such men to be multiplied and combined so that a community might be pervaded by their influence!

Frothingham apparently intended for Channing's reputation to be enhanced by this seeming description of a male Jane Addams, but there are two significant differences between this gifted figment of Channing's imagination and the real Addams, differences that go beyond gender to describe the cultural distance between the leading voice of the American Reformation and the leading exemplar of the religion of democracy. First, Channing's "gifted man" gave the fruit of his education to the circle of uneducated he gathered around him, a one-way delivery of cultural blessings to the needy. This is exactly the sort of charity Addams pointedly criticized as old-fashioned, condescending, and undemocratic. Her settlement was a "reciprocal relation," she explained many times, in which settlement residents received at least as much as they gave. Residents and their neighbors depended on one another for the meaning and value of life rather than creating a dependent relationship of the recipient upon the giver. Addams and her associates did not come to Chicago thinking they were superior to their new neighbors, but rather with the idea that members of the community would themselves teach the residents what they needed to accomplish together. Democracy had ripened between Channing and Addams.[28]

The second major difference between Channing's gifted man and Jane Addams had to do with experience, social experience and the truths that it produced. It really appeared to Channing that "the principles of physical, intellectual, and moral education" could be possessed by that solitary gifted man and then imparted to the uneducated, because the fruits of learning seemed to belong to his social stratum, the Boston elite. Addams had no such certainty about what was true, "assuming that the best teacher of life is life itself," and her life was dramatically broader and more varied than Channing's. She traveled overseas earlier and more often and to a wider array of places, not only England but Russia and Spain as well as India and Egypt and Morocco. She met in those countries and elsewhere in Europe not only literary figures and clergymen but labor activists, politicians, and social thinkers, Fabian socialists like Beatrice and Sidney Webb, members of parliament from multiple countries, Oxford scholars, and Karl Marx's daughter.

She also saw the European poor. The sight of hungry Londoners scrabbling for rotten vegetables in the East End stunned her. She perceived a critical difference between the sort of work "class-conscious Englishmen" did at Toynbee Hall—the first settlement house, at which she volunteered for a stint—and the sort she might do as "a western

American who had been born in a rural community where the early pioneer life had made social distinctions impossible." She thought constantly about perceptions and attitudes, how social training created cultural lenses. Her awareness of the role conditioning played in determining priorities and abilities made her receptive to the many perspectives she encountered abroad as well as at home, where her personal contacts included academics and radicals, religious and political leaders, local and national officials, powerful businessmen and their powerful wives, visiting European royalty, and every president from Roosevelt to Roosevelt. She took in the relative understandings of each of these exposures, but most of all and on a daily basis, she studied her neighbors, immigrants and natives alike, with their skills and traditions learned at home and their values and ambitions practiced in the industrial city. This range of experience was her continuing education, the one that made her qualify whatever truths she had already learned as provisional truths and to stake actions on the collective judgment of this broad spectrum of human perspectives. This, she said, made the work of Hull House valid, and so very different from what Channing had envisioned.[29]

Yet Addams shared Channing's core values and concepts, so her differences from him grew out of that central vision, enacted in an evolved cultural context. She believed in what she called the eighteenth-century "creed of individual liberty," and therefore she opposed coercion, the use of force, and "dogmatism" even when it looked like patriotism, as it did when it stifled free speech during World War I. As Channing had discovered in Virginia and William James backed up with physiological psychology, Addams considered emotion to be "the organic preparation for action." She held "human compassion" as the greatest and most basic of all emotions. Compassion was the opposite of "self-interest," then unfortunately employed as the sole and sufficient justification for action in a twentieth-century society in which the principle of liberty had become "too barren and chilly" rather than productive and vital. She called virtue the "free expression of the inner life," the opposite of conformity. She thought everyone was unique in some way that society really needed. "The most precious moment in human development," she said, and Channing would have agreed, "is the young creature's asser-tion that he is unlike any other human being, and has an individual contribution to make to the world." She loved Wordsworth too, had read his poetry at a younger age than Channing or Mill did, and in her twilight years still quoted him. She even recognized that the modernist youth of that latter day despised Wordsworth's "jingling rhythm," but she insisted how "happy would our natures be, If joy were an unerring light, And love its own security." (To a similar end William James quoted Robert Louis Stevenson: "To miss the joy is to miss all.") For Addams, as for Channing and the free religionists in between them, the surest generator of joy was fellowship, a "fellowship of the deed" that did not imply "similarity of creed" but instead produced steadier and brighter light for the diversity of its members.[30]

Of course Channing dealt only with the diversity among Christians who interpreted the Christian Bible differently. Addams engaged with people in her community from entirely different religious backgrounds and often no religious commitment at all, all of whom found the "vague humanitarianism" of Hull House congenial where its critics tut-tutted its irreligiosity. She met either side of any range with the same expres-sion of her own moral agency as Channing would, however. Once she gave an address and someone in the audience called out that she would be afraid to speak so plainly once she became "subsidized by the million-aires." She answered quickly "that while I did not intend to be subsi-dized by millionaires, neither did I propose to be bullied by workingmen, and that I should state my honest opinion without consulting either of them." The audience of radicals burst into applause and started talking about the danger of tyranny to democratic institutions.[31]

The biggest and most important difference between Addams and Channing had to do with the growth of industrial capitalism. Channing worried about the coercion of slaves by their masters and of Christians by zealous dogmatists. Addams worried about the coercion of everyone, especially the young, by modern industry and the despotic rule of profit. She thought that American politics were out of step with the social conditions of the twentieth century, maladjusted to the massively altered new reality of modern life in which "the real issues are being settled by the great industrial and commercial interests which are at once the products and the masters of our contemporary life." Constitutional rights and privileges won in the eighteenth century and extended over the nineteenth century and into the twentieth were good, she affirmed, but inadequate against a commercial force impervious to the franchise. Her critique was not that of the ideologue but of the empiricist. She and her colleagues observed and, where they could, quantified the effects of industrial work and tenement living on their neighbors, concluding that through coercive forces from advertising to sweated labor, modern industry ruled the lives of the ostensibly free.[32]

The character of her indictment of commercial values begs the old question: Why was there never socialism in America? It is a question that invites a command: define socialism. True, Addams could no more adhere to the socialism derived from Marx and Engels, with its strictly materialist separation of the classes and single determined line of social progress, than Davidson or Salter could, though she read more socialist literature than they, felt its allure more vividly, and spent more time in frank discussion with avowed socialists in her community. But socialists "firmly insisted that fellowship depends upon identity of creed," and Addams saw counterproofs to that creed in every country town and newly mobile immigrant.[33]

Still, she incorporated the socialist critique of the alienation of workers from their product into her recommendation for a more complete education for workers. To be sustainable, their livelihood "must include fellowship as well as the pleasures arising from skilled workmanship and a cultivated imagination." She urged open-mindedness toward Russia after the revolution, pointing to the ideals behind communism, praising the Russian village tradition of self-governance, lamenting the lack of relief provided to the starving Russian people after World War I, and calling for official recognition of the new country. More carefully, knowing her words would not pass muster with doctrinaire socialists, she identified two socialistic currents with which she did identify: "the growing sensitiveness which recognizes that no personal comfort nor individual development can compensate a man for the misery of his neighbors" and "the increasing conviction that social arrangements can be transformed through man's conscious and deliberate effort." These softer, democratically compatible forms of socialism were revolutionary enough for a country in which liberty was supposed to be a birthright. Her social democratic language represents a change of mental awareness that had been developing since the American Reformation and that now, with the modern recognition of interdependence, carried the obligation of action in the direction of social equality for the sake of liberty.[34]

The most obvious place where this type of social democracy was blooming was the church. Or, some churches. What historians call the Social Gospel or social Christianity and identify with liberal Protestants in the decades around the turn of the twentieth century was actually a larger and long-brewing development in American religion in general. Social Christianity diffused Channing's practical Christianity in concert with a movement of British social Christians but more diverse. As Jane Addams observed in her introduction to one of the many books published in the early twentieth century on the relationship between religion and modern society, "Judaism has always upheld the ideals of social justice," which American Reform Jews formalized in their Pittsburgh Platform of 1885. Catholics were early to the defense of workers, visible in the pioneer activism of the Knights of Labor and Pope Pius XIII's 1891 encyclical on labor. Moreover, even among the American Protestants who were concerned with the problems of modern workers—like Rev. Graham Taylor, who wrote a book Addams introduced, *Religion in Social Action* (1913), in the "hope of helping to realise the democracy of religion and the religion of democracy"— alliances across lines of doctrinal difference were a matter of course in the work to which they were devoted. Christians committed to social justice prioritized the public good over orthodoxy. Or monodoxy.[35]

The conference where Addams first presented her address "The Subjective Necessity for Social Settlements" was held at the Plymouth Summer School of Ethics, hosted by the Ethical Culture Society. At least three of the other four presenters were Christians (one Catholic) who evidently did not consider their hosts to be dangerous infidels. Henry Carter Adams wrote the introduction to that volume and explained that the papers within collectively advocated "the democracy of the theorist who asserts for God a common fatherhood, or of the humanist who asserts for man a common brotherhood." This anticipated the slogan of the World's Parliament of Religions, convened at the Columbian Exposition a year later with the aim of "uniting religion against irreligion" under the common "fatherhood of God and brotherhood of man" in order to build a social condition reflective more of divine justice than industrial injustice. At a time when revivalism was growing and the fundamentalist movement beginning—both insisting in overlapping ways on the orthodoxy of the particular evangelical kernel of Reformation Christianity—representatives of a variety of American religions were embracing pluralism, or at least ecumenism, in the service of social activism. Addams described Taylor's reception of socialists and other non-Christians at his settlement house, Chicago Commons, as illustrative of his "religious faith in the unity and solidarity of mankind." Some would say that such a faith is no religion at all, but for Taylor, Addams, and Richard T. Ely—the progressive economist responsible for the publication of *Hull-House Maps and Papers* (1895)—it was the right faith for social action because it excluded no one. Many social Christians used evangelical language and claimed guidance by a divine Christ—such as the most famous ministers in the movement, Washington Gladden and Walter Rauschenbusch—while also speaking hopefully of "moral sentiment" and opposing coercion. Within the growing movement of socially engaged religion, practitioners espoused a range of theological opinions while uniting on the necessity of social action and its relationship to some special sacredness shared by all human beings.[36]

Addams thought this sacred something linked to immortality. The infinite strand of the Reformation Christian faith remained webbed across Christian, postevangelical, and post-Christian forms of that faith in the modern era. A belief in the reality of infinity and of human belonging somehow to that invisible realm united William James, Thomas Davidson, and the like with the purest of evangelicals and strictest of Calvinists. Addams refined her sense of universal human nature down to this "hope of mankind for immortality," a hope she witnessed among many mourners of different cultures and convictions. All showed an "eager determination to hold fast to a link which shall unite those who live in time and space with those who dwell in the timeless unseen."

Thinking of human beings *"sub specie eternitatis,"* Addams—who evidently started reading James after she turned forty, since she quoted his ethical addresses of the 1890s, his *Varieties of Religious Experience*, and his *Pragmatism* in her later works—imagined the perspective on humankind from which all individuals are equal, and equally important for society.[37]

For such equality freedom was necessary, as it had been for the eighteenth-century Reformation Christians who helped create the American Reformation. The core principles of American democracy correlated with the practical effects of Addams's religious conviction. "Democracy believes that the man at the bottom may realize his aim only through an unfolding of his own being," she said, making self-culture a national principle. Therefore moral agency—exercising an autonomous voice in the shaping of society—is necessary, because each "must have an efficacious share in the regulation of his own life." This simple principle describes "our democratic purpose," which is "an attempt at self-expression for each man." The Romantic Christian ideal, turned post-Christian and universal, Addams made into an American national ideal and a religion in and of itself—if religion may be that benevolent ideal from which practical action flows.[38]

If not, Addams was not going to argue about it. She was concerned much less with defining terms and much more with translation between subjectivities in pursuit of common ground. She used the most basic vocabulary she could find in order to cultivate the social ability to act together in light of the consensual judgment of a democratic society. This is why in her *Democracy and Social Ethics* she explained what the corrupt alderman thought, what the new immigrant cared about, and what the reformer believed, so that all may become aware of the values and concepts held by different subjectivities on the social spectrum.

"This is the penalty of a democracy," she acknowledged, "that we are bound to move forward or retrograde together. None of us can stand aside" in this interdependent modern society, for "our feet are mired in the same soil, and our lungs breathe the same air."

Actually believing this powered Addams's reform work. When she said "none" she meant to exclude no one, not to side with workers against management but to find her way into the perspectives of each. Yes, this was where compromise came in, and getting involved in lobbying the government. But for a moral agent like Addams, lobbying could never be pandering. Instead, representing the collective judgment of a range of perspectives to the government became democratic work. She was obliged "to appeal to business men for their judgment and their money, to the educated for their effort and enthusiasm, to the neighborhood for their response and co-operation," she said, a process that "tests the sanity of an idea." Those who really take seriously the innate sanctity of every individual in society must acknowledge that their own convictions, however true they seem, are not the whole truth, and must bend to accommodate or extend themselves in explanation far enough to answer the differing convictions of others.[39]

The democratic process is as unlike the commercial process as the divine right of private judgment is from the doctrine of personal salvation through the death and resurrection of a divine Christ. It is not that they cannot work together—evidently—but from the perspective of Addams and many of her fellow reformers, democracy and capitalism are distinct processes, and although they grew up in America together it was not at all certain that their relationship was entirely harmonious. "All of us forget how very early we are in the experiment of founding self-government," Addams admonished, "and that we are making the experiment in the most materialistic period of all history, having as our court of last appeal against that materialism only the wonderful and inexplicable instinct for justice which resides in the hearts of men." Commercial values often worked against justice, though, faithful to the profit motive alone, and therefore to individualism and self-interest. The problem again was liberty, and with it moral agency. Why did girls become prostitutes? Because commercial values undermine free will. Men who should be protecting them were drawn by the prospect of profit to exploit the weaker sex, who were unsafe on city streets or even in workplaces, subject to abuses of masculine power that Addams sharply contrasted to true manliness. Pimps were "so far from being manly they were losing all virility." Some girls became prostitutes because they were hungry, or because advertising had taught them to desire nice things beyond the means of their factory wages, or because they mistook a brothel for a boardinghouse, or because they trusted someone who was untrustworthy, someone who "seized upon a moment of weakness in a girl" living in a society that then considers her "lost to all decency" forevermore, having given up her basic human right to consent.[40]

Prostitution was only the most egregious form of "commercialized vice," according to Addams, an evil as ancient as slavery and as capable of being overcome by the arising of a new conscience as slavery had been. Every shiny new feature of commercial America—"penny arcades, slot machines, candy stores, ice-cream parlors, moving-picture shows, skating rinks, cheap theatres and dance halls"—also undermined the cause of justice insofar as its only motive was profit. Business enterprises were willing to use "every device known to modern advertising," and their promoters were "careless of the moral effect upon their young customers if they can but secure their money." Addams had no problem per se with such relatively innocent forms of entertainment as motion pictures and plays, but she saw that their being profit-driven rather than justice-driven or truth-driven or even beauty-driven pushed their scriptwriters to favor love stories and their consumers to develop destructive ideas about human relationships. Since the human imagination was such an amazing faculty and the human need for pleasure so primal, Addams found the reign of commercial values distressing. She protested that to "commercialize pleasure is as monstrous as it is to commercialize art." People need both, so they should have both pleasure and art without the distortion of the profit motive.[41]

Addams and her associates provided as much art and pleasure at Hull House as they could—minus the lubricant of alcohol—because their neighbors taught them that art and pleasure were universal human needs, like self-development, expression, agency, meaning, and connection. The Hull House community discovered these needs together by observation and experience.

One of the words that jumps from Addams's pages most often and most puzzlingly is "primitive." In *Democracy and Social Ethics* alone the reader encounters "primitive society," the "primitive" care for "personal decoration over that for one's home or habitat," the "primitive, emotional man," the "primitive man" who had "games long before he cared for a house or regular meals," the "primitive and genuine need" of King Lear for "human contact and animal warmth," the "primitive life" of preindustrial handicrafts, and the "primitive people" of a district who tolerate the Peter Pan ethics of an alderman who lines his pockets with whatever he does not give away as bribes for votes. What she means by the term is somewhere between the primitivism described by the pioneering anthropologist E. B. Tylor, on whom William James drew in formulating his science of religions, and the primitivism of *Tarzan of the Apes* (1912) or that of Picasso. Modernist artists thought something was lost from industrial civilization that could perhaps be appropriated from cultures that had not become deracinated; Jane Addams was no modernist, and no appropriator, but she observed vital features of the preindustrial immigrant cultures in Chicago that she thought younger generations ought to find ways of keeping alive. Handweaving and other artisanal skills particularly attracted her. So did immigrant ethics. Carnal nature was certainly part of basic human nature, she had opportunity to observe again and again, and with it came a touching perennial goodness, a willingness among the poor to sacrifice for their fellows or even of "the girl who overcomes her drink and opium habits, who renounces luxuries and goes back to uninteresting daily toil for the sake of the good opinion of a man who wishes her to 'appear decent,' although he never means to marry her." Addams would not agree with Tylor that Protestant Christian civilization was at the apex of any unilinear arc of human development. She thought that what existed in pre-industrial cultures continued to dwell in modernized ones—and she thought that live germ needed tending.[42]

This is where government came in. Only the modern city, Addams charged, shrugged off its responsibility for its people's primitive needs. Ancient cities had provided festivals on a regular basis, looked after the poor, protected city dwellers from enemies. Now government—the aggregated agency of the people—needed to take back that responsibility and reshape it for modern life. The creation of a government responsive to human needs was urgent, because "unless we establish that humane legislation which has its roots in a consideration for human life, our industrialism itself will suffer from inbreeding, growing ever more unrestrained and ruthless." Modern industry could thrive only if government provided the rule that protected the humanity of modern workers. What Addams called "paternalistic governments" in Europe already did so to a degree that shamed the lagging United States, which needed popular reform rather than big-state decree, because "in a republic it is the citizens themselves who must be convinced of the need of this protection unless they would permit industry to maim the very mothers of the future."[43]

Addams did not use the word "feminist," and her social and political activity was so expansive that she cannot be called an advocate for the rights of women merely—she was garbage inspector for her ward, a founding member of the National Association for the Advancement of Colored People and of the Progressive Party, and much more—but undoubtedly she advocated women's rights in a trailblazing way, both through the suffrage cause and through broader political activity. She was part of a historically novel cohort of men and women who took the justice of women's rights as a matter of established logic awaiting full implementation; even Tolstoy believed women deserved the right to vote. The empirical finding that women's rights meant children's welfare drove activism beyond the franchise. Among her American colleagues outside Chicago, Edith Abbott and Pauline and Josephine Goldmark—the Adirondack companions of William James—made important studies under the auspices of organizations like the National Consumers League. They developed empirical analyses of working conditions and their impact on women that Rev. Graham Taylor drew on in his *Religion in Social Action* and lawyers like Louis Brandeis drew on in their arguments for progressive legislation. Hull House, often called a sociological laboratory, was only one of many enterprises in which early social science was harnessed to public purposes, bringing the civic rights as well as the civil rights of women into the national spotlight. As Addams remembered with pleasure, when she took leadership in the American Women Suffrage Association, she oversaw a diverse coalition that included Scandinavian immigrants—since women there had exercised the municipal franchise since the seventeenth century—and working women, mothers' groups, professionals, property owners, students, and clubwomen. "None of these busy women," Addams explained, "wished to take the place of men nor to influence them in the direction of men's affairs, but they did seek an opportunity to cooperate directly

in civil life through the use of the ballot in regard to their own affairs."
Women are moral agents entitled to government by consent.[44]

Addams used some of her most descriptive prose to represent the
experiences of women in her community at home and at work, experiences she often witnessed personally. Once she came upon a washer-
woman scrubbing the floor of an office building, separated from her
nursing infant for six hours at a stretch. Her front was wet all the way to
her chin. "Her mother's milk mingled with the very water with which
she scrubbed the floors until she should return at midnight, heated and
exhausted, to feed her screaming child with what remained within her
breasts."[45]

Addams understood that, ideology aside, when a mother worked
long industrial hours at low wages, not only was the toll on her family
heavy but naturally the toll on society was as well. Addams knew many
"desperate mothers, overworked and harried through a long day, pro-
longed by the family washing and cooking into the evening." Working
mothers worried about the impact of their absences on their children,
who were then more likely to become wayward. Addams used the words
of H. G. Wells—another James correspondent, known as much for his
social criticism as for his fantastic fiction—to argue that "it is a 'monstrous absurdity' that women who are 'discharging their supreme social
function, that of rearing children, should do it in their spare time, as it
were, while they earn their living by contributing some half-mechanical
element to some trivial industrial product.'" There was an aura of Arts
and Crafts socialism in this critique, but Addams brought it to argue for
social democracy. After detailing the crimes, health problems, and tru-
ancy of the five children of one family she knew, she argued that it
would have been more economical for the state "to have boarded them
with their own mother, requiring a standard of nutrition and school
attendance at least up to that national standard of nurture which the

more advanced European governments are establishing." Her knowledge of the impact on women of irresponsible husbands, not incidentally,
made it "impossible" for her "to write anything which would however
remotely justify the loosening of marriage bonds." Free love was for the
affluent. At the same time, the social ostracism and economic precari-
ousness of illegitimate children and their mothers appeared unjust to
Addams, who recommended following the lead of Germany and Hun-
gary in providing for single women with dependent children without
judgment. She used European comparisons to argue for socially responsible governance.[46]

Addams was not an American exceptionalist, then, save for her
observation that the number and diversity of immigrants to the United
States gave it a continual fresh leavening for its democratic dough. At a
time in American history when Frederick Jackson Turner's assessment
of the newly closed frontier drove some expansionists to look to commercial imperialism for a new Americanizing mechanism, and when
American nativists were fretting over the encroachment on the so-called
Anglo-Saxon by allegedly inferior races and organizing to limit new
immigration by national origin, Addams stoutly advocated for how
immigrants continually reinvigorated the promise of American democracy. While native-born American youth were busier with shopping
than civics, she said, "the real enthusiasm for self-government must be
found among the groups of young immigrants who bring over with
every ship a new cargo of democratic aspirations." Some immigrants
became disillusioned upon finding that "America was wholly commercial in its interests and absorbed in money making," she reported. She
told the story of one suicidal immigrant—"tired of getting seventy-five
cents for trimming a hat that sold for twelve dollars and was to be put
upon the empty head of some one who had no concern for the welfare of
the woman who made it"—to show nativists how shabby their country

appeared to a newcomer who had so recently believed in its promise. Addams argued that immigrants understood American democracy better than any nativist spouting theories about the Anglo-Saxon and the Nordic as truer Americans. When a mayoral candidate started abusing King George on the stump, a gesture "naturally pleasing to the Irish and inevitably highly entertaining to the Germans," the candidate became a champion for the African Americans of Chicago and "embodied for the Slav, the Greek, the Latin, the Turk and all the rest, an assertion that the Anglo-Saxon was no better than he ought to be or at any rate that he would no longer be allowed to dictate what Chicago should teach its school children, whose racial background was as good as anybody's!" The spirit of equality reigned among these diverse city dwellers. Soon the Chicago representatives of "the Council Fire of American Indians" spoke out against "the school histories in which a successful foray of the Red Skins was invariably described as a massacre while one made by the Whites was called a victory over a savage foe." The American Indians pointed out that they themselves, after all, were "the real 100 per cent Americans," if such a concept made any sense at all.[47]

Addams thought the concept of Americanism made sense only insofar as it referred to a commitment to universal human moral agency, which made racial prejudice "the gravest situation in our American life." Discrimination on the basis of race or ethnicity or any other involuntary circumstance corrupted the instincts essential to democracy. "To continually suspect, suppress or fear any large group in a community," she warned, "must finally result in a loss of enthusiasm for that type of government which gives free play to the self-development of a majority of its citizens." She wanted to protect the liberty necessary to the moral agency of African Americans or any other group subject to discrimination on the basis of any factor beyond the control of that group's members. Among global combatants of such prejudice she called out

Gandhi for special praise, in a nice boomerang effect of the American Reformation, since Gandhi's activism by the time Addams noticed it around 1930 already owed a debt to Salter's *Ethical Religion* of 1889. She warned that discrimination robs a society of some of its own best resources "when great ranges of human life are hedged about with antagonism." Most of all, she made self-culture not only an American ideal but also a collective ideal, going beyond individualism to argue that "whatever is spontaneous in a people, in an individual, a class or a nation, is always a source of life."[48]

Addams was no preacher. Rather, she practiced what James called, in one of his letters praising her to a friend, "the Religion of democracy . . . the one which I think makes to me the strongest appeal." This democracy from which James and Addams and many of their peers took their ideal cues was no fixed entity—and never had been. "Democracy like any other of the living faiths of men," Addams said, "is so essentially mystical that it continually demands new formulation." With the help of new believers among immigrants and their novel alliance with laborers, American democracy could become responsible in its government and social fabric for the universal needs made evident by diverse experience.[49]

Individual inner work of realizing the equal worth of others—social ethics, collectively undertaken—was a critical element in the building of this evolved democracy, "the identification with the common lot which is the essential idea of Democracy." As collective judgment becomes government, democracy advances. Yet even though in the modern era tyranny was to be expected from the commercial and industrial quarter rather than ecclesiastical bodies or dogmatic ministers, democratic work remained resonant with that of the practical Christian. The "modern liberal," Addams wrote, "having come to conceive truth of a kind which must vindicate itself in practice, finds it hard to hold even a sincere and mature opinion" if it be one that has no social traction and therefore "can have no justification in works." Modern liberalism could never be an individual affair but only the product of consensus.[50]

A NEW AFFINITY FOR ALL MEN

By the end of the first decade of the twentieth century, Addams could see that, far from being exceptionally advanced in democracy, the United States was in good company in seeking to obtain "the inner consent of the citizen to the outward acts of his government." Moral agency was the basis of modern governance, she said, since "it has long been the aim of our own government and of similar types throughout the world to replace coercion by the full consent of the governed, to educate and strengthen the free will of the people through the use of democratic institutions." More and more, as Addams traveled abroad, received foreign visitors, and talked and read politics and reform with fellow students of human progress, it appeared that all of her favorite causes were being pursued in worldwide movements. Many countries contained voluntary associations for women's rights, industrial reform, and public provision for the people's basic well-being as well as organization against discrimination. These global movements suggested the emergence of "a wider, international morality" that Addams believed really might point to world peace. Even as World War I wrecked many progressive hopes, she and her pacifist colleagues "believed that the endeavor to nurture human life even in its most humble and least promising forms had crossed national boundaries." Now if they could only find a way of making that endeavor practical.[51]

Ever the builder of consensus, Addams looked for allies in hawkish

America. She even signed on to Henry Ford's publicity-seeking Peace Ship in 1915, a fiasco that she luckily was prohibited from boarding at the last minute when an attack of her old spinal problem incapacitated her. She tried to work with President Wilson too, but ultimately saw in him the same prideful disregard for other people's viewpoints as George Pullman had shown. Even her longtime friend and colleague John Dewey did not agree with her "that war, seeking its end through coercion, not only interrupted but fatally reversed [the] process of cooperating good will which, if it had a chance, would eventually include the human family itself." The dwindling number of pacifists in America became more and more dispirited as the war progressed and American involvement became a certainty and then a fact. The absurdity of using coercion to fight coercion isolated pacifists enough to make them doubt their own sanity. But Addams found no reasonable rebuttal in the "dogmatic statements" made by her critics. "We forget," she insisted, "that to obtain the 'inner consent' of a man who differs from us is always a slow process." Forcing obedience does not produce real consent but only future problems.[52]

During the war, Addams and her pacifist colleagues found allies abroad. In 1915 they founded the International Congress of Women to promote neutrality, creating resolutions. Addams personally presented this document to Wilson, who told her three months later that he admired the resolutions more than anything any other body had produced. One of those resolutions opposed "discrimination against human beings on the basis of their race or color," and another presciently held "that no restriction should be placed on the civil or political rights of the Jews." The International Congress of Women met in Zurich and The Hague and urged that a "Society of Nations" be developed, featuring an International Court of Justice and an International Conference that would include women and "deal with practical proposals for international cooperation." Four years later the League of Nations was set up. Addams hoped it would "be founded not upon broken bits of international law, but upon ministrations to primitive human needs." She believed that "primitive human compassion" had "made the folkway which afterward developed into political relationships" and that therefore this most basic and positive human feeling should be made the common rule for international action.[53]

The one way in which America seemed exceptional to Addams—diversity—appeared to be the key to how to make the League of Nations operate effectively. As she had conjectured as early as 1904 and still believed after the armistice, the presence in America of representatives from all the world's nations and their working together for needs that turned out to be universal gave the United States a distinctive experiential basis for working out the conditions of a lasting peace. Addams thought that "our very composition would make it easier for us than for any other nation to establish an international organization founded upon understanding and good will, did we but possess the requisite courage and intelligence to utilize it." Instead, the American people decided against joining the League of Nations, which became lame upon birth.[54]

After the war, Addams traveled vigorously to promote the distribution of relief to the war-torn countries, friends and former foes alike. "Commercial competition" by its nature "could not be trusted to feed the feeble and helpless." Soon the colleagues she had collected through the International Congress of Women formed into the Women's International League for Peace and Freedom (WILPF), with Addams as president. This became her principal pursuit during her last decades. Hull House ran itself by the 1920s, at which point the neighborhood along Halsted Street became considerably less diverse as a result of the National Origins Act of 1924. But WILPF included delegates "from Iceland to Fiji," in Addams's boast, concentrated in Western Europe but global like the just-finished war had been, "made up of people who believe that we are not obliged to choose between violence and passive acceptance of unjust conditions for ourselves or others." The religion of democracy had bubbled up to the international arena.[55]

In her last decade of life, Addams won the Nobel Prize, donated the proceeds to WILPF, advised the architects of the New Deal, wrote many hundreds of thousands of words in correspondence, books, and articles, and traveled. She contemplated the meaning of her life too. She often reflected on her particular experiences and where they seemed to open a murky window onto the universal.

One winter she spent in Egypt. In ancient tombs she saw pictures that aroused in her sudden, crisp memories of her earliest awareness of death. To her surprise, she beheld fears and questions from her childhood wondrously reflected on the painted walls of mastabas thousands of years old. The experience gave her an "abiding sense of kinship" with all human beings. Standing by the bank of the Nile, she experienced two layers of déjà vu at once, vividly remembering her first sight of the Mississippi at age twelve and the queer sensation of having seen it before, upon which the adolescent Addams decided the experience was what Wordsworth had described in his "Ode to Intimations of Immortality":

Our birth is but a sleep and a forgetting:
The soul that rises with us, our life's Star,
Hath had elsewhere its setting,
And cometh from afar.

This link to the infinite through identification with countless unknown others, such as the men she saw in Egypt at work in the fields and the women carrying water, Addams considered an essential part of the "new humanism" of her generation, "the belief that no altar at which living men have once devoutly worshipped . . . can lose all significance for us, the survivors." Past human civilizations were not left behind but included in later cultural forms, leading her to believe that Plato was right when he suggested that "though all else may be transitory in human affairs, the excellent must become the permanent," as she put it in one of her last books, a collection of memorial addresses she had delivered at Hull House for departed loved ones, including Henry Demarest Lloyd and a son of John Dewey.[56]

Of course such a belief was really a hope, one of the ideals on which Addams staked the practice of her adult life. At the end she died of cancer a year after her beloved companion Mary Rozet Smith. Her corpse lay in state for two days in Hull House. Thousands of people paid their respects. "Workmen at dawn, with their dinner-pails . . . children in weeping groups, people of every class and race" came to look at her once more, a colleague recalled. "One old Greek, gazing upon her lovely face, turned to a resident standing near. 'She Catholic?' he asked. 'She Orthodox? She Jewish?' To each question the resident said: 'No.' Whereupon the old Greek said, smiling: 'Oh, I see! She all religions!'" He understood.[57]

CONCLUSION:
AN AMERICAN CENTURY?

When Jane Addams asked government to step into the arena alongside commercial power to service essential human needs, she did not mean it should step in as an opponent, but as a representative of moral interest, the collective good of the people. Like all liberals, and more comprehensively than any liberal before her, she did not favor coercion. This is why in 1935—the year she died—Addams appeared along with Eleanor Roosevelt in a book titled *Why Wars Must Cease*. Addams wanted governments to fill the social gaps that the commercial power could not, to supplement the profit motive with the disinterested motive of simple human welfare. Not only was war obviously destructive of human progress, she thought, but the commercial impulse actually fed the engines of war. Only benevolent governments responsive to the needs of people could preserve human liberty in the modern world.[1]

Her scope was international, aware as she was of movements toward such government in many other countries, but in the United States President Roosevelt adopted some of her ideas and those of other progressives. New Deal legislation vastly increased the activity of the federal government in regulating businesses and relieving basic human want. From that moment forward the word "liberal" became associated with such policies, setting the stage for the politics of the twentieth century and beyond. Roosevelt's 1941 promise that America stood for freedom from want—as well as freedom of speech and religion and freedom from fear—came at a decisive moment. The United States was about to join the worldwide fight against the Nazis and their allies.[2]

Part of the rationale behind the American military effort in World War II came from a newsman who might be called a good liberal in the twentieth-century sense. Henry Luce, son of Protestant missionaries, called on Americans to make the twentieth century an "American Century," one in which the democratic values of the United States were defended and spread with military might. Luce's dream largely came true, and because of the Cold War, the American Century buried the message Addams had tried to deliver about commercialism. Words like "collective" and "the state" became scary. Freedom of speech narrowed. As Soviet "communism" became an ideological enemy of American "democracy," communism came to mean an authoritarian government and a command economy, democracy a government of consent and a free economy. Celebrations of American consumerism then became expressions of American freedom. By the end of the twentieth century, commentators could almost take it for granted that democracy and capitalism went hand in hand.[3]

For Addams, consumerism and the commercial interest were instead drags on freedom, the latest in a long line of determinisms that liberals challenged in defense of moral agency. John Adams had shied away from dogmatic religion and defied a government based on hereditary privilege rather than the consent of citizens. Mary Moody Emerson and William Ellery Channing also rejected autocratic government, extending democracy to religion by defending individual moral agency against the foregone conclusions of predestination and innate, total depravity. Slavery was a deterministic institution, and to a debatable extent so was patriarchy. After the Civil War, the new determinism of materialism, which William James called scientism, then threatened the free will of individuals with the explanatory power of biology that would make all social change the product of impersonal forces. James enlisted the power of the imagination, which Channing and the Emersons had already linked to religion, to restore moral agency. Thomas Davidson faced off against evangelical Christianity and socialism with a democratic deity of individual self-culture, which contested the determinism of class origin and ethnicity with a new social process of interdependent diversities, together producing a higher culture through their interactions. The fixed idea William Mackintire Salter challenged was the laissez-faire state, which pretended that the custom of not protecting laborers' rights was immutable, a natural law like gravity. Industrial capitalism also threatened liberty in the experience of Jane Addams, who saw the profit motive as a fixed idea that bore a haphazard relationship with human well-being, given that commercialism's quickest route to appeal was to play on desire, the basic human craving for pleasure.[4]

Of course, colleagues of Addams and hiking companions of James realized right away that consumer power could be an arm of democracy, which is why they founded the National Consumers League in 1891. Citizens as consumers, or vice versa, also drove the "Don't Buy Where You Can't Work" campaign among the so-called New Negroes of roaring twenties Chicago, who blatantly lived the proud social ethic that Alain Locke described in elegant prose proclaiming the arrival of the cultured, independent-thinking modern African American. Marketers started advertising to middle-class Anglo women in recognition of their purchasing power, and then to more and more demographics, so a sort of democratization of the marketplace gradually followed the integrationist gains in wider American culture.[5]

Those gains came not from daring in the commercial sector, though, but from activism among the legatees of the religion of democracy. "Liberals" they surely were, but they often did not agree with the likes of Luce. Rather than evangelicals they were ecumenical Protestants, liberal Catholics, and Jews, as well as secular humanists, scholars, public intellectuals, activists, artists, and freethinkers of all kinds who carried the banner of moral agency through the rights revolutions of the 1960s all the way to queerness as the ultimate moral agency. Some of them were too captivated by their visions of light to behold that there were real "children of darkness" in the world, said one of their critics, and other liberals were guilty of other sins, but they worked the language of democracy to ask that "America be America again— / The land that never has been yet," in the words of the poet Langston Hughes in 1936. Liberals agreed with a visiting Swedish sociologist in 1944 that the "American creed" of universal liberty and equality clashed with racial prejudice and discrimination. They were moved to action by the prophetic voices of Martin Luther King Jr. and other leaders. Liberal efforts helped make racism a social sin, such that by the twenty-first century an African American could become president and even the most publicly condemned racists knew better than to admit that they adhered to a passé ideology.[6]

The discrediting of white supremacy may be the most significant parcel of liberal common ground cultivated in the twentieth century, but on social questions from gender and sexuality to the environment, liberals built on the American moral tradition they had established over so many decades. Yet to the extent that they condemned not only racism but racists, not only sexism but fellow victims of patriarchy, they disregarded King's core teaching on loving your enemy and betrayed a core teaching from their own tradition. Open-minded inclusivity was more radical than many liberals thought. Secure in the righteousness of their moral commitments—even as a new political movement on their right began successfully branding them as immoral—liberals forgot what Wordsworth had taught, that pride,

> *Howe'er disguised in its own majesty,*
> *Is littleness; that he, who feels contempt*
> *For any living thing, hath faculties*
> *Which he has never used; that thought with him*
> *Is in its infancy.*[7]

Contempt and moral outrage are politically useful qualities with deep historical roots in American intellectual culture going back at least to the abolitionists. Gathering in enclaves of the like-minded was also always part of the culture of lived virtue, although the way liberals aimed to be alike was in independent-mindedness, not in opinions. Yet their critical conversations tended toward consensus, and once there—as on the moral necessity of a public commitment to universal education—liberals cohered into movements, where they sought to build coalitions and popular momentum. Liberal positions then became dogma in those movements. And once liberals became dogmatists, they were no longer pluralists.

Pluralism is a pillar of faith in the religion of democracy. It is not an easy faith and not suited to most people's minds. Pluralism takes a step past multiculturalism, which affirms the vitality and preciousness of every human culture.[8] Pluralism forays beyond countable cultures into infinity, into the unknowable. It is essentially a religious attitude, whether pluralists avow a faith or not, because it includes an intangible something beyond what anyone already knows, what can be named or quantified. In this way it is supernatural. When William James asked his audiences to believe that this is "a democratic universe," he meant one that was both unfinished—infinite—and in need of each individual's unique perspective on what is true and good. Yet he knew his audiences were full of elitists who believed no such thing.

The religion of democracy lives on among activists and religious leaders who engage across lines of difference and blur the boundary between helper and helped. Pluralism continues as a mental habit among scholars whose findings, however rigorously achieved, are always open to criticism and revision, and whose intellectual freedom is somewhat protected from the market. Humility, sincerity, and openness remain virtues even in a postmodern society of spin and hype, flash and glitz. And in a world more than half full of people who do not believe that females are worth as much as males, a world of increasing inequality and ongoing coercion, such liberal virtues are necessary tools so that those who believe in universal equality and freedom can learn to talk with those who do not.

ACKNOWLEDGMENTS

This book was made possible by extraordinary privilege from many quarters. It is a real joy to thank some of those who have sustained this work, even though it is impossible to acknowledge everyone and no one but me is responsible for the inadequacies that remain.

The good public schools of my youth prepared me well to appreciate the rigors of Rice University, where Thomas Haskell made an intellectual historian of me, Richard Wolin showed me the radical contours of social thought, Frank Schubert introduced me to William James, and Terry Doody looked after my reading and my long-term trajectory. My undergraduate education was supported by a donor I never met, Catherine Faye Goodrich, patron of the humanities. During a semester at the University of Melbourne, Patrick Wolfe elegantly modeled how to bring political convictions into historical analysis.

As soon as I landed in graduate school at Boston University, scholars from both inside and outside the university gave me charity as well as latitude. Richard Wightman Fox taught me how to ask historical questions and introduced me to James T. Kloppenberg and David D. Hall, who in different ways and over many years connected me with the sources and methods that became the heart of my scholarly work. Jill Lepore gave me advice and opportunities that I can never repay. Charles Capper exhibited high standards and ready generosity, broadening my horizon immeasurably. These five mentors lit up five unique angles on the dim road ahead.

I have had many great students whose responses to my research have aided the enterprise, but without relief from teaching it never would have been done. Deep thanks to the Center for Religion and American Life at Yale University under the directorship of Jon Butler and Harry S. Stout, who gave me a year to focus on writing during the dissertation stage of the project. The Center for the Study of Religion at Princeton University gave me another lifesaving year during which the outlines of the book slowly emerged. Fellowships are not only sources of funding; they create communities of writers and thinkers whose conversations provide stimulation and comfort through the fluctuations of scholarly confidence. At these institutions, at the Charles Warren Center for the Study of American History at Harvard University, and at the Bay Area Seminar for Early American History, I have valued the fellowship of Carol Anderson, Dee Andrews, Carrie Tirado Bramen, Jessica Delgado, Robin Einhorn, Peter Field, Edie Gelles, Eric Gregory, Philip Haberkern, George Kateb, Kathi Kern, Nicole Kirk, Joseph Mazor, Mark Peterson, Anthony Petro, Manu Radhakrishnan, Ray Raphael, Mark Schmeller, Jeffrey Sklansky, Darren Staloff, Judith Weisenfeld, Caroline Winterer, Walt Woodward, Craig Yirush, and others.

During my three years of teaching in the History and Literature program at Harvard University and at Sonoma State University ever since, students, colleagues, and administrators have sponsored the life of the mind in vital ways. Thanks to the Department of History at Sonoma State for protecting my intellectual freedom and to the School of Social Sciences and other sectors of the university for providing travel grants as well as a crucial sabbatical semester. For encouragement and solidarity at these institutions, at conferences, and elsewhere, I particularly appreciate Robin A. Bernstein, Stephen Bittner, Cynthia Boaz, George Cotkin, Paul Jerome Croce, Leslie Butler, K. Healan Gaston, Dean Grodzins, Andrew Jewett, David Lamberth, Andrew Muldoon, William Clay Poe, Jennifer Ratner-Rosenhagen, Kim Reilly, Michael Robertson, and Leigh Eric Schmidt.

Historical research depends on the stewardship of aging documents at archives. Most of my research was done at the various archives of Harvard University, especially the Houghton Library, where the richness of the holdings is matched only by the professionalism of the staff, among whom Leslie A. Morris went to extra efforts to make the James Library accessible. Other material came from the Sterling Memorial Library at Yale University, the archives of the Society for Ethical Culture in New York City, and the Howard Gotlieb Archival Research Center at Boston University. During periods when a research library was out of reach, the electronic resources of American Periodical Series Online, Early American Imprints, and even Google Books made the old and rare accessible in a wonderfully democratizing way. I am also grateful for the generosity and openness of Hunter Gray, who provided materials from his father's life and trusted my interpretation. The descendants of Charles Bakewell graciously allowed me to see Glenmore, Marc Bernstein helped me navigate Ethical Culture materials, and William Joplin of Putnam Camp and Nina Allen of the Keene Valley Library Archives gave generously to a stranger.

Support also comes in the form of criticism, the most precious gift a scholar can give. I have not done justice to the insights of my readers, but they have been both kind and exacting. For giving their time and expertise to evaluating this book in small pieces and large chunks, I will always be indebted to David D. Hall, Daniel T. Rodgers, Charles Capper, David A. Hollinger, Mark Peterson, Mark Valeri, Daniel Immerwahr, Jonathan Soffer, Sarah T. Phillips, and especially Jill Lepore, who has seen this book at every stage and helped find it a home at Penguin Press. I am grateful to Mally Anderson for her editorial competence, to Scott Moyers for overseeing the series, to Laura Stickney and the editorial board for evaluating my proposal so constructively, and to everyone else involved in the production process.

My privilege has extended beyond the halls of academe. My parents, Margaret and James Kittelson, and my sister, Elizabeth VanVoorhis, gave me more than I can say. Friends have acted like family, especially Bette Dare, Jessica Delgado, Anne and Brian Fitzpatrick, Amie Glass, Sue Hayes and Bill Poe, Adam Lewis, Sophia Reibetanz Moreau, Cynthia and Imari Paris Jeffries, Manu Radhakrishnan, Monica Weinheimer, Marc Wheeler, Diana and Ben H. Winters, and Sarah Wilson-Jones. Robert Moluf, who edited my father's biography of Martin Luther, has given unique support. David Kittelstrom had faith in this book when its author did not, and he continued supporting both long after our partnership changed to coparenting. Many caregivers for our children created the necessary time for toil at my desk, especially Evelyn Strom and Steve Strom, whose cooking also fueled these pages. I owe special thanks to the teachers and communities affiliated with the Foundation for the Preservation of the Mahayana Tradition. To my soccer mates from all over the world, thank you for many joyful moments both on and off the field.

Finally, although all four of my grandparents gave me a great deal, I dedicate this book in part to my paternal grandfather, a great Reformation Christian who has been a beacon for me all my life. The rest is for my children, who I fear have sacrificed for this book, who shed light wherever they go, and who teach me how to learn and how to love.

A.K.
Sonoma County, California
Labor Day 2014

NOTES

PREFACE TO THE PAPERBACK EDITION

1. The Universal Declaration of Human Rights, <http://www.un.org/en/universal-dec laration-human-rights/>, accessed Dec. 6, 2015.
2. Ira Katznelson, *When Affirmative Action was White: An Untold History of Racial Inequality in Twentieth-Century America* (New York: Norton, 2005).
3. Susan Jacoby, "Piety and Politics in America," *The American Prospect* (Spring 2015): <http://prospect.org/article/piety-and-politics-america>, accessed Dec. 6, 2015. Kevin M. Kruse, *One Nation, Under God: How Corporate America Invented Christian America* (New York: Basic Books, 2015). Horace M. Kallen, *Secularism is the Will of God: An Essay in the Social Philosophy of Democracy and Religion* (New York: Twayne, 1954).
4. Margaret Mead and James Baldwin, *A Rap on Race* (Philadelphia & New York: J.B. Lippincott, 1971), 135-36, 67.

INTRODUCTION: AN AMERICAN REFORMATION

1. Ignas K. Skrupskelis and Elizabeth M. Berkeley, eds., *The Correspondence of William James, vol. 8, 1895–June 1899* (Charlottesville: University Press of Virginia, 2000), 254–55. The most recent place this view of the Enlightenment appears is Anthony Pagden, *The Enlightenment: And Why It Still Matters* (New York: Random House, 2013). For a critique of the Eurocentric view of the Enlightenment, see Sebastian Conrad, "Enlightenment in Global History: A Historiographical Critique," *American Historical Review* 117, no. 4 (October 2012): 999–1027. On the place of James in his intellectual culture and the critical question of religion, see David A. Hollinger,

"William James, Ecumenical Protestantism, and the Dynamics of Secularization," in *William James and the Transatlantic Conversation: Pragmatism, Pluralism, and Philosophy of Religion,* ed. Martin Halliwell and Joel D. S. Rasmussen (New York: Oxford University Press, 2014).

2. On how New England Christians always disagreed with one another, see Edmund S. Morgan, *The Puritan Dilemma: The Story of John Winthrop in America* (Boston: Little, Brown, 1958); David D. Hall, *Worlds of Wonder, Days of Judgment: Popular Religious Belief in Early New England* (Cambridge, MA: Harvard University Press, 1990); James William Jones, *The Shattered Synthesis: New England Puritanism Before the Great Awakening* (New Haven, CT: Yale University Press, 1973); Mark A. Peterson, *The Price of Redemption: The Spiritual Economy of Puritan New England* (Stanford, CA: Stanford University Press, 1997). See also William G. McLoughlin, *New England Dissent, 1630–1833: The Baptists and the Separation of Church and State* (Cambridge, MA: Harvard University Press, 1971). Francis J. Bremer, *Puritanism: Transatlantic Perspectives on a Seventeenth-Century Anglo-American Faith* (Boston: Massachusetts Historical Society, 1993).

3. On the prevalence of New England Reformation Christians among Revolutionary patriots, see Mark Valeri, "The New Divinity and the American Revolution," *William and Mary Quarterly* 46, no. 4 (October 1989): 741–69; Donald Weber, *Rhetoric and History in Revolutionary New England* (New York: Oxford University Press, 1988). On the importance of Boston in particular in the Revolution, see Richard Archer, *As If an Enemy's Country: The British Occupation of Boston and the Origins of Revolution* (New York: Oxford University Press, 2010).

   On early uses of the word "liberalism" and the American audience for English liberal thought, see Annabel Patterson, *Early Modern Liberalism* (New York: Cambridge University Press, 1997).

   I adopt the term "American Reformation" from Sydney E. Ahlstrom with Jonathan S. Carey, *An American Reformation: A Documentary History of Unitarian Christianity* (Middletown, CT: Wesleyan University Press, 1985).

4. On religious freedom and the separation of church and state, see Daniel Walker Howe, "Church, State, and Education in the Young American Republic," *Journal of the Early Republic* 22, no. 2 (Spring 2002): 1–24; Perez Zagorin, *How the Idea of Religious Toleration Came to the West* (Princeton, NJ: Princeton University Press, 2003); Chris Beneke, *Beyond Toleration: The Religious Origins of American Pluralism* (New York: Oxford University Press, 2006); Forrest Church, *So Help Me God: The Founding Fathers and the First Great Battle over Church and State* (Orlando, FL: Harcourt, 2007); Stephen Mansfield, *Ten Tortured Words: How the Founding Fathers Tried to Protect Religion in America . . . and What's Happened Since* (Nashville: Thomas Nelson, 2007); David Sehat, *The Myth of American Religious Freedom* (New York: Oxford University Press, 2011).

   For examples of scholarship relying on such a definition of orthodox Protestant Christianity, see Mark A. Noll, *America's God: From Jonathan Edwards to Abraham Lincoln* (New York: Oxford University Press, 2002); D. G. Hart, *The Lost Soul of American Protestantism* (Lanham, MD: Rowman and Littlefield, 2002); E. Brooks Holifield, *Theology in America: Christian Thought from the Age of the Puritans to the Civil War* (New Haven, CT: Yale University Press, 2003). A recent book centering on the distinction between head and heart is Garry Wills, *Head and Heart: American Christianities* (New York: Penguin Press, 2007). The secularization thesis has been surviving empirical beatings at least since Peter L. Berger and Thomas Luckmann published *The Social Construction of Reality: A Treatise in the Sociology of Knowledge* (New York: Doubleday, 1966); recent defenses of the secularization thesis include Steve Bruce, *God Is Dead: Secularization in the West* (Malden, MA: Blackwell, 2002), and Pippa Norris and Ronald Englehart, eds., *Sacred and Secular: Religion and Politics Worldwide* (New York: Cambridge University Press, 2004). One important rebuttal of the idea that secularization accompanied modernity, at least in the history of the United States, is Jon Butler, "Jack-in-the-Box Faith: The Religion Problem in American History," *Journal of American History* 90, no. 4 (March 2004): 1357–78. For more recent treatments beyond the field of U.S. history, see Craig Calhoun, Mark Juergensmeyer, and Jonathan Van Antwerpen, eds., *Rethinking Secularism* (New York: Oxford University Press, 2011), and Ira Katznelson and Gareth Stedman Jones, eds., *Religion and the Political Imagination* (New York: Cambridge University Press, 2011). See also R. Laurence Moore, "Religion, Secularization, and the Shaping of the Culture Industry in Antebellum America," *American Quarterly* 41, no. 2 (June 1989): 216–42.

For a discussion of the intersection of the Enlightenment with Protestant Christianity in America that challenges the head/heart distinction and covers the twentieth century, see David A. Hollinger, "The Accommodation of Protestant Christianity with the Enlightenment: An Old Drama Still Being Enacted," *Daedalus* 141, no. 1 (Winter 2012): 76–88.

See also Brad S. Gregory, *The Unintended Reformation: How a Religious Revolution Secularized Society* (Cambridge, MA: Harvard University Press, 2012).

5. Van Wyck Brooks, *The Flowering of New England, 1815–1865* (New York: Dutton, 1937), 17. F. O. Matthiessen, *American Renaissance: Art and Expression in the Age of Emerson and Whitman* (New York: Oxford University Press, 1941); Lewis Mumford, *The Golden Day: A Study in American History and Culture* (New York: Boni and Liveright, 1926). For the scholarship of the American Renaissance in context, see Charles Capper, "'A Little Beyond': The Problem of the Transcendentalist Movement in American History," *Journal of American History* 85, no. 2 (September 1988): 502–39. See also Joel Myerson, *The American Renaissance in New England* (Detroit: Gale Research, 1978); Myerson, ed., *Studies in the American Renaissance* (Boston: Twayne, 1978–2001); David S. Reynolds, *Beneath the American Renaissance: The Subversive Imagination in the Age of Emerson and Melville* (New York: Knopf, 1988); Jay Grossman, *Reconstituting the American Renaissance: Emerson, Whitman, and the Politics of Representation* (Durham, NC: Duke University Press, 2003).

6. The Enlightenment itself should not be thought of as a secular movement, according to Jonathan Sheehan, "Enlightenment, Religion, and the Enigma of Secularization: A Review Essay," *American Historical Review* 108, no. 4 (October 2003): 1061–80. See also *The Enlightenment Bible: Translation, Scholarship, Culture* (Princeton, NJ: Princeton University Press, 2005). Sheehan's view accords well with the classic account by Henry Farnham May, *The Enlightenment in America* (New York: Oxford University Press, 1976). The contrary position is held most strongly by Jonathan I. Israel, *Radical Enlightenment: Philosophy and the Making of Modernity, 1650–1750* (New

York: Oxford University Press, 2001). See also A. Ferguson, *The American Enlighten-ment, 1750–1820* (Cambridge, MA: Harvard University Press, 1997); Roy Porter and Mikulas Teich, eds., *The Enlightenment in National Context* (New York: Cambridge University Press, 1981); Emmett Kennedy, *Secularism and Its Opponents from Augus-tine to Solzhenitsyn* (Basingstoke, UK: Palgrave Macmillan, 2006).

On moderation in early modern Britain as a strategy of power and domination, see Ethan H. Shagan, *The Rule of Moderation: Violence, Religion, and the Politics of Restraint in Early Modern Britain* (New York: Cambridge University Press, 2011).

7. For a recent innovation on how to define the secular, see Charles Taylor, *A Secular Age* (Cambridge, MA: Harvard University Press, 2007). For the clearest recent examination of secular liberalism, see Alan Ryan, *The Making of Modern Liberalism* (Princeton, NJ: Princeton University Press, 2012). On Samuel Adams, see Gary Scott Smith, "Samuel Adams: America's Puritan Revolutionary," in *The Forgotten Founders on Religion and Public Life*, ed. Daniel L. Dreisbach, Mark David Hall, and Jeffry H. Morrison (Notre Dame, IN: University of Notre Dame Press, 2009), 40–64; Pauline Maier, *The Old Revolutionaries: Political Lives in the Age of Samuel Adams* (New York: Knopf, 1980). My argument adds a religious backstory to the secular under-standing of objectivity most persuasively championed by Thomas L. Haskell, *Objec-tivity Is Not Neutrality: Explanatory Schemes in History* (Baltimore: Johns Hopkins University Press, 1998). This book also relies on the current consensus among histori-ans that American political convictions in the early republic cannot be classified strictly according to either liberalism or republicanism but mixed these traditions with one another and Christianity. See for a start James T. Kloppenberg, "The Virtues of Liberalism: Christianity, Republicanism, and Ethics in Early American Political Dis-course," *Journal of American History* 74, no. 1 (June 1987): 9–33; Joyce Appleby, *Liberalism and Republicanism in the Historical Imagination* (Cambridge, MA: Har-vard University Press, 1992); Robert E. Shalhope, *A Tale of New England: The Diaries of Hiram Harwood, Vermont Farmer, 1810–1837* (Baltimore: Johns Hopkins Univer-sity Press, 2003); Andreas Kalyvas and Ira Katznelson, *Liberal Beginnings: Making a Republic for the Moderns* (New York: Cambridge University Press, 2008).

8. For a more rigorous understanding of the philosophical and political commitments liberals held, see James T. Kloppenberg, *Uncertain Victory: Social Democracy and Progressivism in European and American Thought, 1870–1920* (New York: Oxford University Press, 1986). See also Kloppenberg, "Knowledge and Belief in American Public Life," in *The Virtues of Liberalism* (New York: Oxford University Press, 1998), 38–58. On twentieth-century American liberalism, see Gary Gerstle, "The Protean Character of American Liberalism," *American Historical Review* 99, no. 4 (October 1994): 1043–73. Also David Goodman, "Democracy and Public Discussion in the Pro-gressive and New Deal Eras: From Civic Competence to the Expression of Opinion," *Studies in American Political Development* 18 (Fall 2004): 81–111. For a complemen-tary argument about the religion of democracy, see Jared Hickman, "The Theology of Democracy," *New England Quarterly* 81, no. 2 (June 2008): 177–217. Also Richard Schneirov and Gaston A. Fernandez, *Democracy as a Way of Life in America: A His-tory* (New York: Rutgers University Press, 2013).

9. The language of declension is rife among histories of the Unitarian movement, even by those seemingly sympathetic to the Unitarians; the root text is Conrad Wright, *The*

Beginnings of Unitarianism in America (Boston: Starr King Press, 1955). For examples of the latter charge, see Allen C. Guelzo, "'The Science of Duty': Moral Philosophy and the Epistemology of Science in Nineteenth-Century America," in Guelzo and David N. Livingstone, eds., *Evangelicals and Science in Historical Perspective* (New York: Oxford University Press, 1999), 267–89; John Patrick Diggins, *The Lost Promise of Pragmatism: Modernism and the Crisis of Knowledge and Authority* (Chicago: University of Chicago Press, 1994).

10. Leigh Eric Schmidt, "The Making of Modern 'Mysticism,'" *Journal of the American Academy of Religion* 72, no. 2 (June 2003): 273–302; Schmidt, *Restless Souls: The Making of American Spirituality* (San Francisco: HarperSanFrancisco, 2005); Schmidt, "Cosmopolitan Piety: Sympathy, Comparative Religions, and Nineteenth-Century Liberalism," in *Practicing Protestants: Histories of Christian Life in America, 1630–1935,* ed. Laurie F. Maffly-Kipp, Leigh E. Schmidt, and Mark Valeri (Baltimore: Johns Hopkins University Press, 2006), 199–221; Catherine L. Albanese, *A Republic of Mind and Spirit: A Cultural History of American Metaphysical Religion* (New Haven, CT: Yale University Press, 2006); Schmidt and Sally Promey, eds., *American Religious Liberalism* (Bloomington: Indiana University Press, 2012); Christopher G. White, *Unsettled Minds: Psychology and the American Search for Spiritual Assurance* (Berkeley: University of California Press, 2009); Matthew Hedstrom, *The Rise of Liberal Religion: Book Culture and American Spirituality in the Twentieth Century* (New York: Oxford University Press, 2013). On the therapeutic ethos, see T. J. Jackson Lears, "From Salvation to Self-Realization: Advertising and the Therapeutic Roots of the Consumer Culture, 1880–1930," in *The Culture of Consumption: Critical Essays in American History, 1880–1980,* ed. T. J. Jackson Lears and Richard Wightman Fox (New York: Pantheon, 1983), 1–38. The quotation comes from Robert N. Bellah et al., *Habits of the Heart: Individualism and Commitment in American Life* (1985; Berkeley: University of California Press, 2008), 63–64.

11. The idea that Americans subscribe to a collective civil creed is found in Gunnar Myrdal, *An American Dilemma: The Negro Problem and American Democracy* (New York: Harper, 1944), and named in Robert N. Bellah, "Civil Religion in America," *Daedalus* 96, no. 1 (Winter 1967): 1–21, spawning a great deal of literature. On the disjunction between theory and practice, see Rogers M. Smith, "The 'American Creed' and American Identity: The Limits of Liberal Citizenship in the United States," *Western Political Quarterly* 41, no. 2 (June 1988): 225–51, and Smith, *Civic Ideals: Conflicting Visions of Citizenship in U.S. History* (New Haven, CT: Yale University Press, 1997). For a recent history of human rights that does not include religion, see Lynn Hunt, *Inventing Human Rights: A History* (New York: Norton, 2007), and for a history of human rights that pointedly challenges both Hunt and the importance of the United Nations, see Samuel Moyn, *The Last Utopia: Human Rights in History* (Cambridge, MA: Belknap Press of Harvard University Press, 2010).

12. Ralph Waldo Emerson, *The Complete Works of Ralph Waldo Emerson, vol. 4, Representative Men* (Boston: Houghton, Mifflin and Co., 1904), 5. My method in this book accords with the premise of Daniel T. Rodgers, Bhavani Raman, and Helmut Reimitz, eds., *Cultures in Motion* (Princeton, NJ: Princeton University Press, 2013).

CHAPTER 1 • JOHN ADAMS, REFORMATION CHRISTIAN:
THE PROTESTANT MORAL ETHIC AND
THE SPIRIT OF INDEPENDENCE

1. L. H. Butterfield, ed., *Diary and Autobiography of John Adams* (Cambridge, MA: Harvard University Press, 1961), 3:276. See Peter Shaw, *The Character of John Adams* (Chapel Hill: University of North Carolina Press, 1976). John E. Ferling reconstructs Deacon John Adams's character as well as a historian can using context in "Before Fame: Young John Adams and Thomas Jefferson," in *John Adams and the Founding of the Republic*, ed. Richard Alan Ryerson (Boston: Massachusetts Historical Society, 2001), 72–102; see also Richard D. Brown, "The Disenchantment of a Radical Whig," in the same volume. Ferling's contribution to Adams scholarship also includes *Setting the World Ablaze: Washington, Adams, Jefferson, and the American Revolution* (New York: Oxford University Press, 2000) and *John Adams: A Life* (Knoxville: University of Tennessee Press, 1992). David L. Holmes, *Faiths of the Founding Fathers* (New York: Oxford University Press, 2006), 72–102. On doctrinal diversity in the eighteenth-century Congregational Church, see Patricia Bonomi, *Under the Cope of Heaven: Religion, Society, and Politics in Colonial America* (New York: Oxford University Press, 1986), and Harry S. Stout, *The New England Soul: Preaching and Religious Culture in Colonial New England* (New York: Oxford University Press, 1986); Jon Butler, *Awash in a Sea of Faith: Christianizing the American People* (Cambridge, MA: Harvard University Press, 1990). For an important set of arguments about the diversity of American Christianity in general, see Catherine A. Brekus and W. Clark Gilpin, eds., *American Christianities: A History of Dominance and Diversity* (Chapel Hill: University of North Carolina Press, 2011).

   Lemuel Briant, *The Absurdity and Blasphemy of Depretiating Moral Virtue: A Sermon Preached at the West-Church in Boston, June 18th. 1749. By Lemuel Briant, A.M. Pastor of the First Church in Braintree. [Eight lines of Scripture texts]* (Boston: Printed by J. Green for D. Gookin, in Marlborough-Street, 1749), 27. The early Reformation idea of the right of conscience applied only to the interpretation of the Bible rather than to all of God's revelation; the American Reformation greatly expanded the prerogative of conscience. Thanks to Mark Valeri for help clarifying this point.

2. See David D. Hall, *A Reforming People: Puritanism and the Transformation of Public Life in New England* (New York: Knopf, 2011), xi. On the Forefathers Rock nickname, see *Diary and Autobiography of John Adams*, 3:284. For the essay itself, *A Dissertation on the Canon and Feudal Law*, in *Papers of John Adams*, ed. R. J. Taylor, G. L. Lint, and C. Walker (Cambridge, MA: Belknap Press of Harvard University Press, 1977), 1:111–27.

3. On dignity as a central concept in modern democracy, see Michael Rosen, *Dignity: Its History and Meaning* (Cambridge, MA: Harvard University Press, 2012), and George Kateb, *Human Dignity* (Cambridge, MA: Belknap Press of Harvard University Press, 2011).

4. Adams first reported attending a meeting of the Sons of Liberty in December 1765 and became a regular participant thereafter; *Diary and Autobiography of John Adams*, 1:265–66, 294, 340–42. The meaning of the word "agency" here is different from that used in the provocative and compelling James E. Block, *A Nation of Agents: The American Path to a Modern Self and Society* (Cambridge, MA: Belknap Press of Harvard University Press, 2002). On how Adams understood liberty and its place in his political thought, see C. Bradley Thompson, *John Adams and the Spirit of Liberty*

(Lawrence: University Press of Kansas, 1998). See also Barry Shain, *The Myth of American Individualism: The Protestant Origins of American Thought* (Princeton, NJ: Princeton University Press, 1994).

On "freedom from" and "freedom to," see Isaiah Berlin, "Two Concepts of Liberty" (1958), in *Four Essays on Liberty* (New York: Oxford University Press, 1969).

5. On John Adams's character, see Gordon Wood, "The Relevance and Irrelevance of John Adams," in *Revolutionary Characters: What Made the Founders Different* (New York: Penguin Press, 2006). On the role of English heterodoxy in the American Revolution, see Colin Bonwick, *English Radicals and the American Revolution* (Chapel Hill: University of North Carolina Press, 1977); Knud Haakonssen, ed., *Enlightenment and Religion: Rational Dissent in Eighteenth-Century Britain* (Cambridge: Cambridge University Press, 1996).

6. Max Weber, *The Protestant Ethic and the Spirit of Capitalism* (New York: Scribner, 1930). On Franklin, Edwards, and virtue, see Daniel Walker Howe, *Making the American Self: Jonathan Edwards to Abraham Lincoln* (Cambridge, MA: Harvard University Press, 1997). Howe, like May, is reacting in part to the thesis offered by Alan Heimert, *Religion and the American Mind: From the Great Awakening to the Revolution* (Cambridge, MA: Harvard University Press, 1966).

Here and elsewhere I borrow the resonance of "we" from David A. Hollinger, "How Wide the Circle of the 'We'?: American Intellectuals and the Problem of the Ethnos Since World War II," *American Historical Review* 98 (April 1993): 317–37.

7. *Diary and Autobiography of John Adams,* 1:23. John Adams to Thomas Jefferson, December 12, 1816, in *The Adams-Jefferson Letters: The Complete Correspondence Between Thomas Jefferson and Abigail and John Adams,* ed. Lester J. Cappon (Chapel Hill: University of North Carolina Press, 1959), 2:499.

8. The Briant controversy has been treated in Conrad Wright, *The Beginnings of Unitarianism in America* (Boston: Starr King Press, 1955), 67–72. See also James William Jones, *The Shattered Synthesis: New England Puritanism Before the Great Awakening* (New Haven, CT: Yale University Press, 1973), 132–33. For Mayhew, see Clinton Rossiter, "The Life and Mind of Jonathan Mayhew," *William and Mary Quarterly* 7, no. 4 (October 1950): 531–58, and Charles W. Akers, *Called unto Liberty: A Life of Jonathan Mayhew, 1720–1766* (Cambridge, MA: Harvard University Press, 1964). On the Boston Association of Ministers in this period, see Wright, *Beginnings of Unitarianism,* 67; Sydney E. Ahlstrom with Jonathan S. Carey, *An American Reformation: A Documentary History of Unitarian Christianity* (Middletown, CT: Wesleyan University Press, 1985), 323.

9. William B. Sprague, *Annals of the American Pulpit: Trinitarian Congregational* (New York: Robert Carter and Brothers, 1857), 131–33. William A. Hallock, *The Venerable Mayhews and the Aboriginals of Martha's Vineyard* (New York: American Tract Society, 1874). Hilary E. Wyss, "'Things That Do Accompany Salvation': Colonialism, Conversion, and Cultural Exchange in Experience Mayhew's 'Indian Converts,'" *Early American Literature* 33, no. 1 (1998): 39–61. On many Puritans' skepticism over the possibility of Native American Christianity, see Jill Lepore, *The Name of War: King Philip's War and the Origins of American Identity* (New York: Knopf, 1998). "John Adams to Thomas Jefferson, 28 June 1812," *Founders Online,* National Archives, http://founders.archives.gov/documents/Jefferson/03-05-02-0152. Source: J. Jefferson Looney, ed., *The Papers of Thomas Jefferson,* Retirement Series, vol. 5, *1 May 1812 to 10 March 1813* (Princeton, NJ: Princeton University Press, 2008), 182–86.

10. On Jonathan Mayhew and Harvard, see especially John Corrigan, *The Hidden Balance: Religion and the Social Theories of Charles Chauncy and Jonathan Mayhew* (New York: Cambridge University Press, 1987), and Corrigan, *The Prism of Piety: Catholick Congregational Clergy at the Beginning of the Enlightenment* (New York: Oxford University Press, 1991). On the role of Scottish Common Sense in American theology, see Howe, *Making the American Self,* as well as the work of Mark Noll, notably *America's God.* For an excellent overview, see E. Brooks Holifield, *Theology in America: Christian Thought from the Age of the Puritans to the Civil War* (New Haven, CT: Yale University Press, 2003).

11. Jonathan Mayhew to Experience Mayhew, July 15, 1752, in Mayhew collection at Boston University Archives, box 1, item 35. Experience Mayhew, will, *ibid.,* box 1, item 37. A liberal Christian started the historiography of Mayhew in the Romantic era; Alden Bradford, *Memoir of the Life and Writings of Rev. Jonathan Mayhew* (Boston: C. C. Little, 1838).

12. Jonathan Mayhew to Experience Mayhew, October 1, 1747, in Mayhew collection at Boston University Archives, box 1, item 23. Ann Taves, *Fits, Trances, and Visions: Experiencing Religion and Explaining Experience from Wesley to James* (Princeton, NJ: Princeton University Press, 1999). Briant, *Absurdity and Blasphemy,* 8. On revivals, in addition to Stout, *The New England Soul,* and Butler, *Awash in a Sea of Faith,* see also William G. McLoughlin, *Revivals, Awakenings, and Reform: An Essay on Religion and Social Change in America, 1607–1977* (Chicago: University of Chicago Press, 1978). For the complex response in Boston to the Great Awakening, see especially Mark A. Peterson, *The Price of Redemption: The Spiritual Economy of Puritan New England* (Stanford, CA: Stanford University Press, 1997), 219–39.

13. Charles Chauncy, *The Only Compulsion Proper to Be Made Use of in the Affairs of Conscience and Religion* (Boston: J. Draper, 1739); *Seasonable Thoughts on the State of Religion in New England: A Treatise in Five Parts* (Boston: Rogers and Fowle, 1743). Charles Lippy, *Seasonable Revolutionary: The Mind of Charles Chauncy* (Chicago: Nelson Hall, 1982); Edward M. Griffin, *Old Brick: Charles Chauncy of Boston, 1705–1787* (Minneapolis: University of Minnesota Press, 1980).

14. Maccarty appears in William B. Sprague, *Annals of the American Pulpit* (New York: R. Carter and brothers, 1857–[69]). On the Congregational Way, see Hall, *A Reforming People,* esp. 73–78, 107–11. On Ebenezer Gay, see Robert J. Wilson, *The Benevolent Deity: Ebenezer Gay and the Rise of Rational Religion in New England, 1696–1787* (Philadelphia: University of Pennsylvania Press, 1984). The definition of religion comes from Ebenezer Gay, *Natural religion, as distinguish'd from revealed: a sermon preached at the annual Dudleian lecture* (Boston: John Draper, 1759). Gay may have been exhibiting his Latin scholarship in this definition, as in Latin *religio* means "duty," contrasting with superstition, which was a distinction Reformation Christians like Gay were eager to make; I owe this observation to William Clay Poe III.

15. Mayhew, *Seven Sermons upon the following Subjects* . . . (London: John Noon, 1750), 12; sermons V–VII. Briant, *Absurdity and Blasphemy,* 17, 30. To put this view of Christ in context, see Richard Wightman Fox, *Jesus in America: Personal Savior, Cultural Hero, National Obsession* (San Francisco: HarperSanFrancisco, 2004).

16. Briant, *Absurdity and Blasphemy,* 6, 30; Wright, *Beginnings of Unitarianism,* 224. On liberty of conscience among the early Puritans, see Hall, *A Reforming People,* esp. 46, 50. On right reasoning, Mayhew copied the term down from his reading in Pascal,

suggesting that what some scholars call the Catholic Reformation had a role in the making of the American Reformation as well; Mayhew, *Extracts*, in Mayhew collection at Boston University Archives, box 1, item 10. Michael A. Mullett, *The Catholic Reformation* (New York: Routledge University Press, 1999).

17. Briant, *Absurdity and Blasphemy*, 23.

18. Mayhew, *Seven Sermons*, 3; Briant, *Absurdity and Blasphemy*, 6, 17.

19. Briant, *Absurdity and Blasphemy*, 7, 10, 22, 23.

20. Mayhew, *Seven Sermons,* 5. Henry Farnham May correctly suggests that this road leads to pragmatism in *The Enlightenment in America* (New York: Oxford University Press, 1976), 56–57.

21. Briant, *Absurdity and Blasphemy,* 7, 11; Briant, *Some friendly remarks on a sermon lately preach'd at Braintree, 3d. Parish* (Boston: D. Gookin, 1750), 11.

22. Briant, *Absurdity and Blasphemy*, 23–24, 26, 31.

23. For a start, see Conrad Wright, *The Unitarian Controversy: Essays on American Unitarian History* (Boston: Skinner House, 1994). One element common in the later controversies and missing here is the disjunction between what the church members and the townspeople wanted, which highlighted the tension between Congregational establishment and the Congregational Way.

24. John Porter, *The absurdity and blasphemy of substituting the personal righteousness of men in the room of the Surety-Righteousness of Christ* (Boston: Kneeland, 1750), 4, 5, 15, 22, 29.

25. Briant, *Some friendly remarks,* 8, 27; Porter, *A vindication of a sermon preached at Braintree . . .* (Boston: Kneeland, 1751), 2; Briant, *Some more friendly remarks on Mr. Porter and company* (Boston: D. Gookin, 1751), 24; Samuel J. Niles, *A vindication of divers important Gospel-doctrines, and of the teachers and professors of them, against the injurious reflections & misrepresentations contained in a late printed discourse of the Rev. Mr. Lemuel Briant's* (Boston: Kneeland, 1752), preface 4; Porter, *The absurdity and blasphemy,* 31.

26. *The Result of the Council of a Number of Churches Held at Braintree, Massachusetts, December 5, 1752* (Boston, 1752); emphases in original.

27. Samuel Niles and twelve others, *The Result of a late Ecclesiastical Council* (Boston: s.n., 1753), 2.

28. First Church (Braintree, MA), *The report of a committee of the First Church in Braintree: appointed in March, 1753. To enquire into the grounds of those slanderous reports that had been spread abroad, respecting themselves, and the Reverend Mr. Lemuel Briant, their pastor* (Boston: s.n., 1753); emphasis in original.

29. Briant, *Absurdity and Blasphemy*, 6.

30. Thompson, *John Adams and the Spirit of Liberty,* 6; John Adams to Thomas Jefferson, December 3, 1813, *Adams-Jefferson Letters,* 2:402. Henry May calls free disputes the New England manner in *Enlightenment in America,* 125.

31. *Adams-Jefferson Letters,* 2:405–6. The Latin translation comes from a useful anthology by Bruce Braden, ed., *"Ye Will Say I Am No Christian": The Thomas Jefferson/John Adams Correspondence on Religion, Morals, and Values* (Amherst, NY: Prometheus Books, 2006), 123.

32. Adams to Jefferson, July 18, 1818, *Adams-Jefferson Letters,* 2:527. On Adams giving Mayhew and Chauncy credit, see Corrigan, *Hidden Balance,* 6–7. On Mayhew's discourse and the colonial tensions underlying it, see Chris Beneke, "The Critical Turn:

Jonathan Mayhew, the British Empire, and the Idea of Resistance in Eighteenth-Century Boston," *Massachusetts Historical Review* 10 (2008): 23–56.

33. *Diary and Autobiography of John Adams,* 1:7; Mayhew, *Seven Sermons,* iii; [John Trenchard and Thomas Gordon], *Independent Whig* (London: J. Peele, 1721), xlviii–xlix. On Trenchard and Gordon, see Howe, *Making the American Self,* 13–16; Bonomi, *Under the Cope of Heaven,* 193–95. On how Adams used English political thought, see Annabel Patterson, "John Adams: Reader Extraordinary," in *Early Modern Liberalism* (New York: Cambridge University Press, 1997), 279–305.

34. Mayhew, *Seven Sermons,* v.

35. *Ibid.,* 8, 14, 38–39, 46. See the discussion in Bonomi, *Under the Cope of Heaven,* 196–97; J. C. D. Clark, *The Language of Liberty, 1660–1832: Political Discourse and Social Dynamics in the Anglo-American World* (New York: Cambridge University Press, 1994), 26–27, 168–69, 366.

36. *Diary and Autobiography of John Adams,* 1:8, 28. For more on his context there, see John L. Brook, *The Heart of the Commonwealth: Society and Political Culture in Worcester County, Massachusetts, 1713–1861* (New York: Cambridge University Press, 1989). See also Ray Raphael, *The First American Revolution: Before Lexington and Concord* (New York: New Press, 2002).

37. *Diary and Autobiography of John Adams,* 1:14–15. Thompson, *John Adams and the Spirit of Liberty,* 8–9.

38. On Dedham as exemplary New England town, see Kenneth Lockridge, *A New England Town: The First Hundred Years, Dedham, Massachusetts, 1636–1736* (New York: Norton, 1970).

39. *Diary and Autobiography of John Adams,* 1:10, 43. Norman S. Fiering, "The First American Enlightenment: Tillotson, Leverett, and Philosophical Anglicanism," *New England Quarterly* 54 (1981): 307–44.

40. *Diary and Autobiography of John Adams,* 1:9.

41. *Ibid.,* 1:36–37.

42. *Ibid.,* 1:14, 41. On how Adams held the golden rule as natural law, see Thompson, *John Adams and the Spirit of Liberty,* 23. See also Andy Trees, "John Adams and the Problem of Virtue," *Journal of the Early Republic* 21, no. 3 (Autumn 2001): 393–412.

43. *Diary and Autobiography of John Adams,* 1:41.

44. *Ibid.,* 1:42.

45. *Ibid.,* 1:12, 20, 21n1, 43, 83.

46. *Ibid.,* 1:86, 98–100; Thompson, *John Adams and the Spirit of Liberty,* 22. Richard D. Brown, *Knowledge Is Power: The Diffusion of Information in Early America, 1700–1865* (New York: Oxford University Press, 1989), 82–109.

47. Thompson, *John Adams and the Spirit of Liberty,* 37–38, 49–53.

48. On the rough draft and the role of Adams in the drafting of the Declaration, see Pauline Maier, *American Scripture: Making the Declaration of Independence* (New York: Knopf, 1997), 97–102, 110, 182–84, 241. Thompson, *John Adams and the Spirit of Liberty,* 38–39.

49. John Ferling, "John Adams, Diplomat," *William and Mary Quarterly* 51, no. 2 (April 1994): 227–52 (quotes on 228, 241).

50. Thompson, *John Adams and the Spirit of Liberty,* 197–99.

51. John Ferling, *Adams vs. Jefferson: The Tumultuous Election of 1800* (New York: Oxford University Press, 2004), 26. Stephen G. Kurtz, *The Presidency of John Adams: The Collapse of Federalism, 1795–1800* (Philadelphia: University of Pennsylvania Press, 1957). Shaw, *Character of John Adams,* 106–35.

52. Donald H. Stewart and George P. Clark, "Misanthrope or Humanitarian?: John Adams in Retirement," *New England Quarterly* 28, no. 2 (June 1955): 216–36. Daniel I. O'Neill, "John Adams versus Mary Wollstonecraft on the French Revolution and Democracy," *Journal of the History of Ideas* 68, no. 3 (July 2007): 451–76. On Hannah Adams, see Gary D. Schmidt, *A Passionate Usefulness: The Life and Literary Labors of Hannah Adams* (Charlottesville: University of Virginia Press, 2004). See also the untitled review in the *Monthly Anthology and Boston Review* 9 (August 1810): 116–29, and Leigh E. Schmidt, "A History of All Religions," *Journal of the Early Republic* 24 (Summer 2004): 327–34. Adams to Jefferson, September 14, 1813, *Adams-Jefferson Letters,* 2:372–75.

53. Adams to Jefferson, June 25, 1813, *ibid.,* 2:333–35.

54. Adams to Jefferson, September 15, 1813, *ibid.,* 2:375–77.

CHAPTER 2 · MARY MOODY EMERSON, NATURAL CHRISTIAN: THE CULTURE OF LIVED VIRTUE AND THE FIGHT AGAINST BIGOTRY

1. Mary Moody Emerson to Ezra Ripley, July 25, 1826, in *The Selected Letters of Mary Moody Emerson,* ed. Nancy Craig Simmons (Athens: University of Georgia Press, 1993), 218–19.

2. William Emerson, sermon of 19 August 1764, item 421, Emerson Family Papers (MS Am 1280.235), Houghton Library, Harvard University. Mary Moody Emerson to William Emerson, June 21, 1826, in Simmons, ed., *Selected Letters of Mary Moody Emerson,* 216–17. See also Dean Grodzins, *American Heretic: Theodore Parker and Transcendentalism* (Chapel Hill: University of North Carolina Press, 2002), and George Kateb, *The Inner Ocean: Individualism and Democratic Culture* (Ithaca, NY: Cornell University Press, 1992).

3. Alexandra Oleson and Sanborn Conner Brown, *The Pursuit of Knowledge in the Early American Republic: American Scientific and Learned Societies from Colonial Times to the Civil War* (Baltimore: Johns Hopkins University Press, 1976). Richard D. Brown, *Knowledge Is Power: The Diffusion of Information in Early America, 1700–1865* (New York: Oxford University Press, 1989), and Brown, *The Strength of a People: The Idea of an Informed Citizenry in America, 1650–1870* (Chapel Hill: University of North Carolina Press, 1996). William J. Gilmore, *Reading Becomes a Necessity of Life: Material and Cultural Life in Rural New England, 1780–1835* (Knoxville: University of Tennessee Press, 1989). Joseph Kett, *The Pursuit of Knowledge Under Difficulties: From Self-Improvement to Adult Education in America, 1750–1990* (Stanford, CA: Stanford University Press, 1994). Catherine O'Donnell Kaplan, *Men of Letters in the Early Republic: Cultivating Forms of Citizenship* (Chapel Hill: University of North Carolina Press, 2008).

4. My understanding of M. M. Emerson is deeply indebted to Phyllis Cole, *Mary Moody Emerson and the Origins of Transcendentalism: A Family History* (New York: Oxford University Press, 1998). Mary Moody Emerson, item 579, Emerson Family Papers, 1699–1939 (MS Am 1280.235), Houghton Library, Harvard University. Scholars disagree over whether a term like "feminist," coined in the twentieth century, can even be considered for earlier periods; for two examples of recent scholarship that use the term in full awareness of this fact, both also relevant to the argument of this book, see Sarah Apetrei, *Women, Feminism, and Religion in Early Enlightenment England* (New York: Cambridge University Press, 2010); Arianne Chernock, *Men and the Making of Modern British Feminism* (Stanford, CA: Stanford University Press, 2010).

5. Here lie the origins of the "culture of inquiry" explicated in David A. Hollinger, "William James and the Culture of Inquiry," *In the American Province: Studies in the History and Historiography of Ideas* (Baltimore: Johns Hopkins University Press, 1985), 1–22. On the role of classics in the pursuit of knowledge in the early republic, see Caroline Winterer, *The Culture of Classicism: Ancient Greece and Rome in the Early Republic* (Baltimore: Johns Hopkins University Press, 2002). Henry James in Cole, *Mary Moody Emerson,* 12, 294–95.

6. Mary Moody Emerson to Ralph Waldo Emerson, July 25, 1822, and August 1824, in Simmons, ed., *Selected Letters of Mary Moody Emerson,* 182, 186. Mary Kupiec Cayton, "Who Were the Evangelicals?: Conservative and Liberal Identity in the Unitarian Controversy in Boston, 1804–1833," *Journal of Social History* 31 (1997): 85–107. The American Unitarians were not derived from the English Unitarians, although the two groups were certainly in conversation; for a different view, see J. D. Bowers, *Joseph Priestley and English Unitarianism in America* (University Park: Pennsylvania State University Press, 2007).

7. Mary Moody Emerson to Charles Chauncy Emerson, March 9, 1824, in Simmons, ed., *Selected Letters of May Moody Emerson,* 178. Cole, *Mary Moody Emerson,* 56, 228.

8. Cole, *Mary Moody Emerson,* 61–79. David Hackett Fischer, *Paul Revere's Ride* (New York: Oxford University Press, 1994), 202–12, 312, 394n23.

9. On the role of ministers in the early republic, see Jonathan D. Sassi, *A Republic of Righteousness: The Public Christianity of the Post-Revolutionary New England Clergy* (Oxford: Oxford University Press, 2001). On the Congregational Way, see David D. Hall, *A Reforming People: Puritanism and the Transformation of Public Life in New England* (New York: Knopf, 2011), 28, 73. Simmons, ed., *Selected Letters of Mary Moody Emerson,* 216–17.

10. On public Christianity, see Sassi, *Republic of Righteousness.* On the covenant idea and the widespread departure from the public sphere after the war, see Perry Miller "From the Covenant to the Revival," in *Religion in American Life,* vol. 1, *The Shaping of American Religion,* ed. J. W. Smith and A. L. Jamison (Princeton, NJ: Princeton University Press, 1961); Donald Weber, *Rhetoric and History in Revolutionary New England* (New York: Oxford University Press, 1988); Barry Alan Shain, *The Myth of American Individualism: The Protestant Origins of American Political Thought* (Princeton, NJ: Princeton University Press, 1994). On the role of providential thinking in the construction of American nationhood, see Nicholas Guyatt, *Providence and the Invention of the United States, 1607–1876* (New York: Cambridge University Press, 2007); Ruth

M. Bloch, *Visionary Republic: Millennial Themes in American Thought, 1756–1800* (New York: Cambridge University Press, 1985). On how New England looked different, see Dale S. Kuehne, *Massachusetts Congregationalist Political Thought, 1760–1790: The Design of Heaven* (Columbia: University of Missouri Press, 1996); Mark Y. Hanley, *Beyond a Christian Commonwealth: The Protestant Quarrel with the American Republic, 1830–1860* (Chapel Hill: University of North Carolina Press, 1994).

11. Cole, *Mary Moody Emerson,* 58–62. Amelia Forbes Emerson, ed., *Diaries and Letters of William Emerson, 1743–1776* (Boston: Thomas Todd, 1972). Darren Staloff, *The Making of an American Thinking Class: Intellectuals and Intelligentsia in Puritan Massachusetts* (New York: Oxford University Press, 1988).

12. William Emerson, sermon of 19 August 1764, item 421, Emerson Family Papers (MS Am 1280.235), Houghton Library, Harvard University.

13. *Ibid.* Joseph A. Conforti, *Jonathan Edwards, Religious Tradition, and American Culture* (Chapel Hill: University of North Carolina Press, 1995); George M. Marsden, *Jonathan Edwards: A Life* (New Haven, CT: Yale University Press, 2003); Douglas L. Winiarski, "Jonathan Edwards, Enthusiast?: Radical Revivalism and the Great Awakening in the Connecticut Valley," *Church History* 74, no. 4 (December 2005): 683–739. Cole, *Mary Moody Emerson,* 131–32.

14. William Emerson, sermon of n.d. on Zechariah 9:12, item 435, Emerson Family Papers (MS Am 1280.235), Houghton Library, Harvard University.

15. William Emerson, sermon of 12 December 1772, item 428, Emerson Family Papers (MS Am 1280.235), Houghton Library, Harvard University. Daniel Day Williams, *The Andover Liberals: A Study in American Theology* (New York: King's Crown Press, 1941).

16. Cole, *Mary Moody Emerson,* 60–65, 67.

17. Fischer, *Paul Revere's Ride,* 78–92.

18. *Ibid.,* 204–5.

19. Cole, *Mary Moody Emerson,* 58–62, 73; Fischer, *Paul Revere's Ride,* 204–5.

20. Ralph Waldo Emerson, "Concord Hymn" (1836). Cole, *Mary Moody Emerson,* 65–69.

21. On family government, public sins, and Congregationalist ministers as coleaders with public officials, see Sassi, *Republic of Righteousness,* 20–21, 52–56; Gordon S. Wood, *The Radicalism of the American Revolution,* 1st ed. (New York: Knopf, 1991), 180, 229.

22. Cole, *Mary Moody Emerson,* 68–70. John Demos, *A Little Commonwealth: Family Life in Plymouth Colony* (New York: Oxford University Press, 1970).

23. Cole, *Mary Moody Emerson,* 63, 69–70.

24. *Ibid.,* 63, 69–70.

25. *Ibid.,* 71–75

26. *Ibid.,* 70–71, 74.

27. Ralph Waldo Emerson, "Ezra Ripley, D.D.," in *The Complete Works of Ralph Waldo Emerson, vol. 10, Lectures and Biographical Sketches* (Boston: Houghton, Mifflin and Co., 1909), 380–95. See also the entry describing Ripley as "a MAN, fearless in his duty and determined to walk in the ordinances of his God and Saviour, blameless," in William B. Sprague, *Annals of the American Pulpit or, Commemorative Notices of Distinguished American Clergymen of Various Denominations, from the Early Settlement of the Country to the Close of the Year Eighteen Hundred and Fifty-five*

(New York: R. Carter and brothers, 1857), 120. John Eliot Alden, "Out of the Ashes, a Young Phoenix: Early Americana in the Harvard College Library," *William and Mary Quarterly* 3, no. 4 (October 1946): 487–98. Thanks to Jill Lepore for alerting me to this salient detail.

28. Corrigan, *Prism of Piety*. Conrad Wright, *The Beginnings of Unitarianism in America* (Boston: Starr King Press, 1955). Peter S. Field, *The Crisis of the Standing Order: Clerical Intellectuals and Cultural Authority in Massachusetts, 1780–1833* (Amherst: University of Massachusetts Press, 1998).

29. Robert Middlekauff, "A Persistent Tradition: The Classical Curriculum in Eighteenth-Century New England," *William and Mary Quarterly* 18, no. 1 (January 1961): 54–67. Daniel Walker Howe, "The Cambridge Platonists of Old England and the Cambridge Platonists of New England," *Church History* 57, no. 4 (December 1988): 470–85. Benjamin Whichcote, Aphorism 76, *Moral and Religious Aphorisms* (London: Mathews and Marrot, 1930), 11. Locke praised Whichcote's sermons in a letter to Rev. Richard King, quoted in Whichcote, *Moral and Religious Aphorisms*, xxxii. Jerome Huyler, *Locke in America: The Moral Philosophy of the Founding Era* (Lawrence: University Press of Kansas, 1995). John Marshall, *John Locke, Toleration and Early Enlightenment Culture: Religious Intolerance and Arguments for Religious Toleration in Early Modern and "Early Enlightenment" Europe* (New York: Cambridge University Press, 2006).

30. Stephen L. Darwall, *The British Moralists and the Internal "Ought," 1640–1740* (New York: Cambridge University Press, 1995). G. A. J. Rogers, J.-M. Vienne, and Y.-C. Zarka, eds., *The Cambridge Platonists in Philosophical Context: Politics, Metaphysics and Religion* (Dordecht: Kluwer Academic Publishers, 1997). Benjamin Hoadly, ed., *The Works of Samuel Clarke* (London: J. and P. Knapton, 1738), 1:vi. Wright, *Beginnings of Unitarianism*, 57, 100. Cole, *Mary Moody Emerson*, 95, 124.

31. Whichcote, *Moral and Religious Aphorisms*, xviii–xix, xx–xxi, xxiii–xxiv, xxx, xxxii.

32. *Ibid.,* ix, xxxii 106, 107.

33. *Ibid.,* vii, 37, 106, 132.

34. Huyler, *Locke in America,* 70–74, 98–99. Richard Ashcraft, "Locke and the Problem of Toleration," in *Discourses of Tolerance and Intolerance in the European Enlightenment,* ed. Hans Eric Bödecker, Clorinda Donata, and Peter Reill (Toronto: University of Toronto Press, 2008). John Perry, *The Pretenses of Loyalty: Locke, Liberal Theory, and American Political Theology* (New York: Oxford University Press, 2011). Whichcote, *Moral and Religious Aphorisms,* 42, 113.

35. Simmons, ed., *Selected Letters of Mary Moody Emerson,* 90–92, 201.

36. *Ibid.,* 218–19. For later, transnational considerations of uncertainty, see James T. Kloppenberg, *Uncertain Victory: Social Democracy and Progressivism in European and American Thought, 1870–1920* (New York: Oxford University Press, 1986).

37. Cole, *Mary Moody Emerson,* 164–65. Randolph A. Roth, *The Democratic Dilemma: Religion, Reform, and the Social Order in the Connecticut River Valley of Vermont, 1791–1850* (New York: Cambridge University Press, 1987).

38. Ezra Ripley, *Design and Blessedness of the Bible: A Sermon, Delivered, May 23, 1792, at the Ordination of the Rev. William Emerson, to the care of the Congregational Church and Society at Harvard* (Boston: Isaiah Thomas and Ebenezer T. Andrews, 1792), 6, 7, 16. On occasional sermons, see Sassi, *Republic of Righteousness*.

39. Ripley, *Design and Blessedness of the Bible,* 16, 19.

40. *Ibid.,* 22.

41. Sassi, *Republic of Righteousness,* 22–23.

42. American Academy of Arts and Sciences, Charter of Incorporation, http://www .amacad.org/content/about/about.aspx?d=23; Oleson and Brown, eds., *Pursuit of Knowledge,* 151–63, 168.

43. Cole, *Mary Moody Emerson,* 91–95.

44. *Ibid.,* 111–13, 133, 164–65. Oleson and Brown, *Pursuit of Knowledge,* 168. Wright, *Beginnings of Unitarianism,* 263. Field, *Crisis of the Standing Order*; Kaplan, *Men of Letters.* William Emerson, *An oration pronounced July 5, 1802, at the request of the inhabitants of the town of Boston: in commemoration of the anniversary of independence* (Boston: Manning and Loring, [1802]).

45. On "social segar," *Monthly Anthology and the Boston Review, Containing Sketches and Reports of Philosophy, Religion, History, Arts, and Manners* 2, no. 3 (March 1805): 129. Thanks to Manu Radhakrishnan for the Latin translation. Mary Moody Emerson on Johnson, "To Cornelia," *Monthly Anthology* 2, no. 6 (June 1805): 342. See also Peter S. Field, "The Birth of Secular High Culture: 'The Monthly Anthology and Boston Review' and Its Critics," *Journal of the Early Republic* 17, no. 4 (Winter 1997): 575–609.

46. Elizabeth Palmer Peabody and Margaret Fuller are two notable examples of females who learned Latin; see Bruce A. Ronda, *Elizabeth Palmer Peabody: A Reformer on Her Own Terms* (Cambridge, MA: Harvard University Press, 1999), and Charles Capper, *Margaret Fuller: An American Romantic Life,* vol. 1 (New York: Oxford University Press, 1992).

47. *Monthly Anthology and the Boston Review, Containing Sketches and Reports of Philosophy, Religion, History, Arts, and Manners* 2, no. 3 (March 1805): 129. Thanks to Kagan Senvardarli for explaining the Turkish. Ezra Ripley, *A Sermon Preached on the Completion of the General Repair of the Meeting House in Concord, January 24th, 1792* (Boston: B. Edes and Son, 1792), 18. Mary Moody Emerson to Charles Chauncy Emerson, March 9, 1824, in Simmons, ed., *Selected Letters of Mary Moody Emerson,* 180–81. Ralph Waldo Emerson, "Persian Poetry," *Works, vol. 8, Letters and Social Aims,* 124–49.

48. "Sketches of the Life and Character of Rev. David Tappan," *Panoplist* 1, nos. 1–5 (June–October 1805). "Biographia Americana; or, Memoirs of Distinguished, Professional, or Distinguished Characters in the United States: 7. David Tappan, D.D., A.A.A.S., Hollis Professor of Divinity in Harvard College," *Monthly Anthology* 2, no. 3 (Mar 1805): 123.

49. Wright, *Beginnings of Unitarianism,* 271–73. Ware quoted in Sassi, *Republic of Righteousness,* 157.

50. "Sketches of the Life and Character of Rev. David Tappan," 1, 45.

51. Simmons, ed., *Selected Letters of Mary Moody Emerson,* 32. Doddridge, *The Rise and Progress of Religion in the Soul* (Boston: J. Loring, 1818), 229–31. David Lundberg and Henry F. May, "The Enlightened Reader in America," *American Quarterly* 28, no. 2 (July 1, 1976): 262–93.

52. Cole, *Mary Moody Emerson,* 4, 83, 96–98, 101–7, 256–57. Peter S. Field, *Ralph Waldo Emerson: The Making of a Democratic Intellectual* (Lanham, MD: Rowman and

Littlefield, 2002); Linck Johnson, "Emerson: America's First Public Intellectual?," *Modern Intellectual History* 2, no. 1 (April 2005): 131–51.

53. Letter from Constance, *Monthly Anthology* 2, no. 3 (March 1805): 140–41. For Mary Moody Emerson on Butler, see "The Principle of Action in a Virtuous Agent," *Monthly Anthology* 1, no. 10 (August 1804): 456–57. Jill Lepore, *Book of Ages: The Life and Opinions of Jane Franklin* (New York: Knopf, 2013), 204–5, 216–18.

54. Simmons, ed., *Selected Letters of Mary Moody Emerson*, 54, 64–65, 247, 258–59.

55. Sassi, *Republic of Righteousness,* 122. Wright, *Beginnings of Unitarianism,* 228–89. Josiah Quincy, *The History of the Boston Athenaeum, with Biographical Notices of its Deceased Founders* (Cambridge, MA: Metcalf and Co., 1851). Cole, *Mary Moody Emerson,* 149.

56. Simmons, ed., *Selected Letters of Mary Moody Emerson*, 138, 187–88, 205–7.

57. Mary Moody Emerson, almanac, item 529, Emerson Family Papers, 1699–1939 (MS Am 1280.235), Houghton Library, Harvard University. Jerry Wayne Brown, *The Rise of Biblical Criticism in America, 1800–1870: The New England Scholars* (Middletown, CT: Wesleyan University Press, 1969). Jon H. Giltner, *Moses Stuart: The Father of Biblical Science in America* (Atlanta: Scholars Press, 1988). Mark A. Noll, *Between Faith and Science: Evangelicals, Scholarship, and the Bible in America* (San Francisco: Harper and Row, 1987).

58. On Adam Smith and Madame de Staël, see Andreas Kalyvas and Ira Katznelson, *Liberal Beginnings: Making a Republic for the Moderns* (New York: Cambridge University Press, 2008), 18–50, 118–45. Simmons, ed., *Selected Letters of Mary Moody Emerson,* 182–84, 229.

59. Simmons, ed., *Selected Letters of Mary Moody Emerson*, 258; Cole, *Mary Moody Emerson,* 164.

60. Cole, *Mary Moody Emerson,* 215–19. Mary Moody Emerson, almanac, item 1303, Emerson Family Papers (MS Am 1280.235), Houghton Library, Harvard University.

61. Cole, *Mary Moody Emerson,* vi, 251, 281, 283, 309.

CHAPTER 3 · WILLIAM ELLERY CHANNING,
PRACTICAL CHRISTIAN: UNIVERSAL INNER
DIVINITY AND SELF-CULTURE

1. Mary Moody Emerson to Ralph Waldo Emerson, December 6, 1824, in Nancy Craig Simmons, ed., *Selected Letters of Mary Moody Emerson* (Athens: University of Georgia Press, 1993), 192–94. Elizabeth Palmer Peabody, *Reminiscences of Rev. Wm. Ellery Channing, D.D.* (Boston: Roberts Brothers, 1880), 43, 325, 381. For Unitarian Christianity being known on both sides of the Atlantic, see Dean Grodzins, *American Heretic: Theodore Parker and Transcendentalism* (Chapel Hill: University of North Carolina Press, 2002), 55.

2. For the English Romantics, begin with M. H. Abrams, *The Mirror and the Lamp: Romantic Theory and the Critical Tradition* (New York: Oxford University Press, 1953), and Abrams, *Natural Supernaturalism: Tradition and Revolution in Romantic Literature* (New York: Norton, 1971). The literature on the transatlantic relationship

of the European Romantics with the American Transcendentalists is substantial: Robert Weisbuch, *Atlantic Double-Cross: American Literature and British Influence in the Age of Emerson* (Chicago: University of Chicago Press, 1986), 62–63. Lee Rust Brown, *The Emerson Museum: Practical Romanticism and the Pursuit of the Whole* (Cambridge, MA: Harvard University Press, 1997); Leon Chai, *The Romantic Foundations of the American Renaissance* (Ithaca, NY: Cornell University Press, 1987); Richard Gravil, *Romantic Dialogues: Anglo-American Continuities, 1776–1855* (Basingstoke, UK: Macmillan, 2000); Megan Marshall, *The Peabody Sisters: Three Women Who Ignited American Romanticism* (Boston: Houghton Mifflin, 2005). Tony Tanner, "Notes for a Comparison between American and European Romanticism," *Journal of American Studies* 2, no. 1 (April 1968): 83–103.

3. John White Chadwick, *William Ellery Channing: Minister of Religion* (Houghton, Mifflin and Co., 1903), 174–75. Peabody, *Reminiscences*, 72. On religion in the Romantic movement and era, see Colin Jager, "Romanticism/Secularization/Secularism," *Literature Compass* 5, no. 4 (2008): 791–806.

4. Peabody, *Reminiscences*, 80–81.

5. For Channing's discourse on the "laboring classes," and "Self-Culture," see William Ellery Channing, *The Complete Works of William Ellery Channing: Including the Perfect Life, and Containing a Copious General Index and a Table of Scripture References*, 10th thousand [printing] (London: Christian Life, 1884), 64–79. The Liverpool review is John Hamilton Thom, *The Christian Teacher* I, new ser. (1839): 307–21, cited in Howard M. Wach, "Unitarian Philanthropy and Cultural Hegemony in Comparative Perspective: Manchester and Boston, 1827–1848," *Journal of Social History* 26, no. 3 (Spring 1993): 539–57. William St. Clair, *The Reading Nation in the Romantic Period* (New York: Cambridge University Press, 2004). Channing's milieu is worth considering in light of the strong Anglo-American cultural and intellectual connection of the era; see David D. Hall, "The Victorian Connection," *American Quarterly* 27, no. 5 (December 1975): 561–74; Daniel Walker Howe, *Victorian America* (Philadelphia: University of Pennsylvania Press, 1976); Leslie Butler, *Critical Americans: Victorian Intellectuals and Transatlantic Liberal Reform* (Chapel Hill: University of North Carolina Press, 2007).

6. Ralph Waldo Emerson, "An Address," in *Nature: Addresses and Lectures* (Boston: Houghton, Mifflin, 1876), 121. Elizabeth Palmer Peabody, "Nature," in *Estimating Emerson: An Anthology of Criticism from Carlyle to Cavell*, ed. David LaRocca (New York: Bloomsbury Academic, 2013). Elizabeth Palmer Peabody to Horace Mann, March 3, 1838, in Bruce Ronda, ed., *Letters of Elizabeth Palmer Peabody, American Renaissance Woman* (Middletown, CT: Wesleyan University Press, 1984), 198. Jonathan Messerli, *Horace Mann: A Biography* (New York: Knopf, 1972). Charles Finney, "What a Revival of Religion Is," *Lectures on Revivals of Religion* (New York: Leavitt, Lord and Co., 1835), 9–20. Alexis de Tocqueville, *Democracy in America,* trans. Henry Reeve (New York: G. Dearborn and Co., 1838). James T. Kloppenberg, "Tocqueville, Mill, and the American Gentry," *Tocqueville Review/La Revue Tocqueville* 27, no. 2 (2006): 351–79; Daniel Walker Howe, *The Unitarian Conscience: Harvard Moral Philosophy, 1805–1861* (Middletown, CT: Wesleyan University Press, 1988), 224–26, 366–67. Philip Gura, *American Transcendentalism: A History* (New

York: Hill and Wang, 2007), 46–48, 53–58; Sterling F. Delano, *Brook Farm: The Dark Side of Utopia* (Cambridge, MA: Belknap Press of Harvard University Press, 2004). Carl T. Jackson, *The Oriental Religions and American Thought: Nineteenth-Century Explorations* (Westport, CT: Greenwood, 1981). Peabody, *Reminiscences,* 29.

7. Abraham Lincoln, *The Language of Liberty: The Political Speeches and Writings of Abraham Lincoln,* ed. Joseph R. Fornieri (Washington, DC: Regnery, 2009), 725–33. Robert Bray, *Reading with Lincoln* (Carbondale: Southern Illinois University Press, 2010).

8. John Adams to Thomas Jefferson, November 15, 1813, in *The Adams-Jefferson Letters: The Complete Correspondence Between Thomas Jefferson and Abigail and John Adams,* ed. Lester J. Cappon (Chapel Hill: University of North Carolina Press, 1959), 2:401.

9. Chadwick, *William Ellery Channing,* 6. "William Ellery and others to John Adams," *The Works of John Adams, Second President of the United States: With a Life of the Author, Notes and Illustrations, by His Grandson Charles Francis Adams* (Boston: Little, Brown, 1856), 8:61–63.

10. William Ellery Channing, *Memoir of William Ellery Channing: With Extracts from His Correspondence and Manuscripts,* ed. William Henry Channing (Boston: Crosby, Nichols, and Co., 1848), 1:9–12.

11. Ibid., 1:11–12.

12. Ibid., 1:16–19. Chadwick, *William Ellery Channing,* 7–9. Mark A. Noll, *Princeton and the Republic: The Search for a Christian Enlightenment in the Era of Samuel Stanhope Smith* (Princeton, NJ: Princeton University Press, 1989).

13. Channing, *Memoir,* 1:34–35. Chadwick calls it the "most classical story of Channing's boyhood," in Chadwick, *William Ellery Channing,* 23–24; Peabody, *Reminiscences,* 61–62. David P. Edgell, *William Ellery Channing: An Intellectual Portrait* (Westport, CT: Greenwood Press, 1983); Andrew Delbanco, *William Ellery Channing: An Essay on the Liberal Spirit in America* (Cambridge, MA: Harvard University Press, 1981).

14. David Robinson, ed., *William Ellery Channing: Selected Writings* (Mahwah, NJ: Paulist Press, 1985), 6–7. Delbanco, *William Ellery Channing,* 55–56.

15. Channing, *Memoir,* 1, 32. Herbert Wallace Schneider, "The Intellectual Background of William Ellery Channing," *Church History* 7, no. 1 (March 1938): 3–23.

16. Channing, *Memoir,* 1, 16–17, 22, 29–31.

17. Ibid., 45–64. Delbanco, *William Ellery Channing,* 21–22.

18. Francis Hutcheson, *An Inquiry Concerning the Originals of Our Ideas of Virtue and Moral Good* (1725), quoted in Donald H. Meyer, *The Instructed Conscience: The Shaping of the American National Ethic* (Philadelphia: University of Pennsylvania Press, 1972), 40–41. John Patrick Diggins, ed., *The Portable John Adams* (New York: Penguin, 2004), 407–8. V. M. Hope, *Virtue by Consensus: The Moral Philosophy of Hutcheson, Hume, and Adam Smith* (Oxford: Clarendon Press, 1989). Robert H. Horwitz, *The Moral Foundations of the American Republic* (Charlottesville: University of Virginia Press, 1979). On how the reception of Hutcheson tied into new narratives of American exceptionalism, see J. M. Opal, "The Labors of Liberality: Christian Benevolence and National Prejudice in the American Founding," *Journal of American History* 94, no. 4 (March 2008): 1082–1107. On Scottish Common Sense in context,

see Sophia Rosenfeld, *Common Sense: A Political History* (Cambridge, MA: Harvard University Press, 2011).

19. Francis Hutcheson, *An Essay on the Nature and Conduct of the Passions and Affections* (London: W. Innys, 1756), 313, 318, 320, 331.

20. Channing, *Memoir,* I, 63–64. William Wordsworth, *Ode: Intimations of Immortality from Recollections of Early Childhood* (Boston: D. Lothrop and Co., 1884), 35. Hutcheson, *Essay,* 335.

21. William Ellery Channing, "The Religious Principle in Human Nature" and "The Perfecting Power of Religion," *Complete Works,* 2, 36.

22. Channing, *Memoir,* 1:64. Chadwick, *William Ellery Channing,* 40–41. The enormous literature on pure womanhood begins with Barbara Welter, "The Cult of True Womanhood," *American Quarterly* 18, no. 2 (Summer 1966): 151–74.

23. Channing, *Memoir,* 1:79, 84,

24. *Ibid.,* 1:96, 98–99, 130.

25. Channing, *Memoir,* 1:84, 85. Molly Oshatz, "No Ordinary Sin: Antislavery Protestants and the Discovery of the Social Nature of Morality," *Church History* 79, no. 2 (June 2010): 334–58. Channing, "Slavery," *Complete Works,* 493.

26. On Ferguson, see Andreas Kalyvas and Ira Katznelson, *Liberal Beginnings: Making a Republic for the Moderns* (New York: Cambridge University Press, 2008), 51–87. Channing, *Memoir,* 1:24, 96–97.

27. *Ibid.,* 1:106–7. Mary Moody Emerson, almanac, item 579 folder 3, Emerson Family Papers, 1699–1939 (MS Am 1280.235), Houghton Library, Harvard University. Channing still admired Fénelon three decades later, when he reviewed a new edition of his works for the *Christian Examiner;* reprinted in Channing, *Complete Works,* 407–19.

28. Channing, *Memoir,* 1:107–8. Robert Lovell and Robert Southey, *Poems: Containing the Retrospect, Elegies, Odes, Sonnets & c.* (London: R. Cruttwell and C. Dilley, 1795), 67.

29. William Wordsworth, "Lines Left upon a Seat in a Yew-tree which stands near the Lake of Esthwaite," in *The Poetical Works of William Wordsworth* (Edinburgh: W. Paterson, 1882), 1:96.

30. Channing, *Memoir,* 1:116. Peabody, *Reminiscences,* 134, 449. Thanks to Eric Gregory for helping to quicken this interpretation.

31. Channing, *Memoir,* 1:116–17, 124.

32. *Ibid.,* 1:136–42; Channing, "Christian Worship" (1836), *Complete Works,* 313–14.

33. Channing, *Memoir,* 1:162–65. Peabody, *Reminiscences,* 41–42, 78, 323.

34. Bruce Kuklick, *Churchmen and Philosophers: From Jonathan Edwards to John Dewey* (New Haven, CT: Yale University Press, 1985).

35. Channing, *Memoir,* 1:146.

36. *Ibid.,* 1:345.

37. *Ibid.,* 1:346–48. The contemporary philosopher Richard J. Bernstein characterizes the pragmatic ethos by five interrelated commitments: antifoundationalism; fallibilism; the community of inquirers; contingency; and pluralism. From "Pragmatism, Pluralism, and the Healing of Wounds" (1988), excerpted in Louis Menand, ed., *Pragmatism: A Reader* (New York: Vintage, 1997), 385–90. See also Gail Hamner, *American Pragmatism: A Religious Genealogy* (New York: Oxford University Press, 2003).

38. Channing, *Memoir*, 1:348. Sydney E. Ahlstrom with Jonathan Sinclair Carey, *American Reformation: A Documentary History of Unitarian Christianity* (Middletown, CT: Wesleyan University Press, 1985), 3. Phyllis Cole, *Mary Moody Emerson and the Origins of Transcendentalism: A Family History* (New York: Oxford University Press, 1998), 163.

39. Peabody, *Reminiscences,* 34–36. On historicity among liberal Christians, see Molly Oshatz, *Slavery and Sin: The Fight Against Slavery and the Rise of Liberal Protestantism* (New York: Oxford University Press, 2011). Channing, "Unitarian Christianity," *Complete Works,* 278–88.

40. Channing, *A Sermon, Delivered at the Ordination of the Rev. John Codman: To the Pastoral Care of the Second Church of Christ in Dorchester, Dec. 7, 1808* (Boston: Joshua Belcher, 1808), 4, 6, 7, 9.

41. "Article 7," *Monthly Anthology* (February 1809): 120–21.

42. *Ibid.*, 120. Candy Gunther Brown, *The Word in the World: Evangelical Writing, Publishing, and Reading in America, 1789–1880* (Chapel Hill: University of North Carolina Press, 2004), 2. David Paul Nord, *Faith in Reading: Religious Publishing and the Birth of Mass Media in America* (New York: Oxford University Press, 2004). Thomas A. Howard, *Religion and the Rise of Historicism: W. M. L. De Wette, Jacob Burckhardt, and the Theological Origins of Nineteenth-Century Historical Consciousness* (Cambridge: Cambridge University Press, 2000). William St. Clair, *The Reading Nation in the Romantic Period* (New York: Cambridge University Press, 2004). Catherine O'Donnell Kaplan, *Men of Letters in the Early Republic: Cultivating Forms of Citizenship* (Chapel Hill: University of North Carolina Press, 2008), 14, 197. Neil Brody Miller, "'Proper Subjects for Public Inquiry': The First Unitarian Controversy and the Transformation of Federalist Print Culture," *Early American Literature* 43, no. 1 (2008): 101–35.

43. Simmons, ed., *Selected Letters of Mary Moody Emerson,* 182. Patrick J. Keane, *Emerson, Romanticism, and Intuitive Reason: The Transatlantic "Light of all Our Day"* (Columbia: University of Missouri Press, 2005), 129–31, 136, 305–7. [Richard Henry Dana], "Art. XVI. The Sylphs of the Seasons," *North American Review* 5, no. 15 (September 1817): 365–90. Herbert Baxter Adams, *The Life and Writings of Jared Sparks: Comprising Selections from his Journals and Correspondence* (Boston: Houghton, Mifflin and Co., 1893), 71–74, 553.

44. Peabody, *Reminiscences,* 81.

45. For Catholic attention to Wordsworth, see "The Wisdom and Truth of Wordsworth's Art," Parts I–III, *Catholic World* 38, no. 228, 39, nos. 229–30 (March–May 1884): 738–55; 49–59; 201–17; Thomas O'Hagan, "In the Footsteps of Wordsworth," *Catholic World* 78, no. 465 (December 1, 1903): 310–21. One Methodist called Wordsworth a "Priest of Nature," in "William Wordsworth," *Methodist Review* 19, no. 3 (May 1903): 418–29. Quotation from "The Literature of Nature," *Methodist Review* 20, no. 4 (1904): 558–72.

46. Peabody, *Reminiscences,* 70–76, 142–43. J. Robert Barth, *Romanticism and Transcendence: Wordsworth, Coleridge, and the Religious Imagination* (Columbia: University of Missouri Press, 2003). James Engell, "Biographia Literaria," in *The Cambridge Companion to Coleridge* (New York: Cambridge University Press, 2002); Ronald C. Wendling, *Coleridge's Progress to Christianity: Experience and Authority*

in Religious Faith (Lewisburg, PA: Bucknell University Press, 1995); Mary Anne Perkins, *Coleridge's Philosophy: The Logos as Unifying Principle* (Oxford/New York: Clarendon Press/Oxford University Press, 1994); Douglas Hedley, *Coleridge, Philosophy and Religion: Aids to Reflection and the Mirror of the Spirit* (Cambridge: Cambridge University Press, 2000); Herbert Hovenkamp, *Science and Religion in America, 1800–1860* (Philadelphia: University of Pennsylvania Press, 1978). See also Jeffrey W. Barbeau, "The Development of Coleridge's Notion of Human Freedom: The Translation and Reformation of German Idealism in England," *Journal of Religion* 80, no. 4 (October 2000): 576–94.

47. Hedley, *Coleridge, Philosophy, and Religion,* 8, 36, 102, 221. Rene Wellek, *Confrontations: Studies in the Intellectual and Literary Relations Between Germany, England, and the United States During the Nineteenth Century* (Princeton, NJ: Princeton University Press, 1965). Channing, *Memoir,* 1:151.

48. Mary Moody Emerson to Ralph Waldo Emerson, January 20, 1824, in Simmons, ed., *Selected Letters of Mary Moody Emerson,* 178. Peabody, *Reminiscences,* 171–72. Samuel Taylor Coleridge, *Aids to Reflection, in the Formation of a Manly Character, on the Several Grounds of Prudence, Morality, and Religion,* ed. James Marsh (Burlington, VT: C. Goodrich, 1829), lvii, 7, 35, 65, 127–28, 187.

49. Ralph Waldo Emerson, "The Sovereignty of Ethics," in *Lectures and Biographical Sketches* (Boston: Houghton, Mifflin and Co., 1884), 196; Mary Moody Emerson to Ralph Waldo Emerson, November 7, 1824, in Simmons, ed., *Selected Letters of Mary Moody Emerson,* 194. The discussion here is indebted to James T. Kloppenberg, *Uncertain Victory: Social Democracy and Progressivism in European and American Thought, 1870–1920* (New York: Oxford University Press, 1986), 46–53.

50. Coleridge, *Aids to Reflection,* 21, 102. Kloppenberg, *Uncertain Victory,* 15.

51. Coleridge, *Aids to Reflection,* viii, lx, 3, 21, 37, 364. Wordsworth, *The Prelude,* Book III, line 185. Nancy L. Rosenblum, *Another Liberalism: Romanticism and the Reconstruction of Liberal Thought* (Cambridge, MA: Harvard University Press, 1987); George Kateb, *The Inner Ocean: Individualism and Democratic Culture* (Ithaca, NY: Cornell University Press, 1992).

52. Peabody, *Reminiscences,* 80–81, 292. Channing, "Remarks on Associations" (1829), *Complete Works,* 150. Channing, *Remarks on Creeds, Intolerance, and Exclusion* (Boston: American Unitarian Association, 1830), 3, 5, 7.

53. Peabody, *Reminiscences,* 73, 365–81, 417–23.

54. Channing, "Likeness to God," *Complete Works,* 230–37.

55. Jane Holtz Kay, *Lost Boston* (Boston: Houghton Mifflin, 1999), 30, 95–100, 104, 128.

56. Jonathan D. Sassi, *A Republic of Righteousness: The Public Christianity of the Post-Revolutionary New England Clergy* (Oxford: Oxford University Press, 2001), 68–69, 161–63. Peter S. Field, *The Crisis of the Standing Order: Clerical Intellectuals and Cultural Authority in Massachusetts, 1780–1833* (Amherst: University of Massachusetts Press, 1997).

57. On the Franklin Lectures, see Nian-Sheng Huang, *Benjamin Franklin in American Thought and Culture, 1790–1990* (Philadelphia: American Philosophical Society, 1994), 47–48. Edward Everett's inaugural lecture for the series, "Advantage of Useful Knowledge for Workingmen," explains his goal in extending education as a form of democratic equality; see Everett, *Importance of Practical Education and Useful*

Knowledge (Boston: Marsh, Capen, Lyon, and Webb, 1840), 138–61. On the series as a precursor of the Progressive Era push to extend education to working-class adults, see Sidney L. Jackson, "Some Ancestors of the 'Extension Course,'" *New England Quarterly* 14, no. 3 (September 1941): 505–18. Mary Moody Emerson to Ralph Waldo Emerson, January 20, 1824, in Simmons, ed., *Selected Letters of Mary Moody Emerson,* 178–80. On German universities and American scholars, see Bruce Kuklick, *The Rise of American Philosophy: Cambridge, Massachusetts, 1860–1930* (New Haven, CT: Yale University Press, 1977), 233–35. The argument here strikes a middle ground between that of Sean Wilentz, *The Rise of American Democracy: Jefferson to Lincoln* (New York: Norton, 2005), and Daniel Walker Howe, *What Hath God Wrought: The Transformation of America, 1815–1848* (New York: Oxford University Press, 2007). Bancroft, "The Office of the People," in *Literary and Historical Miscellanys* (New York: Harper and Bros., 1855), 408–75. See the discussion in T. Gregory Garvey, *Creating the Culture of Reform in Antebellum America* (Athens: University of Georgia Press, 2006), 21.

58. Channing, "Self-Culture," *Complete Works,* 64–65, 67, 72.

59. *Ibid.,* 71, 75.

60. *Ibid.,* 64, 66; Jeffrey Sklansky, *The Soul's Economy: Market Society and Selfhood in American Thought, 1820–1920* (Chapel Hill: University of North Carolina Press, 2002).

61. Channing, "Self-Culture," *Complete Works,* 70, 73, 79. William J. Novak, *The People's Welfare: Law and Regulation in Nineteenth-Century America* (Chapel Hill: University of North Carolina Press, 1996).

62. Peabody, *Reminiscences,* 419. Daniel Walker Howe, *Making the American Self: Jonathan Edwards to Abraham Lincoln* (Cambridge, MA: Harvard University Press, 1997), 158–60. Conrad Edick Wright, "Emerson, Barzillai Frost, and the Divinity School Address," *Liberal Christians: Essays on American Unitarian History* (Boston: Beacon, 1970), 41–61. Emerson, "Address to the Senior Class in Divinity," *Works,* 198. Hedge quotation in Bryan F. LeBeau, *Frederic Henry Hedge, Nineteenth Century American Transcendentalist: Intellectually Radical, Ecclesiastically Conservative* (Allison Park, PA: Pickwick Publications, 1985), 116–17. [Frederic Henry Hedge], "Art. VII" [Coleridge's works], *Christian Examiner and General Review* 14, no. 1 (March 1833): 108–29; quotations on 109, 116.

63. Compare the language with Wordsworth's letter to "Mathetes"—the name of an early Christian—which Channing had Peabody read and that criticizes "barren contemplation" because "doubtless to act is nobler than to think." In Samuel Taylor Coleridge, *The Friend: A Series of Essays to Aid in the Formation of Fixed Principles in Politics, Moral, and Religion, With literary Amusements Interpreted* (London: W. Pickering, 1850), 370. *The Common School Journal* 1, no. 1 (November 1838): 4, 8, 9, 14, 15, 73–74. On the common school movement, see Carl F. Kaestle, *Pillars of the Republic: Common Schools and American Society, 1780–1860* (New York: Hill and Wang, 1983).

64. James T. Kloppenberg, "The Canvas and the Color: Tocqueville's Philosophical History and Why It Matters Now," *Modern Intellectual History* 3, no. 3 (November 2006): 495–521. *United States Magazine, and Democratic Review* 1, no. 1 (October/December 1837): 11, 91–108, 319.

65. Kloppenberg, "Tocqueville, Mill, and the American Gentry," 351–81; Kloppenberg, "Life Everlasting: Tocqueville in America," in *Virtues of Liberalism* (New York: Oxford University Press, 1998), 71–81. Sean Wilentz, "Many Democracies: On Tocqueville and Jacksonian America," in *Reconsidering Tocqueville's "Democracy in America,"* ed. Abraham S. Eisenstadt (New Brunswick, NJ: Rutgers University Press, 1988), 207–28. Leo Damrosch, *Tocqueville's Discovery of America* (New York: Farrar, Straus and Giroux, 2010). Tocqueville's correspondence with Sparks and the Sparks essay "Observations on the Town Governments of Massachusetts" are reprinted in Herbert B. Adams, "Jared Sparks and Alexis de Tocqueville," *Johns Hopkins University Studies in Historical and Political Science* 16, no. 12 (December 1898): 569–611. Joseph Tuckerman, *The Principles and Results of the Ministry at Large in Boston* (Boston: James Munroe and Co., 1838), 156. Howe, *Unitarian Conscience*, 224–25. I owe my use of the term "porous" for the Boston liberals' elitism to George Kateb.

66. Howe, *Unitarian Conscience,* 224. R. Laurence Moore, *Touchdown Jesus: The Making of Sacred and Secular in American History* (Louisville, KY: Westminster John Knox Press, 2003). Peabody, *Reminiscences,* 59–60. Alexis de Tocqueville, *Democracy in America,* ed. Francis Bowen (Cambridge, MA: Sever and Francis, 1862), 1:392. Amanda Porterfield, *Conceived in Doubt: Religion and Politics in the New American Nation* (Chicago: University of Chicago Press, 2012).

67. Orestes Brownson, "The Mediatorial Life of Jesus. A Letter to Rev. William Ellery Channing, D.D., June, 1842," in *The Works of Orestes A. Brownson,* ed. Henry F. Brownson (Detroit: T. Nourse, 1901), 4:140–72.

68. Robinson, ed., *William Ellery Channing,* 3; *Gura, American Transcendentalism,* 80. Barbara L. Packer, *The Transcendentalists* (Athens: University of Georgia Press, 2007). Thomas A. Tweed, *The American Encounter with Buddhism, 1844–1912: Victorian Culture and the Limits of Dissent* (Bloomington and Indianapolis: Indiana University Press, 1992), xxx. Arthur Versluis, *American Transcendentalism and Asian Religions* (New York: Oxford University Press, 1993). George Ripley, "Letter to the Church in Purchase Street," in *The Transcendentalists: An Anthology,* ed. Perry Miller (Cambridge, MA: Harvard University Press, 1950), 251–57. Meyer, *Instructed Conscience.*

69. William R. Hutchison, *The Transcendentalist Ministers: Church Reform in the American Renaissance* (New Haven, CT: Yale University Press, 1959). Ronald V. Wells, *Three Christian Transcendentalists: James Marsh, Caleb Sprague Henry, Frederic Henry Hedge* (New York: Columbia University Press, 1943). S. Harris, "The Necessity of Completeness in the Christian Life," *New Englander* 7, no. 27 (August 1849): 369–99. "H" [anonymous author], "Social Reformers," *Harbinger: Devoted to Social and Political Progress* 8, no. 5 (December 2, 1848): 37–38. There is a tremendous literature on antebellum social reform. One good place to begin is Elizabeth D. Clark, "'The Sacred Rights of the Weak': Pain, Sympathy, and the Culture of Individual Rights in Antebellum America," *Journal of American History* (September 1995): 463–93. See also Robert H. Abzug, *Cosmos Crumbling: American Reform and the Religious Imagination* (New York: Oxford University Press, 1994); David A. Zonderman, *Uneasy Allies: Working for Labor Reform in Nineteenth-Century Boston* (Amherst: University of Massachusetts Press, 2011); Jama Lazerow, "Spokesmen for the Working Class: Protestant Clergy and the Labor Movement in Antebellum New

England," *Journal of the Early Republic* 13, no. 3 (Autumn 1993): 323–54; Lewis Perry, *Radical Abolitionism: Anarchy and the Government of God in Antislavery Thought* (Ithaca, NY: Cornell University Press, 1973); John L. Thomas, "Romantic Reform in America, 1815–1865," *American Quarterly* (Winter 1965): 656–74; Ronald G. Walters, *American Reformers, 1815–1860* (New York: Hill and Wang, 1978); Aileen S. Kraditor, *Means and Ends in American Abolitionism: Garrison and His Critics on Strategy and Tactics, 1834–1850* (New York: Pantheon, 1969).

70. On the original song and its many reiterations, see John Stauffer and Benjamin Soskis, *The Battle Hymn of the Republic: A Biography of the Song That Marches On* (New York: Oxford University Press, 2013).

CHAPTER 4 · WILLIAM JAMES, PRACTICAL IDEALIST: THE MAN OF THE WORLD AND THE METHOD OF NATURE

1. The literature on William James is immense. The most comprehensive and astute recent biography is Robert D. Richardson, *William James: In the Maelstrom of American Modernism* (Boston: Houghton Mifflin, 2006). The first biography of James, written by a student of his and still useful, is Ralph Barton Perry, *The Thought and Character of William James,* 2 vols. (Boston: Little, Brown, 1935). Other important approaches to James on which the current chapter draws include Francesca Bordogna, *William James at the Boundaries: Philosophy, Science, and the Geography of Knowledge* (Chicago: University of Chicago Press, 2008); Joshua I. Miller, *Democratic Temperament: The Legacy of William James* (Lawrence: University Press of Kansas, 1997); Richard M. Gale, *The Divided Self of William James* (New York: Cambridge University Press, 1999); Gay Wilson Allen, *William James* (Minneapolis: University of Minnesota Press, 1970); Gerald E. Myers, *William James: His Life and Thought* (New Haven, CT: Yale University Press, 1986); Linda Simon, *Genuine Reality: A Life of William James* (New York: Harcourt Brace, 1998); Eugene Taylor, *William James on Consciousness Beyond the Margin* (Princeton: Princeton University Press, 1996); Daniel W. Bjork, *William James: The Center of His Vision* (New York: Columbia University Press, 1988); George Cotkin, *William James: Public Philosopher* (Baltimore: Johns Hopkins University Press, 1992); Louis Menand, *The Metaphysical Club: A Story of Ideas* (New York: Farrar, Straus and Giroux, 2001); John K. Roth, *Freedom and the Moral Life: The Ethics of William James* (Philadelphia: Westminster Press, 1969); Patrick Kiaran Dooley, *Pragmatism as Humanism: The Philosophy of William James* (Chicago: Nelson-Hall, 1974); Charlene Haddock Seigfried, *William James's Radical Reconstruction of Philosophy* (Albany: State University of New York Press, 1990); Paul Jerome Croce, *Science and Religion in the Era of William James* (Chapel Hill: University of North Carolina Press, 1995); Jacques Barzun, *A Stroll with William James* (New York: Harper and Row, 1983).

2. William James to Alice Howe Gibbens James, July 9, 1898, in Ignas K. Skrupskelis and Elizabeth M. Berkeley, eds., *The Correspondence of William James* (Charlottesville: University Press of Virginia, 2000), 8:390. (Hereafter cited as WJ, *Corr.*)

3. *Ibid.,* 391–92.

4. *Varieties of Religious Experience,* in William James, *Writings 1902–1910* (New York: Library of America, 1987), 219, 296. See Henry Samuel Levinson, *The Religious*

Investigations of William James (Chapel Hill: University of North Carolina Press, 1981); Wayne Proudfoot, ed., *William James and a Science of Religions: Reexperiencing "The Varieties of Religious Experience"* (New York: Columbia University Press, 2004); Charles Taylor, *Varieties of Religion Today: William James Revisited* (Cambridge, MA: Harvard University Press, 2002). On James's religious thought in general, see Bennett Ramsey, *Submitting to Freedom: The Religious Vision of William James* (New York: Oxford University Press, 1993); David C. Lamberth, *William James and the Metaphysics of Experience* (New York: Cambridge University Press, 1999); Lamberth, "Interpreting the Universe After a Social Analogy: Intimacy, Panpsychism, and a Finite God in a Pluralistic Universe," Richard R. Niebuhr, "William James on Religious Experience," and Richard Rorty, "Religious Faith, Intellectual Responsibility, and Romance," all in *The Cambridge Companion to William James,* ed. Ruth Anna Putnam (New York: Cambridge University Press, 1997).

5. WJ, *Corr* 8:390–92.

6. William James, *Writings 1878–1899* (New York: Library of America, 1992), 868. For the legacy of James in twentieth-century social thought, see Trygve Throntveit, "'Common Counsel': Woodrow Wilson's Pragmatic Progressivism, 1885–1913," in *Reconsidering Woodrow Wilson: Progressivism, Internationalism, War, and Peace,* ed. John Milton Cooper Jr. (Washington, DC: Woodrow Wilson Center Press, 2008), 25–57.

7. WJ, *Corr* 11:17. On intellectual community in Keene Valley, see Richard Plunz, ed., *Two Adirondack Hamlets in History: Keene and Keene Valley* (Fleischmanns, NY: Purple Mountain Press, 1999), 191–237.

8. WJ, *Corr* 10:575–76; *Corr* 11:39–40, 438–39. Eldon J. Eisenach, ed., *Mill and the Moral Character of Liberalism* (University Park: Pennsylvania State University Press, 1988). For the legacy of pragmatism across the twentieth century, see David A. Hollinger, "The Problem of Pragmatism in American History," in *In the American Province: Studies in the History and Historiography of Ideas* (Baltimore: Johns Hopkins University Press, 1985), 23–43; James T. Kloppenberg, "Pragmatism: An Old Name for Some New Ways of Thinking?," *Journal of American History* 83, no. 1 (June 1996): 100–38. By "practical idealism" I mean something a bit more technically specific than did the first historian to use the term—about the same period, aptly—Henry F. May, *The End of American Innocence: The First Years of Our Own Time, 1912–1917* (New York: Oxford University Press, 1959).

9. Ralph Waldo Emerson, "Lecture on the Times," in *Nature, Addresses and Lectures* (Boston: Houghton Mifflin, 1876), 277. Elizabeth Palmer Peabody to Elizabeth Curson Hoxie, in Bruce Ronda, ed., *Letters of Elizabeth Palmer Peabody, American Renaissance Woman* (Middletown, CT: Wesleyan University Press, 1984), 454. Richard F. Teichgraeber III, "'Our National Glory': Emerson in American Culture, 1865–82" and "'More than Luther of these Modern Days': The Social Construction of Emerson's Posthumous Reputation," both in *Building Culture: Studies in the Intellectual History of Industrializing America, 1867–1910* (Columbia: University of South Carolina Press, 2010).

10. Henry James, "The Art of Fiction," in *The Portable Henry James* (New York: Penguin, 2004), 435. On Alice James, see Jean Strouse, *Alice James: A Biography* (Boston: Houghton Mifflin, 1980).

11. WJ, *Corr* 4:156, 547–48.

12. Ralph Waldo Emerson, "The Young American," in *Miscellanies; Embracing Nature, Addresses, and Lectures* (Boston: Ticknor and Fields, 1855), 160–61; James's copy of the book is at the Houghton Library at Harvard University, WJ 424.25.12. On the relationship between religion and science before Darwin, see Herbert Hovenkamp, *Science and Religion in America, 1800–1860* (Philadelphia: University of Pennsylvania Press, 1978); Walter H. Conser, *God and the Natural World: Religion and Science in Antebellum America* (Columbia: University of South Carolina Press, 1993); Theodore Dwight Bozeman, *Protestants in an Age of Science: The Baconian Ideal and Ante-Bellum American Religious Thought* (Chapel Hill: University of North Carolina Press, 1977). The literature on Darwin and his reception is enormous; the interpretation here is drawn from, among others, Stephen G. Alter, *Darwinism and the Linguistic Image: Language, Race, and Natural Theology in the Nineteenth Century* (Baltimore: Johns Hopkins University Press, 1999); Peter J. Bowler, *The Non-Darwinian Revolution: Reinterpreting a Historical Myth* (Baltimore: Johns Hopkins University Press, 1988); Gertrude Himmelfarb, *Darwin and the Darwinian Revolution* (Chicago: Ivan R. Dee, 1959); James R. Moore, *The Post-Darwinian Controversies: A Study of the Protestant Struggle to Come to Terms with Darwin in Great Britain and America, 1870–1900* (Cambridge: Cambridge University Press, 1979); Robert J. Richards, *Darwin and the Emergence of Evolutionary Theories of Mind and Behavior* (Chicago: University of Chicago Press, 1987); Jon H. Roberts, *Darwinism and the Divine in America: Protestant Intellectuals and Organic Evolution, 1859–1900* (Madison: University of Wisconsin Press, 1988); Cynthia Eagle Russett, *Darwin in America: The Intellectual Response, 1865–1912* (San Francisco: W. H. Freeman, 1976); Edward A. White, *Science and Religion in American Thought: The Impact of Naturalism* (Stanford, CA: Stanford University Press, 1952); Paul F. Boller, *American Thought in Transition: The Impact of Evolutionary Naturalism, 1865–1900* (New York: Rand McNally, 1969); Morton White, *Science and Sentiment in America: Philosophical Thought from Jonathan Edwards to John Dewey* (New York: Oxford University Press, 1972).
13. [William James], "The Variation of Animals and Plants under Domestication," *North American Review* 107, no. 220 (July 1868): 362–68; James's annotated copy of the book is at the Houghton Library at Harvard University, WJ 516.78.
14. WJ, *Corr* 4:248–51, 309. Merle Curti, *Human Nature in American Thought* (Madison: University of Wisconsin Press, 1980); Bruce Haley, *The Healthy Body and Victorian Culture* (Cambridge, MA: Harvard University Press, 1978); Bordogna, *William James at the Boundaries.*
15. WJ, *Corr* 4:213–14, 247, 300.
16. William James, diary inscribed "Geneve 1859 16 Novembre," and entries for December 21, 1869, and April 30, 1870, in Diary of 1868–70, William James Papers, 1803–1941 (MS Am 1092.9–1092.12), Houghton Library, Harvard University.
17. Friedrich Schiller, "On Grace and Dignity," *Essays Aesthetical and Philosophical* (London: George Bell and Sons, 1910), 171. Jane V. Curran and Christophe Fricker, eds., *Schiller's "On Grace and Dignity" in Its Cultural Context: Essays and a New Translation* (Rochester, NY: Camden House, 2005). [William James], review of H. Bushnell's *Women's Suffrage* and J. S. Mill's *Subjection of Women, North American Review* 109 (1869): 565. WJ, *Corr* 4:300, 370, 389.

18. WJ, *Corr* 4:403. See discussion in Richardson, *William James,* 108–13.

19. The influential depiction of science and religion as at war began in James's time with John William Draper, *History of the Conflict Between Religion and Science* (New York: D. Appleton and Co., 1874). Darwin's theory helped promote the evangelicals' bid to make their version of Protestant Christianity the orthodox one. For one influential interpretation of the late nineteenth century in light of this alleged opposition between religion and science, see Paul A. Carter, *The Spiritual Crisis of the Gilded Age* (DeKalb: Northern Illinois University Press, 1971). See also Frank M. Turner, *Between Science and Religion: The Reaction to Scientific Naturalism in Late Victorian England* (New Haven, CT: Yale University Press, 1974), and J. W. Burrow, *Evolution and Society: A Study in Victorian Social Theory* (New York: Cambridge University Press, 1966). WJ, *Corr* 4:369–71, 570–72. On McCosh and Wright, see diary entry entitled "Evolution and the moral life," from 1875, in William James, *Manuscript Essays and Notes* (Cambridge, MA: Harvard University Press, 1988), 296–98. Thanks to the late James M. Kittelson for the Latin translation.

20. On James's interest in the psychic kind of spiritualism in historical context, see R. Laurence Moore, *In Search of White Crows: Spiritualism, Parapsychology, and American Culture* (New York: Oxford University Press, 1977), and Molly McGarry, *Ghosts of Futures Past: Spiritualism and the Cultural Politics of Nineteenth-Century America* (Berkeley: University of California Press, 2008). On the intellectual dilemma he faced, see Robert Pippin, *Modernism as a Philosophical Problem: On the Dissatisfactions of European High Culture* (Malden, MA: Blackwell, 1999), and Stephen Toulmin, *Cosmopolis: The Hidden Agenda of Modernity* (New York: Free Press, 1990). See also Frank Miller Turner, *Between Science and Religion: The Reaction to Scientific Naturalism in Late Victorian England* (New Haven, CT: Yale University Press, 1974). On the crisis as a neurasthenic episode related to a wider modern crisis in American intellectual life, see T. J. Jackson Lears, *No Place of Grace: Antimodernism and the Transformation of American Culture, 1880–1920* (Chicago: University of Chicago Press, 1981), 47–57.

21. Richardson, *In the Maelstrom of American Modernism,* 103. Max H. Fisch, "Alexander Bain and the Genealogy of Pragmatism," *Journal of the History of Ideas* 15, no. 3 (September 1954): 413–44. William James, April 30, 1870, Diary 1868–1870, in William James Papers, 1803–1941 (MS Am 1092.9–1092.12), Houghton Library, Harvard University. William James, *The Principles of Psychology* (New York: Dover, 1950), 1:121.

22. James, *Writings 1902–1910,* 149–51. Wordsworth, *The Poetical Works of William Wordsworth,* ed. E. de Selincourt and Helen Darbishire (London: Oxford University Press, 1949), 133. William James, April 10, 1872, diary, in William James Papers, 1803–1941 (MS Am 1092.9–1092.12), Houghton Library, Harvard University.

23. *Ibid.* William James, diary excerpt included in letter to Alice Howe Gibbens, June 7, 1877, WJ, *Corr* 4:570-72.

24. Diary entry entitled "Definition of religion," 1873, James, *Manuscript Essays and Notes,* 295–96.

25. WJ, *Corr* 1:215. On James's mental condition, see the biographies of James and Cushing Strout, "The Pluralistic Identity of William James: A Psychohistorical Reading of

The Varieties of Religious Experience," *American Quarterly* 23 (1971): 135–52; Cushing Strout, "William James and the Twice-Born Sick Soul," *Daedalus* 97 (1968): 1062–82. Charles E. Rosenberg, "George M. Beard and American Nervousness," in *No Other Gods: On Science and American Social Thought* (Baltimore: Johns Hopkins University Press, 1978). On neurasthenia as more than just a diagnosis for elites, see F. G. Gosling, *Before Freud: Neurasthenia and the American Medical Community, 1870–1910* (Urbana: University of Illinois Press, 1987). Also worthwhile for putting James's preoccupation with physical health in context is Bruce Haley, *The Healthy Body and Victorian Culture* (Cambridge, MA: Harvard University Press, 1978), and Michael Kimmel, *Manhood in America: A Cultural History* (New York: Free Press, 1996).

26. On the rise of professionalism and the modern university, see Andrew Jewett, *Science, Democracy, and the American University: From the Civil War to the Cold War* (New York: Cambridge University Press, 2012); Burton J. Bledstein, *The Culture of Professionalism: The Middle Class and the Development of Higher Education in America* (New York: Norton, 1976); Bruce Kuklick, *The Rise of American Philosophy: Cambridge, Massachusetts, 1860–1930* (New Haven, CT: Yale University Press, 1977); Walter P. Metzger, *Academic Freedom in the Age of the University* (New York: Columbia University Press, 1955); Laurence R. Veysey, *The Emergence of the American University* (Chicago: University of Chicago Press, 1965); Julie A. Reuben, *The Making of the Modern University: Intellectual Transformation and the Marginalization of Morality* (Chicago: University of Chicago Press, 1996); Daniel J. Wilson, *Science, Community, and the Rise of Academic Philosophy, 1870–1930* (Chicago: University of Chicago Press, 1990).

27. Mrs. John T. Sargent, *Sketches and Reminiscences of the Radical Club of Chestnut Street, Boston* (Boston: James R. Osgood, 1880). WJ, *Corr* 1:251.

28. Letter from William James to Alice Howe Gibbens, March 19, 1876, William James Family Papers, 1803–1941 (MS Am 1092.9–1092.12), Houghton Library, Harvard University. Susan E. Gunter, *Alice in Jamesland: The Story of Alice Howe Gibbens James* (Lincoln: University of Nebraska Press, 2009). R. W. B. Lewis, "The Courtship of William James," *Yale Review* 73 (Winter 1984): 177–98. Simon, *Genuine Reality*.

29. William James to Alice Howe Gibbens James, August 27, 1886, and note by Henry James III, William James Family Papers, 1803–1941 (MS Am 1092.9–1092.12), Houghton Library, Harvard University. WJ, *Corr* 6:267–77. On privacy in the era, see James Turner, *The Liberal Education of Charles Eliot Norton* (Baltimore: Johns Hopkins University Press, 1999), and Rochelle Gurstein, *The Repeal of Reticence: A History of America's Cultural and Legal Struggles over Free Speech, Obscenity, Sexual Liberation, and Modern Art* (New York: Hill and Wang, 1996).

30. [William James], "Women's Suffrage," *North American Review* 109, no. 225 (October 1869): 563. WJ, *Corr* 4:565–70. The literature on separate spheres begins with Nancy F. Cott, *The Bonds of Womanhood: "Woman's Sphere" in New England, 1780–1835* (New Haven, CT: Yale University Press, 1977). To put the James courtship in context, see Karen Lystra, *Searching the Heart: Women, Men, and Romantic Love in Nineteenth-Century America* (New York: Oxford University Press, 1989).

31. John Stuart Mill, *Autobiography,* ed. Harold J. Laski (London: Oxford University Press, 1924), 117.

32. *Ibid.,* 204.

33. *Ibid.,* 157, 158, 160, 204, 206, 210.

34. *Ibid.*, 214, 215.
35. WJ, *Corr* 5:367.
36. William James to Alice Howe Gibbens James, April 11 and 12, 1877; October 8, 1888, William James Papers (MS Am 1092.9–1092.12), Houghton Library, Harvard University. WJ, *Corr* 4:547; *Corr* 5:3. [William James], "Review (unsigned) of R. J. Dugdale, *The Jukes: A Study in Crime, Pauperism, Disease, and Heredity,*" *Atlantic Monthly* 41 (1878): 405.
37. James, *Writings 1878–1899,* 588.
38. *Ibid.*, 907, 983.
39. WJ, *Corr* 5:152–53. Everett later taught "The Psychological Basis of Religious Faith," "The Content of Christian Faith," and "Comparative Religions"; Harvard bulletin for the Philosophy Department for the academic year 1891–92, in the papers of Josiah Royce, Harvard University Archives. William Mackintire Salter—James's brother-in-law and close friend—studied under Everett at Harvard Divinity, calling him "An honored teacher of mine" in "Ethics in the Light of Darwin's Theory," *Ethical Addresses and Ethical Record* 16, no. 8 (April 1909): 229.
40. James, *Writings 1878–1899,* 102, 540.
41. Evangelical Christians also made their arguments scientifically, according to Charles Rosenberg, *No Other Gods: On Science and American Social Thought* (Baltimore: Johns Hopkins University Press, 1976), 76, 267n29. Christopher G. White, *Unsettled Minds: Psychology and the American Search for Spiritual Assurance, 1830–1940* (Berkeley: University of California Press, 2009).
42. James, *Writings 1878–1899,* 544, 548, 551, 562.
43. *Ibid.,* 548.
44. WJ, *Corr* 5:194–96; *Corr* 8:122.
45. For more on James's audience, see Hollinger, "William James and the Culture of Inquiry," in *In the American Province.* WJ, *Corr* 5:217.
46. Franklin B. Sanborn, *Recollections of Seventy Years* (Boston: Richard G. Badger, 1909), 2:485–513. Concord School of Philosophy, *Concord Lectures on Philosophy, Comprising Outlines of All the Lectures at the Concord Summer School of Philosophy in 1882 with an Historical Sketch* (Cambridge, MA: Moses King, 1883). On Hazard, see Elizabeth Palmer Peabody, *Reminiscences of Rev. Wm. Ellery Channing, D.D.* (Boston: Roberts Brothers, 1880), 452. Kuklick, *Rise of American Philosophy,* 57–59. Thomas L. Haskell, *The Emergence of Professional Social Science: The American Social Science Association and the Nineteenth-Century Crisis of Authority* (Urbana: University of Illinois Press, 1977), 212. Austin Warren, "The Concord School of Philosophy," *New England Quarterly* 2 (April 1929): 199–233. Henry A. Pochmann, *New England Transcendentalism and St. Louis Hegelianism: Phases in the History of American Idealism* (Philadelphia: Carl Schurz Memorial Foundation, 1948). Miss Birdseye in Henry James, *The Bostonians* (London: Macmillan, 1886). Elizabeth Palmer Peabody to Mary Peabody Mann, August 1879, *Letters of Elizabeth Palmer Peabody,* 388–89.
47. The 1883 program is in the Thomas Davidson Papers (MS 169), Manuscripts and Archives, Yale University. James, *Writings 1878–1899,* 986–1013. Eugene Taylor and Robert H. Wozniak, *Pure Experience: The Response to William James* (Bristol, UK: Thoemmes Press, 1996); Taylor, *William James on Consciousness Beyond the Margin.* This is happening a quarter century before Freud set foot on American soil; for the

therapeutic dimensions of such a view of consciousness, see Eric Caplan, *Mind Games: American Culture and the Birth of Psychotherapy* (Berkeley: University of California Press, 1998).

48. James, *Writings 1878–1899,* 149–51. William Ellery Channing, *Memoir of William Ellery Channing: With Extracts from His Correspondence and Manuscripts,* ed. William Henry Channing (Boston: Crosby, Nichols, and Co., 1848), 1:185.

49. William James, ed., *The Literary Remains of the Late Henry James* (Boston: Houghton Mifflin, 1884). WJ, *Corr* 8:171. On James's refinement of his *Psychology*, Robert D. Richardson, "Will You or Won't You Have it So?: James on the Will," William James Society centennial symposium, Chocorua, New Hampshire, August 15, 2010.

50. James, *Writings 1878–1899,* 484, 486, 489, 491.

51. *Ibid.,* 495, 502.

52. William James, "Is Life Worth Living?," *International Journal of Ethics* 6, no. 1 (October 1890). Thanks to Anthony W. Smith for bringing this journal to my attention.

53. WJ, *Corr* 8:103–4. This material is worth considering in light of the argument of Ferenc Szasz, *The Divided Mind of Protestant America, 1880–1930* (University: University of Alabama Press, 1982).

54. Howard B. Radest, *Toward Common Ground: The Story of the Ethical Societies in the United States* (New York: Frederick Ungar, 1969). James, *Writings 1878–1899,* 502–3. *Ethical Addresses and Ethical Record* 21, nos. 8–9 (April–May, 1914).

55. James, *Writings 1878–1899,* 450. Andrew C. Rieser, *The Chautauqua Moment: Protestants, Progressives, and the Culture of Modern Liberalism* (New York: Columbia University Press, 2003).

56. WJ, *Corr* 8:172–77. On Delsarte, see Judith R. Walkowitz, "The 'Vision of Salome': Cosmopolitanism and Erotic Dancing in Central London, 1908–1918," *American Historical Review* 108, no. 2 (April 2003): 356–58. The line about bringing a balm to men's lives appeared elsewhere in various phrasing; see "William James Dies: Great Psychologist," *New York Times,* August 27, 1910, 7; M. H. Hedges, "The Physician as a Hero: William James," *Forum* (December 1914): 880; Hedges, "Seeking the Shade of William James," *Forum* (April 1915): 445.

57. WJ, *Corr* 8:157. William Leverette, "Simple Living and the Patrician Academic: The Case of William James," *Journal of American Culture* 6 (Winter 1983): 36–43.

58. See David W. Blight, *Race and Reunion: The Civil War in American Memory* (Cambridge, MA: Belknap Press of Harvard University Press, 2001), on the erasure of slavery, and his essay "The Shaw Memorial in the Landscape of Civil War Memory," for its distinctiveness. The essay can be found in the book that came out of the commemoration of the memorial's centennial, *Hope and Glory: Essays on the Legacy of the Fifty-Fourth Massachusetts Regiment,* ed. Martin H. Blatt, Thomas J. Brown, and Donald Yacovone (Amherst: University of Massachusetts Press, 2001), 79–93, or in expanded form in Blight, *Beyond the Battlefield: Race, Memory, and the American Civil War* (Amherst: University of Massachusetts Press, 2002), 153–69. Blight rightly notes the granting of dignity and "manhood" to the soldiers evident in both the sculpture itself and in the speeches at its dedication. On the 54th in the wider context of Civil War memorials, see Kirk Savage, *Standing Soldiers, Kneeling Slaves: Race, War, and Monument in Nineteenth-Century America* (Princeton, NJ: Princeton University

Press, 1997), especially 192–306. See also Kate Mullis Kresser, "Power and Glory: Brahmin Identity and the Shaw Memorial," *American Art* 20 (2006): 32–57.

59. WJ, *Corr* 3:10. Booker T. Washington, *Up from Slavery* (Toronto, Naperville, Atlanta: J. L. Nichols and Co., 1901). Louis Harlan, *Booker T. Washington: The Making of a Black Leader, 1856–1901* (New York: Oxford University Press, 1972). "Memorable Words," *Century Illustrated Magazine* 54, no. 4 (August 1897): 634; Sarah Wyman Whitman, *The Letters of Sarah Wyman Whitman* (Cambridge, MA: Riverside Press, 1907), 124.

60. WJ, *Corr* 8:242–43, 260–62; *Corr* 3:10. See Booker T. Washington's address in *The Monument to Robert Gould Shaw: Its Inception, Completion and Unveiling, 1865–1897* (Boston: Houghton, Mifflin and Co., 1897).

61. William James, "Robert Gould Shaw," *Memories and Studies* (New York: Longmans, Green, 1911), 35–62.

62. *Ibid*. On the line supplied by Alice Howe Gibbens James, see Henry James III's note in William James Papers, 1803–1941 (MS Am 1092.9–1092.12), Houghton Library, Harvard University.

63. Michael Kazin and Joseph A. McCartin, eds., *Americanism: New Perspectives on the History of an Ideal* (Chapel Hill: University of North Carolina Press, 2006). Nicholas Guyatt, *Providence and the Invention of the United States, 1607–1876* (New York: Cambridge University Press, 2007). Rogers M. Smith, *Civic Ideals: Conflicting Visions of Citizenship in U.S. History* (New Haven, CT: Yale University Press, 1997). Michael Kammen, "The Problem of American Exceptionalism: A Reconsideration," *American Quarterly* 45, no. 1 (March 1993): 1–43. Daniel T. Rodgers, "American Exceptionalism Revisited," *Raritan* 24 (Fall 2004): 21–47; Daniel T. Rodgers, "Theorizing America," *Modern Intellectual History* 1, no. 1 (2004): 111–21. James T. Kloppenberg, "Aspirational Nationalism in America," *Intellectual History Newsletter* 24 (2002): 60–71; Hendrik Hartog, "The Constitution of Aspiration and 'The Rights that Belong to Us All," *Journal of American History* 74, no. 3 (December 1987): 1013–34; Richard Rorty, *Achieving Our Country* (Cambridge, MA: Harvard University Press, 1998); Michael Walzer, *What It Means to Be an American* (New York: Marsilio, 1992); Thomas Bender, ed., *Rethinking American History in a Global Age* (Berkeley: University of California Press, 2002); Martha Nussbaum, *For Love of Country?* (Boston: Beacon, 1996); Jonathan M. Hansen, *The Lost Promise of Patriotism: Debating American Identity, 1890–1920* (Chicago: University of Chicago Press, 2003). Ernest L. Tuveson, *Redeemer Nation: The Idea of America's Millennial Role* (Chicago: University of Chicago Press, 1968). Carrie Tirado Bramen, *The Uses of Variety: Modern Americanism and the Quest for National Distinctiveness* (Cambridge, MA: Harvard University Press, 2000). Paul Revere Frothingham, *William Ellery Channing: His Messages from the Spirit* (Boston: Houghton Mifflin, 1903), 24–25. Daniel Walker Howe, *Unitarian Conscience: Harvard Moral Philosophy, 1805–1861* (Middletown, CT: Wesleyan University Press, 1988), 224–25.

64. Sean Wilentz, *Chants Democratic: New York City and the Rise of the American Working Class, 1788–1850* (New York: Oxford University Press, 1986); David Montgomery, *The Fall of the House of Labor: The Workplace, the State, and American Labor Activism, 1865–1925* (New York: Cambridge University Press, 1987). Roy

Rosenzweig, *Eight Hours for What We Will: Workers and Leisure in an Industrial City, 1870–1920* (Cambridge: Cambridge University Press, 1983). Henry Demarest Lloyd, *Wealth Against Commonwealth* (New York and London: Harper and Bros., 1894). Henry George, *Progress and Poverty* (New York: D. Appleton and Co., 1886). Leon Fink, *Progressive Intellectuals and the Dilemmas of Democratic Commitment* (Cambridge, MA: Harvard University Press, 1997).

65. David S. Reynolds, *Walt Whitman's America: A Cultural Biography* (New York: Knopf, 1995). Michael Robertson, *Worshipping Walt: The Whitman Disciples* (Princeton, NJ: Princeton University Press, 2008). For Whitman in James's writings, see especially *The Varieties of Religious Experience,* in James, *Writings 1902–1910,* 82, 357, 452. See also James, *Writings 1878–1899,* 851–54. William Mackintire Salter, *Walt Whitman: Two Addresses* (Philadelphia: S. Burns Weston, 1899).

66. James borrows this example from the anarchist writer Morrison I. Swift in *Pragmatism, Writings 1902–1910,* 498–99. For an argument that James fits into the anarchist tradition, Deborah J. Coon, "'One Moment in the World's Salvation': Anarchism and the Radicalization of William James," *Journal of American History* 83, no. 1 (June 1996): 70–99.

67. Robert B. Westbrook, *John Dewey and American Democracy* (Ithaca, NY: Cornell University Press, 1991). James T. Kloppenberg shows that James and Dewey in fact made similar contributions to the thought behind social democracy in *Uncertain Victory: Social Democracy and Progressivism in European and American Thought, 1870–1920* (New York: Oxford University Press, 1986). See also Trygve Throntveit, "William James's Ethical Republic," *Journal of the History of Ideas* 72, no. 2 (April 2011): 255–77. WJ, *Corr* 8:279. Bordogna, *William James at the Boundaries.*

68. James, *Writings 1878–1899,* 460, 556, 847, 856, 867. James, *Writings 1902–1910,* 333. Emerson, *Miscellanies,* 100; marked in James's copy. For other interpretations, see Miller, *Democratic Temperament,* and M. C. Otto, "On a Certain Blindness in William James," *Ethics* 53, no. 3 (April 1943): 184–91.

69. James, *Writings 1878–1899,* 847, 856, 860, 867–68, 876–78, 1123–24.

70. *Ibid.,* 708, 868. On intersubjectivity, see Jürgen Habermas, *Between Naturalism and Religion* (Cambridge, UK: Polity, 2008); Habermas, *On the Pragmatics of Communication,* Studies in Contemporary German Social Thought (Cambridge, MA: MIT Press, 1998).

71. James, *Writings 1878–1899,* 880. WJ, *Corr* 8:515–17.

72. It is worth considering the moderate position of James on labor in light of the dominant Protestant work ethic in America; see James B. Gilbert, *Work Without Salvation: America's Intellectuals and Industrial Alienation, 1880–1910* (Baltimore: Johns Hopkins University Press, 1977), and Daniel T. Rodgers, *The Work Ethic in Industrial America, 1850–1920* (Chicago: University of Chicago Press, 1974). On Kallen and Locke, see Menand, *The Metaphysical Club,* 391. John Higham, "Multiculturalism and Universalism: A History and a Critique," *American Quarterly* 45, no. 2 (June 1993): 195–219. David A. Hollinger, *Postethnic America: Beyond Multiculturalism,* 10th Anniversary ed. (New York: Basic Books, 2005).

73. WJ, *Corr* 8:475, 504; *Corr* 10:311. For the anti-imperialist movement in international context, see Michael Patrick Cullinane, *Liberty and American Anti-imperialism, 1898–1909* (New York: Palgrave Macmillan, 2012).

74. James, "Address on the Philippine Question," *Writings 1902–1910*, 1130–35. Hansen, *Lost Promise of Patriotism*, 29–38; Robert L. Beisner, *Twelve Against Empire: The Anti-Imperialists, 1898–1900* (Chicago: University of Chicago Press, 1985).

75. James, *Writings 1902–1910*, 1134–35.

76. *Ibid.* In James's library (at the Houghton Library, Harvard University), see David Hume, *A Treatise of Human Nature* (London: Longmans, Green, 1874), WJ 540.54.2; Hume, *Essays Moral, Political, and Literary* (London: Longmans, Green, 1875), WJ 540.54; John Locke, *An Essay Concerning Human Understanding* (London: William Tegg, 1853), WJ 551.13; Thomas Reid, *Essays on the Intellectual Powers of Man* (Philadelphia: E. H. Butler, 1861), WJ 575.41; Adam Smith, *The Theory of Moral Sentiments* (London: A. Millar, 1761), WJ 581.41. In his opening remarks of the Gifford Lectures, James claimed the Scots to have been the first philosophers he read; James, *Writings 1902–1910*, 11. See also his report to his wife of books he bought in Europe in 1883; WJ, *Corr* 5:415. On the intellectual as a social type, see Christopher Lasch, *The New Radicalism in America, 1889–1963: The Intellectual as a Social Type* (New York: Knopf, 1965).

77. Charles Wollenberg, *Berkeley: A City in History* (Berkeley: University of California Press, 2008).

78. James wrote "practicalism" in the margins of books he read when he recognized elements of this idea; for example in Reid, *Essays on the Intellectual Powers of Man*, ed. James Walker, 113; WJ 575.41 at the Houghton Library, Harvard University. WJ, *Writings, 1878–1899*, 1079–80. F. C. S. Schiller to Alice Howe Gibbens James, December 22, 1911, William James Papers (MS Am 1092.9-1092.12), Houghton Library, Harvard University. Peirce's copy of *Aids to Reflection* is at Widener Library at Harvard University, AC85.P3535.Zz831c.

79. Charles S. Peirce, *Chance, Love, and Logic: Philosophical Essays,* ed. Morris Cohen, with John Dewey (New York: Harcourt, Brace, 1923). Daniel J. Wilson, *Science, Community, and the Transformation of American Philosophy.* A. O. Lovejoy, *The Thirteen Pragmatisms: And Other Essays* (Baltimore: Johns Hopkins University Press, 1963). John Shook, ed., *Early Critics of Pragmatism,* 5 vols. (Bristol, UK: Thoemmes, 2001).

80. "Annie Besant," *Boston Evening Transcript,* March 2, 1898, Mary Baker Eddy scrapbook, Mary Baker Eddy Library, Boston. WJ, *Corr* 10:575; *Corr* 11:39–40. WJ quoted in Henry Steele Commager, *The American Mind: An Interpretation of American Thought and Character Since the 1880's* (New Haven, CT: Yale University Press, 1950), 101.

81. WJ, *Corr* 12:241–44.

82. WJ, *Corr* 8:157.

83. James, *Writings 1902–1910*, 1306, 1312, 1313.

Chapter 5 · Thomas Davidson, Liberal: Freedom, Fellowship, and the Socialization of Self-Culture

1. William James, "A Knight-Errant of the Intellectual Life: Thomas Davidson," *McClure's Magazine* 25 (1905): 3–11.

2. "A Modern Wandering Scholar," *Current Literature* 21, no. 6 (December 1900): 648 (reprinted from the *London Spectator*). Morris R. Cohen, "Some Ideals and

Characteristics of Thomas Davidson," *Alliance Review* (n.d.), clipping in Thomas Davidson Papers (MS 169), Manuscripts and Archives, Yale University. Rodfe Tsedek, "Thomas Davidson," *New York Jewish Herald,* September 14, 1902, in Thomas Davidson Papers (MS 169), Manuscripts and Archives; Yale University. Gaynell Hawkins, "The Influence of a Life: Thomas Davidson, Gifted Teacher, Produced Educated Adults," *Journal of Adult Education* 1, no. 3 (June 1929): 268–70. Louis I. Dublin, "Thomas Davidson, Educator for Democracy," *American Scholar* 2 (April 1948): 201–11. Albert Lataner, "Introduction to Thomas Davidson's 'Autobiographical Sketch,'" *Journal of the History of Ideas* 18, no. 4 (October 1957): 529. (Hereafter cited as Davidson, "Autobiographical Sketch.")

3. Thomas Davidson, *Education of the Wage-Earners: A Contribution Toward the Solution of the Educational Problem of Democracy,* ed. Charles M. Bakewell (New York: Burt Franklin, 1904), 142.

4. Thomas Davidson, "Is Life Worth Living?," *International Journal of Ethics* 6, no. 2 (January 1896): 231–35. Davidson, "Human Immortality: Two Supposed Objections to the Doctrine," *International Journal of Ethics* 9, no. 2 (January 1899): 256–59. William Knight, *Memorials of Thomas Davidson: The Wandering Scholar* (London: T. Fisher Unwin, 1907), 137–38. Thomas Davidson, "Address," *Proceedings of the Free Religious Association* (1882); Francis Ellingwood Abbot to Thomas Davidson, February 9, 1890, and William Mackintire Salter to Davidson, February 24, 1890, in Thomas Davidson Papers (MS 169), Manuscripts and Archives, Yale University.

5. Davidson, "Intellectual Piety," 6. Davidson, "American Democracy as a Religion," *International Journal of Ethics* 10 (October 1899): 26.

6. Knight, *Memorials of Thomas Davidson,* 75.

7. John Dewey, *A Common Faith* (New Haven, CT: Yale University Press, 1934). This is distinct from the civil religion described by Robert N. Bellah and many others, but not unrelated. See Russell E. Richey, *American Civil Religion* (New York: Harper and Row, 1974); Raymond J. Haberski, *God and War: American Civil Religion Since 1945* (New Brunswick, NJ: Rutgers University Press, 2012).

8. Davidson, *Education of the Wage-Earners,* 204. Rodfe Tsedek, "Settlement Work and the Davidson Method," *Daily Jewish Herald,* November 26, 1902, in Thomas Davidson Papers (MS 169), Manuscripts and Archives, Yale University.

9. Davidson, "Autobiographical Sketch," 531. W. H. G. Armytage, "Thomas Davidson, Anglo-American Educator," *History of Education Journal* 2, no. 3 (Spring 1951): 75; Knight, *Memorials of Thomas Davidson,* 10. The claim of Davidson's illegitimacy appears in Norman Mackenzie, "Percival Chubb and the Founding of the Fabian Society," *Victorian Studies* 23, no. 1 (Autumn 1979): 37. Max Weber, *The Protestant Ethic and the Spirit of Capitalism* (New York: Scribner, 1930), chapter 5.

10. Davidson, "Autobiographical Sketch," 531. Ignas K. Skrupskelis and Elizabeth M. Berkeley, eds., *The Correspondence of William James* (Charlottesville: University Press of Virginia, 2000), 12:604. (Hereafter cited as WJ, *Corr.*) A similar American novel that William James also read and praised is Harold Frederic, *The Damnation of Theron Ware* (1896); see WJ, *Corr* 8:397, 616.

11. Samuel Butler, *The Way of All Flesh* (Ware, UK: Wordsworth Editions Limited, 1994), 218, 234.

12. Davidson, "Autobiographical Sketch," 531–32. C. C. Everett, *Fichte's Science of Knowledge: A Critical Exposition* (Chicago: Griggs, 1884). Anthony LaVopa, *Fichte: The Self and the Calling of Philosophy, 1762–1799* (New York: Cambridge University Press, 2001). On de-Christianization, David A. Hollinger, "Jewish Intellectuals and the De-Christianization of American Public Culture in the Twentieth Century," in *Science, Jews, and Secular Culture: Studies in Mid-Twentieth Century American Intellectual History* (Princeton, NJ: Princeton University Press, 1996).

13. Davidson, "Autobiographical Sketch," 532. Auguste Comte, *Introduction to Positive Philosophy*, trans. Frederick Ferré (1830; New York: Bobbs-Merrill, 1970). Mary Pickering, *Auguste Comte: An Intellectual Biography* (New York: Cambridge University Press, 1993–2009). T. R. Wright, *The Religion of Humanity: The Impact of Comtean Positivism on Victorian Britain* (New York: Cambridge University Press, 1986). David W. Levy, *Herbert Croly of the New Republic: The Life and Thought of an American Progressive* (Princeton, NJ: Princeton University Press, 1985). Jane Addams, *Twenty Years at Hull-House* (New York: Penguin, 1998), 58.

14. "Some Notes on Missouri: The Heart of the Republic," *Scribner's Monthly* 8, no. 3 (July 1874): 257–85. Ralph E. Morrow, *Washington University in St. Louis* (St. Louis: Missouri Historical Society Press, 1996). Henry A. Pochmann, *New England Transcendentalism and St. Louis Hegelianism* (Philadelphia: Carl Schurz Memorial Foundation, 1948). Charles Milton Perry, *The St. Louis Movement in Philosophy, Some Source Material* (Norman: University of Oklahoma Press, 1930); James A. Good, "'A World-Historical Idea': The St. Louis Hegelians and the Civil War," *Journal of American Studies* 34, no. 1 (December 2000): 447–64.

15. Davidson, "Autobiographical Sketch," 532. Pochmann, *New England Transcendentalism and St. Louis Idealism*, 66, 114–15.

16. James McGrath Morris, *Pulitzer: A Life in Politics, Print, and Power* (New York: HarperCollins, 2010).

17. *Ibid.*, 40–42. Pulitzer is also credited with putting up the money for the Breadwinners' College in Pochmann, *New England Transcendentalism and the St. Louis Hegelians*, 76–77.

18. Morris, *Pulitzer*, 42. WJ, *Corr* 5:347, 380. Donald Yacovone, "'Surpassing the Love of Women': Victorian Manhood and the Language of Fraternal Love," in *A Shared Experience: Men, Women, and the History of Gender*, ed. Laura McCall and Donald Yacovone (New York: New York University Press, 1998). Lawrence Birken, *Consuming Desire: Sexual Science and the Emergence of a Culture of Abundance, 1871–1914* (Ithaca, NY: Cornell University Press, 1988). George Chauncy, *Gay New York: Gender, Urban Culture, and the Makings of the Gay Male World, 1890–1940* (New York: Basic Books, 1994). Michael Robertson, *Worshipping Walt: The Whitman Disciples* (Princeton, NJ: Princeton University Press, 2008), 8, 140–68, 176, 184–88, 215.

19. Thomas Davidson, "Love's Last Suit," *Saturday Evening Post*, March 9, 1878; Davidson, "Love Sonnet," *ibid.*, April 6, 1878. Knight, *Memorials of Thomas Davidson*, 24.

20. William James in Knight, *Memorials of Thomas Davidson*, 111–12. Mrs. John T. Sargent, *Sketches and Reminiscences of the Radical Club of Chestnut Street, Boston* (Boston: James R. Osgood, 1880), 334–38.

21. Knight, *Memorials of Thomas Davidson,* 369–70. Davidson, "On Prof. Tyndall's Recent Address," publication inscrutable, 1874, 361–70, in Thomas Davidson Papers (MS 169), Manuscripts and Archives, Yale University.

22. Davidson, "Autobiographical Sketch," 534. On Amson, including the poem, Knight, *Memorials of Thomas Davidson,* 128–29, 140. The book is Thomas Davidson, *The Parthenon Frieze and Other Essays* (London: Kegan Paul, Trench, 1882).

23. Davidson, "Autobiographical Sketch," 532–35. Thomas Davidson, "An Interesting Personal Interview with Pope Leo XIII," *Boston Daily Advertiser,* July 13, 1880; WJ, *Corr* 5:130–131n. Program for the Concord Summer School of Philosophy (1883), in Thomas Davidson Papers (MS 169), Manuscripts and Archives, Yale University.

24. Davidson, "Autobiographical Sketch," 534. WJ, *Corr* 5:199, 499–500. William James, "The Philosophical System of Antonio Rosmini-Serbati," *Nation* 35 (1882): 313. Thomas Davidson, *The Philosophical System of Antonio Rosmini-Serbati* (London: Kegan Paul, Trench, 1882), 25, 108, 257; WJ 841.77.

25. Davidson, "Autobiographical Sketch," 534.

26. Knight, *Memorials of Thomas Davidson,* 16–25.

27. *Ibid.* Fellowship of the New Life, Constitution, and Davidson, "Stones for Bread," *Index* 16 (1884): 111–12, in Thomas Davidson Papers (MS 169), Manuscripts and Archives, Yale University.

28. Percival Chubb to Thomas Davidson, March 30, 1890, in Thomas Davidson Papers (MS 169), Manuscripts and Archives, Yale University. Knight, *Memorials of Thomas Davidson,* 16–25. Edward R. Pease, *History of the Fabian Society* (London: Fabian Society, 1925), 26–28. George Bernard Shaw, *Essays in Fabian Socialism* (London: Constable and Co., 1932), 135–37.

29. Thomas Davidson, "The Democratization of England," *Forum* 21 (1896): 460–70. Knight, *Memorials of Thomas Davidson,* 54. Davidson, "The Moral Aspects of the Economic Question," *Index* 1886, in Thomas Davidson Papers (MS 169), Manuscripts and Archives, Yale University. On the ASSA, see Thomas L. Haskell, *The Emergence of Professional Social Science: The American Social Science Association and the Nineteenth-Century Crisis of Authority* (Urbana: University of Illinois Press, 1977); William Leach, *True Love and Perfect Union: The Feminist Reform of Sex and Society* (New York: Basic Books, 1980). For a broader treatment, see Dorothy Ross, *The Origins of American Social Science* (New York: Cambridge University Press, 1991).

30. John L. Thomas, *Alternative America: Henry George, Edward Bellamy, Henry Demarest Lloyd and the Adversary Tradition* (Cambridge, MA: Belknap Press of Harvard University Press, 1983), 6–17, 53, 118–24.

31. Table of Contents, *Journal of Social Science, Containing the Proceedings of the American Association of Social Science* 27 (October 1890): 3. See also Robert V. Andelson, ed., *The Critics of Henry George: An Appraisal of their Strictures on Progress and Poverty,* 2 vols. (Malden, MA: Blackwell, 2003–4). Louis Hartz, *The Liberal Tradition in America: An Interpretation of American Political Thought Since the Revolution* (New York: Harcourt, Brace and World, 1955). The book has spawned a great deal of commentary, critically analyzed in Mark Hulliung, ed., *The American Liberal Tradition Reconsidered: The Contested Legacy of Louis Hartz* (Lawrence: University Press of Kansas, 2010). The broader literature on liberalism is truly enormous. See the perspectives in the special issue on national and

transnational liberalism, *Intellectual History Newsletter* 24 (2002). WJ, *Corr* 10:200. Letter to the editor, *The Open Court* 2, no. 31 (1888): 5. Thomas, *Alternative America,* 119.

32. Davidson, "The Single Tax," *Journal of Social Science* 27 (October 1890): 8–15.

33. Davidson, "Property," *Journal of Social Science* 22 (June 1887): 107–12. Davidson's rhetoric here supports the argument of Robert Bannister, *Social Darwinism in Anglo-American Thought* (Philadelphia: Temple University Press, 1979).

34. Stow Persons, *Free Religion: An American Faith* (New Haven, CT: Yale University Press, 1947), 14–17. Robert H. Wiebe, *The Search for Order, 1877–1920* (New York: Hill and Wang, 1967); Haskell, *Emergence of Professional Social Science.* See also Alexandra Oleson and John Voss, eds., *The Organization of Knowledge in Modern America, 1860–1920* (Baltimore: Johns Hopkins University Press, 1967); Alan Trachtenberg, *The Incorporation of America: Culture and Society in the Gilded Age* (New York: Hill and Wang, 1982).

35. Elizabeth Palmer Peabody, *Reminiscences of Rev. Wm. Ellery Channing, D.D.* (Boston: Roberts Brothers, 1880), 169, 173–75, 394. On the relationship of Channing and other liberal Christians to the religions of India, see Spencer Lavan, *Unitarians and India: A Study in Encounter and Response* (Boston: Beacon, 1977); Robert D. Baird, ed., *Religion in Modern India* (New Delhi: Manohar, 1981). William R. Hutchison, *The Modernist Impulse in American Protestantism* (Cambridge, MA: Harvard University Press, 1976). David M. Robinson, "'A Religious Demonstration': The Theological Emergence of New England Transcendentalism," and Dean Grodzins, "Theodore Parker and the 28th Congregational Society: The Reform Church and the Spirituality of Reformers in Boston, 1845–1859," both in *Transient and Permanent: The Transcendentalist Movement and Its Contexts,* ed. Charles Capper and Conrad Edick Wright (Boston: Massachusetts Historical Society, 1999), 49–120. See also Perry Miller, ed., *The Transcendentalists: An Anthology* (Cambridge, MA: Harvard University Press, 1950).

36. Peabody, *Reminiscences,* 174–75; emphases in original.

37. O. B. Frothingham, "Secular Religion," *The Index* 1, no. 2 (1870): 5. Persons, *Free Religion,* 39–41. Sydney E. Ahlstrom with Jonathan Sinclair Carey, *American Reformation: A Documentary History of Unitarian Christianity* (Middletown, CT: Wesleyan University Press, 1985), 256–57. This episode is worth considering in light of the argument advanced by R. Laurence Moore, *Religious Outsiders and the Making of Americans* (New York: Oxford University Press, 1986).

38. Joseph Henry Allen, *Our Liberal Movement in Theology, Chiefly as Shown in Recollections of the History of Unitarianism in New England* (Boston: American Unitarian Association, 1882); Allen, *A Historical Sketch of the Unitarian Movement Since the Reformation* (New York: Christian Literature, 1894). Jabez T. Sunderland, *The Liberal Christian Ministry* (Boston: G. H. Ellis, 1889). Frederick B. Mott, *A Short History of Unitarianism Since the Reformation* (Boston: Unitarian Sunday-School Society, 1893). Minot J. Savage, *Our Unitarian Gospel* (Boston: G. H. Ellis, 1898). William Channing Gannett, *A Hundred Years of the Unitarian Movement in America, 1815–1915: The Story, the Difficulties, the Outlook* (n.p., 1915?). Charles Graves, *A History of Unitarianism* (Boston: American Unitarian Association, 1917). Earl Morse Wilbur, *Our Unitarian Heritage: An Introduction to the History of the*

Unitarian Movement (Boston: Beacon, 1925). Charles Harold Lyttle, *Freedom Moves West: A History of the Western Unitarian Conference, 1852–1952* (Boston: Beacon, 1952).

39. Thomas Davidson, *The Positive Virtues* (Chicago: Open Court, 1887). *The New Ideal* 1, no. 3 (May 1888): 36. Paul Carus, "11th Anniversary Commemoration," *Open Court* 11, no. 1 (January 1887): 4–5. M. D. Leahy to Thomas Davidson, May 23, 1887, in Thomas Davidson Papers (MS 169), Manuscripts and Archives, Yale University. One important treatment of the rise of post-Christianity in this period is James Turner, *Without God, Without Creed: The Origins of Unbelief in America* (Baltimore: Johns Hopkins University Press, 1985).

40. Thomas Davidson, Address, *Proceedings of the Free Religious Association* (1887): 68–72. "Nature-Deep," *The New Ideal* 3, no. 4 (February 1890): 46–47. O. B. Frothingham, *Transcendentalism: A History* (New York: G. P. Putnam's Sons, 1876). Thomas Wentworth Higginson, *The Sympathy of Religions* (Boston: Free Religious Association, 1876). *Freedom and Fellowship in Religion: A Collection of Essays and Addresses* (Boston: Roberts Brothers, 1875), 358–59. On Higginson, see George M. Frederickson, *The Inner Civil War: Northern Intellectuals and the Crisis of the Union* (New York: Harper and Row, 1965); Butler, *Critical Americans*. On Ingersoll, see Susan Jacoby, *Freethinkers: A History of American Secularism* (New York: Metropolitan Books, 2004).

41. Abbot, *The Index* 1, no. 1 (1870): 1–3, 7. W. Creighton Peden, *The Philosopher of Free Religion: Francis Ellingwood Abbot* (New York: P. Lang, 1992). Sydney E. Ahlstrom and R. Bruce Mullins, *The Scientific Theist: A Life of Francis Ellingwood Abbot* (Macon, GA: Mercer University Press, 1987).

42. Ahlstrom and Mullins, *The Scientific Theist*, 43. Abbot, *Scientific Theism* (Boston: Little, Brown, 1885). WJ, *Corr* 6:100, 101. Abbot, *The Way Out of Agnosticism; or, the Philosophy of Free Religion* (London: Macmillan, 1890); Abbot, *Professor Royce's Libel: A Public Appeal for Redress to the Corporation and Overseers of Harvard University* (Boston: G. H. Ellis, 1891); Abbot, *Is Not Harvard Responsible for the Conduct of Her Professors, as Well as of Her Students?* (Boston: G. H. Ellis, 1892); Abbot, *The Syllogistic Philosophy, or Prolegomena to Science* (Boston: Little, Brown, 1906). Abbot, *If Ever Two Were One: A Private Diary of Love Eternal*, ed. Brian A. Sullivan (New York: Regan, 2004).

43. F. E. Abbot to Thomas Davidson, February 8, 1885, in Thomas Davidson Papers (MS 169), Manuscripts and Archives, Yale University. Untitled article on the Concord School's demise, *Current Literature* 3, no. 4 (October 1889): 281. "The Summer School," *The Dial* 18, no. 215 (June 1, 1895): 2.

44. For a contemporary description of leisure in the Adirondacks with references to Wordsworth, Davidson, and Putnam Camp (but notably not to William James), see J. Osgood, "Picnicking in the Adirondacks," *Outing: An Illustrated Magazine of Recreation* 14, no. 4 (July 1889): 284–89. Knight, *Memorials of Thomas Davidson*, 63–73. WJ, *Corr* 8:523. Karl Jacoby, "Class and Environmental History: Lessons from the 'War in the Adirondacks,'" *Environmental History* 2, no. 3 (July 1997): 324–42. David Strauss, "Toward a Consumer Culture: 'Adirondack Murray' and the Wilderness Vacation," *American Quarterly* 39, no. 2 (Summer 1987): 270–86. Philip G. Terrie,

Contested Terrain: A New History of People in the Adirondacks (Syracuse, NY: Syracuse University Press, 1997).

45. Thomas Davidson, "The Kingdom of Heaven," *Christian Union* 43, no. 3 (January 15, 1891): 82–84.

46. Thomas Davidson, "The Ethics of an Eternal Being," *International Journal of Ethics* 3 (April 1893): 336–51.

47. WJ, *Corr* 8:262. Thomas Davidson, *The Philosophy of Goethe's Faust*, ed. Charles M. Bakewell (Boston: Ginn and Co., 1906), 24, 25, 155. "Is Goethe's *Faust* Out of Date?" *Current Literature* 44, no. 6 (June 1908): 632–34. Henry Van Dyke, "On the Study of Tennyson," *Century Illustrated Magazine* 42, no. 4 (August 1891): 502–11. "Rousseau as an Educator," *The Critic* 33, no. 854 (July/August 1898): 93–94.

48. Davidson, *Philosophy of Goethe's Faust,* 15, 58, 145. Davidson is arguing here against the critical take on liberalism later developed by C. B. MacPherson, *The Political Theory of Possessive Individualism: Hobbes to Locke* (Oxford: Clarendon, 1962).

49. *Ibid.*, 3, 9n, 15, 29, 30, 40, 57, 141.

50. Thomas Davidson, "The Creed of the Sultan: Its Future," *The Forum* 22 (October 1896): 152–63. Davidson, "The Brothers of Sincerity," *International Journal of Ethics* 8, no. 4 (July 1898): 439–60. Davidson, *A History of Education* (New York: Charles Scribner's Sons, 1901), 28, 87.

51. Davidson, *History of Education,* 168, 169. Davidson, "The Creed of the Sultan," 157, 163, 164.

52. Jane Rendall, *The Origins of Modern Feminism: Women in Britain, France, and the United States, 1780–1860* (London: Macmillan, 1985). Barbara Taylor, *Mary Wollstonecraft and the Feminist Imagination* (New York: Cambridge University Press, 2003). Daniel I. O'Neill, "John Adams versus Mary Wollstonecraft on the French Revolution and Democracy," *Journal of the History of Ideas* 68, no. 3 (July 2007): 451–76. Eileen Hunt Botting and Christine Carey, "Wollstonecraft's Philosophical Impact on Nineteenth-Century American Women's Rights Advocates," *American Journal of Political Science* 48, no. 4 (October 2004): 707–22. Howard M. Wach, "A Boston Vindication: Margaret Fuller and Caroline Dall Read Mary Wollstonecraft," *Massachusetts Historical Review* 7 (2005): 3–35. Andrew Delbanco, *William Ellery Channing: An Essay on the Liberal Spirit in America* (Cambridge, MA: Harvard University Press, 1981), 40. Peabody, *Reminiscences,* 86–87. Advocates of women's rights tended toward heterodox spiritual practices, including spiritualism; Ann Braude, *Radical Spirits: Spiritualism and Women's Rights in Nineteenth-Century America* (Bloomington: Indiana University Press, 1989); Beryl Satter, *Each Mind a Kingdom: American Women, Sexual Purity, and the New Thought Movement, 1875–1920* (Berkeley: University of California Press, 1999). On the Brahmo Samaj, see David Kopf, *The Brahmo Samaj and the Shaping of the Indian Mind* (Princeton, NJ: Princeton University Press, 1979). Sargent, *Sketches and Reminiscences,* 95–104. *The Index* 1, no. 27 (July 22, 1870): 5. S. Margaret Fuller, *Woman in the Nineteenth Century* (New York: Greeley and McElreth, 1845); developed from "The Great Lawsuit: Man versus Men, Woman versus Women" of 1843. See discussion in Charles Capper, *Margaret Fuller: An American Romantic Life* (New York: Oxford University Press,

1992) 2:6–19. Susan A. English, "The Education of Women in Ceylon," *The New Ideal* 2, no. 7 (July–August 1890): 338–39.

53. Knight, *Memorials of Thomas Davidson,* 76. Thomas Davidson, "The Task of the Twentieth Century," *International Journal of Ethics* 12 (October 1901): 23–43; first given before the Philadelphia Ethical Society, in Thomas Davidson Papers (MS 169), Manuscripts and Archives, Yale University. Charlotte Perkins Gilman, *The Living of Charlotte Perkins Gilman: An Autobiography* (Madison: University of Wisconsin Press, 1991), 231. Gilman, *Women and Economics: A Study of the Economic Relation Between Men and Women as a Factor in Social Evolution* (1898; Berkeley and Los Angeles: University of California Press, 1998), 279.

54. Davidson, *Philosophy of Goethe's Faust,* 42, 43. Davidson, "American Democracy as a Religion," 39.

55. Davidson, "American Democracy as a Religion," 26, 28–29, 31, 32.

56. *Ibid.,* 37–38. Useful for context here is Kathryn J. Oberdeck, *The Evangelist and the Impresario: Religion, Entertainment, and Cultural Politics in America, 1884–1914* (Baltimore: Johns Hopkins University Press, 1999).

57. Knight, *Memorials of Thomas Davidson,* 72, 81.

58. Davidson, *Education of the Wage-Earners,* 53, 97–98, 177.

59. *Ibid.,* 53, 64n.

60. Howard B. Radest, *Toward Common Ground: The Story of the Ethical Societies in the United States* (New York: Frederick Ungar, 1969), 124; David A. Hollinger, *Morris R. Cohen and the Scientific Ideal* (Cambridge, MA: MIT Press, 1975), 26–27. Joseph Kett, *The Pursuit of Knowledge Under Difficulties: From Self-Improvement to Adult Education in America, 1750–1990* (Stanford, CA: Stanford University Press, 1994), 102–330. Marc Stears, *Progressives, Pluralists, and the Problems of the State: Ideologies of Reform in the United States and Britain, 1909–1926* (New York: Oxford University Press, 2002). Fred M. Schied, *Learning in Social Context: Workers and Adult Education in Nineteenth Century Chicago* (DeKalb: Northern Illinois University Press, 1993). Walter A. Wyckoff, *The Workers: An Experiment in Reality,* 2 vols. (New York: C. Scribner's Sons, 1897–98); see James, "What Makes a Life Significant."

61. Davidson, *Education of the Wage-Earners,* 103.

62. *Ibid.,* 119, 182. Anzia Yezierska, *Bread Givers: A Novel: A Struggle Between a Father of the Old World and a Daughter of the New* (Garden City, NY: Doubleday, Page and Co., 1925).

63. Davidson, *Education of the Wage-Earners,* 108, 117, 205.

64. *Ibid.,* 148. Rodfe Tsedek, "Thomas Davidson," *New York Jewish Herald* (1902), clipping in Thomas Davidson Papers (MS 169), Manuscripts and Archives, Yale University.

65. Davidson, *Education of the Wage-Earners,* 208.

66. *Ibid.,* 174.

CHAPTER 6 · WILLIAM MACKINTIRE SALTER, NEW LIBERAL:
ETHICAL CULTURE AND SOCIAL PROGRESS

1. William Mackintire Salter, "Dr. James on the Feeling of Effort," *Unitarian Review* 16 (December 1881): 544–51. Ignas K. Skrupskelis and Elizabeth M. Berkeley, eds., *The*

Correspondence of William James (Charlottesville: University Press of Virginia, 2000), 5:141–44, 210–13. (Hereafter cited as WJ, *Corr.*)

2. WJ, *Corr* 5:477.

3. *Ibid.*, 5:503; 6:85–86, 310. Copy of deed and plan from July 30, 1897, photographs in author's possession.

4. William Mackintire Salter, "Ethical Religion," in Salter, W. L. Sheldon, and S. B. Weston, *The Ethical Movement: Its Philosophical Aims, Its General Aims, Its Relation to Christianity, Unitarianism, and Free Religion* (Boston: George H. Ellis, 1884), 5. On Chicago and progressive reform, see for a start Michael Willrich, *City of Courts: Socializing Justice in Progressive-Era Chicago* (New York: Cambridge University Press, 2003); Richard Schneirov, *Labor and Urban Politics: Class Conflict and the Origins of Modern Liberalism in Chicago, 1864–1897* (Urbana and Chicago: University of Illinois Press, 1998); Georg Leidenberger, *Chicago's Progressive Alliance: Labor and the Bid for Streetcars* (DeKalb: Northern Illinois University Press, 2006); Andrew Wender Cohen, *The Racketeer's Progressive: Chicago and the Struggle for the Modern American Economy, 1900–1940* (New York: Cambridge University Press, 2004); Laura M. Westhoff, *A Fatal Drifting Apart: Democratic Social Knowledge and Chicago Reform* (Columbus: Ohio State University Press, 2007); Christopher Robert Reed, *The Chicago NAACP and the Rise of Professional Black Leadership, 1910–1960* (Bloomington: Indiana University Press, 1997); Elizabeth J. Clapp, *Mothers of All Children: Women Reformers and the Rise of Juvenile Court in Progressive Era America* (University Park: Pennsylvania State University Press, 1980).

5. WJ, *Corr* 6:290.

6. William Mackintire Salter, *Nietzsche the Thinker: A Study* (New York: Henry Holt, 1917), 473.

7. "Notes and News," *The Dial* (October 11, 1917): 362. Sales of *Nietzsche* in Salter Papers, Ethical Culture Society Archives, New York City.

8. A. W. Coats, "Henry Carter Adams: A Case Study in the Emergence of the Social Science in the United States, 1850–1900," in *On the History of Economic Thought* (London: Routledge, 1992), 1:365–85. Philip D. Jordan, *William Salter: Western Torchbearer* (Oxford, OH: Mississippi Valley Press, 1939); James Hill Langdon, *Reverend William Salter, D.D., 1821–1910: Minister of the Congregationalist Church and Society of Burlington, Iowa, 1846–1910* (Des Moines, IA: s.n., 1911); William Salter, *Sixty Years and Other Discourses with Reminiscences* (Boston: Pilgrim Press, 1907).

9. Johnson Brigham, *Iowa: Its History and Its Foremost Citizens* (Chicago: S. J. Clarke, 1918), 1:206. Hill, *Rev. William Salter,* 607.

10. On liberal theology and the West, see William R. Hutchison, *The Modernist Impulse in American Protestantism* (Cambridge, MA: Harvard University Press, 1976). Jordan, *William Salter,* 148–60. William Mackintire Salter, *The Great Rebellion in the Light of Christianity* (Cincinnati: American Reform Tract and Book Society, 1864). Salter, *The Life of James W. Grimes, Governor of Iowa, 1854–1858; A Senator of the United States, 1859–1869* (New York: D. Appleton and Co., 1876).

11. Howard B. Radest, *Toward Common Ground: The Story of the Ethical Societies in the United States* (New York: Frederick Ungar, 1969), 62–63. William Mackintire Salter, "Another View of Newman," *The Arena* 22 (September 1891): 475–86.

12. Salter, "Another View of Newman," 475, 481–82.

13. *Ibid.*, 476–78, 483. John Henry Newman, *An Essay in Aid of a Grammar of Assent* (New York: Catholic Publication Society, 1870), 115; James's copy of the book is at the Houghton Library at Harvard University, WJ 559.95. The reason I claim James read the book around the same time as Salter is because James noted inside the cover his parents' address, which pins his acquisition of the book to the 1870s; other notations suggest that he revisited the book while preparing for his Gifford Lectures, at which point he acquired a later work of Newman's as well, *Lectures on the Doctrine of Justification* (London: Longmans, Green, and Co., 1897), WJ 559.95.2. James, "The Will to Believe," *Writings 1878–1899* (New York: Library of America, 1992), 463. The faith-ladder is in *A Pluralistic Universe* (1909), found in James, *Writings 1902–1910* (New York: Library of America 1987), 779.

14. Henry Neumann, *Spokesmen for Ethical Religion* (Boston: Beacon, 1951), 90–97. James Frank Hornback, "The Philosophic Sources and Sanctions of the Founders of Ethical Culture" (PhD thesis, Columbia University, 1983). Richard F. Teichgraeber III, *Building Culture: Studies in the Intellectual History of Industrializing America, 1867–1910* (Columbia: University of South Carolina Press, 2010). William Mackintire Salter, *On a Foundation for Religion* (Boston: G. H. Ellis, 1879), 29. Abbot's copy is Phil 8510, Harvard University.

15. William Mackintire Salter, *The Ethical Movement, Its Philosophical Basis, Its General Aims, Its Relation to Christianity, Unitarianism, and Free Religion: Three Addresses Before the Free Religious Association, Boston, May 30, 1884* (Bristol, UK: Bristol Selected Pamphlets, 1884), 17. Salter, "Do the Ethics of Jesus Satisfy the Needs of Our Time?," *The Index* (December 14, 1882). Salter, *Ethical Religion* (Boston: Roberts Brothers, 1889), 317.

16. "Chicago Ethical Society," 9–20, Folder I, Chicago—Wallerstein History, in Salter Papers, Ethical Culture Society Archives, New York City. Radest, *Toward Common Ground,* 14–25. Joseph Chuman, "Between Secularism and Supernaturalism: The Religious Philosophies of Theodore Parker and Felix Adler" (PhD dissertation, Columbia University, 1994).

17. Benny Kraut, "Judaism Triumphant: Isaac Mayer Wise on Unitarianism and Liberal Christianity," *AJS Review* 7 (1982): 179–230. Leonard J. Mervis, "The Social Justice Movement and the American Reform Rabbi," *American Jewish Archives* 7 (June 1955): 171–230. Hirsch explicitly disagreed with "that great man, Felix Adler," in Hirsch, "Judaism and Modern Religion," in *My Religion* (New York: Macmillan, 1925), 291. Stephen Wise to Thomas Davidson, September 29, 1898, in Thomas Davidson Papers (MS 169), Manuscripts and Archives, Yale University. Morris Cohen, *The Faith of a Liberal* (New York: Henry Holt, 1946). For more on Hirsch and the Reform Judaism of the era, see Tobias Brinkmann, *Sundays at Sinai: A Jewish Congregation in Chicago* (Chicago: University of Chicago Press, 2012). See also Naomi W. Cohen, "The Challenges of Darwinism and Biblical Criticism to American Judaism," *Modern Judaism* 4, no. 2 (May 1984): 121–57; Lila Corwin Berman, "Mission to America: The Reform Movement's Missionary Experiments, 1919–1960," *Religion and American Culture* 13, no. 2 (Summer 2003): 205–39.

18. William Mackintire Salter, *Christmas from an Ethical Standpoint* (Chicago: Society for Ethical Culture, 1889), 14. Emily Mace, "Cosmopolitan Communions: Practices of

Religious Liberalism in America, 1875–1930" (PhD dissertation, Princeton University, 2010).

19. William Mackintire Salter, *Moral Aspiration and Song* (Philadelphia: Ethical Addresses, 1905); Salter, *The Lack of Joy in Modern Life and the Need of Festivals* (Philadelphia: S. Burns Weston, 1900); Salter, ed., *Ethical Songs* (Philadelphia: S. Burns Weston, 1906). Radest, *Toward Common Ground*, 307–12. David A. Hollinger, *After Cloven Tongues of Fire: Protestant Liberalism in American History* (Princeton, NJ: Princeton University Press, 2013). *Pilgrim Hymnal* (Boston: Pilgrim Press, 1958), 424.

20. William Mackintire Salter, *Objections to the Ethical Movement Considered* (Chicago: Radical Review, 1884), 29–30. "Its Followers Seek for 'Pure Religion' in Ethical Culture: Society Founded on the Ideal Pronounced by Emerson Strives to Materialize Its Visions," *Chicago Tribune,* May 21, 1913, in Salter Papers, Ethical Culture Society Archives, New York City. Salter, *Why Unitarianism Does Not Satisfy Us* (Chicago: Max Stern, 1883).

21. William Mackintire Salter, *The Basis of the Ethical Movement* (Chicago: Max Stern, 1883), 15, 19, 22.

22. *Ibid.,* 12–13, 15–17. Salter's use of the term "inward monitor" reflects the religion of democracy's roots in the American Reformation; William James used the same term in his conclusion to *The Varieties of Religious Experience;* James, *Writings 1902–1910,* 463.

23. Salter, "Do the Ethics of Jesus Satisfy the Needs of Our Time?"; emphasis in original; offprint in Salter Papers, Ethical Culture Society Archives, New York City.

24. Richard Schneirov and John B. Jentz, *Chicago in the Age of Capital: Class, Politics, and Democracy During the Civil War and Reconstruction* (Urbana: University of Illinois Press, 2012). Mitchell Newton-Matza, *Intelligent and Honest Radicals: The Chicago Federation of Labor and the Politics of Progression* (Lanham, MD: Lexington Books, 2013). Dominic A. Pacyga, *Polish Immigrants and Industrial Chicago: Workers on the South Side, 1880–1922* (Chicago: University of Chicago Press, 2003). Hartmut Keil and John B. Jentz, eds., *German Workers in Industrial Chicago, 1850–1910* (DeKalb: Northern Illinois University Press, 1983). Bessie Louise Pierce, *A History of Chicago,* vol. 3, *The Rise of a Modern City, 1871–1893* (New York: Knopf, 1957), 237–40.

25. Edward Bellamy, *Looking Backward, 2000–1887* (Boston: Ticknor, 1888). Upton Sinclair, *The Jungle* (New York: The Jungle Publishing Co., 1906). Theodore Dreiser, *Sister Carrie* (New York: Doubleday, Page and Co., 1900). William T. Stead, *If Christ Came to Chicago: A Plea for Union of All Who Love in the Service of All Who Suffer* (Chicago: Laird and Lee, 1894). Carl Sandburg, "Chicago," in *Chicago Poems* (New York: Henry Holt, 1916), 3–4. On Stead and others, see Paul Boyer, *Urban Masses and Moral Order in America, 1820–1920* (Cambridge, MA: Harvard University Press, 1978). Gay Wilson Allen, *Carl Sandburg* (Minneapolis: University of Minnesota Press, 1972).

26. Robert E. Weir, *Beyond Labor's Veil: The Culture of the Knights of Labor* (University Park: Pennsylvania State University Press, 1996). Richard Schneirov, *Pullman, Illinois: Company Town* (Alexandria, VA: Alexander Street Press, 2007). Richard T. Ely, "Pullman: A Social Study," *Harper's New Monthly Magazine* 70 (February 1885): 452–66.

27. Daniel T. Rodgers, "In Search of Progressivism," *Reviews in American History* 10, no. 4 (December 1982): 113–32. Hirsch, *My Religion*, 134. John L. Thomas, *Alternative America: Henry George, Edward Bellamy, Henry Demarest Lloyd and the Adversary Tradition* (Cambridge, MA: Belknap Press of Harvard University Press, 1983), 73–75. Robert B. Westbrook, *John Dewey and American Democracy* (Ithaca, NY: Cornell University Press, 1991), 49–50. Charles Howard Hopkins, *The Rise of the Social Gospel in American Protestantism, 1865–1915* (New Haven, CT: Yale University Press, 1940). Henry F. May, *Protestant Churches and Industrial America* (New York: Harper and Row, 1949). Jean B. Quandt, *From the Small Town to the Great Community: The Social Thought of Progressive Intellectuals* (New Brunswick, NJ: Rutgers University Press, 1970). Robert M. Crunden, *Ministers of Reform: The Progressives' Achievement in American Civilization, 1889–1920* (New York: Basic Books, 1982). Alan Dawley, *Struggles for Justice: Social Responsibility and the Liberal State* (Cambridge, MA: Belknap Press of Harvard University Press, 1991). Richard Wightman Fox, "The Culture of Liberal Protestant Progressivism," *Journal of Interdisciplinary History* 23, no. 3 (Winter 1993): 639–60. Leon Fink, *Progressive Intellectuals and the Dilemmas of Democratic Commitment* (Cambridge, MA: Harvard University Press, 1997). Nancy Cohen, *The Reconstruction of American Liberalism, 1865–1914* (Chapel Hill: University of North Carolina Press, 2002). Michael McGerr, *A Fierce Discontent: The Rise and Fall of the Progressive Movement in America, 1870–1920* (New York: Free Press, 2003). Andrew Feffer, *The Chicago Pragmatists and American Progressivism* (Ithaca, NY: Cornell University Press, 1993).

28. Many of Salter's addresses were published by Charles H. Kerr, whose story helps open up this nexus of liberal religion and radical politics. See Allen Ruff, *"We Called Each Other Comrade": Charles H. Kerr & Company, Radical Publishers* (Urbana and Chicago: University of Illinois Press, 1997). The association of liberalism and radicalism among thinkers was argued without the religious dimension by Christopher Lasch, *The New Radicalism in America, 1889–1963: The Intellectual as a Social Type* (New York: Knopf, 1965). For a deeper history, see Craig J. Calhoun, *The Roots of Radicalism: Tradition, the Public Sphere, and Early Nineteenth-Century Social Movements* (Chicago: University of Chicago Press, 2012). See also David Kadlec, *Mosaic Modernism: Anarchism, Pragmatism, and Culture* (Baltimore: Johns Hopkins University Press, 2000). Another view is Brian Lloyd, *Left Out: Pragmatism, Exceptionalism, and the Poverty of American Marxism, 1890–1922* (Baltimore: Johns Hopkins University Press, 1997).

29. William Mackintire Salter, *The Social Ideal* (Chicago: Max Stern, 1883), 7, 15. Salter, *The Problem of Poverty* (Chicago: Radical Review Print, 1884), 8, 20.

30. Salter, *Problem of Poverty*, 31. Salter, *First Steps in Philosophy (Physical and Moral)* (Chicago: Charles H. Kerr, 1892), 77n.

31. Bruce C. Nelson, "Revival and Upheaval: Religion, Irreligion, and Chicago's Working Class in 1886," *Journal of Social History* 25, no. 2 (Winter 1991): 233–53. Alexander Trachtenberg, *The History of May Day* (New York: International Press, 1947). David Montgomery, *The Fall of the House of Labor: The Workplace, the State, and American Labor Activism, 1865–1925* (New York: Cambridge University Press, 1987). For the eight-hour movement in Worcester, Massachusetts, see Roy Rosenzweig, *Eight*

Hours for What We Will: Workers and Leisure in an Industrial City (New York: Cambridge University Press, 1983).

32. Blaine McKinley, "'A Religion of the New Time': Anarchist Memorials to the Haymarket Martyrs, 1888–1917," *Labor History* 28, no. 3 (1987): 386–400.

33. Nell Irvin Painter, *Standing at Armageddon: The United States, 1877–1919* (New York: Norton, 1987). Paul Avrich, *The Haymarket Tragedy* (Princeton, NJ: Princeton University Press, 1984). James Green, *Death in the Haymarket: A Story of Chicago, The First Labor Movement, and the Bombing that Divided Gilded-Age America* (New York: Pantheon, 2006). Carl S. Smith, *Urban Disorder and the Shape of Belief: The Great Chicago Fire, the Haymarket Bomb, and the Model Town of Pullman* (Chicago: University of Chicago Press, 2007). Schneirov, *Labor and Urban Politics,* 194–99.

34. William Mackintire Salter, *The Cure for Anarchy* (Chicago: H. M. Shabad and Co., 1887), 3, 5.

35. Salter, *The Cure for Anarchy,* 5–7, 13. Salter, *What Shall Be Done with the Anarchists?* (Chicago: The Open Court, 1887). WJ, *Corr* 6:290. Henry David, *The History of the Haymarket Affair: A Study in the American Social-Revolutionary and Labor Movements* (New York: Russell and Russell, 1936), 393–425. Thomas S. Engeman, "Religion and Politics the American Way: The Exemplary William Dean Howells," *Review of Politics* 63, no. 1 (Winter, 2001): 107–27. Howard A. Wilson and W. D. Howells, "William Dean Howells's Unpublished Letters on the Haymarket Affair," *Journal of the Illinois State Historical Society* 56, no. 1 (Spring 1963): 5–19. On Voltairine de Cleyre, see Leigh E. Schmidt, "The Parameters and Problematics of American Religious Liberalism," in *American Religious Liberalism,* ed. Leigh E. Schmidt and Salley Promey (Bloomington: Indiana University Press, 2012), 1–16.

36. Salter brings up the anarchists and Chicago businessmen in *Freedom of Thought and of Speech* (Chicago: Charles H. Kerr, 1892); he criticizes the apology of one of the Illinois judges in "Gary vs. the Supreme Court," *Liberty (Not the Daughter but the Mother of Order)* 9, no. 41 (June 10, 1893): 1. Salter, "Aspects of the Social Question: The Chicago Conferences. Economic Conferences Between Business Men and Workingmen," *Unitarian Review* 30, no. 2 (August 1888): 163–77. Also Salter, "Second Thoughts on the Treatment of Anarchy," *Atlantic Monthly* 89 (May 1902): 581–88. Neumann, *Spokesmen for Ethical Religion,* 95–96. Victoria Bissell Brown, *The Education of Jane Addams* (Philadelphia: University of Pennsylvania Press, 2004), 251–52, 266, 280.

37. John F. Turner and Thomas W. Allinson, ed., *Chicago Ethical Society, 1882–1916: Historical Sketch of Its Organization and Activities* (pamphlet, 1916). *Relief Works* (Chicago, n.d.), in Salter Papers, Ethical Culture Society Archives, New York City. Radest, *Toward Common Ground,* 63–66, 79, 154.

38. WJ, *Corr* 6:78, and 8:5. Radest, *Toward Common Ground,* 66–70. Stuart M. Blumin, *The Emergence of the Middle Class: Social Experience in the American City, 1760–1900* (New York: Cambridge University Press, 1989). Sven Beckert, "Propertied of a Different Kind: Bourgeoisie and Lower Middle Class in the Nineteenth-Century United States," in *The Middling Sorts: Explorations in the History of the American Middle Class,* ed. Burton J. Bledstein (New York: Routledge, 2002), 285–95.

39. On Lloyd, see Thomas, *Alternative America,* esp. 73–74, 81–82; Schneirov, *Labor and Urban Politics,* 266; and Shelton Stromquist, *Reinventing "The People": The Progressive Movement, the Class Problem, and the Origins of Modern Liberalism, The Working Class in American History* (Urbana and Chicago: University of Illinois Press, 2006), 24. *The Ethical Record* 1, no. 1 (April 1888). Thomas Davidson to Henry Demarest Lloyd, November 29, 1896, Thomas Davidson Papers (MS 169), Manuscripts and Archives, Yale University.

40. Robert Rydell, *All the World's a Fair: Visions of Empire at America's International Exhibitions, 1876–1919* (Chicago: University of Chicago Press, 1984). Relevant chapters are in Alan Trachtenberg, *The Incorporation of America: Culture and Society in the Gilded Age* (New York: Hill and Wang, 1982), and Gail S. Bederman, *Manliness and Civilization: A Cultural History of Gender and Race in the United States, 1880–1917* (Chicago: University of Chicago Press, 1995).

41. William Mackintire Salter, "Moral Forces in Dealing with the Labor Question," *International Journal of Ethics* 5, no. 3 (April 1895): 296–308.

42. William Mackintire Salter, *Bad Wealth: How It Is Sometimes Got* (Philadelphia: S. Burns Weston, 1896). Salter, *Anarchy or Government?: An Inquiry in Fundamental Politics* (New York and Boston: Thomas Y. Crowell, 1895), 11, 53, 88–89, 145, 147, 154; emphases in original. M. Swift, "A Generation Without Prospects," *Open Court* 2, no. 72 (January 10, 1889): 1412. On Swift, see Fink, *Progressive Intellectuals,* 7–8; Coon, "'One Moment in the World's Salvation,'" and Kadlec, *Mosaic Modernism,* 23–24.

43. Salter, *Anarchy or Government?* 11.

44. W. J. Ashley, "Anarchy or Government?: An Inquiry in Fundamental Politics," *International Journal of Social Ethics* 6, no. 3 (April 1896): 395–99. "Social and Economic Studies," *Chautauquan* 23, no. 3 (June 1896): 382. Frank Chapman Sharp, "Anarchy or Government?: An Inquiry in Fundamental Politics," *Philosophical Review* 6, no. 1 (January 1897): 101–2. Frank H. Brooks, ed., *The Individualist Anarchists: An Anthology of Liberty (1881–1908)* (New Brunswick, NJ: Transaction, 1994), 29–38.

45. William Mackintire Salter, *Ethical Religion* (Boston: Roberts Brothers, 1889), 78–79. Salter, "What Is the Real Emancipation of Woman?," *Atlantic Monthly* (January 1902): 28–35.

46. William Mackintire Salter, "Ethics and Woman," *The New Ideal* (April 1890): 176–77. Salter, "A Marriage Address," *Open Court* 2, 39 (1888): 1319–20. Salter, *Walt Whitman: Two Addresses* (Philadelphia: S. Burns Weston, 1899), 11, 29–30.

47. William Mackintire Salter, *Ethics and Philosophy* (Philadelphia: Conservator, 1891), 3, 8. On Traubel and the Whitman fellowships, see Michael Robertson, *Worshipping Walt: The Whitman Disciples* (Princeton, NJ: Princeton University Press, 2008), 232–76.

48. William Mackintire Salter, "Horace Traubel," *Forum* (February 1914): 313–14.

49. *Ibid.,* 313.

50. Henry James, Horace Greeley, and Stephen Pearl Andrews, *Love, Marriage, and Divorce, and the Sovereignty of the Individual* (Boston: Benj. R. Tucker, 1889). John C. Spurlock, *Free Love: Marriage and Middle-Class Radicalism in America, 1825–1860* (New York: New York University Press, 1988). Richard Wightman Fox, *Trials of Intimacy: Love and Loss in the Beecher-Tilton Scandal* (Chicago: University of Chicago Press, 1999), 73–76, 234–36. See especially Fox, "New Baptized: The Culture of

Love in America, 1830s to 1950s," in *Religion and Cultural Studies,* ed. Susan L. Mizruchi (Princeton, NJ: Princeton University Press, 2001), 110–39.

51. Hendrik Hartog, *Man and Wife in America: A History* (Cambridge, MA: Harvard University Press, 2000). Priscilla Yamin, *American Marriage: A Political Institution* (Philadelphia: University of Pennsylvania Press, 2012).

52. Salter, "Horace Traubel," 314. Salter, "What Is the Real Emancipation of Woman?," 30. Radest, *Toward Common Ground,* 69, 159.

53. Patrick Wolfe, *Settler Colonialism and the Transformation of Anthropology: The Politics and Poetics of an Ethnographic Event* (New York: Cassell, 1999). Salter, *Social Ideal,* 12. On the Indian Rights Association and Protestant-led assimilationism in general, see Henry E. Fritz, *The Movement for Indian Assimilation, 1860–1890* (Philadelphia: University of Pennsylvania Press, 1963); Frederick E. Hoxie, *A Final Promise: The Campaign to Assimilate the Indians, 1880–1920* (Lincoln: University of Nebraska Press, 1984); William T. Hagan, *The Indian Rights Association: The Herbert Welsh Years, 1882–1904* (Tucson: University of Arizona Press, 1985); Edmund J. Danziger Jr., "Native American Resistance and Accommodation During the Late Nineteenth Century," in *The Gilded Age: Essays on the Origins of Modern America,* ed. Charles W. Calhoun (Wilmington, DE: Scholarly Resources, 1996), 163–84. On the construction of Indians as vanishing, see Brian W. Dippie, *The Vanishing American: White Attitudes and U.S. Indian Policy* (Middletown, CT: Wesleyan University Press, 1982). See also Patrick Wolfe, "Land, Labor, and Difference: Elementary Structures of Race," *American Historical Review* 106, no. 3 (June 2001): 866–905. On the cultural devastation caused by the move to reservations, Jonathan Lear, *Radical Hope: Ethics in the Face of Cultural Devastation* (Cambridge, MA: Harvard University Press, 2006).

Elizabeth Palmer Peabody, notably, defended Native American rights but opposed the idea that they should give up their culture, allying with Indian activist Sarah Winnemucca; see Frederick E. Hoxie, *This Indian Country: American Indian Activists and the Place They Made* (New York: Penguin Press, 2012).

54. Wolfe, "Land, Labor, and Difference," 869. Hoxie, *A Final Promise,* 20.

55. Hoxie, *A Final Promise,* 3–5, 15, 17–29; Fritz, *Movement for Indian Assimilation,* 26; Hagan, *Indian Rights Association,* 5–6.

56. On education in the Ethical Culture Society, see Radest, *Toward Common Ground,* 100, 103, 213. Felix Adler, "A New Experiment in Education," *Princeton Review* (1882); Mabel R. Goodlander, *The First Sixty Years: An Historical Sketch of the Ethical Culture Schools, 1878–79-1938–39,* in Ethical Culture Society Archives, New York City. Lloyd to Davidson, October 19, 1888, in Thomas Davidson Papers (MS 169), Manuscripts and Archives, Yale University. The pamphlet Lloyd had just read is probably Davidson, *The Conditions, Divisions, and Methods of Complete Education* (New Jersey: The Orange Chronicle, 1887): 6–35.

57. Horace M. Kallen, "Democracy vs. the Melting Pot," in *Culture and Democracy in the United States* (New York: Boni and Liveright, 1924). David A. Hollinger, *Postethnic America: Beyond Multiculturalism,* 10th Anniversary ed. (New York: Basic Books, 2005); Daniel Greene, "A Chosen People in a Pluralist Nation: Horace Kallen and the Jewish-American Experience," *Religion and American Culture* 16, no. 2 (2006): 161–93. For another view, see Everett Helmut Akam, *Transnational America: Cultural*

Pluralist Thought in the Twentieth Century (Lanham, MD: Rowman and Littlefield, 2002).

For the wider progressive context of the adoptions sponsored by the IRA, see Christine Stansell, "Women, Children, and the Uses of the Streets: Class and Gender Conflict in New York City, 1850–1860," *Feminist Studies* 8 (1982): 309–35; Linda Gordon, *The Great Arizona Orphan Abduction* (Cambridge, MA: Harvard University Press, 1999); Susan Tiffen, *In Whose Best Interest: Child Welfare Reform in the Progressive Era* (Westport, CT: Greenwood, 1982); LeRoy Ashby, *Saving the Waifs: Reformers and Dependent Children, 1890–1917* (Philadelphia: Temple University Press, 1984); Linda Gordon, *Heroes of Their Own Lives: The Politics and History of Family Violence* (New York: Viking, 1988).

58. WJ, *Corr* 9:233–34.

59. This and most subsequent information about John Randall Salter comes from personal correspondence with his son, Hunter Gray, in author's possession. Some documents are available on his Web site: http://hunterbear.org/James%20and%20Salter%20and%20Dad.htm. On the Salters' longing for a child, see WJ, *Corr* 9:243–44.

60. On Dewey's sons' deaths, see WJ, *Corr* 10:502–503n.

61. Carl T. Jackson, "The Meeting of East and West: The Case of Paul Carus," *Journal of the History of Ideas* 29, no. 1 (January–March 1968): 73–92. William H. Hay, "Paul Carus: A Case-Study of Philosophy on the Frontier," *Journal of the History of Ideas* 17, no. 4 (October 1956): 498–510.

62. The growing literature on Eastern religions in the West includes Thomas A. Tweed, *The American Encounter with Buddhism, 1844–1912: Victorian Culture and the Limits of Dissent* (Bloomington and Indianapolis: Indiana University Press, 1992); Carl T. Jackson, *The Oriental Religions and American Thought: Nineteenth-Century Explorations* (Westport, CT: Greenwood, 1981); Richard King, *Orientalism and Religion: Postcolonial Theory, India, and "The Mystic East"* (New York: Routledge, 1999); Robert S. Ellwood Jr., *Alternative Altars: Unconventional and Eastern Spirituality in America* (Chicago: University of Chicago Press, 1979); Wouter J. Hanegraaff, *New Age Religion and Western Culture: Esotericism in the Mirror of Secular Thought* (New York: E. J. Brill, 1996); Holly Edwards, *Noble Dreams, Wicked Pleasures: Orientalism in America, 1870–1930* (Princeton, NJ: Princeton University Press, 2000); J. J. Clarke, *Oriental Enlightenment: The Encounter Between Asian and Western Thought* (New York: Routledge, 1997); Stephen Prothero, *The White Buddhist: The Asian Odyssey of Henry Steel Olcott* (Bloomington: Indiana University Press, 1996); Suzanne Marchand, "German Orientalism and the Decline of the West," *Proceedings of the American Philosophical Society* 145, no. 4 (December 2001); Marchand, "Philhellenism and the *Furor Orientalis*," *Modern Intellectual History* 1, no. 3 (2004): 331–58. Another crucial text is Eric J. Sharpe, *Comparative Religion: A History* (LaSalle, IL: Open Court, 1986).

63. Davidson, *A History of Education* (New York: Charles Scribner's Sons, 1901), 45. Lillian Brown-Olf, "Moods in the Museum Before a Chinese Shrine," *Verse by Members of the Women's Club of the Chicago Ethical Society* (n.d., in Ethical Cultural Society Archives, New York City).

64. The story of James praising Buddhism to the Sri Lankan monk Anagarika Dharmapala appears in Rick Fields, *How the Swans Came to the Lake: A Narrative History of Buddhism in America* (Boulder, CO: Shambhala, 1981), 131. James, *Writings*

1902–1910, 466. James got some of his sense of Buddhism from Harold Fielding-Hall, *The Soul of a People* (1898), a book on Buddhism in Burma that James read with such joy that he told his wife it was "destined to help dispel the blindness" (WJ, *Corr* 8:518). In *Soul of a People*, karma is described as holding "that whatever is done or left undone inevitably reacts upon the character, affects for weal or for woe the destiny of the soul." See a review of the book that was in Salter's folder on Buddhism, "A New Inter-, pretation of Buddha's Teachings," *Religion and Ethics* (November 1908): 539–41. Steve Odin, *The Social Self in Zen and American Pragmatism* (Albany: State University of New York Press, 1996).

65. Salter, *The Basis of the Ethical Movement*, 9.

66. Salter, "Moral Forces on Dealing with the Labor Question," 306. Salter may have gotten the Buddhist renunciation of private salvation from "A Vow from a Buddhistic Liturgy," *The Index* 1 (1870): 7.

67. "Creeds and Criminality," *Public Opinion*, November 25, 1887, in Salter Papers, Ethical Culture Society Archives, New York City.

68. Radest, *Toward Common Ground*, 67, 154, 168. William Mackintire Salter, *Imperialism* (Chicago: Alfred C. Clark, 1899); Salter, "The Negro Problem: Is the Nation Going Backward?," *Ethical Addresses and Ethical Record* 10, no. 9 (May 1903): 163–80. Salter, *First Steps in Philosophy* (Chicago: Charles H. Kerr, 1892), 106, 155.

69. William Mackintire Salter, "Mr. George Bernard Shaw as a Social Critic," *International Journal of Ethics* 18, no. 4 (1908): 455. Salter, "Schopenhauer's Contact with Pragmatism," *Philosophical Review* (March 1910): 137–53. Salter, "Schopenhauer's Type of Idealism," *The Monist* 21, no. 1 (January 1911): 2–5. Salter, *Nietzsche*, 20. On Nietzsche and his American reception, see Jennifer Ratner-Rosenhagen, *American Nietzsche: A History of an Icon and His Ideas* (Chicago: University of Chicago Press, 2012).

70. Salter, *Nietzsche*, 338.

71. *Ibid.*, 338, 473. James, *Writings 1878–1899*, 875. Thanks to Katherine Kelly for first drawing my attention to this crucial line in James.

72. Radest, *Toward Common Ground*, 83–95. Letter from A. Sabro, in Salter Papers, Ethical Culture Society Archives, New York City; also M. K. Gandhi, "God and Congress," *Young Idea* (March 5, 1925), clipping enclosed in letter from Henry Neumann to Mary Salter, May 20, 1925, in Salter Papers. Salter, *What Is Americanism?* (New York: American Ethical Union, 1924), 23–24.

73. Emerson, transcribed in Salter's hand in his folder on Nature Study, in Salter Papers, Ethical Cultural Society Archives, New York City. Salter, "Another View of Newman," 486.

CHAPTER 7 · JANE ADDAMS, SOCIAL DEMOCRAT: UNIVERSAL NEEDS AND THE COOPERATIVE ROAD TO INTERNATIONAL PEACE

1. Ignas K. Skrupskelis and Elizabeth M. Berkeley, eds., *The Correspondence of William James* (Charlottesville: University Press of Virginia, 2000), 10:121, 124, 129. (Hereafter cited as WJ, *Corr*.)

2. Jane Addams, *Democracy and Social Ethics,* ed. Charlene Haddock Seigfried (Urbana and Chicago: University of Illinois Press, 2002), 7. (Hereafter cited as Addams, *DSE*.)

3. Howard B. Radest, *Toward Common Ground: The Story of the Ethical Societies in the United States* (New York: Frederick Ungar, 1969), 65, 155. On Davidson, see Jane Addams, *Twenty Years at Hull-House* (New York: Penguin, 1998), 63–64; see also Addams, "Jane Addams's Own Story of Her Work: Fifteen Years at Hull House," *The Ladies' Home Journal* 23, no. 4 (March 1906): 13–14. WJ, *Corr* 11:313.

4. Addams, *DSE,* 5, 119, 120.

5. Addams, *Twenty Years at Hull-House,* 16.

6. Jane Addams, *Forty Years at Hull-House: Being "Twenty Years at Hull-House" and "The Second Twenty Years at Hull-House"* (New York: Macmillan, 1935), 458. Addams, *Peace and Bread in Time of War* (Boston: G. K. Hall, 1960), 133. WJ, *Corr* 10:124. Her personal friendships with criminals appear, among other places, in Addams, *Newer Ideals of Peace* (New York: Macmillan, 1907), 58–59.

   Two excellent recent biographies of Addams are Victoria Bissell Brown, *The Education of Jane Addams* (Philadelphia: University of Pennsylvania Press, 2004), and the two volumes by Louise W. Knight, *Citizen: Jane Addams and the Struggle for Democracy* (Chicago: University of Chicago Press, 2005), and *Jane Addams: Spirit in Action* (New York: W.W. Norton, 2010). Still useful is Allen F. Davis, *American Heroine: The Life and Legend of Jane Addams* (New York: Oxford University Press, 1973). See also Mary Jo Deegan, *Jane Addams and the Men of the Chicago School, 1892–1918* (New Brunswick, NJ: Transaction, 1998); Daniel Levine, *Jane Addams and the Liberal Tradition* (Madison: State Historical Society of Wisconsin, 1971); Allen F. Davis, *Spearheads for Reform: The Social Settlements and the Progressive Movement, 1890–1914* (New York: Oxford University Press, 1964); Marilyn Fischer, Carol Nackenoff, and Wendy E. Chmielewski, *Jane Addams and the Practice of Democracy* (Urbana: University of Illinois Press, 2008); Eleanor J. Stebner, *The Women of Hull House: A Study in Spirituality, Vocation, and Friendship* (Albany: State University of New York Press, 1997).

7. The residents, *Hull-House Maps and Papers* (Urbana and Chicago: University of Illinois Press, 2007), 59. In her autobiography, Addams doubled the number of nationalities represented in the neighborhood: Addams, *Twenty Years at Hull-House,* 176. Other quotations in this paragraph come from *ibid.*, 55, 183, 255. On the diversity of approaches under the broad tent of progressive reform, see Jennifer Fronc, *New York Undercover: Private Surveillance in the Progressive Era* (Chicago: University of Chicago Press, 2009), and Robert D. Johnstone, *The Radical Middle Class: Populist Democracy and the Question of Capitalism in Progressive-Era Portland, Oregon* (Princeton, NJ: Princeton University Press, 2003).

8. Jane Addams, *The Spirit of Youth and the City Streets* (New York: Macmillan, 1917), 20, 70. WJ, *Corr* 12:384.

9. Addams, *Newer Ideals of Peace,* 11, 14. Isaiah Berlin may have been the first to formally specify the necessity of pluralism for modern liberalism; see George Crowder, *Isaiah Berlin: Liberty and Pluralism* (Malden, MA: Polity, 2004). See also Robert B. Talisse, *Pluralism and Liberal Politics* (New York: Routledge, 2012), and John Gray, *Enlightenment's Wake: Politics and Culture at the Close of the Modern Age* (New York: Routledge, 1995).

10. Jane Addams, *Peace and Bread in Time of War* (Boston: G. K. Hall, 1960), 151.

11. Addams, *Twenty Years at Hull-House*, 26.

12. The Quaker business is ably treated in Brown, *Education of Jane Addams*, 22, 305n46–47. For the Hicksite movement, see H. Larry Ingle, *Quakers in Conflict: The Hicksite Reformation* (Knoxville: University of Tennessee Press, 1984).

13. Addams, *Twenty Years at Hull-House*, 19, 30, 33.

14. *Ibid.*, 19. Addams, *DSE*, 68. On Addams's participation in the American importation of European social reforms in the Progressive Era, see Daniel T. Rodgers, *Atlantic Crossings: Social Politics in a Progressive Age* (Cambridge, MA: Belknap Press of Harvard University Press, 1998). On Mazzini and Fuller, see Charles Capper, *Margaret Fuller: An American Romantic Life, vol 2., The Public Years* (New York: Oxford University Press, 2007), 316–24. Hansen, *Lost Promise of Patriotism*, xiv–xvi.

15. Addams, *DSE*, 68–69.

16. *Ibid.*, 36. On how the private domestic sphere for women carried over into social reform, see Robyn Muncy, *Creating a Female Dominion in American Reform, 1800–1935* (New York: Oxford University Press, 1991).

17. Addams, *Twenty Years at Hull-House*, 48. For more on Mitchell and Gilman, see Helen Lefkowitz Horowitz, *Wild Unrest: Charlotte Perkins Gilman and the Making of "Yellow Wallpaper"* (New York: Oxford University Press, 2010).

18. Addams, *Twenty Years at Hull-House*, 35–36, 38, 41–42. On the role of literature in Addams's life and that of her community, see Barbara Sicherman, *Well-Read Lives: How Books Inspired a Generation of American Women* (Chapel Hill: University of North Carolina Press, 2010), 135–92.

19. Addams, *Twenty Years at Hull-House*, 38. For some of the contrasts and tensions between evangelical Christianity that included social work and social Christianity like that of Addams, see Torben Christensen and William R. Hutchison, eds., *Missionary Ideologies in the Imperialist Era, 1880–1920* (Aarhus, Denmark: Forlaget Aros, 1982).

20. Henry Carter Adams, ed., *Philanthropy and Social Progress* (New York and Boston: Thomas Y. Crowell, 1892), 17.

21. William James, "What Makes a Life Significant," *Writings, 1878–1899* (New York: Library of America, 1992), 868–69. Percival Chubb, "Tolstoy on Ethics and Religion," *Ethical Record* 2, no. 3 (February–March 1901): 114–16. W. T. Sheldon, "Count Tolstoy from an Ethical Standpoint," *Ethical Record* 2, no. 2 (July 1889): 65–82. Apparently Tolstoy admired the Ethical Culture movement and particularly Felix Adler as well, reading a number of the publications of the New York Ethical Society, according to Andrew Dickson White, "Talks with Tolstoy," *McClure's Magazine,* cited in *Ethical Record* 11, no. 5 (June–July 1901): 200–203. Leo Tolstoy, *My Confession,* trans. David Patterson (New York: Norton, 1983), 70. Addams, *Twenty Years at Hull-House,* 55–56, 172. This account contains one of Addams's misprisions, for she said she read Tolstoy's *My Religion* directly after college, but that was eight years before it was published. More likely is that she read *My Confession* first, but she still could not have gotten an edition of that until, at the very earliest, three years after graduating from Rockford.

22. Leo Tolstoy, *What Then Must We Do?,* ed. Aylmer Maude (London: Oxford University Press, 1935), 171.

23. *Ibid.,* xviii.

24. Addams, *Twenty Years at Hull-House*, 172. For more on their relationship, see James Cracraft, *Two Shining Souls: Jane Addams, Leo Tolstoy, and the Global Quest for Peace* (Lanham, MD: Lexington Books, 2012).

25. Addams, *Twenty Years at Hull-House*, 177, 179. The experience of such workers three decades later comes vividly to light in Tillie Olsen, *Yonnondio: From the Thirties* (New York: Delacorte Press, 1974).

26. Addams, *Twenty Years at Hull-House*, 181.

27. On the snare of preparation, see *ibid.*, chapter 4.

28. WJ, *Corr* 11:69. Paul Revere Frothingham, *William Ellery Channing: His Messages from the Spirit* (Boston: Houghton Mifflin, 1903), 39–40. Addams in Adams, ed., *Philanthropy and Social Progress*, 2; Addams, "Charitable Effort," *DSE*, 11–34. For a current manifestation of the vision of Addams, see Jay Readey and Jeff Pinzino, "Set Up Hull Houses for 2013: Jane Addams' Plan for Chicago Offers Modern Inspiration," *Chicago Tribune*, November 20, 2013, http://articles.chicagotribune.com/2013-11-20/news/ct-houses-plan-chicago-hull-future-innovation-pers-20131120_1_hull-house-hull-house-first-settlement-house.

29. Addams, *Twenty Years at Hull-House*, 30.

30. Addams, *Newer Ideals of Peace*, 40, 41. Addams, *Peace and Bread in Time of War*, 90, 192. Addams, *A New Conscience and an Ancient Evil*, 11, 144. Addams, *The Spirit of Youth*, 8, 20, 124. Addams, *Second Twenty Years*, 194. James, *Writings 1878–1899*, 847. Addams, *Twenty Years at Hull-House*, 58, 124, 150.

31. Addams, *Twenty Years at Hull-House*, 102, 124.

32. Addams, *Newer Ideals of Peace*, 42. Addams, *Spirit of Youth*, 7, 127.

33. James T. Kloppenberg, "*Requiescat in Pacem*: The Liberal Tradition of Louis Hartz," in *The American Liberal Tradition Reconsidered: The Contested Legacy of Louis Hartz*, ed. Mark Hulliung (Lawrence: University Press of Kansas, 2010), 90–124. Addams, *Twenty Years at Hull-House*, 124–25.

34. Interdependence as a feature of modern history is argued persuasively in Thomas Haskell's *The Emergence of Professional Social Science: The American Social Science Association and the Nineteenth-Century Crisis of Authority* (Urbana: University of Illinois Press, 1977), as well as his contributions to the debate over antislavery in essays collected in *Objectivity Is Not Neutrality: Explanatory Schemes in History* (Baltimore: Johns Hopkins University Press, 1998).

35. Graham Taylor, *Religion in Social Action* (New York: Dodd and Mead, 1913), viii, xvii, xx. On the possible derivation of American Social Gospel from British Social Christianity, see William R. Hutchison, "The Americanness of the Social Gospel: An Inquiry in Comparative History," *Church History* 44 (September 1975): 1–15. On Judaism, see Leonard J. Mervis, "The Social Justice Movement and the American Reform Rabbi," *American Jewish Archives* 7 (June 1955): 171–230. On Catholics, see Deirdre M. Moloney, *Catholic Lay Groups and Transatlantic Social Reform in the Progressive Era* (Chapel Hill: University of North Carolina Press, 2002). Other helpful sources for understanding the movement, including Addams's role in it, begin with Charles Howard Hopkins, *The Rise of Social Gospel in American Protestantism, 1865–1915* (New Haven, CT: Yale University Press, 1940), and include Donald K. Gorrell, *The Age of Social Responsibility: The Rise of Social Gospel in the Progressive Era, 1900–1920* (Macon, GA: Mercer University Press, 1988); Susan

Curtis, *A Consuming Faith: The Social Gospel and Modern American Culture* (Baltimore: Johns Hopkins University Press, 1991); Janet Forsyth Fishburn, *The Fatherhood of God and the Victorian Family: The Social Gospel in America* (Philadelphia: Temple University Press, 1981); Ronald C. White Jr., *Liberty and Justice for All: Racial Reform and the Social Gospel, 1877–1925* (San Francisco: Harper and Row, 1990); Ralph E. Luker, *The Social Gospel in Black and White: American Racial Reform, 1885–1912* (Chapel Hill: University of North Carolina Press, 1991); Gary J. Dorrien, *Social Ethics in the Making: Interpreting an American Tradition* (Malden, MA: Wiley-Blackwell, 2008); and Dorrien, *The Making of American Liberal Theology: Imagining Progressive Religion, 1805–1900* (Louisville, KY: Westminster John Knox Press, 2001).

36. Addams, ed., *Philanthropy and Social Progress,* xi. On the World's Parliament of Religions, see Grant E. Wacker, "A Plural World: The Protestant Awakening to World Religions," in *Between the Times: The Travail of the Protestant Establishment in America, 1900–1960,* ed. William R. Hutchison (New York: Cambridge University Press, 1989), 253–77; Richard Hughes Seager, *The World's Parliament of Religions: The East/West Encounter, Chicago, 1893* (Bloomington: Indiana University Press, 1995); Amy Kittelstrom, "The International Social Turn: Unity and Brotherhood at the World's Parliament of Religions, Chicago, 1893," *Religion and American Culture* 19, no. 2 (2009): 243–74. Walter Rauschenbusch quoted in Paul Boyer, *Urban Masses and Moral Order Order in America, 1820–1920* (Cambridge, MA: Harvard University Press, 1978), 239.

37. Addams, *The Excellent Becomes the Permanent,* 4, 10.

38. Addams, *Forty Years at Hull-House,* 383.

39. Addams in Addams, ed., *Philanthropy and Social Progress,* 24, 25. Addams, *DSE,* 112.

40. Addams, *A New Conscience,* 9, 108, 143.

41. Addams, *Spirit of Youth,* 98, 160–61. Addams, *A New Conscience,* 158.

42. Addams, *DSE,* 18, 20, 21, 26, 45, 81, 110. Addams, *Spirit of Youth,* 40. E. B. Tylor, *Primitive Culture: Researches into the Development of Mythology, Philosophy, Religion, Arts, and Custom* (New York: Henry Holt, 1874). Bernard McGrane, *Beyond Anthropology: Society and the Other* (New York: Columbia University Press, 1989). Gail Bederman, *Manliness and Civilization: A Cultural History of Gender and Race in the United States, 1880–1917* (Chicago: University of Chicago Press, 1995).

43. Addams, *Spirit of Youth,* 148, 149.

44. Addams, *Twenty Years at Hull-House,* 220.

45. *Ibid.,* 117.

46. *Ibid.,* 271. Addams, *A New Conscience,* 115, 116. Addams, *The Long Road of Woman's Memory,* 40–42.

47. Addams, *Spirit of Youth,* 147. Addams, *Forty Years at Hull-House,* 266–67.

48. *Ibid.,* 401. This relates closely to the essential point made in David A. Hollinger, *Postethnic America: Beyond Multiculturalism,* 10th Anniversary ed. (New York: Basic Books, 2005).

49. WJ, *Corr* 10:129. Addams, *Spirit of Youth,* 146.

50. Addams, *DSE,* 9. Addams, *Peace and Bread,* 150.

51. *Addams, DSE,* 3, 82, 112.

52. *Ibid.,* 3, 104–5.

53. *Ibid.*, 89–90, 113, 255, 257, 263.
54. *Ibid.*, 113.
55. *Ibid.*, 87, 253–54.
56. Addams, *Long Road of Woman's Memory,* 75. Addams, *The Excellent Becomes the Permanent* (New York: Macmillan, 1932), 13.
57. Addams, *Forty Years at Hull-House,* 454.

CONCLUSION: AN AMERICAN CENTURY?

1. Carrie Chapman Catt, Mrs. Franklin D. Roosevelt, Jane Addams, Judge Florence E. Allen, Mrs. Wm. Brown Meloney, Dr. Alice Hamilton, Mary E. Woolley, Florence Brewer Boeckel, Emily Newell Blair [and] Dorothy Canfield Fisher, *Why Wars Must Cease,* ed. Rose Young (New York: Macmillan, 1935). On the relationship between commercialism and war, see Jane Addams, *Newer Ideals of Peace* (New York: Macmillan, 1907), 223.
2. David M. Kennedy, *Freedom from Fear: The American People in Depression and War, 1929–1945* (New York: Oxford University Press, 1999).
3. Alan Brinkley, *The Publisher: Henry Luce and His American Century* (New York: Knopf, 2010). Elaine Tyler May, *Homeward Bound: American Families in the Cold War Era* (New York: Basic Books, 1988). The most provocative association of democracy with free-market capitalism appears in Francis Fukuyama, *The End of History and the Last Man* (New York: Free Press, 1992). Such an association was far from a foregone conclusion, according to Howard Brick, *Transcending Capitalism: Visions of a New Society in Modern American Thought* (Ithaca, NY: Cornell University Press, 2010).
4. For wider cultural unease about the modern consumer ethos, see William Leach, *Land of Desire: Merchants, Power, and the Rise of a New American Culture* (New York: Vintage, 1993), and Daniel Horowitz, *The Morality of Spending: Attitudes Toward the Consumer Society in America, 1875–1940* (Baltimore: Johns Hopkins University Press, 1985).
5. Landon R. Y. Storrs, *Civilizing Capitalism: The National Consumers League, Women's Activism, and Labor Standards in the New Deal Era* (Chapel Hill: University of North Carolina Press, 2000). Davarian L. Baldwin, *Chicago's New Negroes: Modernity, the Great Migration, and Black Urban Life* (Chapel Hill: University of North Carolina Press, 2007). Alain Locke, ed., *The New Negro: An Interpretation* (New York: A. and C. Boni, 1925). The most far-reaching argument for consumerism as a form of citizenship is Lizabeth Cohen, *A Consumer's Republic: The Politics of Mass Consumption in Postwar America* (New York: Vintage, 2004).
6. On the social activist commitments of ecumenical Protestants, see David A. Hollinger, "After Cloven Tongues of Fire: Ecumenical Protestantism and the Modern American Encounter with Diversity," *Journal of American History* 98, no. 1 (June 2011): 21–48. K. Healan Gaston, "Demarcating Democracy: Liberal Catholics, Protestants, and the Discourse of Secularism," in *American Religious Liberalism,* ed. Leigh E. Schmidt and Sally Promey (Bloomington: Indiana University Press, 2012), 337–58. The "children of darkness" line comes from Reinhold Niebuhr, a theologian critical of mid-twentieth-

century liberals and the Social Gospel; see Richard Wightman Fox, *Reinhold Niebuhr: A Biography* (New York: Pantheon, 1985). Gunnar Myrdal, *An American Dilemma: The Negro Problem and American Democracy* (New York: Harper, 1944). On how the black prophetic tradition of the civil rights movement won over liberals, see David L. Chappell, *A Stone of Hope: Prophetic Religion and the Death of Jim Crow* (Chapel Hill: University of North Carolina Press, 2004). Ashley Southall, "Counterpoints to Offensive Remarks," *New York Times*, April 27, 2014, SP7.

7. Wordsworth, "Lines Left upon a Seat in a Yew-tree."

8. For complementary steps past multiculturalism, see David A. Hollinger, *Postethnic America: Beyond Multiculturalism,* 10th Anniversary ed. (New York: Basic Books, 2005), and Kwame Anthony Appiah, *Cosmopolitanism: Ethics in a World of Strangers* (New York: Norton, 2007).

INDEX